VO[ICES]
FROM THE
THIRD
REICH

VOICES FROM THE THIRD REICH

AN ORAL HISTORY

Johannes Steinhoff
Peter Pechel
Dennis Showalter

DA CAPO PRESS • NEW YORK

Library of Congress Cataloging in Publication Data

Steinhoff, Johannes.
Voices from the Third Reich: an oral history / Johannes
Steinhoff, Peter Pechel, Dennis Showalter.—1st Da Capo Press ed.
    p.   cm.
Includes index.
ISBN 0-306-80594-4
1. Germany—History—1933-1945. 2. World War,
1939-1945—Personal narratives, German. 3. Interviews—Germany.
I. Pechel, Peter. II. Showalter, Dennis E. III. Title.
DD256.5.S764   1994
943.086′092′2—dc20   94-19111
[B]   CIP

First Da Capo Press edition 1994

This Da Capo Press paperback edition of *Voices from the Third Reich* is an
unabridged republication of the edition published in Washington, D.C.
in 1989. It is reprinted by arrangement with Regnery Gateway.

Published by Da Capo Press, Inc.
A Subsidiary of Plenum Publishing Corporation
233 Spring Street, New York, N.Y. 10013

Acknowledgments

The authors wish first of all to extend thanks to their interview partners. Their willingness to share memories that are as painful as they are compelling made this book possible. Particular gratitude goes to the *Verband der Kriegs- und Wehrdienstopfer* and its Executive Director, Hans-Ulrich Greffrath, to Dr. Hugo Stehkämper and the Cologne Municipal Archives, to Drs. Werner Röder and Herrmann Weiss, of the *Institute für Zeitqeschichte,* Munich, and to Ludwig Freiherr von Hammerstein-Equord, Lilo Clemens, Johannes Völkers, Anna Sibylle Apfelstedt, Alfred Etzold, and Ursula Randt. Hans-C. von Carlowitz of Vienna, Dr. Bernard Schmitt of Metz, and Dr. Giuseppe Bisignano of Bruneck, South Tyrol, helped assemble the "part-time Germans." Manfred Sadlowski and Mönch Verlag also provided much help in the project's early stages.

Among our direct collaborators, Ulrike Jäschke transcribed the interview tapes. Monica Houston-Wäsch contributed as translator and typist. Dierdre Baca and Barbara Cavender joined us to assist in typing the final manuscript. Ursula Steinhoff bore with grace two years' reliving of World War II and the Nazi era. Clara Anne Showalter understood and accepted the absences and abstractions of her husband, as did John and Clara Kathleen of their father.

Wendy Rubin has been from the beginning an invaluable member of the team. She kept the rest of us on track and up to the mark. Her skills as a translator, her organizing ability, and her dedication to the project's success have done much to make the book what it is. We thank her for her participation.

And we must also thank our editors—Harry Crocker, Joseph Harriss, and Franz Oppenheimer (who was also our lawyer)—whose devoted service helped us finish the job.

Contents

PREFACE

by
Helmut Schmidt

Historiography must be based on documents and objects. The latter make it possible to draw conclusions even from periods and developments that are not supported by documentary evidence. Historiography, nonetheless, is an art, not a science. It is the art of understanding past events. It is also the art of omitting and distilling facts—particularly for those periods for which a great number of documents and testimonies are available. Furthermore, it is the art of narrating history. It is the grouping of facts into periods, the recognition of inherent laws. Finally, it is the art of judging historical events and the people who acted in them. From the classical Greek and Roman historians to the present, from Ranke or Tocqueville to Spengler or Toynbee, historiography has also always been a combination of philosophy and history. But whether considered science, art, or philosophy: no one who writes about history can do without documentary evidence.

One hundred and fifty-seven German witnesses of World War II speak in this book. Because they recollect events of four or five decades ago, their stories should be judged and evaluated with some caution. Few people willingly reveal errors or failures that occurred in earlier phases of their lives; for many there are subjective reasons that prevent them from recognizing the limits of their objectivity. Those who have read Churchill's and de Gaulle's memoirs know that an individual's national or personal point of view inevitably influences retrospective self-assessment.

The fortuitous nature of one's personal environment, including our upbringing and education, our parents and their friends, our own friends and companions, and, above all, the tasks imposed on us in the past, influence the interpretation and recollection of events in which we were personally involved. A former general sees the events of the war and their context differently from a private, or from his wife and children, who were then in the cellar of their burning apartment house. But they all also see past events inevitably under the influence of what they have experienced and learned over the course of the many decades that have passed since then. The testimony of each is especially influenced by the degree of maturity and judgment each had reached at the time of the experience that he now relates—so many, many years later. Someone who became an adult in 1933 when Hitler came to power experienced the war differently from someone who became an adult during the war—and at any rate differently from someone who became an adult only twenty, thirty, or forty years later. The student generation of 1968 in the Federal Republic of Germany and elsewhere in Europe chose moral standards for political and governmental actions as well as standards for individual conduct, standards that for the most part were completely unknown to a 20-year-old German in 1938.

Every generation is inclined to apply its own standards to the actions of past generations. Consequently, some of today's young Germans find it difficult to understand the blind obedience of those young Germans who had to endure the war either as soldiers at the front or as civilians at home. I have the impression that former soldiers from the other side of the many fronts of World War II understand the behavior of their then German enemies better than our own sons and daughters do today. Some of the latter believe us when we say that only very few of us were convinced Nazis, but they insist that we justify why we were not members of the resistance. They have grown up in a free society, one in which one need not endanger one's life or show great courage to demonstrate at the fence of an airport, at a nuclear power station, or at a missile base—or even to resort to violence. Hence they believe that such "resistance" should also have been demanded from us in the Third Reich. They lack the experience of a totalitarian dictatorship, of a totalitarian state and its absolute control of information and education. Those who remind them today that democratically passed constitutional laws require compliance and obedience are generally accused of wanting to turn back the clock. Turn it back to what? To the Nazi-state? Or to the Weimar democracy? Some of the Germans of '68, and especially the subsequent Red Army Faction, believed it their moral duty to comply only with those laws the significance, application, and morality of which they could understand and accept. They had been educated for freedom. But this education ended once more in utter perversion. Those young Germans had become the prey of a utopian ideology of anarchy, in a way similar, but opposite, to that of their fathers who had become the victims of another perverted ideology, namely that of blind obedience.

Most soldiers under Hitler's high command were not Nazis. But their background and education as well as the state's omnipotence had made it their duty to serve their country—always and especially when at war. In the first years of the Nazi era, many of those who were already adults in 1933 or who were on the threshold of adulthood had succumbed to Hitler's suggestive power and his great success in overcoming enormous, depressing unemployment; but euphoria vanished, at the latest, when Germany invaded the Soviet Union. Everyone, including elementary school children, knew something about Napoleon's march to Moscow and its catastrophic outcome, a knowledge that was a warning signal for most. Yet, most Germans remained convinced of their duty to fight for their country.

The majority of the men and women in the resistance also shared that conviction. They were prepared to commit high treason—to remove Hitler and the Nazi-dictatorship—but they were not ready to commit treason in the sense of delivering their fatherland to its enemies in a war. They were patriots—and they were heroic patriots. Initially, there were only a few who believed that they should accept even the defeat of Germany for the higher purpose of removing Hitler's inhuman dictatorship. Among those, Jewish Germans and other victims of Hitler's persecution were naturally relatively numerous. Germans who had managed to emigrate or flee in time, thus escaping extermination in the concentration camps, belonged to that group. The majority of Germans, however, hoped for an early and lenient peace. Until then, they were ready to carry on for many years and to do their duty.

But what was a German's duty at the time of Hitler's World War? How could we Germans find out what it was? The member of the resistance who was prepared to commit high treason against the leadership and the regime did what he considered his moral duty, no less than the member of the resistance who was ready to commit treason against his very country. But millions of German soldiers also believed that they were doing their duty serving as anti-aircraft gunners, lance corporals, or commanding generals fighting in Russia, Africa, the Ardennes, or Germany's own burning cities. Just as German air-raid wardens and civilians in business and industry felt that they were doing their duty.

As Germans we might call World War II the tragedy of our sense of duty. For generations Germans had been far more successfully educated for doing their duty than for exercising individual political and moral judgment. Hitler used and abused our sense of duty. Only a few had the judgment to recognize a moral duty superior to the one we had been indoctrinated with.

We can speak of heroism whenever the performance of recognized or accepted duties means imminent danger to body and life. But heroism presupposes fear. The actions of a person who shows absolutely no fear in the face of danger are not heroic, they are simply foolish. During Hitler's World War, there was much fear, but there were also many people who overcame their fear in order to do their duty. There were innumerable varieties of heroism in the cities of the homeland as well as at the fronts.

Most of the heroes, however, never considered themselves such. Only a few wanted to be heroes. The kind of heroism promoted by Hitler was only a relatively minor success. Only a few believed in the "heroic" ideal—the longer the war lasted, the less they did so. As a school boy, I had read Carlyle's *On Heroes, Hero Worship and the Heroic in History*. The book appeared to me highly artificial. At the same time, I found Remarque's *All Quiet on the Western Front* in my father's bookcase—and Remarque seemed to me incomparably more credible. In fact, World War II was even more appalling than World War I as described by Remarque. I was one of the many millions of Germans who had no ambition to become a hero. But at the same time, I was one of the many millions who took pains to do his duty.

I was one of those Germans who reached adulthood only after I had become a soldier. But during the eight years I served as a soldier, I did not gain much additional political judgment. I became one of the millions of opponents to the regime, but at the same time, I was one of the millions who did not know what could or should be put in its place. Only as a prisoner of war did I understand the principles and values of a democratic society and a democratic constitutional state. Most of my generation went through a similar experience, and for those among us who had to endure Soviet captivity for years, the process of learning and understanding was particularly difficult. One positive thing, however, most Germans seem to have carried away from their wartime experience, was a realization that we are responsible for one another and that we must help one another. This commandment, which at various times has been called fraternity, solidarity, or comradeship, is one of the two values we have gained directly and existentially from the war. In today's society of superabundance, this value is threatened.

The other value is the ideal of individual freedom. During the Nazi era and especially during the war those who had to learn to conceal their opinion and to bite their tongue were not in need of "reeducation" with regard to the cardinal value of freedom of opinion. Apart from that, however, we Germans had a lot to learn after the end of the war and the end of the Nazi era. Meanwhile—compared with the first German attempt to establish a democracy during 1919 to 1933 and even more so with Bismarck's empire of 1871 to 1918—we have been able to establish a democratic constitutional state in the Federal Republic of Germany that so far has been uniquely successful. In doing so we have learned from our former enemies, mostly from the Americans, the English, and the French. This state does not have any common ideological commitment beyond or above the fundamental principles of our Basic Constitutional Law. Its citizens are free to choose and develop their personal religious, philosophical, and political beliefs. The Germans speaking in this book—each of them in a different way and based on their different personal beliefs—have participated in building this state to the end that the horrors of the past should never recur.

True, this state has a significant flaw. It is not a national state of the Germans, but only a part of such a state. We Germans cannot remedy this flaw. The division of Europe, of Germany, and of Berlin, is maintained by the Soviet Union with great military power. The Soviet Union's great armament and drive to expand under Stalin, Khrushchev, and Brezhnev, have led the western democracies to the realization that a balance of military power is necessary for maintaining peace in Europe and that this balance is impossible without a considerable contribution to defense from the 60 million people of the Federal Republic of Germany. This is the reason why the German Federal Armed Forces have been in existence since 1955. At about the same time, within the Soviet sphere of influence, the so-called People's Army of the 16 million people of the German Democratic Republic has been built. Officers and generals who had once served together in Hitler's armed forces, participated in the creation of both German armies.

The arming of both German states against each other, or more precisely, the integration of the two new German armies into opposing international systems of alliance, thus began as early as ten years after the end of Hitler's World War. The German Democratic Republic was not the German fatherland, but neither was the Federal Republic of Germany. Where was the German fatherland? The fatherland was nothing but a wishful inner concept. So, what was the patriotic duty of a draftable German when there was no fatherland to defend? Many old wounds from the conflict between the duty imposed by the state and a self-recognized moral duty were opened again.

The Germans on the one side are told that it is their duty to defend the reality of socialism and its "achievements." I do not dare to estimate how many of them inwardly believe that. They are probably a minority. Yet, the overwhelming majority complies with the law of their state. Which one of us, who lives in security and freedom, has the right to reproach them for doing their duty, or to summon them to heroic resistance? The Germans in the German Democratic Republic have been cast from one dictatorship into another. Who has the temerity to condemn from a safe distance the conduct of people who must live under a dictatorship?

The other Germans are told that they must be ready to defend freedom, individual dignity, and democracy. I believe that this is right. But I must confess that in the course of the 1950s—when I was hoping for a unification of the two separated German states—I had to overcome considerable initial inner doubts before I could totally agree with this maxim. True, I liked being a member of the German Federal Parliament, but even as late as the end of the 1960s, I again struggled with myself for a long time before I accepted the appointment as Minister of Defense and thereby—by virtue of the constitution—the control and command of the German Federal armed forces, because I knew that, even at that time, many a German was still plagued by the same doubts I myself had overcome during the 1950s. Still, thereafter I served in this office with pleasure and devotion. I knew the generals and officials, Steinhoff, Kielmannsegg, Baudissin, Maiziere, Wirmer, and many of the others who during fifteen years had created and shaped the armed forces of the Federal Republic (the *Bundeswehr*). I knew I could rely on their loyalty to the constitution.

And today, twenty years later, everyone can rely on the armed forces' loyalty to the constitution. And soldiers can rely on not having to serve under a commander who might give unconstitutional or immoral orders. The internal structure of today's *Bundeswehr* is categorically different from that of the *Wehrmacht* in which my generation served. The basic ethical spirit of the *Bundeswehr* is unique among the German armies of this century—it is not a patriotic army of the fatherland, but a patriotic army of the constitution. And as an instrument of military defense, it is also one of the best armies in the world.

Almost all of the architects and pedagogues of the German Federal armed forces as well as its political commanders were men who had fought as soldiers in Hitler's World War; some of them came from the resistance, others from the Führer's headquarters. All of them had to face the necessity of defining anew the duties of a soldier and therefore also their own. The actual result in the form of the *Bundeswehr* permits us to conclude that they brought not only negative experiences back from the war, but that they were also willing and able to learn from their experiences, and that they had preserved enough human and moral integrity during the war to do so—in spite of Hitler. Many Germans, whether in private life, in business, in the universities, in the civil service, in the churches, in the trade unions and associations, or in politics, have kept their human and moral integrity—despite Hitler's dictatorship and his war.

The old saying that men make history is truer when turned around. Historical circumstances form men. For most of his life, the margin of possible decisions an individual can make is very small. But it is almost always possible for an individual to behave decently toward his fellow men. I am convinced that the majority of Germans did behave decently during World War II—considering the all too human weaknesses that none of us can escape.

True, there were also many swine and many criminals. A criminal who voluntarily confesses his guilt is a rarity—except in a courtroom during a trial. A swinish character who is not personally brought to trial will hardly ever confess his vile and immoral activities of the past, especially many years later. But the rest of us, the great mass of ordinary people, we, too, tend to forget those human shortcomings for which we should really blame ourselves. And when we cannot forget, we tend to gloss over or to find excuses in the external circumstances of that time. Nobody who could not cope with a difficult situation is fond of finding himself a weakling.

Therefore, the testimonies in this book must be read with some detachment. But after all, all historically significant documents must be read with critical detachment for they almost always say very little about the motives and feelings of the people concerned. Yet, this book is a deserving experiment. The reader will understand that the selection of contributors has inevitably—though unintentionally—influenced the general impression; he will assume that the individual contributors, had they had more time and space for their statements (abridged by the editors), would possibly have placed one or the other accent differently. That they were all willing to answer questions appears to me in itself deserving of our gratitude.

Brutal dictatorships of all kinds force upon people patterns of behavior that they would under normal circumstances consider

totally unusual, unappealing, and even profoundly repulsive. This
was true when Christianization was imposed throughout Europe with
a cross in the one hand and a sword in the other, it was true under the
Inquisition, and it was once again true when the European colonial
powers of the 18th and 19th centuries imposed their rule on foreign
countries. Today, the same is true under dictatorships such as those of
Burma, Rumania, and Chile. It was equally true under the dictatorships of Hitler and Stalin.

For everyone—even for the people living under a totalitarian
dictatorship—the Prussian philosopher Immanuel Kant laid down
the moral principle according to which everyone must behave in such
a way that his behavior can also serve as a maxim for the behavior of
all. But it was easier for this great philosopher of the Age of Enlight-
enment to formulate his "categorical imperative" in the abstract than
it was to adhere to it when at the mercy of the life-threatening Nazi
regime.

A Note on Procedures

Adolf Hitler and the Nazis still fascinate American readers. Forty-four years after its downfall, books about the Third Reich continue to appear with predictable regularity. Why publish another one? Because National Socialism did not exist in a vacuum. The German nation, the German people, brought Hitler to power. They cheered his triumphs. They bore the burden of his war. They participated in his crimes. They were also his victims. This book is their story.

We originally intended to produce an oral history that would present the genesis of the Third Reich as well as its downfall. But we found that few people who, as adults, witnessed the rise of the Nazis and were responsible for voting Hitler into power are still alive and able to communicate.

This study therefore presents the second generation of the National Socialist era. Most of the men and women whose stories made this book were children or teenagers when Hitler came to power; few were older than 21. Emigration was impossible. The Third Reich became their world. By the start of World War II they were old enough to kill and be killed, yet still too young for their opinions to be consulted. War formed their memories and shaped their lives. Taught to react to orders and slogans, they learned to think for themselves as the Reich crumbled. Millions were drafted into the Wehrmacht. Some fought to the end in the ranks of the SS. Others found their way into the resistance.

All emerged bearing not only the physical and psychological scars of defeat, but also the burden of their parents' decisions. For it is one of history's ironies that Hitler achieved the opposite of his goals. Instead of dominating the globe, Germany was divided and emasculated. Instead of disappearing from history, the Jews became a moral focal point of Western civilization. And instead of a master race, today's Germans are scapegoats.

It took two of us, Gen. Steinhoff and Dr. Pechel, almost two years to collect the interviews presented here. We traveled extensively, particularly to Berlin, Hamburg, Munich, Cologne, and Vienna, which were where most of the contributors lived. Since the Austrians, the people from Alsace-Lorraine, and those from the South Tyrol were considered Germans either before or during the war, it was also necessary to talk to survivors among these "part-time Germans." For obvious reasons it was impossible to interview people within the Communist part of Germany, the German Democratic Republic.

Although we knew at the outset the names of many of those we wanted to interview, a real breakthrough in locating others occurred when Steinhoff wrote a short article, "War Victims and Survivors," describing the book project in the monthly paper of Germany's largest veterans' organization. The reaction to this invitation to contact us was spontaneous and overwhelming. Our mail box overflowed.

The vast majority of the interviews were tape recorded. A few contributors preferred to make only a few oral remarks, but in addition gave us written memoirs, letters, or essays to include in our "oral history."

Nobody whom we approached refused to be interviewed. Since the majority were over 60 years old—many were in their seventies— they were inclined to open their hearts. We felt that for them it was a relief, almost like shedding a burden. In fact, we questioned our subjects occasionally with great reluctance, because we felt that the experience was becoming too painful for them. Many, both men and women, could not continue and had tears in their eyes. In a few cases they turned away, saying "I cannot do it, I cannot continue. . . ." One should bear in mind that almost every person in Germany now over 60 years old was in one way or another involved in war activities, either as a soldier, a *Volkssturm* member, a victim of bombardment, or a worker in a weapons factory. Some of the interviews were conducted in unusual circumstances. For instance, Leo Welt was interviewed by Steinhoff while sitting in the corner of a big, noisy tent during an industrial exhibition in Turkey. Pechel managed to persuade von Witzleben to cross the border between West and East Berlin and tell him his story in the lobby of a hotel. But most of the contributors preferred to speak to us in their own homes. The interviews lasted an average of two hours and twenty minutes.

This wartime generation does not always tell us what we might wish to hear. But in these interviews the Third Reich's last survivors came to terms with their experience. Heroism and egoism, self-sacrifice and self-deception—all are present in these pages. Our conclusions emerge in the epilogue. It is up to the reader to challenge or to accept them.

The Rejected Republic

For most of the men and women telling their stories in this book, the rise of the Third Reich was a logical result of the aftermath of the First World War. Germans rushed to the colors in 1914, convinced that they were defending their homeland against an overwhelming coalition of enemies. Germany's collapse four years later reflected not so much principled rejection of the existing order as the temporary exhaustion of people strained beyond their limits.

The Weimar Republic proclaimed in 1918 bore the burdens of a lost war. The peace settlements destabilized Europe by replacing the Habsburg Empire with an unstable constellation of new states. In Germany the Versailles Treaty was widely seen as a dictated peace, designed to keep the country in permanent subjection by reducing its army to a token force of 100,000 men, by requiring heavy reparations payments, and by imposing on Germany the sole moral responsibility for beginning the World War.

Weimar captured neither minds nor imaginations. For too many of its citizens the Republic was a way station to something better. Its first president, Friedrich Ebert, was dismissed by critics on the right and on the left as a former harness maker, a mediocrity with neither style nor ability. Intellectuals scorned a system that seemed determined to make Germany safe for little fat men with briefcases. Interest groups fought for power in a parliamentary system where cabinets rose and fell for the most trivial reasons. Many bureaucrats and generals, opposed in principle to democracy, observed the confusion with grim satisfaction.

The German Empire's decision to finance the First World War by printing and borrowing money began an inflationary spiral that continued under the Weimar Republic. By November 1923, the mark was at an absurd 4.2 billion to the dollar. Such an exchange rate made money meaningless. While some groups profited, the savings of Germany's middle class vanished. Values of thrift and hard work became irrelevant. The Republic eventually succeeded in stabilizing its currency. But Germany's economy remained characterized by high unemployment, low profits, and negative balances of payment through the 1920s.

Instability became crisis as the Great Depression hit Germany. Instead of an overnight cataclysm, as in the U.S., Germans had up to eighteen months to watch their economy collapse. The Republic's economy failed not with a bang, but with a whimper, slowly grinding to a halt as everybody looked to his own affairs. In the winter of 1931, almost five million Germans were out of work. The number fell by one million during the summer, but the decline was temporary. By February 1932, over six million men and women, ten percent of the entire population, stood in unemployment lines. Hundreds of thousands more had stopped trying to find work, or never started.

On September 14, 1930, 6.4 million Germans cast ballots for the National Socialist German Workers' Party and its leader, Adolf Hitler. Even before the Depression, the Nazis had established themselves as Germany's major protest party. Now they moved into Germany's political mainstream, not with threats of destruction, but with promises to make things better. The country needed a sense of community, thundered Nazi orators, a will to cooperate in a common cause. Instead of facing each other as adversaries, Germans had to become comrades.

It was a simple appeal, but speeches and rallies, parades and conferences, spread it to every corner of a tired, frightened country. The Nazis' confidence was inspiring at a time when few seemed willing or able to take action of any kind. Germans began speaking of *Massenrausch*—the mass intoxication of Hitler supporters.

The appeal of National Socialism was not universal. The Nazis were unable to elect Hitler president over the incumbent, aged hero Field Marshal Paul von Hindenburg, in April 1932. In July the party's

Reichstag vote peaked at 37 percent. This was enough to keep Germany in a state of turmoil. It was not enough to bring Hitler to power without help from the men around Hindenburg. Their hope was somehow to attract Hitler's voters while getting rid of Hitler himself. Ultimately they accepted both, hoping that political responsibility would tame Hitler. On January 9, 1933, Adolf Hitler was appointed Chancellor of Germany.

THEO HUPFAUER

Born 1906; joined the Nazi Party in 1930; deputy to the minister for armaments and ammunition, Albert Speer, 1944 to 1945; from 1945 to 1948 was a witness for the defense at the Nuremberg trials; later became an industrial manager and lives in Munich.

"The German government, Kaiser and all, was a total failure."

I entered secondary school, the *Gymnasium,* in 1917, during the First World War. It was a boarding school, and included several so-called "special classes," young officers already too badly wounded to go back to the front, who had been discharged and were now working for their "Wartime" or "Emergency" *Abitur* diploma. These ex-officers were outspoken on one point: the German government, Kaiser and all, was a total failure. "We soldiers," they said, "saw to it that in the whole war not an enemy set foot in Germany. We were betrayed by the Kaiser and the politicians."

That naturally made a deep impression on the younger boys, who until then had no interest at all in politics. Now we were confronted with it every day. In about 1920, when I was 15 years old, I joined a right-wing youth group directed by Vice-Admiral von Trotha. He was an officer from the old Imperial Navy and an active opponent of the Weimar Republic. We often made trips to other parts of Bavaria to meet other chapters of the group, which included quite a few grown-ups. These weren't just field trips; they were political rallies.

The great inflation after World War I hit us hard when our classmates had to leave the *Gymnasium* because their parents couldn't finance it any longer. German citizens were impoverished from one day to the next. A bread roll cost as much as 20 million marks. Mailing a letter cost 100 million. A quart of milk cost 300 million marks. Even after the currency reform in 1923, when one billion paper marks was made equal to one new mark, those who didn't own furniture or other material possessions were very poorly off. This politicized us even more.

In 1926, I entered the university of Würzburg. It seemed natural for me to join a duelling fraternity. Its motto was "Honor, Freedom, Fatherland"—still the motto today. Once again, I was automatically involved in politics.

In contrast to some of the other fraternities which were more socially minded, ours was patriotically oriented, and this was heavily stressed. I remember reading something like this: "National Socialism was not born in Munich, but in Versailles." Everything that happened after World War I was a product of the Treaty of Versailles. That so-called "peace" dictated by the winning side radicalized the whole political atmosphere in the 1920s. Radicalization implies extremes. In Germany, these extremists were the National Socialists on the right and the Communists on the left. Election figures for these years show that all the other parties lost votes and the extremists kept growing.

The radicalization of politics got worse after 1928 as unemployment increased. That meant that the competition between parties became increasingly fierce. In the end, there were no longer political assemblies in one hall or another, but parades like military maneuvers, and large-scale street fights. All the young men were involved. That was when I joined the Nazi Party, in 1930. To me, the old-line conservative parties were too tame, too "establishment." They were for old men who had lost their fire, but not for a young man ready and willing to do something! In 1931, I joined the SS.

JUTTA RÜDIGER

Born 1910; from 1937 to 1945, head of the Nazi League of German Girls; worked as a psychiatrist after the war; now resides in Bad Reichenhall, Bavaria.

"We said, 'This is the only possible answer to Bolshevism.' "

I was born in 1910, and I still remember the soldiers marching off to war in 1914—the bands playing, the cavalry with their lances. But when I think of my childhood, 1923 was the most important year. Everyone was against the Versailles Treaty. Even as children we were told, "Never forget it; always think about it; never talk about it." The French occupied Düsseldorf, and they could be brutal—even sadistic. For example, a student with only one leg, a veteran from the war, was walking down Düsseldorf's main street and a French soldier deliberately bumped into him so that he fell flat on his face.

In 1923, the Ruhr was occupied. And the Rhinelanders, who really are an easy-going people, not at all chauvinistic, began to react, especially the workers. There was a separatist movement, but they were regarded as rabble, bought and paid for by the French.

All of these things strengthened my nationalism. And then came the economic depression and unemployment. I was a student at the University of Würzburg, and my father was an electrical engineer. One day they told him, "Herr Rüdiger, you're going to have to accept a very large salary reduction to keep your job." He had to borrow from his younger brother, who was single, to keep me in school. It hurt his pride, and it hurt mine.

One day some friends took me to a meeting of National Socialist students. I was greatly impressed. There were people who always quarreled about everything, students from the duelling fraternities, from the regular fraternities, students who didn't belong to any organizations. And here they were, all in harmony. What you have to understand is that we really had two camps in Germany, the national and the socialist. And the Communists were making converts among the socialists for their Bolshevik program. The Nazis told us that Hitler had learned a great truth from his experiences in the war: The important thing was not whether someone had money or a title, but whether he contributed to the well-being of his people. Hitler said nationalism and socialism should be identical. The nationalist should be there for every one of his countrymen and socialism must be adapted to the nature of a people. Thus, National Socialism.

For us it meant comradeship—solidarity, you might call it today. The concepts really impressed us. We said, "This is the only possible answer to Bolshevism." And that's how I came to join the National Socialist German Students' League.

OTTO KUMM

Born 1909; a trained printer, became one of the most highly decorated surviving senior officers of the Waffen-SS; last commander of the SS armored division Leibstandarte Adolf Hitler; *later returned to work as a printer in Offenburg, Baden, where he resides.*

"One could try the Communists or join the Nazis."

From 1925 to 1929 I was a printer's apprentice, and then I spent a year travelling through Germany on foot. I saw almost all of the country. Each region has a beauty of its own. But in 1930 we already had almost three million unemployed, half of industry was at a standstill. Endless lines of emaciated, hungry people stood around on the streets. It was a miserable picture, especially in the cities. Later, in 1932, there were six million unemployed. Along with the dependent families, this added up to a third of our population.

I visited political gatherings whenever and wherever possible: political assemblies ranging from the far right to the far left. After listening to what was said, I came to the conclusion that—given the fact that millions of Communist Germans already looked to the Soviet Union as their fatherland—there were two options. One could try a new beginning with the Communists under Russian leadership, or join the National Socialists who were working to free the country from the stranglehold of the Versailles Treaty and make it independent once again. I couldn't see any third option back then, and I guess millions of other Germans couldn't either. That's why I joined the SA in October 1930, without being a committed National Socialist. I told myself there was only this one chance: to support this party in the hope that Adolf Hitler and his movement would make a new start.

I was in the SA for a year, but it seemed a little soft to me, too undisciplined. So I applied to the SS and was accepted. It was still a very small group, sifted from the SA with the purpose of protecting the Party, especially the Party leadership, in public. That's why we had the name *Schutzstaffel,* abbreviated to SS. I was at several of the larger rallies in Hamburg. It was our job to shield the podium, accompany the speakers to and from their cars, guard their hotel, and so on. Together with the SA, we would also go on so-called propaganda marches through all the quarters of Hamburg, and often things would get pretty lively. Hamburg was a red city, even after 1933. I can well remember Bloody Sunday in Hamburg-Altona, when entire blocks were occupied by armed Communists, firing into our column from the roofs. We had 13 or 14 dead that day.

Sure, today you can ask what we were doing in these working class areas in the first place. Well, the National Socialists were a workers' party, with the prime goal of winning over the German worker. You could only persuade these people if you had something to offer, and kept doing it. And as a matter of fact, the great majority of SA and SS members in later years came from the opposite camp. They'd been converted.

ROLF JOHANNESSON

Born 1902; career naval officer under Weimar
and the Third Reich; after the war joined the
Federal Republic's navy; retired as rear admi-
ral; lives in Hamburg.

"There wasn't a worker's son among us."

I was 16 years old when I joined the Kaiser's navy as a cadet. I grew up in a German Empire fascinated by the sea, and never wanted to be anything but a sailor. I joined my first ship as a cadet in Kiel just in time for the mutiny in November 1918. Revolution was spreading like wildfire from city to city, as far as Bavaria. The High Command, without even consulting the government, ordered the fleet to make a final sortie against the British Navy. Some of the crews mutinied and refused to take the ships to sea.

I was on the *Schlesien,* an old battleship used to train cadets. All around us we saw red flags. Our captain ordered us to get underway, and we left harbor five minutes before the mutineers closed the booms. One of our lieutenants proposed dismissing the unreliable men, allowing anyone who wanted to leave the ship to go, and setting course for Kiel with whomever was left. When we mustered, we had 326 men left out of 741. But 73 of these were officers and petty officers; 202 were cadets like me. Only 42 sailors and 9 stokers, 51 enlisted men, stayed with the ship.

On November 9, we learned that the Kaiser had abdicated, that a republic had been proclaimed, and that Germany had asked for an armistice. A whole world collapsed. Three weeks later, the local revolutionary council told us cadets to go home.

I enrolled at the University of Berlin on December 1, 1918. Most of us were still wearing uniforms; the atmosphere in the classrooms was that of the trenches—sober, serious, comradely. But it was a semester of discontent. Revolutionaries occupied buildings. Troops loyal to the government marched through the streets of Berlin. When I heard that a naval assault company was being raised to protect East Prussia from the advancing Soviets, I volunteered. This was one of the best decisions I have ever made in my life.

We were sent to Courland in the Baltic States. I remember being under fire for the first time, and the little clumps of dirt thrown up by machine gun fire. We held our positions until things stabilized. In retrospect, I can say, and not without a little pride, that I did my part to ward off the Bolsheviks.

In February 1921, I rejoined the navy as a cadet. So many of its officers had been involved in plots against the Weimar Republic that new faces were essential. Relations between the officers and enlisted men were exemplary. They set patterns for the Wehrmacht that had a lot to do with the German soldier's excellent fighting record in World War II. We junior officers also got along well among ourselves— there was no personal ambition in a navy that was forbidden by the Versailles Treaty to get any bigger.

We officers did not think of ourselves as political, but we were always involved with politics. Once the President of the Republic, Friedrich Ebert, visited our training ship and was introduced to us cadets. He shook hands with each of us and asked how our fathers earned their living. There wasn't a worker's son among us.

Another side of the navy's class structure showed when Defense Minister Wilhelm Groener boarded my torpedo boat to avoid crossing the Polish corridor on his way to East Prussia. He sat with us four officers down in the mess. He asked each of us what we earned, and none of us could give him an answer. Money was not important to us. A bit exasperated, he said, "How am I supposed to raise your salaries if no one will tell me what he earns?" Where do you find such dedicated officers nowadays?

WERNER BARTELS

Born 1902; World War I veteran; aircraft engineer and test pilot; airline pilot in South America; recalled to the Luftwaffe in 1940; shot down over Britain and later exchanged for a British pilot; after the war was a company representative; lives in Bonn.

"In 1920, because of my reactionary intriguing, I was forced to leave the army."

During World War I, I was drafted at the age of 15 into the auxiliary services and helped unload the wounded whenever a hospital train came in. That was in 1917. A year later, I became a dispatch rider in a field artillery battery. The Germans had already started to retreat by the time I got to the front. With my dispatch bag and my mess kit in hand, I ran back and forth between our battery and the various withdrawing units. I ran because we didn't have any more horses by then. Most of them had either landed in a cookpot or had been butchered to make sausage.

The only thing the withdrawing troops were really interested in was getting home respectably, without a revolution, but we were surprised by a revolution after all. Nevertheless, we continued to march back in organized formations. We even marched into Dessau to the sounds of band music. No one wanted to accept the fact that the war was lost and, moreover, that the country had left its army in the lurch. That's more or less why the *Freikorps* came into existence. I for one, chose to enlist in the *Freiwilliges Landesjägerkorps,* which was under General Märcker's command. If we couldn't live under the monarchy, then we certainly wanted to live in an honest and decent national state. Then in 1920, because of my reactionary intriguing and involvement in the Kapp Putsch, I was forced to leave the army.

GOTTFRIED FÄHRMANN

Born 1923; fighter pilot in the only jet fighter unit of the Luftwaffe; became a high ranking civil servant after the war; resides in Munich.

"Jobs were scarce, and they paid nothing."

I grew up in the 1930s, alone with my mother. My father, who had worked in my grandfather's factory, died two months before my birth. At that time, social welfare or insurance for the self-employed did not exist, and my mother was left penniless. We moved in with my grandmother, who owned a small jewelry shop. As young as I was, I have a very good recollection of the economic situation during those years. Often after school I would run home and ask, "Did you sell anything today?" The answer was usually, "Only repair work for 30 pfennigs."

When I was 7 years old, we lived practically next door to the employment office. I had to walk past it every day on my way to school, and the number of people lined up waiting for work was incredible. There was a pub on the corner, and I still have vivid recollections of seeing women there, with their children, keenly watching over their husbands in an attempt to keep them from going in and drinking up what little money they had.

I had two good friends in elementary school. One had a father who lost an arm in World War I. He worked as a doorman, and was among the first to be let go when the economic crisis began. My other friend's father was also out of work. He earned a little by gathering up used toothpaste tubes. We helped him to cut up the tubes and remove the remaining contents, which he then sold as chalk. During this time, in 1929, my grandfather's factory went bankrupt as well.

In 1932, I entered secondary school. Even then, the differences in the political views of our teachers were very obvious. They were outspoken and debated openly with one another. In 1933, I joined the Hitler Youth, *Jungvolk,* and stayed a member until 1938. I received my secondary school diploma and decided to go to trade school. I found a position as a technical apprentice, which at that time wasn't the easiest thing to come by. Jobs were scarce to begin with, and they paid nothing.

We young people felt it was high time someone brought the situation under control. We were all fascinated when, after regular elections had been held, our highly respected President, von Hindenburg, appointed Adolf Hitler Reichs-Chancellor in the Garrison Church in Potsdam. I vividly recall Hitler bowing deeply to Hindenburg. In my mind, this gesture resulted in the identification of National Socialism with Prussia and Germany. It is simply wrong to categorize all Germans as Nazis because they loved their country.

KLAUS VON BISMARCK

Born 1912; great-nephew of Chancellor Otto von Bismarck; highly decorated infantry officer; after the war was director-general of Germany's largest radio and television station; president of the Goethe Institute; resides in Munich.

"The first president was a proletarian."

There were very few Nazis among the *Krautjunker* "hillbilly aristocrats" in eastern Pomerania. They were, for the most part, monarchists who failed to grasp the essence of the Weimar democracy due to their blindness to history and their continued adherence to the monarchy. As monarchists, they maintained their traditional approach to the privileges of owning land in Prussia. Thus they lived in a sort of reservation for aristocrats.

On the other hand, the aristocrats in Pomerania were poor in contrast to those in Silesia, East Prussia, and the Saar area. They arose at 5 A.M. with everyone else—even though they were the owners—and harnessed the horses. And their wives worked into the night balancing the books. But most of these men had naturally been officers in the Prussian Guards, and the mantelpieces above their fireplaces were appropriately adorned with the silver ashtrays and cognac goblets exchanged with their fellow officers. In other words, this was their world, a world miles from the reality of Weimar. To them, the Weimar Republic was a socialist and clerical state, and Ebert, the first president, was a proletarian. They also considered the *Gauleiter* and other classes who came into existence during the Third Reich as satraps, and rejected them as well.

WILHELM FISCHER

---

*Born 1916; fought in Russia; surrendered to
the Red Army in 1945; retired civil servant;
lives in Cologne.*

"We soon stopped laughing."

Before 1933, the Nazis' comical salute was considered a joke. But we
soon stopped laughing. I will never forget the first time I saw this
salute, in 1928 or 1929. I stood waiting at a streetcar stop, the Mass
was over, and a young man in normal Sunday clothes stood next to
me. A streetcar came, and a fellow got out wearing a brown shirt, a
red armband with swastika, and leggings. The two men looked at
each other, threw up their arms, and loudly shouted "Heil Hitler!"
Several older people shook their heads but didn't say anything. I was
12 years old at the time and had no idea what it meant. I asked my
father at home. He only smiled and said, "You can forget those
assholes; they'll come to their senses." How is it said in Latin?
"Errare Humanum est."

MARTIN KOLLER

Born 1923; son of a Protestant pastor; flew tactical reconnaissance missions on the Russian front, losing one leg; joined the Bundeswehr as a civil servant after the war; lives in Troisdorf, Rhineland.

"The combat soldier was an ideological symbol for us."

When I was born in southern Germany the second son of six children, a bottle of milk cost several million marks. My father had been a soldier in the First World War and saw action at Verdun. The combat soldier was an ideological symbol for us. But my father was a monarchist at heart; he was very critical of the takeover by Hitler and the brownshirts. When Hitler came to power I was 10 years old.

Father was a Protestant minister, and, as minister's kids, we were part of the upper class. I had a classical humanistic education at a well-known school.

Then the radio era began. I remember my father bringing home a box one day and setting it up high enough so that we couldn't fiddle with it. He turned some knobs and it began to sputter and crack. All at once the world barged into our living room. From there I followed the events of the Day of Potsdam, as it was called in 1933. You could hear the bells ringing, the marching music playing, and then "the Führer, the Führer." These were our first impressions of a new technology that let us take part in what was happening in the world. Or so we thought. Now I know the Nazis very consciously used this new instrument to influence the masses.

Like all boys back then, we belonged to a youth group. There were the Socialists, there were the Communists. Even then the Hitler Youth was in existence, and the *Jungstahlhelm,* soldiers' kids who wore field-gray uniforms. All of these groups were military-oriented. Their members wore uniforms, buckles, and shoulder straps. We had blue shirts and wore armbands with an oak leaf cross, symbol of the Christian Boy Scouts.

The various groups used to wage real gang wars. We used to call these wars "field games" because we went out to the fields and forests to fight. Once my brother was badly beaten up and was spitting out his teeth. He said one word that I will never forget: "fascists." I had never heard this word before. But all that ended in 1934, when all youth groups were dissolved by a national decree, and everybody had to join the Hitler Youth, or the so-called "State Youth." Suddenly we were a Hitler Youth troop.

Before graduation, I had already applied to be a professional soldier in the Luftwaffe because I wanted to fly. That must have been around the beginning of 1939. Then the war broke out, and there was no school, as such, any more.

PETER HERZ

Born 1930; son of an anti-Nazi socialist; lives in Cologne and is an employee of the city.

"There was a tin Hitler with a moveable arm."

We lived in a typical workers' district. I spent my free time during the week with my classmates, and I spent Sundays with my father at the local soccer club matches. It was a typical workers' organization. The high point was always Sunday evening, when we got together in the club's small meeting hall and ate sausages and potato salad and drank a big mug of beer.

The SA tavern was only a short distance away. The SA members often left there late and drunk and came over to our clubhouse to raise hell. But they were usually driven off with table and chair legs. My father usually led the counterattack.

I got my first impression of National Socialism as a child, when I saw SA model soldiers in a store window. There was also a tin Hitler with a moveable arm. A few days later these tin soldiers were parading through the streets in the flesh. They always carried the party flag right up front, and everyone had to greet them with a tip of the hat or a raised arm, just like that tin Hitler in the showcase.

HANS HERWARTH VON BITTENFELD

Born 1904; attached to the German Embassy in Moscow before 1939; a junior officer in the Wehrmacht; returned to the Foreign Service of the Federal Republic; served, among other posts, as ambassador to Great Britain; now lives in Bavaria.

"Nobody wanted to identify with the Weimar Republic."

In my opinion, the reason for Hitler's rise to power was the failure of the bourgeois parties, in particular the wait-and-see demeanor of the Social Democrats. They were not accustomed to assuming power and bearing responsibility. And although they never gave Brüning their vote of confidence, they never blocked his executive authority. Secondly, the bourgeois parties failed in that they were incapable of creating a defensive front against either National Socialism or Communism at a time of very high unemployment. Add to those factors the psychological burden of the Treaty of Versailles, and you had strong support for National Socialism and Communism.

The worst thing was that, aside from the Social Democrats and the German People's Party, nobody wanted to identify with the Weimar Republic. This was a very grave error.

PART I

THE
MASTER
OF
EUROPE

CHAPTER 1

Corps of Vengeance

"You will be my corps of vengeance," Luftwaffe chief Hermann Göring told a group of junior officers in 1936. But public support for nationalism and rearmament stopped far short of enthusiasm for actual war. One million eight hundred thousand Germans had fallen in 1914–18. Hitler, himself a front-line veteran, insisted that his own war experiences were the Reich's best guarantee of peace. He was widely believed by people unable to credit the idea that anyone who had been "out there" would willingly risk a repetition.

The first four years of National Socialism were years of triumph in Germany. The Enabling Act of March 1933, which concentrated almost all political power in the hands of the new Führer, was approved by over 80 percent of the Reichstag. The Nazi New Order projected an image of energy and determination. Even Hitler's murder of a number of political opponents, including the SA leaders, in the Blood Purge of 1934, was widely interpreted as a sign of his intention to guarantee stability. A national labor service to absorb teenage males; public work projects, particularly the autobahns, to provide jobs for their fathers and older brothers; military expansion leading to full rearmament—for all these, Hitler took the credit. As the economy boomed, millions of Germans agreed that "we have our Führer to thank."

In contrast to the Soviet Union, where enemies of the regime were defined objectively by class identity, the Nazis acted on the principle that no morally sound German would consciously remain aloof from the developing national revolution. The brown terror of the early 1930s was now official. But the Nazis preferred to consolidate their position at the grass roots through a policy of *Gleichschaltung* (coordination). This meant giving every possible everyday activity a National Socialist identity. Choral groups, gymnastic societies, all the voluntary associations which dominated the social life of neighborhoods and small towns in Germany, were "invited" to cooperate. Youth organizations were dissolved, their members forced into the League of German Girls and the Hitler Youth. After 1933, many prominent local Nazis were neither ideologues nor opportunists, but the kind of energetic good citizens to be found at the heart of any community anywhere. Their participation enhanced the regime's credibility as Hitler moved Germany closer to war.

The reintroduction of conscription in March 1935, was merely a down payment to the generals for their support since 1933. Army, navy, and the newly created independent air force under Hermann Göring, all prepared wish lists. But for all Göring's boasts that the new Germany wanted guns instead of butter, Hitler never trusted the masses who cheered him so loudly. The Nazi leader refused to mobilize the economy for war. As late as 1942, the Reich was producing a broad spectrum of consumer goods, but far from enough arms.

The weapons that existed reflected less coherent strategic planning and national policy than questions of what was available, or what satisfied egos, or what could be produced cheaply and quickly. For the sake of competing with Great Britain, the navy concentrated on battleships. For the sake of numbers, twin-engined bombers were built instead of larger, longer-ranged aircraft. For the sake of haste, the armored divisions went to war with most of their tanks mounting nothing heavier than 20-millimeter cannon.

But if the Wehrmacht was relatively well equipped compared to its principal rivals, neither Hitler nor his generals was ever quite sure what to do with the hardware. For the military professionals, rearmament had been an end in itself since 1918. Strategic planning took second place, particularly among a new generation of generals obsessed with the technical capabilities of their weapons. Germany's commitment to a medium-range air force, epitomized by Göring's cancellation of an embryonic four-engined bomber program in 1937, reflected Hitler's belief in the deterrent, that is to say the political, effect of air power. Göring ignored strategic forces and effective fighter forces for air defense. The refusal of both Nazis and soldiers to develop a comprehensive approach to strategy would contribute much to the ideologization of Germany's war, with will power expected to replace rational calculation.

Nazi Germany's foreign policy was initially designed to take advantage of Europe's fear of another war and Europe's indecision about what to do with Germany. Between 1933 and 1938, it seemed that everything so long denied to Weimar was granted on demand to the Nazis. Hitler withdrew from the League of Nations and its disarmament conference with no more than token protests. In March 1936, German troops entered the Rhineland, demilitarized by the terms of Versailles. France was unable to react without general mobilization. Britain was unwilling "to fight a man for going into his own back yard." Four months later, the outbreak of civil war in Spain gave Hitler the chance to test his new military machine. The Wehrmacht's Condor Legion provided invaluable air and ground support for Francisco Franco's Nationalists. Cooperation in Spain also improved relations with Italy, whose dictator, Benito Mussolini, still viewed Hitler as more rival than colleague. By 1937, the Rome-Berlin Axis was a fact of Europe's diplomatic life, and Adolf Hitler stood at the focal point of the continent.

Even these triumphs were mere preliminaries. In November 1937, the Hossbach Conference, so called after the officer who kept its minutes, indicated Hitler's intention to turn east, where the real opportunities lay. In March 1938, the Austrian government succumbed to German pressure. Two months later Hitler issued secret orders to the Wehrmacht: prepare to occupy the Sudetenland and crush Czechoslovakia.

He met little opposition. Many prominent critics of Hitler's movement left Germany when the Nazis took power. Active resistance was initially confined to the left—Communists and some Social Democrats, along with a few intellectuals who refused to emigrate. Not until 1936 did it begin to emerge among other sectors of the population: Christians who decided that the Reich's behavior reflected fundamental immorality rather than temporary lapses; soldiers, civil servants, journalists, and diplomats who realized that the New Order meant a new war. As yet their numbers were few. The officer corps in particular was enjoying its new status and its expanded responsibilities.

In 1938, the Czechoslovak crisis did generate discussion within the General Staff about removing Hitler. But the reasons were more pragmatic than moral: Hitler was risking the wrong war at the wrong time. Senior officers rejected tentative proposals for a *coup* on the grounds that they believed the Wehrmacht's junior officers and enlisted men were so influenced by National Socialism that they were likely to refuse to act against the regime. This guaranteed Hitler a continued free hand.

The Führer was disappointed when France and Britain capitulated unconditionally at the Munich Conference in September 1938. British Prime Minister Neville Chamberlain spoke of "peace in our time." Six months later, Hitler occupied what remained of Czechoslovakia. Then Poland received a list of demands. The Polish government, supported by France and Britain, refused them. On September 1, 1939, Hitler had his war.

JOHANNES STEINHOFF

Born 1913; fighter pilot seeing action in the Battle of Britain, the Soviet Union, Africa, Italy, and France; wing commander, First Jet Wing; awarded Knight's Cross with Oak Leaf and Swords; after the war worked as an advertising agent, then rejoined the Luftwaffe, becoming Chief of Staff; Chairman of NATO's Military Committee; lives in Wachtberg-Pech, Rhineland.

"We were the 'guarantors of the future.' "

I entered the service in Stralsund on the Baltic Sea on April 20, 1934. My group—there were 176 of us—later became known as "Göring's Cadets." We were all to become pilots in the new German Luftwaffe. We were virtually never influenced by politics. The so-called political officers were non-existent at that time. The first time I was directly confronted with politics was when Joseph Goebbels gave a fiery speech during a visit to our crew in 1934. In retrospect, I must say he put on a really good show, a masterpiece of polemics.

I then became a naval fighter pilot. We flew our pants off. Politics was a completely different world and one we didn't bother with. We were proud. We were pampered. We were the "guarantors of the future." Göring's air bases were conceived in typical Third Reich style—very modern and comfortable, almost luxurious.

My class of lieutenants was the first Luftwaffe "mass production of officers" in the Third Reich. We were ordered to Berlin in 1936. Göring was to speak to us in the Prussian parliament building. Inside, the building's huge amphitheater was filled to capacity. At least 1,000 young lieutenants were there. Göring spoke for about an hour. He had gained a tremendous amount of weight. He wore a blue-gray uniform and red-spurred Russian leather boots. He declared revenge and retaliation against the enemies of the last war. Of course we had respect for this man, a *"Pour le Mérite"* pilot himself during the First World War. His behavior was theatrical. He used popular terms, speaking of disgrace, humiliation, the Reich's right to "living space," and he promised retaliation. When he closed with "and you will one day be my corps of vengeance," there probably wasn't a single person in attendance who wasn't totally motivated to give his utmost in support of this regime.

PETER PETERSEN

Born 1926; served at the end of the war in the elite Grossdeutschland *Division; was a "true believer" until the end; after the war became a long-time member of the Bundestag active in improving German-Jewish relations; a market researcher today, he lives near Stuttgart.*

"I really wanted to join the SS. They were the elite."

I was sent to a "Napola" at the beginning of the war. A Napola was a *Nationalpolitische Erziehungsanstalt,* a political training school. I wound up there after a commission had gone through secondary schools and chosen young boys who were blond, athletic, and who also had above-average grades. About 1,000 youths were sent to the school for a week-long test. They accepted 200.

The Napola was completely different from regular schools. We had horses, we had sailboats, and we were the elite. We were proud of being soldiers, of wanting to help the Führer attain the final victory, of our medals and recognition. It was taken for granted that most of us would volunteer for the SS on graduating.

I really wanted to join the SS. They were the elite and they had the best-looking uniforms. But then I had an upsetting experience. One of my friends, who was two years older than I was, came back in 1942 to visit his old school. He had become what I wanted to become. He was an *SS Untersturmführer,* but he had completely changed his personality. When I mentioned this to him, he made me swear that I would never repeat his story as long as he was alive. I kept my promise.

He told me that he had been at the front and had taken prisoners. He asked the battalion staff what he should do with them. The Waffen-SS general in command of the sector said, "shoot them."

My friend then protested that the prisoners were not partisans, but regular soldiers, and that he could not legitimately shoot them. He was ordered back to the battalion, where he received a terrible bawling out. He was told that he would learn that this was no kindergarten war. He would be sent to take command of a firing squad where he would be shooting partisans, German deserters, and who knows what else. He told me that he had not had the courage to refuse to obey this order, since he would have been shot. Then he returned to the front. Later, when we heard that he had been killed, we had a memorial ceremony. He had "fallen on the field of honor."

THEO LOCH

Born 1919; volunteered for the Waffen-SS;
after the war was a newspaper and television
journalist active in the movement for European
unity; lived in Cologne until his death in 1987.

"My generation was raised to die."

I was 11 years old when Hitler came to power. My father was a government official in the German state of Baden. In 1934, he had a monthly net income of 350 marks. Even considering the higher buying power of the mark in those days, the question of how we would make it to the end of the month was very important.

In 1933, when I was in my first year at the *Gymnasium,* I was in a youth group. I greatly enjoyed the trips, the camping out, and everything that the group had to offer. In 1934, my parents read that a "Napola," a political training school, was to be founded at Lake Starnberg, near Munich. The school was to accept athletically talented youth with an academic bent, who would be trained "in a healthy, natural, National Socialist manner." The tuition would depend on the parents' income. My mother wrote to this school, and I was accepted out of a great number of applicants. The question of party membership was unimportant; my father was not a member.

My life until 1945 can be explained only in terms of my training at this school. There was a great deal of pressure on the students from the very beginning. It was of central importance to be a good comrade. The teachers were all young; all were civil servants who had absolutely no experience working with children.

The school was a cross between a cadet institution and an upper-middle-class boarding school. We even played golf there. I don't know who said that my generation was raised to die, but it was true. Nothing was said at the school about preparing us to die, but we were told to be ready for the great test. In 1938, I traveled to the U.S. as part of a school exchange program. In 1937, our school had brought over two Americans who lived with us and wore our uniforms. One of them was from Choate and the other was from Andover. Two students from our school were then selected to go to the States. One of them was later shot down over the Mediterranean. I was the other one.

America was another world. The Americans welcomed us with open arms. They were interested in Germany and made comparisons between Germany and Roosevelt, between the New Deal and the German labor service, and between the roadbuilding programs in the U.S. and Hitler's attempts to deal with unemployment. One thing that made me think a great deal was the "Crystal Night" of November 9, 1938. Even Americans who were very friendly toward Germany said, "Not this. This we can't understand."

After the war, when I met another former Choate student, a Jew who is now a lawyer in the U.S., he asked me, "Theo, did you ever consider how many Jews there were in Choate at the time?" I told him that I had never thought about the matter.

EGON BAHR

*Born 1922; officer candidate and anti-aircraft
gunner; had to leave the service because of his
Jewish descent; postwar journalist and later
member of the West German Bundestag; Social
Democratic expert on security and defense
issues; former cabinet minister; architect of
Ostpolitik; resides in Bonn.*

"As a part-Jew I could be a soldier, but not an officer."

As a teenager in the Third Reich, I was pulled two ways. I remember
when the Nazis took power my father said, "That means war." And
then it was 1936, and still no war. The old people didn't know what
they were talking about. Everything was fabulous! Then we occupied
the Rhineland, and everything was very fine indeed. On the one hand
I was proud of my country. On the other hand, I knew that for my
family, and maybe for me, it would be terrible if everything kept on
going the way it was.

My father was a teacher in Torgau, in Thuringia. But my mother
was half-Jewish, and that was enough to get my father thrown out of
his job in 1938. We moved to Berlin, and he went to work in a
factory. It was easier to escape notice there than in a small town like
Torgau.

I joined the Luftwaffe because I didn't want to march. I was sent to
Belgium for basic training, but my real turning point came when I
was sent to officer's training school. The cadets were a normal cross-
section. All of us knew who was a Nazi, and we were careful around
Nazis—so careful that they were in danger of being isolated because
of their beliefs! Then I got a letter from my father: "The *Gau* Racial

Research Office has discovered your ancestry." Officially I was one-quarter Jewish. Naturally, I reported this to my commanding officer. He found the whole thing disgraceful. He relieved me from duty, and planned to court-martial me for "attempting to infiltrate the Wehrmacht."

But the other officers at the school were decent men, and their reports were enough to quash the court-martial proceedings. My record showed I hadn't "infiltrated" anywhere. My papers showed from the beginning that I had a Jewish grandmother, only no one had ever noticed. According to regulations, they should never have accepted me for officer's training in the first place. As a part-Jew, I could be a soldier, but not an officer.

To save everybody's face, I was just discharged as unworthy to be a soldier of the Third Reich.

HERIBERT SUNTROP

Born 1928; makes his home in Cologne.

"We had become somebody again!"

We won international races on land, on the water, and in the air. During the Olympic Games it rained medals. Meanwhile, there was a rapid decrease in unemployment and an improvement in the social situation of classes of society that previously had been poor. There was also a Nazi program for the improvement of the quality of life (*Kraft durch Freude*). Not surprisingly, all of this led to public enthusiasm, or at least sympathy, for the new regime and the new state.

I can remember moments very well when self-confidence—even euphoria—suddenly emerged. For example, I remember the day when people on the street suddenly called out, "The Zeppelin is coming, the Zeppelin is coming!" Everyone looked up at the sky, filled with pride at this technical wonder the Germans had created. The next day, we heard about the first place finishes of our racing cars. The day after that, our glider pilots made new record flights. At a major international flying event in Switzerland, our bombers flew faster than the other bombers in the competition. The entire world envied us for these achievements. We had become somebody again!

ALBERT BASTIAN

Born 1927; Hitler Youth and war volunteer; lost a leg in 1945; after the war was employed by the Federal Postal Service; makes his home in Pirmasens, Palatinate.

"The Führer expects you boys to be quick as greyhounds, tough as leather, and hard as Krupp steel."

I was ten years, ten months, and eighteen days old when I had to make my first political decision. It was the morning after Crystal Night, the night of November 9, 1938, when all the synagogues in Germany went up in flames; when the windows of countless Jewish shops were smashed by the National Socialists; when thousands of Jews were arrested and taken to concentration camps.

It was still dark outside when I woke and heard a strange man's voice coming out of the kitchen. A stranger in our house in the middle of the night?

It was Levi, the Jewish livestock dealer to whom my father always sold the calves; the Jew who supplied us with pork lard all year and always said to my mother, "Ma'am, if you don't have money now, pay what you can, there's no rush. Your boys need something to chew on." A Jew, a Jew—it kept running through my head. I was not at all happy that he was sitting in our kitchen.

In the spring of 1938, two Labor Service camps were erected not far from our village. I had become friendly with two of the troop leaders who always took me with them on their Sunday patrols along the border. Their comments about the Führer, the Treaty of Versailles, the purpose and meaning of the Labor Service, and the German youth which would restore Germany's honor made an impression on me.

I had already been a member of the *Jungvolk* for ten months. In our small village on the French border, the leader of the *Jungvolk* group was our teacher. He had already talked to us about the Jews: "The downfall of Germany in the First World War. You have to fight them wherever you can—these capitalists, these blood-suckers, who are only concerned with their profit, who don't work but only deal in trade." We boys had the task of convincing our parents not to do business with Jews. And here was this Jew sitting in our kitchen. Levi wanted to get away to France. He had already sent his family to safety there in the spring of 1938.

I was in despair. Although my father opposed my teacher and refused to buy me a brown shirt, I respected my teacher. He was big and strong. "The Führer," my teacher said, "expects you boys to be quick as greyhounds, tough as leather, and hard as Krupp steel." And here was my father, a friend of Jews. I just couldn't figure it out.

When it got dark, my father took Levi across the border. When he came back my mother asked him, "Are you sure nobody saw you?" "You can rest assured," my father told her, and at that moment I saw a smile light up my mother's face. And for the first time in my life I wished I wasn't my parents' son.

ROLF JOHANNESSON*

"This was a terrible repeat of the botch-up in 1914."

I can no longer recall my exact feelings and thoughts when Hitler came to power, but they certainly were positive. Very few suspected that the medicine taken on January 30, 1933, would turn out to be deadly poison which would ultimately destroy the Reich.

In the spring of 1933, Hitler made one of his first speeches to the armed forces, and he chose the navy. He came to our base. The men were lined up three ranks deep; the center remained open. I stood on the right as commanding officer and was able to observe everything exactly. In his brown, poorly tailored party uniform and high boots of thick, soft leather, Hitler didn't impress me in the least. His speech was feeble. His escorts consisted of several good-looking young men. I was irritated by the cloud of perfume they left when they passed by.

Hindenburg died on August 2, 1934. While previously our oath was always made to *"Volk und Vaterland,"* now it was "absolute obedience to Adolf Hitler."

Later, I acted as an expert witness and a military film censor for military courts. I could not permit any films showing wealthy spies drinking champagne with beautiful women. I had just banned a French film which united these three taboos into one colorful adventure. General Werner von Blomberg, the War Minister, viewed the film with me in Goebbel's private film studio. Blomberg said, "Let's lift the ban on this one. Essentially it's about love, and one should not forbid love." At the time I hadn't the slightest notion that Blomberg's affair with a prostitute was about to destroy his career.

My tour of duty in Berlin was during the time of the gigantic rearmament. Orders to establish new regiments, training grounds,

* Biography on page xxx.

and headquarters, came across my desk on a daily basis. The expansion, however, did not coincide with an expansion of our reputation inside the country. Observer officers reported continual excesses by party officials and SS formations. I left Berlin feeling dubious about the future.

I thought an officer should seize every possible chance to experience a war, and the Spanish Civil War was going on. On July 10, 1937, I left Berlin under a false name and flew via Rome to Seville in a Ju-52. I was supposed to head the intelligence and sabotage unit of the Condor Legion.

When the Italian infantry in Spain was involved in a surprise firefight, some of its officers lost their heads. Eye-witnesses reported that the younger men threw themselves down on the ground, crying. The Italian troops were lazy and vain in comparison to the modest, tattered, and non-military appearance of the Spanish. It was the Germans who made a really first-class impression.

I got to know Göring at closer range in April 1939. I had returned from Spain to take command of a new destroyer. My ship was assigned to escort Göring to a meeting with Franco. He didn't sail with us, but on the liner *Huascaran* on a course to the west, to the Balearic Islands, where we waited for Franco without avail. He had obviously changed his mind; he always came up with new excuses for his absence.

In the evenings, we were always Göring's invited guests. When we complained about the problems we were having with our new ships, he said, "Your complaints about the technical deficiencies are justified. Since we've achieved everything we wanted, we would be crazy to start a war. In the event that the situation does come to a head, Hitler is going to send me to London. It's common knowledge that Ribbentrop is too dumb for the job of ambassador to England."

At the time, I was totally convinced that Göring was airing his honest opinion. His appearance was impressive; big blue eyes; a round but pleasant face; a large and impressive figure; and short little fingers. When he came on board my ship and ceremoniously inspected the ranks—well, I had never seen my men so radiant. The man definitely possessed charisma. One night after dinner we sat on the deck of the *Huascaran,* Göring bundled up in his white coat sipping strawberry punch. Suddenly he disappeared. He had taken a big bowl of punch down to the crew in the engine room.

In June 1939, I took part in a Berlin victory parade staged by the Condor Legion. We marched through the Brandenburg Gate and were received by Hitler, Göring, and Ribbentrop. So you see, I was once able to march through the streets of Berlin as a victor after all, adorned with a German and a Spanish medal.

Behind the parades, the navy's situation was bad. When Chamberlain announced a new British armaments program shortly after the Munich Agreement in 1938, Hitler reacted very harshly. A new naval construction plan was the result, and it was aimed at England. Nevertheless, this so-called Z-plan still acknowledged the precedence of the army and Luftwaffe. In my eyes, this was a terrible repeat of the botch-up in 1914, with the same catastrophic results. The naval balance looked like this: the British had 12 battleships, 9 aircraft carriers, and 184 destroyers. Germany had no comparable battleships, no aircraft carriers, and only 22 destroyers with unreliable engines.

I was captain of the destroyer *Erich Steinbrinck*. At 9 A.M. on September 4, 1939, we received the order to head toward Swinemünde to refuel because we were to be sent into the North Sea. Towards 1:00 A.M. on September 5, we reached Swinemünde. We will never forget this last night we had with our families. The future was like a nightmare to us. Now our opponent was a mighty naval power. When I met my wife that night, she told me, "Finis Germaniae."

JUTTA RÜDIGER*

"I was somewhat shaken—my hand kissed by the Führer!"

National Socialism attracted many women who were not ordinary housewives impressed by Hitler's talk about "children, church, and kitchen." I finished my studies and became one of the first social psychologists in Germany. I was a practicing psychologist when I joined the League of German Girls in 1933. Two years later I was asked if I wanted to work for the League full time. I had done a lot of work with young people, and thought that this would be a good way to spend a few years.

By 1937, I was head of the organization—at the ripe age of 27. I took over something my predecessor had already begun, something new in a youth movement, physical training. Before that, the girls had sports only in secondary schools. So we gave them a lot of opportunities, and they participated enthusiastically. We also tried to see that *every* girl got job training. Earlier this wasn't the case. Either they were from "good families" and did nothing, or they were unskilled workers. We in the League were determined that every girl should be able to stand on her own feet, whether she was married or not.

Before 1933, the youth movement had been a kind of elite. We wanted to bring in everybody, all the boys and girls. That was the goal of Baldur von Schirach, head of the Hitler Youth. His idea was to have one comprehensive youth movement. Even the youngest would learn to give up her selfish wishes, to see that even the smallest task was part of her responsibility to the people. And we succeeded.

At the same time, that brought the risk of too much collective experience. I told Schirach that once the girls had learned to be part

* Biography on page xxvii.

of a group, from age 17 on, they should be able to develop their appropriate tendencies and talents individually. Schirach was very attracted by the idea. He spoke of individuals bound to a community. And I still find that a good goal today: individual personalities who still have a sense of responsibility to the whole. That was the basis of our work in the League of German Girls. Schirach stressed gymnastics. He said, "It doesn't matter how high a girl jumps, or how far she puts the shot, but that her body develops properly, harmoniously."

Schirach had a streak of genius. Every conference with him, once you got to know him, was an experience. He came from a very cultivated family. His mother, and his grandmother on his father's side, were Americans, so he was three-quarters American. I remember being invited to his house in 1938. His mother was there as a guest, as was his sister, an opera singer who had just returned from a concert tour in the U.S. She told us it was horrible what was being said about Germany, and her mother suddenly burst into tears and said there was going to be another war between Germany and America. Of course I didn't believe it.

I first met Hitler personally in 1931 in Düsseldorf. His sonorous voice impressed me. I felt, "Here is a man who thinks not of himself, but of Germany!"

I met Hitler for the second time seven years later, in 1938. He gave a reception for his high party officials, and Schirach invited me and a colleague from a branch of the League. We considered wearing our new uniforms, which had been designed by a fashion house in Berlin. But we changed our mind and wore evening dresses instead.

When we went up the stairs to the reception hall, there stood Hitler! Alongside him was a master of ceremonies who announced the guests as they arrived. We were formally presented, and Hitler kissed the ladies' hands! I was somewhat shaken—my hand, kissed by the Führer! Then a bit later he said he would like to see our uniforms, so we went back to the hotel and changed.

When we returned, there was only a small group around Hitler. I got the impression then that he was somehow shy and inhibited around women. After dinner he moved from table to table, and when he got to ours he looked me and my colleague up and down and said,

"I've always told the Mercedes people that a good motor isn't enough. You need a good body too." He leaned forward a bit and said, "But a good body alone isn't worth anything either." Then he left. Mercedes cars were his great love; I suppose he thought he was honoring us with the comparison.

Until 1945 that was our picture of Hitler. He could hold people spellbound, but still had a sense of humor and knew how to laugh.

We didn't go to war with any great enthusiasm, but we thought Hitler was right. We had reports of how Germans in Poland were being persecuted, and how the Poles were saying, "On to Berlin!" We were told Hitler's first demands were moderate, that he only wanted the Polish Corridor. There was even a joke about Hitler telling a Polish countess: "Madame, I don't want your whole castle; I'll be satisfied with the corridor." We didn't believe Hitler wanted a bigger war. Then France and Britain declared war on us. Schirach called the leaders of the Hitler Youth and the League of German Girls together. He told us it was going to be a long, hard war. "It can last seven years," he said. "As long as the Englishman smokes his pipe by the fireplace, things will be all right. But when he puts his pipe aside and climbs into the trenches, it will be a hard fight. You'll live to see Berlin in flames!"

Our mouths hung wide open! We were shocked, but it helped prepare us for what was to come.

WILLI WEISSKIRCH

Born 1923; infantryman in World War II; was wounded three times; after the war was a journalist and later a member of the Bundestag; today is the Soldiers' Welfare Commissioner (Wehrbeauftragter) of the Federal Republic in Bonn.

"Hitler is the Chancellor now, and that means war, son!"

Two key events made considerable impressions on me. The first occurred on January 31, 1933. I had read the newspaper that morning. In one of the columns, in heavy type, was a headline: *Hitler Reichskanzler.* "Hindenburg has appointed Adolf Hitler *Reichskanzler.* . . ." I read it, but, as a ten-year-old, didn't think twice about it. Then my father came home from work and immediately asked me for the newspaper. He read the article and suddenly exclaimed, "Oh my God! Now there'll be a war!" I asked him how he knew there was going to be a war, and he replied, "Here it is, right here in black and white! Hitler is the Chancellor now, and that means war, son!"

That was one experience. The other happened a few weeks earlier—during the presidential election of 1932. We kids in Brüning's Center Party had stickers—the kind you have to lick—with a picture of Hindenburg's head and the slogan: "Hitler stands for Bolshevism; vote for Hindenburg!" I remember asking my father what Bolshevism was. He replied, "Son, I don't know of any other way to explain it but that it's chaos and total confusion. Hitler's election will lead to Bolshevism and then ultimately to war!"

In 1934, guards began appearing in front of the two Jewish stores in our town. They were butcher shops. One was Abraham Winter and the other was Aaron Neuhaus. We patronized Aaron Neuhaus' shop simply because the liverwurst tasted better, but we occasionally bought from the Winters, who lived across the street from us. Aaron Neuhaus was a veteran of World War I and had received the Iron Cross First Class. He had had the medal and the certificate framed, and they hung on his wall. Now it was announced that the SA would be sent in on Saturday to keep people from buying in his store. That was a warning to the two butchers, and they didn't even open up. Since they were closed on Saturday, everybody shopped there on Friday. My mother sent me over with a list of things to buy. Aaron Neuhaus took the list, filled my mother's order, and gave me a wiener. Then he gave me a hearty pat on the shoulder and said, "Willi, you're a good kid. Stay the way you are and give your parents my best greetings!"

They're all gone, all dead, all destroyed! By the time Crystal Night happened, we had moved. My father had been transferred. I often thought: I wonder what the Neuhauses and the Winters are doing?

HELMUT SCHMIDT

Born 1918; officer in the anti-aircraft artil-
lery; after the war became a career politician
(SPD) and a member of the Bundestag; is the
former Federal Minister of Defense and of
Finance and Economic Affairs; was a Chan-
cellor of the Federal Republic from 1974
through 1982; resides in Hamburg.

"Since I was the captain of the club, I automatically became a Hitler Youth leader."

I grew up in a very lower-middle-class family. My father's natural father was a Jew, and his mother was from Mecklenburg. My grandfather, who was actually my father's foster father, was an unskilled longshoreman who spoke only dialect. My father was able to work himself up and out of this class. Not only did he become an apprentice, which at this time was unheard of, but he became an apprentice in a law firm. Apparently he must have made an impression on somebody because he was ultimately given a scholarship. He entered a teachers college and majored in elementary education. After the First World War ended, he continued with his studies in night school and eventually received a degree in economics. He then became a certified business and economics teacher. During the first 40 years of his life my father had succeeded in rising out of the lowest class of the proletariat into the bourgeoisie. He was, therefore, in a position to send his two sons to higher schools.

My father's political influence on me, his oldest son, was minimal. He didn't believe in political activities by youth. He even forbade me to join a youth group, which was an extremely popular thing to do at the time. Naturally, he refused to let me join the Hitler Youth. He couldn't, however, prevent my school's rowing club from being incorporated into the Hitler Naval Youth in 1934. Since I was the captain, the president, of the club, I automatically became a Hitler Youth leader.

My parents avoided any political involvement after the Nazis came to power and the Nuremberg Laws went into effect. It was obvious that they wanted nothing to do with the Nazis. I knew how terrified they were of somehow someone finding out that they had been concealing their Jewish descent.

My father sent me to a school that even by today's standards would be considered extremely progressive. Some of the teachers were Communists, some were Nazis, some were German Nationalists, while others were anti-Semites. But none of this mattered much to us, because they were all dedicated educators. Strong emphasis was placed on the more artistic subjects such as music, art, sketching, and literature. We spent many, many school hours in these subject areas. All of this influenced me in developing a great interest for modern and expressionist art, and for music, baroque as well as modern.

Our time at school was shortened by one year, because Adolf Hitler needed soldiers. As a result, we all received our diplomas one year early. My parents had told me that according to the Nuremberg Laws, I was a one-quarter Jew, so I decided to leave Germany. I was in contact with the German Shell Oil Company and had intentions of going to Indonesia where they were drilling for oil. But nothing came of it.

Because I had changed my mind about going to Indonesia, and I wanted to study, I decided to enlist and get the two years I had to serve in the military over with. I wanted to study either in Munich or in Vienna. I planned to study simultaneously at the Technical University and the Arts Academy, and in no way did I want my studies to be interrupted by the draft. So in 1937, I volunteered to serve the mandatory two years.

During my two years as a draftee, I spent one year as a rank-and-file gunner. I was a Private First Class during the following six months, and an NCO the last six months of my initial tour of duty. All this time I was planning to become an architect. I sought out friends and contacts accordingly.

I had no real ambition as far as the military was concerned. I didn't have the slightest interest in achieving any great accomplishments or becoming somebody. The fact that I became a reserve officer was due to my previous education. Promotion to reserve officer was largely an automatic process for those of us who had the *Abitur*. Of course, I didn't have any complaints about becoming a reserve officer, but I never had any interest in becoming a career officer. I wanted to be an architect. Then the war started. As young as I was, I only hoped that the episode wouldn't last too long.

INGE AICHER-SCHOLL

Born 1917; her sister and brother were key members of the White Rose resistance group; they were condemned to death by the Volksgerichtshof *and executed on February 22, 1943; now lives in Bavaria.*

"From that day on, I was afraid of prison."

Shortly before the Nazi takeover, we moved to Ulm. There were five of us brothers and sisters. I was 16, Hans 15, and Sophie was 12 years old. Politics became an issue for the first time in our lives. There was a great deal of talk about the fatherland, of comradeship, of the love of our homeland and the unity of the German people. It impressed us because we loved our home very much; also our home in the larger sense, the fatherland, though we wouldn't have been able to say why. And Hitler, or so we heard, wanted to bring greatness, fortune, and prosperity to this fatherland. He wanted to see that everyone had work and bread, that every German became a free, happy, and independent person. We thought that was wonderful, and we wanted to do everything we could to contribute. So it was no wonder that all five of us joined the Hitler Youth.

We just could not understand why our father was against it from the beginning. He even compared Hitler to the Pied Piper. All of his attempts to hold us back failed in the face of our excitement.

Hans was the first to have doubts. They were little things, but they added up: an injustice toward one of his friends here, the ban on the books of his favorite poet, Stefan Zweig, there. This seed of doubt soon sprouted in all of us. On one of our spring walks we had a long discussion with our father, who explained to us what was really going on in Germany. He said that Hitler wanted war. This conversation made father and us friends again, and the family became a small, secure island in a world that was becoming increasingly strange and hard to understand. It wasn't as if Hans decided from one day to the next that he was against National Socialism; it was a gradual development. Although Hans was a year younger than me, he had an aura; what he had to say interested you.

One morning in the autumn of 1937, the Gestapo knocked at our door just as Sophie was ready to leave for school. Elisabeth, our middle sister, had already left home to complete her studies as a kindergarten teacher. Werner, Sophie, and I were there when the two Gestapo men arrived—they usually operated in twos. They searched the apartment, confiscated our diaries, and took us away. I was 19 years old.

The Gestapo took only us children, not our parents. We were accused of continuing the activities of disbanded youth groups. They kept us in the local Gestapo prison at Ulm that day, and when it got dark they put us into an open truck and drove us to Stuttgart on the newly finished Autobahn. Of course, we weren't dressed warmly enough, and the next morning we arrived helter-skelter at the Gestapo headquarters. They put each of us into a separate cell. We were completely flabbergasted. We could not take it very seriously. We knew that we had not done anything bad, so we thought we would just be interrogated and set free again.

They left me sitting in that cell for eight days before coming to question me. I heard footsteps above me and footsteps in the court-yard. Once I heard a woman's voice which I thought could be my mother's. Perhaps they had picked her up too. And sitting there in prison, I wondered if they had already shot my father. Heaven only knew. I was very afraid of what would happen to my brother Werner; he was only 15. I was only 19 at the time, and it was such a shock that from then on I was always afraid. I was afraid of anything that might lead to my being taken to prison again, and that was exactly what they wanted.

On the last day, I was called for questioning—two Gestapo men once again—and they asked about all kinds of things. At one point, I said that I had read a tiny article in the newspaper about a resistance group in Berlin. And the Gestapo men asked me what I thought resistance was. I answered that I thought resistance was against bad people. With that they roared with laughter, and thought I was so naive that I would not be able to tell them much at all.

Gradually, I learned that the more naive, the more innocent and stupid you answered, the better. When they burst out laughing, I laughed along with them. And then they let me go, after I signed a paper which said that I would not discuss this interrogation with anyone, and if I did, it would be grounds for another arrest. I signed it, and they let all of us go.

But from that day on, I was afraid of prison, and this fear made me very timid and passive, just completely inactive.

My father was arrested in early February 1942, picked up in the early morning, the second time for our family. I was just coming back from a visit in Munich and my mother met me at the door: "Your father has just been taken away by the Gestapo." As she spoke, another Gestapo man, who had just finished searching the house, appeared. He had rooted through all of our books. He asked us a few questions. He wanted to know names. He even asked us for the address of Rainer-Maria Rilke. Thank God I told him that Rilke had long been dead. And then the Gestapo man seemed to lose interest.

I wanted to bring a few things to the prison for my father. I happened to see him being escorted between two Gestapo men. His face was pale as a sheet, and he looked at me mutely. Later we learned that one of his employees had reported him. She had asked him what he thought of the war and of Hitler. He said he thought Hitler was the biggest scourge with which God had ever punished humankind, and if he didn't end the war soon the Russians would be sitting in Berlin inside a few years. She had talked about this, probably with the district Nazi officers, and they had informed the Gestapo. Naturally, this kind of testimony by an employee carried a lot of weight. In August 1942, my father was tried and sentenced to four months in prison. At that, he got off fairly easily. It could have been much worse.

MSGR. ERICH KLAUSENER

Born 1917; his father, active before 1933 in the Catholic Center Party, was murdered by the Nazis in 1934; drafted into the army; when the war ended, moved to Berlin and became a priest; died 1988.

"A priest should be with a dying man!"

I was 17 years old in 1934, and was a student in the high school in Lietzensee. It was 30 June, the last day of school before summer vacation. At home, we always waited until my father, a senior official in the Ministry of Traffic and Postal Affairs, arrived before we ate our lunch. But he didn't come. We received a strange telephone call around 3:30 that afternoon. The person said someone had called and told him something had happened to my father at the ministry. My mother frantically tried to get in touch with my father's superior, Eltz von Rübenbach, who finally agreed to talk to her. But he was hesitant and intimidated, and didn't know any of the details.

We went to the ministry ourselves. The thing that astounded us the most was that a cabinet minister like Eltz von Rübenach was totally helpless and did not want to put his life in jeopardy. Two SS men armed with rifles stood in front of the office where my father had been shot. They had been ordered to shoot anyone who tried to gain entrance to the room. No one dared to even try. Eltz von Rübenach wasn't willing to take the slightest step to help us at all. I said to him, "You're a Catholic! You know a priest should be with a dying man! If we could only send in a priest!" He stood there totally confused and couldn't begin to understand how I could even ask such a thing of him. After we realized that there was absolutely nothing we could say or do, we went back home.

Toward the middle of the next week, we found out that the SS had cremated my father's remains. Even everything concerning the urn burial was hush-hush. In the end, we did have a fairly open ceremony. The solidarity of the Catholic Church was apparent from the very beginning. Not one person backed off from us or pretended they didn't want to have anything to do with us. Everyone knew that the reports pertaining to my father's death were all stinking lies. We knew for a fact that the bishop supported my father 100 percent. The Papal Nuncio, Eugenio Pacelli, who later became Pope Pius XII, did too.

Why my father was killed is a very difficult question to answer. One could conclude that personal revenge was the primary motive. My father had been responsible for a meeting of 60,000 Catholics in Berlin a week before his death. He had given a speech which, in Göring's opinion, had motivated the people to unite in a way that was by no means in line with what the National Socialists professed. At the time, this was the only mass gathering to take place without the overwhelming presence of the National Socialists.

Göring saw my father only once. Göring told him, "You bourgeois have only stuck pins in us. We National Socialists are going to fight back with our fists!"

Why the Catholic Church did not take an open stand against Hitler is not an easy question to answer. It was known that Cardinal Graf Preysing and the other leaders of the Catholic community in Berlin did not agree with Hitler and tried to find a path for the Church, and the poor souls who belonged to the Church, to follow in this situation. I know that Monsignor Adorf, one of Preysing's closest assistants, maintained that you couldn't place more of a burden on people who already have a heavy burden to carry, especially when you didn't have to carry it yourself. I was very much aware of the dilemma of our bishops at that time. Preaching a sermon is so confoundedly simple. Afterwards you get supporting letters. But the bishop insisted: "What burden am I placing on those who listen to the sermon and try to live accordingly? They are not all saints, and do not have a call to martyrdom."

MARIANNE HOPPE

Born 1911; movie and stage actress; met both Hitler and Goebbels; after the war continued to act in many films and television series; lives in Bavaria.

"This man was sickening. I left and never went back."

I was young and pretty, I think you could say that. I had made two or three films when I received the phone call: "The Führer would like to invite you to dinner." Leni Riefenstahl, Sybille Schmitz, and a few other well-known actresses were there. Hitler sat across from me and didn't talk at all. Actually, we were all pretty quiet. After dinner, we stood up and he said to me, "I am glad you were able to come. May I show you my apartment?" I said, "Yes, that would be nice." After he showed me a few rooms, he opened the door to another. "This is my bedroom," he said. "Oh," I said, "how gloomy." I will never forget it; the room was really dismal. "Can't you do something to cheer this room up?" I asked. "No" was the only thing he said.

Hitler in person made just about the same impact on me as his picture on a postcard did. As a man, he had absolutely no flair, at least, not to me. People talked about his sincere interest in the arts. He had his own concept of the arts and he was most likely interested in that, but it wasn't our kind of art. I was invited back much later. And what happened on that evening is a really strange story. The film *The Rebel* was being shown. It was about the people's revolt in the Tyrol against the French in 1809. In one scene, the French army had to march through a very narrow pass. From above, the Tyrolians had set up some boards loaded with stones. When the French came through, the Tyrolians cut the ropes, and all of the rocks fell on the French. Hitler became terribly excited and started to rub his knee. He started to moan as the rocks started to roll. I don't know if he was crazy or what, but he had a kind of orgasm.

I remember standing up in the dark room. This man was sickening. I left and never went back.

One day in 1936, the doorbell rang. There was an SS soldier at the door. "Hello," he said, "the Reich Propaganda Minister is on his way up the steps." And a few moments later, he really was there. The driver went back downstairs and Goebbels walked into my apartment and closed the door. I was 25, old enough, you'd think, but I was still relatively naive. In a situation like that you're speechless, totally baffled. What was I going to do? How was I going to get this man out of here?

Goebbels sat down and said he thought the two of us could get together, and he hoped we could make some kind of arrangement. For example, he told me he was giving a speech in Dresden, and would naturally have a plane ready to fly me there. "You fly over, I'll give my speech, and then we'll dine together." I began to feel a bit queasy and thought: "He can't really mean he's going to pick me up with an airplane and flowers. Surely others will be going along too!" Although it wasn't easy, I told him, "You know we both have our reputations to lose. I don't think it will work out." I had a reputation to lose in any case, something I had absolutely no desire to do. Then I had to think of a way to get him out of my apartment. He started to make advances. He told me how much influence he had in the film industry, and so on. I didn't like that one bit. He was trying to blackmail me! I don't think I was really aware of what I was saying, but I told him, "And you seriously think I would fall for a person like you?" Hearing that, he turned pale, took his cap, and left.

OTTO KUMM*

"The Waffen-SS had nothing to do with the concentration camps; we were soldiers."

We SS men didn't become soldiers for career reasons, but out of necessity. Germany was surrounded by enemies, and the Reich had to be protected from outside forces if it was to be built up from the inside. That's why we became soldiers, and for no other reason. I don't believe I would have spent my life in the military. As every officer had to, I signed up for 25 years, but I really doubt whether I would have stayed on. I have to say I liked being a soldier, no doubt about that, but I didn't see it as a career, more as a mission.

What we envisioned right along with the great majority of our people was a Reich with national sovereignty and social justice. We felt both of these goals were being reached more and more in the late 1930s. We had no cause for any kind of doubt, because our commanders were so deeply rooted not only in the German military, but also in National Socialism and the meaning it had for all of us. That's probably also a reason why the Waffen-SS accomplished such outstanding achievements during the war. We didn't have a single commander who questioned the higher leadership. Sure, we had some second thoughts at the end of the Western campaign in 1940, when we let the British get away, but these didn't last long. They were superficial and didn't cause us to question Hitler or his genius. The

---

* Biography on page xxviii.

real doubts only came much later, at the end of the war, but then they came in force.

The Waffen-SS had nothing to do with the concentration camps; we were soldiers. From 1934 onwards, there were the SS General Service troops, the later Waffen-SS. They were separate from the "Death's Head" battalions, which were the guard battalions for the concentration camps. Their service was not considered military service like ours. The "Death's Head" division was set up at Dachau in 1940, after the Polish campaign. But these troops were guard units which had nothing to do with the internal operation of the concentration camps. They knew as little as we did about what was going on inside those camps. Inside, there was only a small camp command post, consisting of maybe 12 men. That was all the SS actually had in the camps: just the commander with his staff from the general SS.

When the SS General Service Troops were re-named Waffen-SS after the French campaign, all of the other SS organizations were included under the term Waffen-SS in order to keep them from being drafted into the regular armed forces. That's how the men of the "Death's Head" nominally became members of the Waffen-SS. The Waffen-SS had its own regiments and divisions, its own officer training schools, and its own replacement battalions, all directly under the direction of the highest SS authority. The other troops were subordinate to completely different administrations, and they had nothing to do with the real Waffen-SS.[1] The nominal grouping together has the bitter disadvantage for us today that people say we were all Nazis. But we considered ourselves to be soldiers, exclusively. We wanted nothing to do with what happened in the concentration camps, for God's sake! And I would never have lent myself to anything like that!

---

[1] For a clearer analysis of the relationship of the Waffen-SS to the camp system see Charles Syndor, *Soldiers of Destruction: The SS Death's Head Division, 1933–1945* (Princeton: Princeton University Press, 1977).

WOLFGANG STRESEMANN

*Born 1904; son of former German Reichs-
Chancellor Gustav Stresemann; emigrated to
the United States in 1939; later returned to
West Germany and became superintendent of
the Berlin Philharmonic Orchestra; resides in
Berlin.*

"It wasn't long before everything German was damned."

I was a musician, and not particularly active politically. Nevertheless, as the son of Gustav Stresemann, one of the Weimar Republic's
leading political figures, I was something of a marked man in Hitler's
Germany. I finally decided to emigrate to the United States in 1939.
For months before there was not a single social event in Berlin where
someone didn't seek me out to say: "If only your father were still
alive, none of this would be happening."

In the States, I had some of my biggest confrontations with other
German emigrants. Emigrants were ultimately more patriotic than
most others in the United States. They all lived in the same area of
New York City, and eventually became more American than the
Americans. Their obvious hate went so far that they discontinued
speaking German altogether. Husbands and wives spoke to one
another with horrendous accents in English, Goethe's language no
longer good enough to claim as their own. I believe that deep down
underneath, these people had been so hurt, as Germans, that as a
result they only felt terrible hatred for a country they now wanted to
see destroyed.

Initially, it was a different story in Washington. Roosevelt was a
gambler of sorts. He had a superficial quality to his character. He was

a phenomenal personality who enjoyed a tremendous amount of popular support, but had little understanding of either economics or foreign affairs. His New Deal was a great slogan, but Roosevelt basically had little idea himself of what the program was really about. He had not the slightest notion of foreign policy, and little knowledge of history. He concerned himself only superficially with things of this nature. The fact that he was re-elected for a fourth term was due to the war.

Once the Americans became engaged in the war, a flood of anger emerged. First it was directed at anyone who even resembled a Japanese. As you can imagine, it wasn't long before everything German was damned as well.

Americans are probably the most patient of all people, but when they get pushed far enough, watch out, especially if you're on their list of enemies. Hitler sure found that out.

HANS HERWARTH VON BITTENFELD*

"My oath of loyalty was not a matter of concern to me."

In 1939, I took part in the secret negotiations which resulted in the German-Soviet Nonaggression Pact. The decisive motive from Hitler's standpoint was to cover his back. He was in no way daunted by the British guarantee to Poland. The French had already given Poland a guarantee, but this did not impress him either. It did have an effect on him when the British and the French began to negotiate a security pact with the Soviets. This made Hitler nervous because he would then have three world powers against him, and that was too many. So the race began between Hitler, the British, and the French to win Stalin's favor.

* Biography on page xxxix.

It was a competition that Hitler naturally won, because he offered Stalin everything that czarist Russia had lost at the end of World War I: the Baltic States, Bessarabia, and, I believe, half of Poland. Compared to that, what the British and the French had to offer was peanuts.

Stalin was also disappointed that he was not invited to the Munich Conference in 1938. He believed that because the issue revolved around a Slavic state, Czechoslovakia, that he should have been consulted. He distrusted the British and the French in the first place, and he was negatively impressed when they failed to respond after Hitler reunited Austria with the German Reich. All this greatly disappointed him.

Back in 1939, I do not believe any of us ever assumed this pact would be broken by either side. We actually believed it served the interests of both countries. It only became apparent to us later that Hitler regarded it as a provisional agreement. In the end, he returned to the old idea laid down in *Mein Kampf,* to crush the Soviet Union. He also had some strange ideas I believe he expressed in this way: "The Soviet Union grows more and more powerful every year. According to human expectation and the lessons of history, my successor will be a weak man. Therefore I must eliminate this threat to Germany and Europe now, before the Soviet Union becomes stronger, and before a weak successor governs Germany."

Right up until the last moment in May of 1941, our ambassador to Moscow tried to convince Hitler that the Soviet Union had no intention of getting involved in a war against the Reich. He pointed out time and again that the Soviets had fulfilled their treaty obligation to the letter, with shipments, not only of grain, but of war-essential raw materials. And the reports from von Köstring, the German military attaché in Moscow, revealed that the Red Army was a significant factor in terms of defense, but incapable of making an offensive move.

It is sometimes suggested that Köstring did not report accurately and that he did not warn Hitler sufficiently. That is wrong. Köstring had a very clear picture of the military situation. It was a difficult problem. He did not dare portray the Soviet Union as either too weak or too strong, but he tried very hard to present an accurate picture. When he met Hitler in East Prussia after the war broke out, Hitler offered him the supreme command of the troops that were to be deployed as garrisons from Astrakhan to Archangel, after victory over the Soviet Union. Hitler assumed this would be taken care of in a matter of weeks. Köstring answered, "First of all, the Russian winter is very hard and one should not underestimate Russian resistance." And he added, "The Russian bear has been hit over the head once, and has awakened from hibernation. If he is hit on the head again, he will rear up on his hind legs, and then things will become really unpleasant." Consequently, von Köstring was relieved of his command.

I had an American friend named Chip Bohlen who was an attaché at the American Embassy in Moscow. I informed him of the secret negotiations. Bohlen didn't believe me. He said, "Herwarth is beginning to imagine things, he's drunk too much whiskey again, or who the hell knows what else." And these were my exact words, "You don't believe me? Well, I'll let you know what and when something is happening." I began to inform him on a regular basis, and I gave him all the details because he found it all so incredible. But the United States was simply not involved in world politics. The American Embassy always took its time reporting back to Washington. Things that we reported immediately took them about two weeks.

According to the laws of the Third Reich, what I was doing was most certainly treason, but that didn't bother me. My disapproval was much too strong to do otherwise. Allow me to put it this way: It was not so much a rejection of Hitler personally as it was an attempt to protect Germany from being entangled in another two-front world war which we would surely lose. My conviction was, "For God's sake, it will mean the downfall of Germany." So it was not necessarily the intention of countering Hitler, but of saving the fatherland from an imminently dangerous situation.

My oath of loyalty was not a matter of concern to me. I swore an oath to Germany. And I had the distinct feeling that Hitler had already broken his oath several times by then. I sensed that Hitler was a menace to Germany. I recalled what my recruit training officer had once said in regard to following orders: "Orders are to be carried out without question unless you are ordered to commit a crime or if your commanding officer is obviously insane." In my opinion, both applied in this case.

SIGISMUND VON BRAUN

Born 1911; entered the Foreign Service during the war; brother of Wernher von Braun; after the war was the West German ambassador in Paris and later at the United Nations; resides in Bonn.

"He was really only interested in making it to the stars."

My younger brother was Wernher von Braun, who was known for his success in rocket research. He already dreamed of travelling to the moon and the stars at the age of seven. I can still remember what happened one day when we lived in Berlin. We launched a fireworks rocket from one of those little kiddie wagons with the assumption that it would probably only reach the speed of a pedestrian. It didn't turn out exactly that way. Before we knew it, it had flown out of our hands and crashed through our greenhouse window; the cauliflower was literally covered with broken glass. It was the first time my father was to foot the bill for rocket development.

Wernher was actually a gifted engineer. Politics did not interest him in the least. During the time when he developed the V-1 and V-2, he was really only interested in making it to the stars. He said that what he was doing was also a means of developing rockets so that someday they could reach space.

Apart from that he had a natural talent for public relations. He knew exactly what to say to the Germans and what to say to the Americans to get ahead in his field, which meant getting to the moon one day. I visited him a few months before he died of cancer and he was already quite weak. He said to me: "You know, actually I am dying with the feeling of having achieved what I set out to do as a boy, to enable a human being to land on the moon."

CHAPTER 2

"Jews, Get Out!"

Germany's Jews were among its best citizens. They had taken advantage of legal emancipation and an open society to make contributions in every aspect of the country's economic, cultural, and intellectual life. Twelve thousand had been killed in action in World War I, one of the highest casualty rates of any European minority. But success generated hostility. Jews were criticized by German Gentiles for doing *too* well, and for dominating key professions such as law and medicine. The so-called *Ostjuden,* Jewish immigrants from eastern Europe, were attacked even by German Jews as outsiders always ready to bend the rules for their own benefit.

While anti-Semitism was neither unfamiliar nor uncongenial in Germany, served as a main political course it was unappealing. Its adherents tended to be dismissed as fanatics as soon as they sought to translate principle into reality. At the same time, because anti-Semitism was so common and so relatively ineffectual, its existence in the Nazi program was not enough to dissuade Germans from supporting the party for other reasons.

The Nazi seizure of power was followed by a series of "wild" or unauthorized anti-Semitic actions ranging from window-breaking to murder. Then on April 1, 1933, Hitler ordered a national boycott of Jewish businesses and Jewish professionals. The spectacle of armed stormtroopers threatening corner grocery stores and old women did nothing to enhance the Nazi image at home or abroad. The boycott was, however, a signal that the New Order meant what it said about Jews having no place in Germany.

An increasing number of Jews sought to emigrate if they could meet the stringent conditions imposed both by the Reich and by prospective host countries, especially the United States. Others remained, refusing to be driven from their homeland by forces they still considered temporary. Soon, they reasoned, the real Germany would arise and put an end to this brown blight. In the meantime, Hitler announced the Nuremberg Race Laws of September 1935.

This legislation legitimized and simplified a growing body of specific legal and political decisions on the "Jewish question." It deprived most Jews of their German citizenship. It forbade marriages between Christians and Jews. It legally defined "Jews" and "half-breeds" (*Mischlinge*), children or grandchildren of mixed marriages. For "the protection of German honor," it forbade Jews to employ Gentile housemaids under 45 years of age.

Paradoxically, these laws were welcomed by some German Jews because they *were* laws. They gave Jews standing, however limited, in place of the previous two years of uncertainty. But the idea of a state based on just laws, the *Rechtsstaat,* the pride of Germans for centuries, was gone beyond recall. From 1935 to 1938, the net around the Jews was drawn even tighter. Businesses and personal property were confiscated, or their sales forced at ridiculously low prices. Jewish doctors and Jewish lawyers were forbidden to practice their professions. Identity cards and passports were marked with a "J." Male Jews with "German" first names were required to add "Israel" to their names; women were forced to assume "Sara."

GASTON RUSKIN

Born 1924; deported to Auschwitz; emigrated to Argentina, but returned to Berlin, where he lives today.

"The Tora Scrolls had been peed on."

Persecution of the Jews actually began as early as 1933. My grandfather was a master glazier. He had had his own little shop in Berlin since 1920. He and his family had all emigrated to Germany from the province of Posen in Poland. Because of inflation, the compensation they received for leaving their homes and farms was almost nothing.

I remember very clearly that in 1933, the Nazis were already beating people up. That year, an SA man put a sign in front of my grandfather's store which read, "Don't buy from Jews." Then he went around the back of the store and knocked on the door. My grandfather opened the door and greeted the man. That guy beat up my 60-year-old grandfather and left him lying there on the ground. Fortunately, his son-in-law just happened to come by and the SA guy ran off.

The Jews were persecuted again on November 9, 1938, known as "Crystal Night." I remember that that afternoon after school I went to our synagogue. Because it was in a house where other people lived, it hadn't been burned down. But I was shocked when I saw our synagogue from the inside. The thing most sacred to all Jews, the Tora Scrolls, were rolled out all over the floor and had been peed on. It's true! I never saw that synagogue again. I never went back.

In 1940 I quit school, one year before receiving my *Abitur* diploma. My non-Jewish friends all got their *Abiturs*. I was 16 years old and began an apprenticeship in the Jewish community. All Jewish schools were closed by April 30, 1941. All vocational schools were shut down as well. Jewish children had no place to go to school, they no longer received any kind of education. The Nazis didn't want to give them any opportunity to educate themselves. All Jews were forced to work. The Jewish community did try at least to open a kindergarten for the younger children who couldn't stay at home alone because their parents and older brothers and sisters were out performing forced labor.

ARNOLD BIEGELEISEN

Born 1908; was a Jewish clerk with good prospects until the Nazis took power; emigrated to Argentina; returned to Berlin after the war.

"Since you continue to employ Jews, we can no longer do business with you."

I was 25 years old and employed as a clerk when trouble began in 1933. I held a good position. But when Hitler arrived on the scene, my career plans went up in smoke.

On the whole, everyone at work was really nice to us. Besides myself, one other Jew was employed there. There was only one individual who caused us any problem. He had been a staunch Social Democrat, and was one of the first to cross over to the other side. He pressured everyone, we Jews included, into buying the *Stürmer,* a virulently anti-Semitic Nazi publication. He always laughed ironically when we let ourselves be intimidated into buying the paper. One day in 1934, the Gestapo showed up looking for an employee who was known to be a Social Democrat. They had apparently already searched the man's house. Our *Stürmer* colleague informed the Gestapo that our building had a back door, and advised them to place a guard there right away so the man they were looking for could not escape. Jewish stores and businesses were first boycotted on April 1, 1933. SA men stood in front of smeared display windows carrying signs which read, "Don't buy from Jews." My mother, who didn't look Jewish at all, was stopped by an SA guard after leaving one of the shops. He said, "You see the sign, but you go in anyway!" We didn't take the warnings and threats seriously. At that time, we were still permitted to move around freely.

Our company began making Nazi insignia. One day, one of our customers from Munich showed up and saw me working there. I overheard him talking to the company owner. "Since you continue to employ Jews, we can no longer do business with you," he said. After that incident, my colleagues warned me every time they saw a customer coming, and I would run and hide in the bathroom. This continued until the day in April 1935, when the customer from Munich showed up again. I wasn't able to hide fast enough, and he saw me. He went directly to the management and roared, "If you think you're pulling the wool over my eyes, you're wrong! You are still allowing Jews to work here!" The company let me stay until December, but then the boss told me, "I'm sorry, but you will have to go."

I received unemployment compensation for a while, but soon decided to leave Germany. In 1936, with 10 marks cash and 20 marks for my fare, I boarded a ship for Argentina. I was single and couldn't speak any foreign language.

DOROTHEA SCHLÖSSER

*Born 1921; half-Jewish, she survived the war
as a singer and afterwards became a theatrical agent; lives in Berlin.*

"There are Jews and there are Christians,
but worst of all are the half-breeds."

My aversion to Hitler began with a remark made by the principal of
my school. He said, "There are Jews and there are Christians, but
worst of all are the half-breeds." That really hit home! Usually I
thought I stood above such insults, and more often than not I actually
made fun of the Nazis. I didn't take them seriously. I considered them
funny little brown delinquents, more comic than dangerous. And that
was a mistake too many of us made. Focusing mainly on their
repulsive and obnoxious qualities, we failed to sense how dangerous
the Nazis really were. But this time I was shocked at my principal's
remarks, because they were obviously directed at me. I did get my
Abitur, but I cried a lot during that period. I used to look at myself in
the mirror and think, "Are you really that horrible?" After a while, I
really almost believed myself to be inferior.

The laws dealing with half-Jews were harsh. In order to attend a
university, one had to possess documentation that one was Aryan. I
used my father's papers, and it's a wonder that they let me finish at all.
Initially, I wanted to study law, but I knew that was impossible. Since
my mother's side of the family was very musical, I was more than
happy to continue with my studies in that direction. But all of my
instruction was private; I received no official diploma.

I had to have Aryan documentation for everything, even when
getting my driver's license. That was the first and only time I ever

forged any documents in my life. I was asked if I was Aryan, to which I replied, "yes." After all, I did need to drive a car.

Most of all, I wanted to make sure nothing happened to my mother. We were always able to hide her. She must have lived in 20 to 30 different apartments, always running from one to the next, always hidden by other people. The last place I lived was on the Kurfürstendamm. Hitler's chief interpreter also lived in our building. His girlfriend lived on the same floor I did, and after every bombing attack, he came to see if she was still alive. He would also warn us in the event any deportation of Jews was planned, so that I had time to get my mother out of sight. Anyone caught hiding Jews was sentenced to death.

Jews who thought they were welcome in Germany, Jews who were Germans themselves, couldn't comprehend what was happening to them. They refused to believe it. Once, the best-known gynecologist in Berlin, a good friend of my mother's, called to ask her to visit him and his wife so they could say good-bye. My mother assumed they had received permission to leave the country. They said their farewells, and two days later the doctor and his wife were found dead. They had committed suicide. That sort of thing was not uncommon.

HANNS PETER HERZ

Born 1927; survived the war in Germany as a "half-Jew"; after the war served as a senior government official; today makes his home in Berlin.

"We won't go into the swimming pool with a half-Jew."

My first inkling of the Weimar Republic's instability was on May 1, 1932, when I was five years old. The Social Democrats and the *Reichsbanner* met for the 1st of May rally. My father took me to the assembly and said, "Look at everything very carefully, and tell me later if you see anything odd." I noticed that they'd rolled up their flags and banners and marched off with them tucked under their arms. When asked if I'd noticed anything I said, "Yes, they marched with their flags rolled up, and usually they hold them up high." "That's right, son," my father said. "Remember that. They're Social Democrats and they don't want to be provoked by the Nazis. That's why they carry their principles rolled up under their arms." That was one impression of the Weimar Republic I've never forgotten.

Starting after 1933 we didn't belong anymore. They broke our kitchen windows and the glass in our front door. On the wooden part of the door they scrawled a Star of David and wrote *"Juden raus!"* (Jews, get out!)

I started secondary school in 1938. The teacher put a boy beside me whom I found to be the most unlikeable person I'd ever met. Yet just four weeks later he was my best friend. He did a lot to help me get over this mentality of cringing and taking it all. You see, I was constantly being teased and beaten up by classmates—being called Jew, *"artfremd"* (freak), and so on. Then my friend started punching me until I learned to hit back. After that, I knocked a tooth out of the next guy who tried to beat me up; that stopped the beating for awhile. I was eleven years old.

The following year, something happened that I'll never forget, because it showed Nazis could have two sides. A boy named Lippert, the youngest son of the Nazi mayor of Berlin, joined our class; he sat right behind me. One day after recess—right before German class— I came into the classroom and found a Star of David scribbled on my desk bench. And in the few minutes that I sat at my desk with my back turned, he wrote "JEW" on the back of my jacket.

Our German teacher walked into the classroom. He saw it and came over to me, "Stand up! Who did that?" I was afraid to tell on a high-ranking Nazi's son and said, "I don't know." "Fine," said the teacher, "Then you'll get paddled." My friend stood up and said, "It was Lippert!"

The teacher said, "Lippert! Get the sponge, wet it, wipe off the bench, clean off his jacket, and then bring me the sponge." When Lippert gave him the sponge, the teacher squeezed it out and slapped Lippert right and left across the face. He said, "I don't want this happening in my classroom again." Turning to me he said, "The next time you 'don't know' who it was, you'll get it too!"

But there were other teachers. We had a tough, hard-core Nazi as a physical education and swimming teacher. The first day we had to put on our bathing trunks and stand alongside the pool. When we were all lined up, he said, "Herz, step forward. And you stay there. We won't go into the pool with a half-Jew." From then on I spent swimming class, two hours every week, standing at the edge of the pool in my trunks. I didn't learn to swim until 1963.

My father tried to leave Germany several times with a brother and a cousin, in 1934, 1936, and 1937. They sent 300 letters all over the world. The responses they got were the basis of our stamp collection. Among the letters were ones to the United States. The Americans wrote back to say that it would be all right for us to immigrate if we found someone to give us an affidavit. Such an affidavit cost a thousand dollars back then—per person. We talked to a friend of friends who lived in the States. He was willing to give my father an affidavit, but not for the whole family. We turned him down. We would have had to come up with the ticket money as well. We'd written the American government and we'd gotten an answer: they weren't prepared to give my father special placement in the quota rules. The USA had a very rigid quota for Germans, and no exceptions were made for German Jews. In retrospect, it may have been a good thing. Still, we had to acknowledge that people willing to help didn't exactly come a dime a dozen.

INGE SCHILZER

Born 1921; emigrated to Palestine illegally in 1940 and returned from Israel to Germany in 1960; moved to Berlin where she resides today.

"Everyone was staring at me: a Jewish girl in a BdM uniform!"

My parents were practicing Jews. I was therefore raised a Jew, and never considered myself to be out of the ordinary because of it. I was active in a Jewish youth group, but I attended a Christian school with all the other children. For me, there was absolutely no difference.

In 1933, I went to a girls' high school. One day I was met at the main entrance of the school and told, "Go home! You can't come here anymore! You're a Jew!" So I went home. Every evening after that I used to look up at the stars and think to myself, "Now your life is washed up." I realized that every goal I had set for myself was totally unreachable. From then on I knew that what I had decided to do with my life, the plans I had made, even as a 10-year-old, would never become reality. Even today, I still have difficulty in coming to terms with the change of course that my life so suddenly took.

My father was one of the first who lost his job because he was a

Jew. He was also one of the first who was made to perform forced labor. It's true that Hitler had the new autobahns built in part by prisoners. My father was one of them, performing hard labor without pay.

I was probably one of the first to read *Mein Kampf.* I even understood it. It's strange that other people failed to understand it as well. Hitler did everything he said he would do. It was so obvious. Since Hitler predicted it, I wasn't surprised when the situation in Germany did brighten up for a while.

When I realized that my parents were in no position to help me out of my dilemma concerning school and my future, I decided at the age of 15 to take matters into my own hands. I realized later on that I did some pretty dumb things.

In September 1939, Mussolini came to Berlin. I don't know why, but I just had to see him. He wasn't even that good-looking. I was attending a vocational school at the time, and had a classmate who was in the League of German Girls, the BdM. She had had to join the BdM, and wore their uniform. I also wore a uniform, the same one as all Jewish girls in our youth group: the traditional navy blue skirt and white blouse. My girlfriend and I decided to exchange uniforms. I wore the BdM uniform, and she wore mine. Then we ran off to catch a glimpse of Mussolini.

There wasn't much room to move around, and I was shoved in between two SA men. Everyone had their right arm raised in the Hitler salute. There was no way I was going to raise my arm. I knew that probably no one would notice me anyway, they were all looking at those two idiots. On the way home I was almost trampled to death; people everywhere were pushing and shoving. I finally broke free, and ran home faster than I had ever run before. I reached our street, and forgetting that I still had the BdM uniform on, I couldn't figure out why everyone was staring at me. A Jewish girl in a BdM uniform! My mother almost had a heart attack when she saw me.

LOTHAIRE LEVY

---

*Born in 1923 to Jewish parents; family fled to
France after Hitler came to power; escaped
after the German invasion and fought with the
Free French; today owns a large department
store in Metz, France.*

"My father was wounded and taken prisoner
by the Russians."

I was born on July 28, 1923, in the Saarland, approximately two
miles from the Lorraine border. I lived and went to school there until
I was 10 years old. My father, being Jewish, sensed immediately that
Hitler's election meant that he would bring about a revolution in
Europe, especially in Germany. He said, "We're not going to wait
around for the elections here in the Saarland to take place.[1] We're
moving to Metz, in France." That's how I ended up in Metz.

I had to learn French. Until then, I had only spoken German. I
couldn't even say yes or no in French. I attended high school until
1938. In September of 1938 we had our first real shock: Hitler
occupied parts of Czechoslovakia, the Sudetenland. Then Chamberlain went to Munich to sign a temporary peace agreement. The war
started a year later.

My father was born in 1895. His mother died two years afterwards. He was raised by his 16-year-old sister, the eldest of the six
children. When he was 13, he was sent to Trier to begin his apprenticeship. He was drafted at the age of 19 and sent to the Russian front.

---

[1] By the terms of the Versailles Treaty, the Saarland was made economically part of
France and put under League of Nations administration for 15 years. At the end of that
time a plebiscite would determine its future. In January 1935, the citizens voted
overwhelmingly for reunion with Germany.

He was wounded only three weeks later—he had taken a shot in the mouth—and was taken prisoner by the Russians. He spent three years in Siberia. In 1919, he was part of a prisoner exchange and landed in Königsberg, today Kaliningrad, in the midst of the German revolution. Before that, he had also experienced the Russian revolution.

He was still a young man when he returned home, where he lived for two years before he got married. Then, because of inflation, the money he had been able to save was almost worthless. He lost just about everything. The only thing he could afford to buy when he got married was a bedroom set—that was all! He worked very hard until 1933. And in 1933, we moved to Metz. He continued to work for three more years until he was told he couldn't anymore, and he was denounced by people for no reason at all. In 1939, he was arrested because he was still a German citizen. He was sent to work in a French military labor camp for foreigners. In 1942, he managed to escape. He came to Lyon and stayed with us until 1944, when he and my mother fled to Switzerland. They weren't welcome there either, and ended up being interned. They didn't come back home until August 1945. My father was finally a free man, but he died the very same year.

KLAUS SCHEURENBERG

*Born 1925; deported with his family to There-
sienstadt in 1943; was ordered to help in the
construction of a hide-out for the infamous
Eichmann; he survived and returned to Berlin
after the war.*

"I had absolutely no idea what a *Saujude* was."

My father was, like many middle-class German Jews, a naive,
unpolitical individual. When Hitler came to power, he created a new
decoration, the Front Fighter's Cross, in an effort to demonstrate his
affinity with the combat veterans of World War I. The cross was sent
to everyone who had fought on the front in the last world war, along
with a huge certificate that read, "My dear comrade. . . ." The Nazis
didn't have a list of who was Christian and who was Jewish yet, so my
father was sent one. After he got it my father said, "Hitler can't be all
that bad. He hasn't done anything to me. Look, he's even awarded me
this medal." How naive! This thing really closed his eyes to a lot for a
long time. When he finally woke up and saw that everything wasn't so
rosy after all, it was much too late to do anything.

Through the German Jewish Alliance, he wrote a letter to his
brother and sister in the United States. He had financed both of their
trips at a time when he was still financially well off. When the Jewish
Alliance asked my aunt and uncle in America if they would sign an
affidavit which meant that they would have to accept financial
responsibility for us for one year, they replied that they weren't in a
position to do so. What they didn't know was that by refusing to
sponsor us, they had as much as signed our death warrants.

Until Hitler came, I went to a normal elementary school in Berlin.

It's astounding how quickly things changed after Hitler. Our physical education teacher showed up to school every day wearing a Nazi uniform. Even though I was a good gymnast, he said to me and another classmate, who wasn't that athletic, "Out, you Jew-boys!" We all had to be present for the flag-raising ceremony which took place every day during recess. We stood there at attention and had to sing the Horst Wessel song. And when the flag went up, everybody shot out their right hand and held it up high. The P.E. teacher saw me do this along with the rest of the kids. In front of everybody, he came over and gave me a murderous beating. "You Jew-boy!" he screamed. "You're not allowed to give the German salute. And who do you think you are, singing the national anthem and the Horst Wessel song?" I started to cry. I was only eight years old. "I'm German too!" I cried back. He screamed even louder, "What? You're a German? You're a *Saujude!*" I had absolutely no idea what a *Saujude* was.

That's why I went to my religion teacher and asked her what a *Saujude* was. What was a Jew? She said, "But you know what a Jew is. On Friday nights you light the candles and you keep the Sabbath day holy." "Sure we do," I said, "doesn't everyone?" "No," she told me, "only Jews." And then she told us something about our history. I can still see her today, the way her deep black eyes glistened when she told us we were the chosen people. What she said did a lot for my self-confidence. But she went on to tell us that we were also predestined to suffer. That's actually when I began to take interest in Judaism and what it was all about.

I started going to the Jewish school. On November 9, 1938, the principal came to our classroom and told us there were anti-Jewish demonstrations taking place. She said, "Quickly, you are all to go straight home and wait until we tell you you can come back to school. Don't come back before then!" The children in surrounding Aryan schools had gotten the day off and were told to go over to the Jewish school and beat up the Jewish kids. But we had courage. We got our bicycles, made the girls walk in the middle, and with our bicycle pumps in our hands, we fought our way through. They hadn't expected us to hit back; they had always been told that all Jews were cowards. I got hit in the head with a rock. I was so concerned with getting myself out of there in one piece, I didn't even realize my head was bleeding.

I didn't go straight home; I went to the synagogue first. It had been burning since the night before. I did not dare cry because I would have betrayed myself. There was a Jewish shoe store right next to the synagogue. An eight-year-old boy was crawling through the broken display window. A woman was waiting for him on the street. "Look, Mom!" he said. "Look at these great shoes I just stole!" The mother said, "Silly, you have shoes for two left feet. Now go right back in there and get the right shoe." A policeman was standing next to the woman, making sure that everything was all right.

HELMUT SCHMOECKEL

Born 1917; one-quarter Jewish; a U-boat commander during the war; afterwards joined the Bundeswehr; lives in Bonn.

"I looked like any other blond Hitler Youth."

My home, my school, and the *Marine-Bund* were the pillars of my early life. We read Dwinger, Rilke, Beumelburg, and other patriotic poets in school, but literature didn't interest me that much. In the *Marine-Bund* (Navy League) we all wore navy uniforms with short pants. It was a former navy commander's organization to improve young people's upbringing. We had a very close camaraderie and did lots of interesting things. We learned Morse code, lamp and flag signalling, and nautical science, but we didn't have anything to do with arms. It was only logical that I join the navy afterwards.

In 1935, the Nuremberg Laws went into effect. At the time, I really wasn't fully aware of actually what was going on. I guess I'd heard one thing or another about Aryan laws, but whether they were passed or not really wasn't any concern of ours, or so I thought.

I signed up for the navy in 1936. Everything went fine until one day I was informed that I'd been discharged. I mean, I looked like any other blond, curly-haired Hitler Youth, and took it for granted that my Aryan *Nachweis* was no problem. But my father had been reactivated as a colonel and had to submit evidence of Aryan heritage, including that of my mother's side of the family. It turned out that although my grandfather's parents had married as Christians, both of them had come from Jewish families. My grandfather was a *Volljude* (100 percent Jewish) by blood.

My father called me home and explained that I'd been discharged. I was completely shocked, but that's the way it was. So I decided to study mechanical engineering, and started as an apprentice, first with Siemens in Berlin, and then at the German shipyards in Kiel. It was a pretty tough time for me because I was dressed as a dock worker, and I had to watch my comrades walk off ships all spruced up as navy lieutenants. But they were still nice to me. Even though they knew why I'd left, they still treated me like one of the gang.

Around that time, my father filed a petition for my reinstatement. In July 1939, this was approved and I had the chance to go back to the navy.

LILO CLEMENS

Born 1928; lived through the war as a "half-Jew" (Mischling), then emigrated to Israel; returned to Berlin in 1974, where she continues to live today, working as a social worker.

"The war is really over when you can buy a loaf of white bread and eat it all by yourself!"

I was 11 years old when the war broke out. My family had lived in the same house in the Alt-Moabit district of Berlin for decades. So we were well known in the shops—the dairy, the bakery, the butcher shop, and so forth. I did a lot of the shopping myself. I had two ration cards marked with a "J" for Jews. One was mine and the other belonged to my father. My mother's ration card was normal. The shopkeepers always placed my mother's card on top of the other two so the other customers in the store couldn't see that I had cards for Jews. And whenever there weren't too many customers around, the baker would usually throw in an extra wedge of bread, or his wife would add an extra roll. At the time, I remember dreaming, "If you ever live to see the end of the war"—something no one really believed—"then you'll know it's really over when you can go and buy a loaf of white bread and eat it all by yourself!"

I was always hungry back then. Not at the beginning, say in 1939 or 1940, but beginning in 1941, I can tell you we knew what it was like to be hungry. A loaf of bread was cut up every morning into so many slices. Whoever got the end piece the day before couldn't have it the following day. It was awful. We each got, maybe, three pieces of bread a day. My father had to get through the entire day on that, and he was doing hard manual labor. How my mother was able to survive, I'll never know. She always gave one of us an extra slice from her portion, and she worked all day long too. Our big meals usually consisted of turnips with water or water with turnips. It was really a treat when there were two potatoes in the pot as well.

My Jewish father was the type who said, "If we do everything they ask of us, what can they do to us? I'm no longer allowed to broadcast on the radio, I'm not allowed to write, and they've taken away my job. What more can they do to us?" My uncle, my father's only brother, emigrated to Argentina in 1938. His wife worked in the Jewish Agency's emigration office. I remember her calling us and asking, "Listen, is there anything I can do for you? Do you want to get out?" My father was agitated, "What? Leave Germany? I don't see what for! Wherever you are, it is always the same harassment!" That was my father. Yet he wasn't a German nationalist either. His family had just lived in Germany as Germans for so long that he considered himself to be the typical "German citizen of Jewish faith." [1]

---

[1] The self-description favored by assimilated and acculturated Jews under the Second Empire and the Weimar Republic.

MARIANNE REGENSBURGER

Born 1921; former schoolmate of Henry Kissinger; being Jewish, she emigrated with her family in 1939, first to Britain, later to the United States; returned to Germany after the war and became a television personality; makes her home in Berlin.

"Even with blonde hair, you'll never be an Aryan."

I'm originally from Fürth, in Bavaria, just like Henry Kissinger. In fact, his father was my math teacher. Henry was in a grade between my sister and me. I remember he was called Heinzi and was known to be a tattletale.

I first found out I was Jewish when I was a young child, a preschooler. I must have been around five years old. I was walking down the street and when someone called me a "stinking Jew" I had no idea what that was. I went home and asked what they meant. My parents were both totally assimilated Germans, and reluctantly explained what was going on. My father claimed to be an atheist. The only time he ever put his foot inside a synagogue was on Memorial Day, and then he wore all of his insignia and medals from World War I: two Iron Crosses, his pilot's wings, a Bavarian distinguished service medal, a wound badge, and I don't know what else.

It must have been around 1933 when I entered an all-girls high school. Even then, I still didn't know much about my identity or heritage. I pressed on as if nothing were wrong, and even took part in our school's Christmas play. Someone denounced this, and an article about me appeared in the *Stürmer* newspaper. I was the ripe age of 12. This was bad because my parents, especially my mother, were proud that I had been chosen to participate in the manger scene. My mother really gave me a beating. It was as if I had afflicted the family with bad luck.

Another time my mother dyed my hair. I only recall her washing my hair with something that smelled absolutely horrible. All of a sudden my hair was a completely different color. I'd always had medium brown hair, and now I was a strawberry blonde. I remember my teacher telling me, "Even with blonde hair, you'll never be an Aryan." It was so embarrasing, and it took weeks for me to convince my mother never to dye my hair again. I assume my mother did that so that I would look Aryan. It was a foolish attempt to fit in with the others. This actually goes to show how non-political German Jews really were. The attempts to adapt, to fit in with the others, no matter what, certainly had to do with the fact that we no longer identified with Judaism.

I did things out of pure defiance. I kept going to church and to the theater. While my parents were making preparations to emigrate, I remember strolling through Nuremberg and Fürth with one of those huge Telefunken radios. It had been strictly forbidden for Jews to possess a radio of any kind. Anyway, I lugged this thing back home and listened to both the BBC and Radio Moscow, which was also illegal. Naturally, I didn't understand a word of the broadcast from Moscow.

We emigrated at the end of March 1939. I was 18 years old. At the border an SA man came over—he must have been a customs inspector—and grabbed my suitcase with both hands and dumped the entire contents on the ground. It wasn't a very pleasant experience, especially since I had hidden a 100 mark bill in the sole of one of my shoes. Officially, we were only allowed to take 10 marks out of the country. All of a sudden, I started to cry. I stood there in the hallway and cried because I didn't have a visa and was about to be shipped off on another train. I repacked my suitcase and went back. The SA man and another man came over and tried to console me: "Don't worry, it's not all that bad. One day you will surely come back here."

HANS RADZIEWSKI

Born 1924; was betrayed as a Jew by another Jew to the Gestapo; deported to Auschwitz; survived and returned to Berlin, where he was a social worker after the war; lives in Berlin.

"If you run away again, they will be shot."

At the end of 1938, there was only one career classification for Jews in Berlin, and that was "Jewish worker." Engineers, lawyers, real estate agents, whatever, were prohibited from continuing with their careers. Only a rare few could, some doctors, for example. So you saw street sweepers who used to be judges, doctors, lawyers, teachers, and so on. This was because it had become next to impossible to leave the country.

To ask a Jew why he didn't emigrate was futile. First of all, people who have lived in a place for decades, who have their retirement pension or a small income—where were they supposed to go and what were they supposed to do? A healthy single person who still has his life before him can manage such a move. But a whole family? I was the oldest of five children. My father was badly disabled in the First World War. Where were we supposed to go? To get to the United States, we needed 4,000 marks times six—24,000 marks. That was a fortune.

After my father was interned in the camp in Sachsenhausen—I was also in Sachsenhausen for two weeks—we wanted to get out and try and get to the United States. This was in November 1938, and, of course, it was much too late.

My father originally came from Posen province, which used to be part of Western Prussia. After World War I was lost, the entire family opted for Prussia. My father got married in Berlin in 1915, completed his *Abitur,* and volunteered for military service, something most everyone did at the time. He was the youngest of four brothers, and all of them enlisted. Two of them were killed in the war. This wasn't anything special, you just wanted to be as German as everyone else. If Hitler hadn't started his fanatic anti-Semitism, I would probably have been just as good a soldier for the fatherland as my own father had been.

I attended a Jewish secondary school where we were taught by outstanding Jewish instructors who were no longer permitted to teach at "Aryan" schools. We were not, however, allowed to graduate. At that point I asked my father if I couldn't please go into gardening. We didn't get much to eat, and my father was quite happy when I came home with a couple of vegetables in my pocket now and again.

Next I worked at the Jewish cemetery from July 1939 to the end of December 1940. After that I was at the labor exchange for two days. On the second day, a big burly man in a Nazi uniform came in. He owned a furniture factory, and I asked if he could use me. He asked what my occupation was, and I told him I was a carpenter. He took me.

Later he said to me, "Hans, you're a big, fat liar!" I asked what he meant, and he answered, "You're no carpenter!" And I said, "No, but I'm a gardener." He said, "Okay, from now on you take care of my garden."

My parents were picked up by the Gestapo on October 24, 1942. I went to the police about it and had to stay at the station. We all ended up on the deportation train. Our train left the Berlin-Grünewald station early on a Monday morning, October 26. During the night, shortly after we crossed the Oder River, I jumped out of the train while we were crossing a bridge. I got back home two days later. I phoned the furniture company and went back to work.

The owner's daughter-in-law asked what was wrong. I said, "Frau Diko, I was deported, but I ran away." "I'll have to tell my father-in-law about this right away," she told me. But they never did anything about it. My work was still there, and I continued to glue furniture together. They were happy I was back, and I did a good job.

One day I was gluing when the daughter-in-law ran in. She said, "The SS is here, and they are picking up all of our Jewish workers."

She pressed 100 marks into my hand, and as dirty, as smeared up as I was, I ran out through the back courtyard with a tool kit still in my hand, and climbed over a fence.

After that I had to rely on friends. It was always prearranged; I could come back on this or that day at such and such a time. Sometimes I was out of Berlin, and other times I stayed in an apartment in the city. I usually didn't go anywhere until evening. I could warm myself, get something to eat, and have a place to sleep. The people who helped me were all Aryan colleagues from work. They knew very well that they were seriously endangering their own lives by helping me. During air raids, they went down to the basement and I stayed behind in the apartment. That didn't bother me. After all, what more could happen to me? On the contrary, it was something of a reprieve; during a raid no one could come and arrest me.

A few times in March, when the weather was cold, I went to the Jewish cemetery. I took a blanket and some bread—whatever I could get on the black market, whatever somebody had given me—down to a tomb. I would put the blanket over my head and wait until it was dark. I had to disappear again before it got light, because that's when the first workers arrived.

At times I would visit old customers of the furniture factory, people whose addresses I knew. I rang the doorbell and asked them if they still needed the cupboard or whatever they had ordered from us a while back, or if they needed anything repaired. Generally, there was something that needed to be glued together, and then I got lunch and coffee. The people didn't know I was a Jew, and they were pleased that the firm had sent someone by. Naturally, they asked me why I wasn't in the service, and then I had to make something up.

There were traitors among the workers, you see, Jewish hirelings who were sent out on the street by the Gestapo to catch people. At the end of March, a Jewish acquaintance stopped me on the street and said, "How are you?" I was really glad to see him. "Fine, thanks," I answered. "Do you want a cup of coffee?" "Yes, I could use one," I said. And all at once I was arrested. They had been sent out by the Gestapo—Jews!

The Gestapo officer who interrogated me handed me some photographs and asked, "Do you know these people?" "Yes," I said, "they are my brothers and sisters." And then he said, "If you run away again, they will be shot!"

RICHARD LÖWENTHAL

Born 1908; active in the resistance until his emigration to Britain in 1935; returned to West Germany after the war; a political scientist well known for his numerous books, is a professor at the Berlin Free University; resides in Berlin.

"My presence had become a danger to my comrades."

Due to my past involvement in the Communist and Socialist left, I was part of the resistance movement from the very beginning of the Third Reich. I even joined the ranks of the leadership in 1935, when our organization was undergoing a critical phase. It was then that my "illegal" friends advised me to leave the country, not so much because I was in any real immediate danger myself, but because my presence had become a danger to my comrades.

You've got to understand that these illegal groups met, four or five members at a time, in various apartments to talk about the events going on in the country. It was an ironclad rule at the start of every meeting that we raised a question: If the police appear on the scene, how did we come to know one another, and what are we doing? And if it's a group consisting of four workers and one Jewish intellectual, these questions simply had no safe answers. That was why I came to pose a threat to those close to me.

CHAPTER 3

Blitzkrieg

Germany went to war for the second time in a quarter-century with a mixture of disbelief and determination. For the men in uniform, this time there was no talk of a "fresh and joyful" war. A clumsily faked attack on a Silesian radio station and episodic outbreaks of violence against German nationals in Poland generated no crusading enthusiasm. Troops moving through Berlin on the way to the front were not greeted with the hysterical cheering of 1914. In silence, thousands of men and women watched the tanks and trucks roll by. But in that silence was the beginning of a conviction more powerful than the superficial patriotism of World War I, a feeling that had nothing to do with Hitler or National Socialism. It was the determination, as yet unspoken, that this time the homeland would not experience the consequences of defeat.

Poland's collapse in less than a month surprised even the Wehrmacht generals. The quick German victory owed less to new techniques of warfare than to the imbalance of forces between the combatants. The German-Soviet Nonaggression Pact of August 8, 1939, left Poland exposed from both sides. Her French and British allies remained passive at a time when Germany's western frontier was virtually defenseless. Hitler's luck held even after Poland's collapse. Blitzkrieg in the East became Sitzkrieg—phoney war—in the West. The victorious Wehrmacht had a full winter to train and to modernize its equipment.

To the experts of the General Staff, a drive across the open terrain of Belgium and northern France in the pattern of August 1914, initially seemed to present the greatest chance of success. The alternative proposal of a thrust through the center, pitting internal-combustion engines against the wooded, broken ground of the Ardennes, caught not only Hitler's imagination, but Chief of Staff Franz Halder's as well. For all its risks, it seemed an alternative to getting stuck once more in the mud of Flanders.

On April 9, 1940, Germany invaded Norway and Denmark. Hitler preempted a British move into Scandinavia by making Narvik and the North Cape major German naval bases. On May 10, the Wehrmacht launched its main offensive into France and the Low Countries. The French army was not, as some have said, prepared only to fight the last war. But it lacked the capacity to react to the lightning-fast German combination punches. Neither did individual French and British soldiers possess the firepower and the tactical skill of their German counterparts. German officers led from the front and exercised initiative instead of waiting for orders.

Thrown off balance in the first days of the German offensive, the Western Allies never recovered. On May 14, the Luftwaffe bombed Rotterdam when orders cancelling the mission were not received. The next day the Dutch army surrendered. On May 28, Belgium's King Leopold took his country out of the war. The best French and British troops were destroyed in a series of vicious encounters, or driven into the sea at Dunkirk.

The successful evacuation of Dunkirk was also a military disaster, leaving the British Isles virtually defenseless. But the Wehrmacht lacked the strength to pursue two simultaneous offensives. The tanks and dive bombers turned from the Dunkirk pocket to drive France out of the war and to her knees. On June 22, 1940, the French government signed an armistice at Compiègne—in the same railroad car where a German delegation signed the armistice of November 11, 1918.

History seemed to have turned full circle. Places whose names a quarter-century ago had been symbols of a generation's sacrifice— Verdun, Ypres, Vimy, Arras—had fallen into German hands like beads pulled from a string, hardly rating a line in the official report. Casualties had been lower than in 1870, fewer than 10,000 dead. All the images were of not merely victory, but conquest. Laughing men in field-gray uniforms rode tanks past seemingly endless columns of shabby, unshaven prisoners. German soldiers marveled at the sights of Paris, or tested their high school French in local bistros. German officers stood in line to receive their generals' stars or marshals' batons.

One enemy remained: Great Britain. The German army's newly acquired confidence could not bring tanks and guns across the few miles of water separating the combatants. The German navy, which would normally carry the brunt of preparing any landings, had been crippled during the Norwegian campaign. That sideshow had been undertaken at least partly because of the navy's conviction that Scandinavian bases were necessary to support the offensive against Britain's economy. By the time the bases were secured, however, the navy had lost most of its ships.

This put a double burden on the Luftwaffe. Not only would it have to obtain initial air superiority, but it also would have to sustain the invasion against what was sure to be desperate British resistance. For the first time in the war, the Wehrmacht was unable to maintain the initiative. In the six years of its existence, the Luftwaffe had developed no strategic concept, no doctrine of how to maintain a strategic offensive. Göring and his senior advisors failed to concentrate on key objectives. Instead, the focus of the attacks was constantly shifting, from radar stations and air fields, to the British fighter force itself, to the docks, and then the streets, of London.

The Luftwaffe lacked the striking power, the reserves, and the supply structure to implement such a random approach. Its twin-engine bombers could neither defend themselves nor carry enough tonnage to justify their increasingly heavy losses. The Luftwaffe's first-line fighter, the Me-109, was at least as good as its great rival, the Spitfire. But the Me-109 had originally been designed to operate over German air space. Like all single-seaters of the day, it lacked range. Its pilots flew and fought always with one eye on their fuel gauges.

The Battle of Britain was the first battle in history fought entirely in the air, and among the last characterized by a certain chivalry between the combatants. Strategy, technology, and the skill and determination of the RAF, combined to deny the Luftwaffe the first requirement of a successful invasion, air superiority. In the fall of 1940, the Germans withdrew their invasion force from the Channel coast.

But the Battle of Britain was more than an operational defeat. It cost the Luftwaffe many of its best crews and its most promising junior leaders. It began the process of attrition that eventually reduced the Wehrmacht to a shell. And it strengthened Hitler's determination to concentrate on destroying National Socialism's main political enemy, Communist Russia.

The blitzkrieg achieved one more set of triumphs in Western Europe. Hitler regarded the Mediterranean as a strategic dead end, and would probably not have moved south had it not been for his Italian ally. Mussolini, eager to establish an independent sphere of influence, had declared war on France and Britain only days before France's collapse. Since then his armies had met nothing but disaster.

German expansion into the Mediterranean was more than just a rescue operation. Italy's ambitions posed at least a potential threat to Germany's own position in southeastern Europe. Rumania and Hungary moved into the Nazi camp in 1940, Bulgaria—much less willingly—in 1941. But anti-Axis generals of the Yugoslav army reacted to their king's acceptance of a German alliance by staging a coup on March 27, 1941.

Hitler responded with a blitz into Yugoslavia and Greece. Belgrade was bombed into submission by the Luftwaffe on April 6. Three weeks later, German tanks rolled into Athens. On May 20, the Greek and British troops who had managed to escape to the island of Crete were surprised in what was then the greatest airborne operation in history. German paratroopers and glider infantry took the island with 6,000 casualties in some of the war's bitterest close fighting. And the Wehrmacht paid for the Balkan campaign with six weeks' delay in mounting the riskiest operation in Germany's military history: the invasion of Russia.

KLAUS VON BISMARCK*

**"We were highly impressed with ourselves—
our vitality, our strength, and our
discipline."**

The war began for me in 1939, despite the fact that I found Goebbels' inflammatory remarks about the "aggressive" Polish people and their anti-German riots hard to believe. I had the feeling the Poles did not pose a threat to us. I personally felt no hatred for the Poles. There weren't any Poles in Pomerania, nor did I know any. Nevertheless, I had the distinct feeling the time had come for me to do my duty as a soldier.

When did I have my first doubts? It was in the beginning, in Poland. I began to suspect that something was wrong when I realized what a poor, victimized country Poland actually was. The old women I saw poking around in the burned churches somehow just did not fit the picture painted by Nazi propaganda.

The soldiers themselves weren't exactly ecstatic about the war, nor did they really believe the propaganda they heard. On the other hand, they didn't believe they were doing anything that was wrong. At the time, we were all captivated by the situation. We were highly impressed with ourselves—our vitality, our strength, and our discipline. The moment you, as an officer, received a command position, you had the feeling you were leading in a ten-mile run. A command position also provided an officer with a perfect moral cover: "We can't do anything about it, it has to be this way."

I know today that I was abused. My military idealism was abused, the idealism which represented Prussian tradition.

---

* Biography on page xxxv.

MAX MAYER

*Born 1913; served as a test pilot at Peene-
münde, the Reich's missile test ground; active
after the war in the Federal Republic's aero-
space program; resides in Bonn-Bad Godesberg.*

"Peenemünde was wonderfully equipped,
typically Luftwaffe."

Once when we visited my father at work, three bright red biplanes
flew low over the roofs. This was naturally fascinating and of colossal
interest to us youngsters. Sometime later, the first electric railway
line between Munich and Regensburg was opened. My brother, a
friend, and I went to see it. We were standing at the train overpass
when we saw something strange in the distance. It looked like a big
cloud which slowly turned out to be a Zeppelin. It was a majestic
sight to see it flying over the steeples of Regensburg.

My father was a patriot. When the national anthem was played,
tears would run down his cheeks. This basically describes my environment the day Hitler came to power on January 30, 1933.

My studies continued at the university, and we students weren't
under any political pressure. The party was recruiting at the university, but very few of us joined. My family never even owned a copy of
Mein Kampf, let alone read it. I still haven't read it to this day. The
first time I saw it was after the war.

Today no one would dare propose labor service. But voluntary
labor service wasn't such a bad thing, just as the household year for
young girls wasn't. It's something that would surely do young people
today some good before they go out into life and into careers.

Considering my interests, I naturally joined the German Air
Sports Club. I flew my first basic-training flights in small gliders.

I went to Berlin during the summer of 1936, during the Olympics.

Berlin was a whirlwind of excitement. There was brilliant sunshine and a fantastic atmosphere. I went to the Olympic Games and saw the water sports. I saw divers do somersaults from the 30-foot board. The crowds were ecstatic; everyone was cheering. My training as an aeronautical engineer and test pilot was of course very attractive. I started in Bremen with the Focke-Wulf company. Then I went for further flight training to the German Research Establishment for Aeronautics in Braunschweig. There I met Professor Gödert, who later worked at the Arnolds Engineering Center in Tullahoma, Tennessee. I met lots of people during that time. That was actually the great thing about this education: you were never in one section for more than a few months, and you got an overall picture through active participation in different assignments.

In 1938, I was offered a job at the Peenemünde rocket center. It was all very secret and we weren't allowed to talk about it. I was invited to go up and take a look around. I was curious to see what the area and the people were like there.

I finished my flight training in Braunschweig, and in December of 1938 I went up to Peenemünde on my motorcycle via Berlin. The guard took me directly to my quarters. It was a bachelor's apartment, perfectly set up—the kind you dream about. I went to the canteen to get something to eat. There were lots of friendly people sitting together at a large round table. There was *Flugbaumeister* Reins, Wernher von Braun, Dr. Thiel, Dr. Hermann from the simulator, and they all greeted me right away. I got to know Wernher von Braun that first evening. We all lived in the same building, House 5. We later called it the "bull pen" because, for the most part, only unmarried men lived there.

The primary reason for Peenemünde was that, in the early 1930s, the Army Ordnance Department wanted to circumvent the Versailles limitations on artillery range. At that time, the maximum range permitted was something like 20 to 22 miles. There was a captain in the Ordnance Department in Berlin by the name of Dr. Dornberger. He met a few rocket enthusiasts, so naturally he also knew both Oberth and Rudolf Nebel. The department wondered if artillery ranges couldn't be extended using this technology. They were all just rocket fans who wanted to do things like send mail by missile and fly to the moon.

Had these people gone to the authorities with their ideas—back then that would have been the German Ministry of Transport—they wouldn't have gotten a penny's worth of funding for their projects. So they had to count every cent and try out their ideas on their own launch pad. Finally, Dornberger took them under his wing and authorized some funds if they continued research on solid-fuel and liquid-fuel rockets. At first they used an army testing site at Kummersdorf. When Kummersdorf became too small, they moved to Peenemünde.

When I arrived in Peenemünde in 1938, a completed air strip and hangars, administration buildings, cafeterias, and housing already existed. It was wonderfully equipped, typically Luftwaffe. Everything was beautifully done. Even by today's standards it was a superbly equipped and functioning test site. The residential buildings were done up like villas. Imagine going to a place like that as a young man! We could fly there, go sailing in the Baltic, and we were researching new frontiers. How could we possibly not like it?

After work, we usually sat around and talked. The men from Peenemünde East, who over at Oye Island had developed the A-2 and then the A-4 (forerunner of the V-2), always spoke of their ambitions. "If we could only get up higher!" they said. "If we could only one day do what Professor Oberth dreamed of! If we could make it to the moon, what an experience that would be for humanity."

We developed and tested so-called stand-off weapons, which were actually flying bombs such as the HS 293 that were released beyond the range of the anti-aircraft weapons protecting the target. The principle was to follow a tracer flare from the cockpit as soon as it was launched. We tested wireless guidance by remote radio control. We even tested guidance by television! That was in 1942! From a height of up to 5 miles, we could hit targets of 15 × 15 feet from a distance of 10 miles. We were also highly successful with the use of the *Fallbombe* (the S01400X). This was dropped from an altitude of at least 15,000 feet, and guided to the target by the bombardier through radio or wire remote control.

All told, 450,000 tons of shipping were to be sunk with these weapons during the war.

The sinking of the Italian battleship *Roma,* for example, was spectacular. On the night of September 10, 1943, it left the port of

Livorno to join the Allies. A German bomber discovered the *Roma* on its way to Malta and sank her, lock, stock, and barrel. Two thousand sailors drowned.

We also tested the rocket-powered Messerschmitt 163 during the war, and got it ready for front use. At the time, it was the only rocket plane in the world. However, it was a very vulnerable target after it exhausted its fuel supply, and had to glide back to earth. Another project at Peenemünde was a long-distance unmanned aircraft, a flying bomb: the so-called V-1. What is interesting is that such a weapon had already been suggested shortly after the war broke out. But the project was scrapped because, with the means at our disposal, we couldn't get the desired target accuracy. Therefore it was classed as an area weapon, and the Wehrmacht didn't want to employ such weapons, because they would mean civilian casualties. But British attacks on cities in the Ruhr led to the directive to develop it after all, in May or June 1942. By 1944, when the invasion of Normandy took place, 5,000 of them were ready for action. In addition, there were the tests of the "piggy-back" system; an unmanned Ju-88 carrying a four-ton bomb with a manned FW 190 fighter on top controlling the launch. Certainly its accuracy wasn't very good; it really was an area weapon which was also very vulnerable.

Then came the night of August 17, 1943. It was a wonderful night with a full moon. I had just gotten back on a flight from Friedrichshafen on Lake Constance. We had eaten together and were sitting up around midnight eating the plums I had brought back with me. Suddenly, the alarm sounded. The sirens were wailing and there was a massive attack right over our heads; 650 four-engine British bombers dropped their bombs on us—an area 500 yards wide and a little over a mile long. We had a bunker near our quarters, in the center of the administration area. When the attack was over, everything was on fire. Dornberger had to run to the bunker in his socks; he'd forgotten his boots. Lieutenant Colonel Stahms, who had lost a leg landing a Ju-88, lost his artificial leg in the fire. Approximately 765 people died during the attack. Although some of the army's sector was damaged, the rest of the plant was pretty much intact. The test site in Peenemünde West was left untouched.

WALTER KNAPPE

Born 1916; drafted into the Luftwaffe in 1939; shot down twice and captured three times by three different armies; after the war was a manager at the Siemens Company; resides in North Rhine Westphalia.

"He died fighting for Germany."

I was drafted in 1939. I was a POW three times. I was shot down twice, and three times I had to make emergency landings.

I was trained as a navigator. At the beginning of May 1940, we saw action in the West, at Rotterdam and over Dunkirk. On one mission we got separated from our squadron and were attacked by two French fighters. Both of our engines caught fire and we had to make a crash landing in Belgium.

When we landed, we were enveloped in a heavenly calm. It didn't last long. There was a whistling, and bullets hit the wing and the cockpit. I saw that it was dangerous in there and time to get out. Our radioman and the pilot were already out. With one jump I was out and running in the direction of my comrades—hands up, of course. And then the three of us were standing with upraised hands in front of the aircraft, looking at nothing but rifle barrels. Our captors weren't wearing uniforms. Suddenly I felt a sharp blow in the shoulder, a shot that went clean through. Hot blood ran down into my clothes, and I staggered. The civilians rushed us, robbed us of everything we had, and cursed us.

We were turned over to the French and questioned by one interrogator after the other. Then we were separated. I was taken to a field hospital near Dunkirk. I was rescued when Dunkirk was taken. During all of this, I had one experience I will never forget. There were wounded French, British, Germans, and North Africans in this hospital. The packs lined up in rows were treated as common property. I took a French pistol, and others picked up guns, but no one harmed anyone else. We had become a community.

When I was freed, I was taken by hospital train to Germany. I cannot describe the feeling I had as I neared the German border as a wounded soldier coming home from captivity. We were speechless when the first flowers were put into our hands.

After I recovered, I flew once again as a navigator in a bomber. I was a German doing my part for the Reich. I couldn't understand how some people could even begin to doubt the prospects for final victory, or how they could question the justice of the war.

I returned to the squadron I had been assigned to during the campaign in France. Our unit had lost 17 of its 27 aircraft; there were only ten of the old crews left. The next missions we flew, the Battle of Britain, were tough. We flew by day and by night. Once, one of our engines caught on fire as we were returning from Liverpool. It's pretty tricky trying to fly a JU-88 with only one engine, but we made it home.

I was shot down the night of October 31, 1940. I woke up several days later in a British hospital. I had a brain concussion, a fracture at the base of the skull, and arm and leg fractures. My three crew members had died on the way to the hospital. As I was told later, the doctors had worked hard to save me since I had shown signs of life. They succeeded in pulling me out of a coma that lasted eight to ten days. I had to be fed intravenously.

A German Jewish woman living in England was sent to help me learn to speak again. She gave me the feeling that it was important to speak. I felt as if I were learning to talk all over again.

In the hospital, I felt quite a sense of *esprit de corps* with the British there. All of the soldiers had come from Dunkirk. Although I was their prisoner, we didn't live together as enemies, but as soldier comrades. The experience of war brought us together.

The Red Cross took my personal data and reported it to Germany. When November had come and gone and my squadron had received no word of my whereabouts, they turned in a death report: "He died fighting for Germany." Fortunately, my parents later heard by way of the Red Cross that a Walter Knappe, seriously wounded, was in British captivity.

I was shipped to Canada in 1942. We landed at Halifax and travelled west by train. We arrived in Quebec after dark. What a surprise it was to see all the bright lights! In Germany everything was blacked out, of course. We were devastated, and we could not possibly understand how, now that the U.S. and Canada were in the war, we could possibly be victorious. How could we win against such superior power?

We began to doubt our leaders, and we found ourselves saying, "How can a relatively small country—even if it is called 'Greater Germany'—possibly defend itself against enemies on every front? How could it even protect itself within the borders of the Reich?" We really began to realize the size of North America when we travelled by fast train for days, heading west, all the way to Alberta. The country seemed endless—it simply went on, day in and day out. I began to realize that our leaders were not only impulsive, but they were also wantonly and rashly foolish. These feelings stayed with me until I was included in a prisoner exchange. Those of us who were exchanged were wrecks physically, and sometimes mentally. But while we were not our old selves, we still wanted to get home to help our country.

FERDINAND KRONES

Born in 1918 in Austria; a tanker during the war; after the war was a teacher; resides in Vienna.

"Hitler wanted to make a gesture to Britain."

The alert sounded on the morning of May 9, 1940. Our tanks were refueled and the crews were issued ammunition. That evening we drove toward the border via Kyllburg in the Eifel Mountains. We reached northern Luxembourg at about 5:00 A.M. On the 10th, the day the war with France began, we drove over mountainous roads and high passes. We reached southern Belgium on the morning of the 11th. It was the city of Bastogne.

Shortly before we reached Sedan, we received a radio message from our company commander, a very well-educated man: "We are now at the spot where in 1870 Napoleon III surrendered his sword to Bismarck and said, 'Since I did not have the pleasure of dying at the head of my troops, I present your excellency with my sword.' " And Bismarck graciously asked him to keep his sword "as a symbol of respect for the bravery of the French soldiers."

This time we took everyone by surprise. About halfway between Bastogne and Saint Quentin there was a French military exercise ground, where soldiers were training. The British soldiers there were completely unaware that the troops approaching were neither French nor British, but German. They continued their exercises until suddenly a German tank was 500 yards away from them. They were captured without a shot being fired.

Afterwards, our division arrived at the farthest western point of the encirclement at Dunkirk. Suddenly we were ordered to stop and the British were allowed to evacuate most of their troops to England. I still cannot figure out whether this decision was made by the army command, or whether it came straight from the top. My personal guess is that Hitler wanted to make a gesture to Britain, by making it possible for them to retreat without a fight. This was a gesture to the "blood relatives," our English cousins.

But that was something we didn't understand at the front. We were advancing very successfully, and we all wondered, why stop now?

WERNER BARTELS*

"We were the first pilots to walk down the Champs Elysées, and we planned to be the first to walk down Bond Street."

I remained an officer in the reserves the entire time I worked for the aircraft industry as a civilian. I was called for temporary duty as a pilot in a fighter wing in 1940. I was on active duty long enough to fly the first missions against France on May 10, 1940. I was the wing's chief technical officer, and ended up flying during the entire French campaign alongside General Galland, a captain at the time. He and I were the first pilots to walk down the Champs Elysées after France capitulated. We made plans to be the first ones to walk down Bond Street in London as well. In fact, it didn't take long for me to get to London after all—only I wasn't a victor, I was a prisoner.

I got hit during our first major raid against the docks of London, July 20, 1940. We were heavily outnumbered by the Spitfires we met in the air. It was obvious that they were out to get Galland. Before I knew it I had a Spitfire on my tail, and my leg was all but shot off. A whole group of muscles was just gone. One hand was also shot to pieces. In addition to all of this, I had been hit in the head. I felt for my crotch. If there was nothing there, I saw no reason to land. But my "family jewels" were okay, so I decided to try somehow to crash-land the plane. Near Ramsgate, I saw a house that had a huge red cross painted on its roof. I managed to fly underneath some drooping telegraph wires and belly-land the plane in a field of cabbages and potatoes. I started to lose consciousness the minute I landed. I had lost so much blood, it's amazing that I was capable of landing the plane at all!

The next thing I knew, I was being put on a stretcher and driven

---

over dirt roads to the hospital. I was given a blood transfusion in the operating room and lost all consciousness after that. When I came to, I saw that my right leg was fully casted and hanging in traction. One side of the cast had been left open, and tubes had been shoved deep into my thigh to drain the pus. They had my arm hanging high and had bandaged my head. I looked like a living cast.

In 1941, I was transported to Canada. I was in the same railroad car with Captain von Werra when we crossed the U.S.-Canadian border and he jumped out of the window and fled. A motion picture was made about him, called "The One Who Got Away."

In 1942, a Red Cross commission consisting of doctors from neutral countries went through the military hospitals to select which of the severely wounded would be part of a prisoner exchange. I was one of those picked. In July 1943, I was sent to Edinburgh. From there, I went by hospital ship to Göteborg in Sweden. The ferry from Stettin on the Baltic Sea, carrying a corresponding number of British prisoners, also arrived in Sweden where the exchange took place.

All of us prisoners, Germans and Brits, were hanging around in front of the ships when along came the British brigadier who, along with the German colonel and the commander of the harbor, had been involved in the exchange. The Swedes had given us something to drink, and for two hours we had really boozed it up. In fact, we were stinking drunk. At any rate, here comes this Tommy with his typical stiff stride and his swagger stick under his arm. He looks at one of the British officers and says, "Captain, do you know that there is a war going on against Germany?" He really jumped on the guy. The British officer had lost a leg. "Yes, sir!" he said. But he was stinking drunk too and still hanging on to me to keep from keeling over! It was great!

We finally arrived back in Germany. I couldn't believe what had happened to our country in so short a time. I couldn't help crying. I spent many, many sleepless nights just lying there thinking and crying about what had happened.

JOHANNES STEINHOFF*

"I realized that Göring was obviously an amateur, and I began to hate him."

I didn't have to wait long for my next meeting with the supreme commander of the Luftwaffe. I had been tasked with setting up Germany's first night fighter squadron. I must admit that I didn't have the slightest idea of how to hunt down enemy aircraft in the dark of night. And my superiors—including Göring—knew even less, much less. During the first months of the war and after the campaign in Poland, we were stationed at an air base near Bonn. We tried flying our Messerschmitt 109s, a single-seater aircraft, after dark. When I say dark, I mean pitch-black. All the German cities had their lights off. We weren't very successful at it, and it's a miracle in itself that I survived at all.

I was ordered to Berlin for a meeting about our night fighters, or rather our non-functioning night fighters. You see, British bombers had reached the Reich's capital, and were dropping—at least in the beginning—pamphlets. That made Göring mad! He had boasted that his name would be Hermann Meier if Allied bombers ever reached Berlin. (Later on, he was in fact ironically referred to as Hermann Meier.)

I will never forget that meeting. We all sat around an enormous round table. Everything in the room seemed to have oversized medieval dimensions. The huge chandelier hanging from the ceiling was made out of a wagon wheel. The chairs were covered with thick yellow leather. The masterpiece was in the middle. The back of that chair had to have been at least six feet high. That was where Göring sat. We were a small group: Göring, three or four generals, and finally me.

* Biography on page 7.

Göring lit up a Virginia cigar and lectured for at least half an hour. What he had to say sounded like the script of a movie about World War I: biplanes looping, attacking from below, flying so close that the pilots could see the whites of their enemy's eyes. I couldn't stand it any longer. After all, I was the only one present who had actually flown any night missions. I dared raise one finger. There was dead silence. Göring looked at me in astonishment. He pointed his cigar at me giving me permission to speak. I simply said that everything had changed. We flew at much higher altitudes. We wore oxygen masks. Furthermore, we had no navigational aids and the cities had been blacked out. The only way we could spot the enemy was if he just happened to be picked up by a searchlight.

That's as far as I got. Göring gestured with a wave of his cigar that I had said enough. "Young man," he said, "young man, you still have a lot of experience to gain and a lot to learn before you think you can have your say here. Now why don't you just sit back down on your little rear end." At that moment I realized that the man was obviously an amateur, and I began to hate him.

Shortly afterwards, I was thrown out of the night fighting business. If it hadn't been for the fact that I already had won a few dog fights, I would have probably disappeared from the face of the earth. But before I knew it, I was given a day fighter squadron based near Calais. The Battle of Britain had begun.

In retrospect, I must say that those four months—that is, from the beginning of August to the beginning of November—were the most trying, both psychologically and physically, I was to experience throughout the entire war. It was strictly a battle between two air forces, and was unique in that the other world powers did not get involved. It was a battle in which very young men fought like medieval knights. Both sides not only recognized, but also adhered to the rules of fair play.

The expectations the Luftwaffe's leaders placed on us were outrageous. Two to three times a day we found ourselves either over the Channel, over London, or somewhere over the British Isles, engaged in heavy air-to-air combat with British fighters. As luck had it, it was our wing's job to escort our bombers. We had orders to avoid combat; our job was strictly to make sure the bombers made it to their targets.

But the German Luftwaffe lost a substantial number of its young pilots during these months of the war because of its equipment. When the Luftwaffe became involved in the war, its resources were minimal. Strategic bombers were non-existent. The fighters, which were expected to provide the bombers with protection, didn't have much range. In addition to this, Göring, on several occasions, took it upon himself to change target sites at random for no apparent reason. By the middle of September, it was all too obvious that we were fighting a losing battle.

I personally believed that the outcome of this air battle was a major turning point in the war. From that moment on, I knew we had lost control of the third dimension: the air space over Europe. I had already taken part in the campaign in France, the destruction of Rotterdam, and the occupation of Scandinavia. In terms of air warfare, all of this had been child's play. Now the situation was dead serious.

MARIANNE HOPPE*

"Somehow Göring was never able to detach himself from World War I."

What kind of man was Göring? We saw him once or twice a year. My husband was the superintendent of the Prussian State Theater at the time, and had to report to Göring, who was the Prussian Minister President. He presented himself as a genial good fellow, the kind who always picks up the check. And considering his past—he was a superb pilot during World War I—I guess you could say he deserved a certain amount of respect. How he came to join the Nazi Party, and how he came to get himself involved in that dreadful party business, I

---

* Biography on page 31.

have no idea. It was probably because they needed someone with his charisma.

Göring was a very jovial man. He was friendly. The atmosphere in his home was, you could almost say, cozy, even if the women were all sitting around the table formally dressed, wearing their ermine stoles. He was absolutely harmless, at least that's the appearance he gave. But he knew exactly what was going on. He knew everything. I experienced a wonderful scene during one of our visits. Göring's young nephew, a pilot, was there on leave. Göring started talking about flying to England in large formations, and so on. The nephew suddenly turned white as a ghost. He stood up and said, "That's not true! Those planes we have to fly are all nothing but a bunch of old crates. We are going to get ourselves shot down." Göring turned pale and said, "If what you're saying is what's going around in the officers' clubs, then I can only ask where would we be today if we had talked like that during the First World War?" "Yes," I said, "and just where are we today?" Somehow Göring was never able to detach himself from World War I.

WOLFGANG PREISS

Born 1910; anti-aircraft gunner during the war; a well-known actor famous for playing German generals in such films as The Longest Day *(TV version) and* The Winds of War; *lives in Baden-Baden, Baden.*

"Jewess Trudel Kahn went as a Portuguese *señhora* to Munich with a special SS pass."

One day I walked down the Champs-Elysées with a friend of mine, Hannes Steltzer. There were beautiful women, expertly made-up, everywhere in Paris. The first time you visit Paris, you are totally intoxicated by the city. We pointed out the beautiful women to each other—look at this one, look at that one. He said to me, "Look at her!" I look and say, "Trudel!" and she says, "Wolfgang!"

After my *Abitur,* I had gone to Munich to study German literature and theater. Later, I took drama classes and there I met Trudel Kahn, a Jewish girl. She studied with me and we both received degrees in 1932. After that we lost touch. And then in Paris, there she was, suddenly standing in front of me. And she told me an unbelievable story:

After we passed our exams in 1932, I accepted a part immediately, and she stayed in Munich where she met a young brewery owner from Nuremberg. They fell in love, got married around the end of the year, and lived in Nuremberg. Then came the Third Reich. Slowly things began to change: she was a "Full Jew." Her husband managed to hold things off for a while one way and another. He knew some of the party bigshots. But soon even his good connections didn't help anymore. So first they formally separated; then they officially divorced but continued to live a married life. Then at one point she said she couldn't stand it anymore; there was no sense in it. Back then people still thought this Hitler apparition couldn't last forever. She'd been in Paris as a dancer once and said, "Listen, I'll go to Paris again. We'll write each other until this nightmare is over, and then everything will be like before."

She went to Paris, and in the beginning she wrote her husband every day. But she never got a letter from him, and he never got one from her. Time went by. She began her life again as a *chanteuse* and danced in some cabarets. Around this time she met a Portuguese. He was somewhat older than she—she was 23—but he was a good man who fell head over heels in love with her. He proposed, and Trudel Kahn went to Portugal with *Señhor* Fernandez and got married. The marriage went well, though more on a companionship basis, and after nine months they separated as friends.

She went back to Paris, now as Dolores Fernandez, with a Portugese passport. She rejoined her cabaret, and then the war broke out. German troops marched into Paris, and one of the first German soldiers she saw on the street was her ex-husband. They started married life again where they'd left off four or five years before.

As a brewery owner, her ex-husband was liquor supplier for the troops—especially for the officers. So of course he attended parties and receptions accompanied by his "Portugese girlfriend." The gents were thrilled. She was so attractive, and spoke German so fluently. When SS officers asked her why her German was so good, she told them she had studied in Munich and, moreover, had "planned a trip to Munich a few years ago to visit some old friends, but unfortunately the war got in the way." The SS officers responded immediately with, "It would be a pleasure and an honor for us to arrange a trip to Munich for you."

And that was how the Jewess Trudel Kahn went as a Portuguese *señhora* to Munich with a special SS pass. She had somehow found out that her mother had been sent to Dachau, and she tried to get in contact with her. But soon a friend who worked in one of the party offices warned her, "Trudel, somehow somebody's noticed; you better get out of here!" So she went back to Paris. In the meantime, her husband had been sent to the Russian front where, I believe, he was killed. She never heard from him again.

In 1955, I was acting at the Munich *Kleine Komödie* in the play "Dial 'M' for Murder." On the first night, I received a huge bouquet—from Trudel Kahn, who had returned to Germany after the war.

LOTHAIRE LEVY*

"They had been German soldiers in the First World War and French soldiers in 1939!"

Even though we were living in France, my father was still a German citizen. And because he was German, he was interned at the beginning of the war when all Germans living in Metz were arrested. My

* Biography on page 51.

stepmother took me, my grandparents, and the rest of the family to Dijon, about 120 miles south of Metz. Then, in May 1940, Hitler attacked France, and I fled on my bike to Lyons, where I had an uncle. One uncle of mine was a French soldier; two other uncles were taken prisoner by the Germans. They had been German soldiers in the First World War and French soldiers in 1939! The Germans arrested my uncles in May 1940, and they showed up in Lyon in 1941. Even though they were Jews, the Germans had released them because they had fought in the First World War.

I was 17. I worked in Lyon until 1942, when the Germans arrived. I knew the moment had come to do something. So I fled over the Pyrenees into Spain. There, I was thrown in jail because I had illegally crossed the border. Although I was never sentenced, I spent six months in prison. But there were certain people in Spain who arranged for us to be exchanged.

I set out for Casablanca via Portugal, and joined up with the Free French forces. In Morocco we formed the famous Second Armored Division under General Leclerc.

There were German POWs in North Africa, and they were really glad to be prisoners; it meant that the war was over for them. They kept pestering us: "Are we going to the States? Are you sure we are going to the States?" All, even the Germans we took as prisoners in Normandy, wanted to know if they were going to be sent to the United States. That was all they ever talked about.

From Morocco, we went to England by ship, where we stayed until we could set out for Normandy. We fought in Normandy and took part in the liberation of Paris. From there we fought our way across the Vosges Mountains to Strasbourg, and finally to Stuttgart. We reached Berchtesgaden during the very last days of the war.

KARL SCHULZE

Born 1914; a captain in the paratroopers; fought in Crete and Italy, and was part of the operation that rescued Mussolini; later joined the Bundeswehr, and today makes his home in Oberachem, Rhineland.

"We jumped right into enemy positions."

I was a member of the paratroops, and my last rank was captain. I was called to service a little late, and because the French campaign was over so quickly, we young officers were afraid the war would be over without our having had a chance to prove ourselves. The only way out seemed to be the paratroops.

I first saw action in Greece. Our task was to stop the British retreat at the Corinth Canal, and that's what we did. My battalion was supposed to build a bridge at the canal's eastern exit in case the existing bridge was destroyed. Our assault engineers had taken that bridge in a surprise raid. They landed by cargo glider and removed the demolition charges. Unfortunately, they left the explosives on the bridge, and the defending British troops on the opposite shore hit one of these charges and blew it up.

I also jumped at Crete with the 1st Battalion of the 2nd Parachute Regiment. Along with some support troops, we were supposed to take the airstrip at Rethymnon so that air landings could take place. However, the British put up such stiff resistance that we suffered very high casualties and failed to take it. We jumped right into enemy positions which hadn't been detected by aerial reconnaissance.

We were usually dropped at 1,000 to 1,500 feet, an altitude at which the planes were very vulnerable. The pilots had seen that there was very heavy defensive fire over the target area, so they had us jump a few miles in front of the intended drop zone. That was a short distance for the pilots, but now we had to reach the drop zone on foot before we could attack. We did gain some ground, but later in the morning we were overrun in a surprise counterattack by the New Zealanders. I was badly wounded and taken prisoner. But all told, the Crete operation was a success. Our troops later took the island, and I was free again.

KARL-HEINZ REINTGEN

Born 1916; director of a military radio station during World War II; introduced the famous World War II song, "Lili Marlene"; after the war became vice president of Radio Saarbrucken; lives in Saarbrucken.

"Mr. Lili Marlene"

In April 1941, at the beginning of the Balkan campaign, I was ordered to report to a Colonel Kratzer at Army Supreme Command. Colonel Kratzer took one look at me and came straight to the point: "You're a radio broadcaster!" I said, "Yes, sir." Then he told me I was to fly to Zagreb to take over the radio station there. I had barely gotten to Zagreb when I received a teletype that read: "Lieutenant Reintgen, you are to assume command of the station in Belgrade immediately." So we got back in the plane and took off again.

In Belgrade the station building had been totally destroyed, but the transmitter was still operational. It didn't take long to find a new building and to begin to broadcast. We had a total supply of 54 records, no news ticker, and we were expected to be on the air 20 hours a day. I decided to send one of my people to the German radio station in Vienna. At first, the people in Vienna refused to relinquish any of their own records, except for those that had been banned by Goebbels as harmful to morale. At my request, the man I sent returned with some of the banned records. One of them was "The Song of a Sentry"—the Lili Marlene song. We broadcast this song constantly, at least once an hour. Everybody wanted to hear it. I got so sick of the record, I stopped playing it on the air. We got an immediate flood of complaints and protests, including a letter from a listener in Hamburg, of all places. Only then did we realize that when we transmitted at night, not only could the Balkans tune in, but that all of Germany could pick us up as well.

We knew we had to come up with the most effective way to use the song. Then it dawned on me that the ideal time to play it would be three minutes before our 10 P.M. news broadcast. Everyone listened to the 10 o'clock news. We aired messages and greetings from front soldiers to their families and friends back home and vice versa. And then I said: "And now just for you, for everyone here and there—'Lili Marlene.' "

You can't imagine how successful this was. We received at least 10,000 letters a week. All in all, we received millions of letters—all because of Lili Marlene. I aired this program over 1,000 times. It had international ties, because the Allied troops also heard it.

I once received a letter from the United States addressed only to "The Sentry." It somehow made it to Belgrade. Enclosed were five dollars with a request to give a special greeting to someone. This individual had tuned in to our short wave channel which reached as far as the U.S. east coast.

Another time, three German soldiers marched in with a British pilot who'd been shot down. He told me his wife listened to our program every night, as did many people in England when it was time for "Lili Marlene." His wife was pregnant and due to give birth the following week. He asked me if it was possible to let her know that he was all right and was a prisoner—in English. I told him I'd do it. Naturally there was an incredible commotion afterwards, but that really didn't bother me.

High German officers, General Beyerlein of the Africa Corps, for example, told me that every night at three minutes to ten, everyone on both sides ceased fire to listen in. Even Churchill was supposed to have said that it would be most amusing if Lili Marlene ended up being the only thing left to survive the Nazis.

Major General Rudolf Schmundt, Hitler's aide-de-camp from the Wehrmacht, called Hitler's attention to this popular song aired by the military station in Belgrade. Hitler so liked the song that he had Schmundt get him the record. He was as captivated by the melody as he was by the text. He thanked Schmundt with the words, "Schmundt, this hit will not only enrapture the German soldier, it will probably outlive us all." How right he was.

When I went to the United States after the war, I was greeted with the headline, "Mr. Lili Marlene. . . ." At least it was *Mister*.

CHAPTER 4

The Part-Time Germans

In the fall of 1940, Adolf Hitler had the opportunity to consolidate rule over a continental empire unmatched since the days of Napoleon. Nazi influence in the Balkans grew by the week. The government of Vichy France was eager to assume the role of a client state. Mussolini's Italy and Franco's Spain were vulnerable to German pressure. And the dictator's bandwagon attracted an increasing number of riders from outside the Reich's original borders.

These "part-time Germans" were the legacy of almost a thousand years of emigration that left pockets of German-speaking men and women scattered across eastern Europe. They were also the creation of a peace settlement that redrew the map of Europe to the systematic advantage of its non-Germanic peoples. The Slavic states of post-1918 Europe were strongly nationalistic, and made corresponding demands on their ethnic minorities. The new relationships would have been difficult even had the Germans possessed far less sense of their own cultural superiority. But in Poland, in Czechoslovakia, even in an Alsace restored to France, tensions festered.

The Republic of Austria, created as a separate country in 1919 from German remnants of the Habsburg Empire, was a major source of irredentism. A third of this dwarf state's population lived in Vienna; the rest eked out a living from tourism, subsistence farming, and small-scale industry. Austria's markets as often as not lay behind new frontiers and high tariffs. *Anschluss*, union with Germany, had widespread public support despite its prohibition by the Versailles

Treaty. After 1933, Austria's citizens were further influenced by Nazi propaganda—particularly by descriptions of the good life in Hitler's Reich. When Hitler bullied Chancellor Kurt von Schuschnigg into accepting the entry of German troops in March 1938, they were greeted with applause and flowers.

Czechoslovakia had also been created out of the old Habsburg Empire. Its Germans, concentrated in the mountainous north and east, the Sudetenland, were never completely integrated into the new state. They had never been a part of Germany either, but this did not prevent Hitler from using their grievances as an excuse for dismembering Czechoslovakia in 1938. Like the Austrians, the Sudeten Germans enthusiastically accepted the benefits of integration into the Reich.

An indication of Hitler's further plans for these ethnic Germans came in the South Tyrol. This region, annexed by Italy after World War I, had been subjected by Mussolini to far more rigorous cultural discrimination than anything occurring in democratic Czechoslovakia before 1938. Hitler kept his silence, particularly after the formation of the Rome-Berlin Axis. Italy's major concession involved allowing any South Tyrolians who so wished, to move to Germany. An overwhelming majority opted for the Reich. The Brenner Pass remained the official boundary between Italy and Greater Germany until 1943, when Italy's King went over to the Allies.

The beginning of the Tyrolians' arrival coincided with Nazi plans for a massive resettlement of "Germanic" peoples. From the Baltic States, from Transylvania, from everywhere in southeastern Europe, families were moved by truck, rail, and wagon train to new homes in occupied Poland: homes whose Polish and Jewish owners had been expelled.

For this there was a price—a blood price. The Reich's part-time Germans either became eligible for conscription, or were "allowed" to volunteer for the SS. The same alternatives awaited the Alsatians, who changed flags for the third time in a century when their province was reannexed in 1940. Initially, the Wehrmacht had put strict limits on the manpower available for Himmler's household guards. Enlisting racially suitable foreign volunteers seemed an ideal way to evade domestic restriction. Beginning in 1940, the SS began recruiting in

Scandinavia and the Low Countries. Vichy France too had its share of administrators who hoped participation in a war with Russia would enhance the status of their new regime. The number of Western European recruits remained small. The SS Viking Division, often credited with consisting primarily of blond, blue-eyed Scandinavians, had a considerable percentage of German volunteers. Other foreigners also found their way into Himmler's empire. The "Byzantine SS" ultimately included Latvian, Estonian, Hungarian, and even Galician units.

A special category of part-time Germans emerged after the invasion of the Soviet Union. From the first months of the campaign, manpower-short Wehrmacht units informally integrated Russian prisoners into their ranks as supply and service troops. These *Hilfswilligen,* or *HIWIS,* were eventually included in wartime tables of organization. Some simply preferred serving the Germans to life in a POW camp. Others, however, were committed anti-Stalinists or anti-Communists.

As the 1942 offensive penetrated the Cossack and Muslim areas of southern Russia, Wehrmacht ranks were swelled by companies and battalions, then divisions and corps, of volunteers fighting under German colors for liberation from Soviet rule. In 1943, captured Russian General Andrei Vlasov took the process a step further by calling on all Russians to join his Liberation Movement. By that time, however, the mass of Russian people had been alienated beyond redemption by a brutal German occupation.

In describing the part-time Germans as participants in a European crusade against Bolshevism, postwar apologists exaggerate their numbers and misrepresent their aims. The presence of tens of thousands of foreigners in Wehrmacht ranks suggests instead Hitler's power to appeal to hopes and discontents even outside Germany. These volunteers would be bitterly disappointed.

JOHANN ALLMAYER-BECK

Born 1919; Austrian citizen; served in the Wehrmacht; currently lives in Vienna; is an historian.

"National Socialism has to be an improvement."

It was a mistake for Hitler to occupy Austria. It would have been enough just to threaten with the *Anschluss*; everything would have worked out Hitler's way all by itself. The party gained power very quickly here; it could rely on the masses for support. Not that they had all become Nazis; on the contrary, estimates show that only about 20 percent were actually Nazis. The rest were people with the old yearning for the resurrection of the First Reich, the Holy Roman Empire of the German Nation.

The myth of the Reich played a large role for historically-oriented people who thought that the old glory of the Empire—in which Austria played a very prominent role—would return. Of course, the memory of fighting side by side with Germany in the First World War was yet another reason. Furthermore, there was the desire to get rid of the Treaty of St. Germain, so that we wouldn't be looked at as the leftovers of the Habsburg Empire anymore. Initially too, many people on the left said, "Now we're finally rid of this conservative, clerical regime. National Socialism has to be an improvement."

The union opened economic opportunities for the Austrians, and provided many jobs. Rearmament created full employment. People were either not aware of what was going on, or they didn't believe it was possible that one man could and would consciously steer a country into a war.

There was surely a latent anti-Semitism in Austria. In Vienna, for example, there was a large Jewish bourgeoisie which was quite well integrated. But before and after World War I, many Jews from the East migrated to Austria, eastern, orthodox Jews. Naturally they lived here as a foreign element, an alien minority which aroused the envy of small shopkeepers. They were immediately recognized as a danger by the native Jewish bourgeoisie. Anti-Semitism was probably somewhat stronger in Vienna than in the rural provinces like the Tyrol or Steiermark, where there were virtually no Jews. This was the tragic side of the *Anschluss:* that this primitive anti-Semitism was allowed to be activated so quickly.

FERDINAND KRONES*

"An overwhelming majority of the Austrian population voted for the *Anschluss.*"

Today, people claim that Austria was the first victim of Hitler's politics, that Austria was raped by Germany. That's not true. As early as 1919–20, parts of Austria held plebiscites. An overwhelming majority of the population, an average of 95 percent, voted for *Anschluss* to the German Reich in an absolutely free vote, with a secret ballot and no outside influence.

The active political parties at the time were not only in favor of *Anschluss,* and encouraged their members to vote for it, but they called for union with Germany as part of their platforms.

Anschluss was forbidden by the Allies, and was then not permitted in the Peace Treaty of St. Germain. Given the political and military situation at the time, Austria was forced to submit. But naturally the *Anschluss* lived on in people's minds. It was strengthened when unemployment and the general economic picture became so bad that

---

* Biography on page 76.

it looked as though unification with the newly flourishing German Reich was the only way Austria could be saved.

Economic need was certainly a strong motive for the *Anschluss.* When Hitler became Chancellor in 1933, Austria had a higher percentage of unemployment than Germany. Nevertheless, I personally consider one of the key motives to be something which delved deeper into the human soul: the strong feeling of national identity with the Reich. What was left of Austria after World War I wanted to be more than the rump of a vanished empire.

The majority of patriotic Austrians welcomed the union with often tearful joy. And the youth organizations in Austria, including the Catholic ones and a majority of the Socialist ones, were for the *Anschluss,* if not for Adolf Hitler.

In 1938, I was drafted into a German division stationed in Vienna. I always thought of myself as a soldier of the German Wehrmacht in service to the Greater German Empire. There were even many young Jews who thought in terms of a greater Germany. And I know in Austria that there were Jews who supported the Reich, but could no longer participate after 1938 because of Nazi racial policies. There were Jewish members of student fraternities who still had duelling scars on their faces, and yet could no longer work with their German nationalist friends.

There were intellectual and political elements within Austria in favor of the *Anschluss,* but opposed to National Socialism and Adolf Hitler's politics. There were also people—even among those with a concept of greater Germany—who were for the *Anschluss* only on the condition that Austrian autonomy be preserved within the framework of a Greater German Empire. These people believed in a legitimate, democratic, Christian, and federal *Anschluss,* but not in the violent measures used by Hitler.

These measures challenged the Austrian identity, which was an enormous political mistake. Hitler was obsessed with the belief that the German empire he had dreamed of in his youth could only be achieved through his own political actions. He acted as if there had never been a German people or a German history for 1,000 years before him.

Hitler's crushing of Austria stemmed from his experiences as a destitute young man in Vienna when he acutely felt the lack of adequate social welfare programs. I think his feelings of hatred toward Austria were best expressed by his eliminating the concept "Austria" (*"Österreich"*) from German history by replacing it with "Ostmark" (Eastern Region).

ERICH KERN

Born in 1919 in Austria; master sergeant in the army from 1938 to 1945; after the war, a sales representative; lives in Bonn.

"Hitler was greeted with tumultuous jubilation."

After I finished my apprenticeship as a baker in 1938, I was sent to Graz. Hitler visited Graz on March 10, 1938. At this time, the city of Graz had approximately 250,000 inhabitants. It seemed as if every one of them went out to greet the Führer. We stood on the street for seven hours until Hitler finally arrived. He was greeted with tumultuous jubilation. The rejoicing went on into the night. Hitler stayed at the Park Hotel, and thousands of people swamped the place and cheered all day and all night. We young people were full of hope and believed that a new time was coming, that there would be work and bread for all.

Austria was in the worst possible economic condition at the time. Children from poor backgrounds had absolutely no chance to obtain any advanced education; only the privileged could afford it. Austria was a class state.

Austrians were very poor when I was a baker's apprentice; some peasants couldn't even afford to pay for three rolls. I sometimes gave them a roll for lunch. In the winter, the town set up "warming rooms" where the townspeople could get warm. We stole coal with a hand-drawn cart from the freight train station. Things improved after Hitler took over.

Germany was already flourishing when Hitler came to Austria. We heard that everything was going well there. Of my four brothers, one went to Germany before the annexation and found work digging out the lead at public firing ranges. He then returned with the storm troopers, the SA. We believed in Germany. We became soldiers out of conviction; we wanted to do our duty for our country. We had no way of knowing that we were being so cheated. I believe that we were a cheated and betrayed generation. Did we have an alternative? I say no.

HANS-C. VON CARLOWITZ

Born 1917; professional soldier in the armored forces; after the war became an Austrian citizen and moved to Vienna, where he works as a sales representative.

"In the field there wasn't the slightest difference between the Austrians and the Reich Germans."

In March 1938, my division, the 2nd Armored Division, was given the order to march into Austria. On the 13th, my unit was moved to Vienna and remained there. At the time, I was 21 years old and had just become a lieutenant.

Marching into a German-speaking country as a Reich German gave me a feeling of being an eyewitness to history. Already in the outskirts of Vienna we were welcomed by the inhabitants *en masse*—most surely in ignorance of what was to come and, in my opinion, primarily out of economic need. But they also welcomed us with a surprising historical awareness of the commonalities between our countries.

Wherever we went, in groups or individually, there was not a single man among us who did not make friendly contacts immediately. Families readily took us in; we said to each other, "It's just like being home in Germany here."

The poverty in Austria was very apparent. I recall being assigned to bring 12 of my regiment's soup kitchens to Floridsdorf, a workers' suburb of Vienna, where unemployment was particularly rife. The images I retained of people of all classes on this occasion seared me like a hot iron. Absolute poverty and sheer physical want prevailed.

Another example of this: In the autumn of 1938, we received our first Austrian recruits. Most of them were from Vienna, and had signed up for the tank troops with the appropriate attitude—good will and no difficulties. However, the physical condition of these young men, many of whom came from working-class homes, presented some problems. They were so weak that our regimental commander, breaking with all Prussian military practice, ordered an hour in bed during the afternoon for these young men for eight weeks. This particular order was unique, but exemplified the situation in Austria at the time.

We noticed very quickly that the physical condition of these men improved rapidly, and that they could keep up better with the rigorous physical strain of tank training. When war broke out, they repaid our efforts.

In the field there wasn't the slightest difference between the Austrians and the Reich Germans. I can easily recall an emaciated, scrawny young guy in particular, who joined us in 1938. After heavy losses of officers on the night of September 7, 1939, in southern Poland, he took his BMW 750 motorcycle and drove it into a small pocket three times to rescue wounded. He was the first recruit in our regiment to be decorated with the Iron Cross. Much later, in the second half of the Russian campaign, he was discharged from the army because it turned out that he was half Jewish!

THEO HUPFAUER*

"All the bishops raised their right arms in the Nazi salute."

I was sent to Vienna after the *Anschluss* in 1938 to help set up the German Labor Service there. One day, a friend of mine who was working for Bürckel, the Reich commissioner of Vienna, came to me and said he had a really dumb assignment, and asked whether I would come along. We got into the car, and I said, "Where are we going?"

"We're going to see Cardinal Innitzer," he said.

"What am I supposed to do?" I asked.

He answered, "You're Catholic. You know how to act around them."

On the way there, he let me read a proclamation calling for support of the *Anschluss* in the upcoming plebiscite. When I asked what was supposed to be done with it, my friend said, "Innitzer and all the bishops are supposed to sign it."

"They're never going to do it!" I said. "Do you really think you can negotiate this?"

"I have to," he replied. "Bürckel is too cowardly to go himself."

We were very warmly greeted by the Cardinal, and then my friend gave him the document. He read it. Without changing his expression, he said that he found it very interesting, but it was not something he was authorized to deal with alone. The Austrian bishops would need to confer on this. Then I said, "Yes, your Eminence, you will have to call a bishops' conference." He agreed. There were only 14 days left until the plebiscite, so I said, "Your Eminence, the other bishops should be here by the day after tomorrow at the latest."

---

* Biography on page xxv.

We returned two days later. As we went up the stairs to the episcopal palace, my friend asked me how you were supposed to greet Catholic bishops. I said, "Klaus, just don't give them a Nazi salute! After all, we want something from them. A polite bow should suffice."

A little priest opened a side door for us and admitted us to a room where six or seven bishops were sitting. We stood in the entrance way and gave them a polite bow, whereupon all the bishops stood up and raised their right arms in the Nazi salute. Under my breath, I hissed, "Klaus, it looks like they want something from us, too."

And that's the way our negotiations began. It was a very rational, precise discussion. Naturally they proposed some alterations, but for us what mattered was that the bishops signed a document saying they were in favor of union with the German Reich.

ANDREAS MEYER-LANDRUTH

Born 1932 in Tallinn, Estonia; as a child was part of the great wartime migration of German people, first from Estonia to Poland, then from Poland to Germany; entered the diplomatic service after the war; is presently serving for the second time as the Federal Republic's ambassador to the Soviet Union.

"A Pole was hanged in the marketplace."

I was born in Reval (Tallinn), the capital of Estonia. My family, ethnic Germans, had lived in the Baltic region since the 19th century. Ever since German crusaders attempted to Christianize this area, 700 years ago, after they had failed to re-conquer the holy places of

Christendom, there has been a constant stream of German settlers into the Baltic.

My grandfather emigrated to Estonia in the 1870s. He had been a bank employee in Lübeck and lost his job during an economic crisis. He got a job at a bank specializing in agricultural loans, at a time when new techniques, in threshing machines, for example, were revolutionizing farming. He later became the director of a bank, and he kept his position until the Bolshevik revolution in 1917. The bank's assets had largely been in Russia. They included investments in the trans-Siberian railway and were lost when Estonia became independent.

Ethnic Germans had always had special privileges in the Baltic. They had special legal rights. They had their schools and churches. This culture survived the First World War.

My father was active in public life. He was in the town council, and he was a member of the so-called "cultural administration," which was in charge of the school system, and which sought to preserve German identity.

The real difficulties arose with the Nazi government's policy of cultivating German culture in foreign countries. This led to tensions with the native population and with the Estonian administration. In Latvia, the tensions were even stronger.

The three countries created when the Baltic region became independent, Estonia, Lithuania, and Latvia, the so-called "potato republics," were healthy countries, and their populations lived well. Baltic independence lasted only 20 years, until what for us was the real beginning of the Second World War: the Hitler-Stalin Pact, signed in Moscow on August 23, 1939. Although these three states were situated east of the new border created by the Pact treaty, it contained a secret additional clause, according to which the Baltic Germans would have the option of emigrating before Soviet domination became complete.

At that time, there were approximately 80,000 ethnic Germans living in the Baltic countries who wished to emigrate. They did not want to repeat their experiences living under the Russians in the First World War. Some of these Germans went to Sweden and some to Great Britain, but most went to Germany. I was ten years old when we sailed to Stettin as part of an operation organized by Heinrich Himmler under the motto "home to the Reich." Upon disembarking, we realized we had been tricked, since we were not in Germany itself. We wound up in freshly occupied Poland, in Posen. We slept in schools, on straw. The situation was extremely difficult. My father had stayed behind in Estonia to finish up some business, and my mother and brother and sister and I were completely at a loss. My mother cried from morning until night, and we had absolutely no idea what would become of us.

After a while, things returned somewhat to normal. We were settled in small towns in Poland. The nobility was sent to the country. There were factories in the towns, and my father managed one of them until the end of the war. This was under a so-called "interim administration." All property rights were to be settled after the war.

The region enjoyed remarkable stability. I went to school. Often I went to the country on weekends, and during the week our family took in Baltic children who lived in the country and who went to school in the city.

Although we had peace where we lived, we had a number of very unpleasant experiences. A Pole who had supposedly profiteered in grain was hanged in the marketplace, and we children were assembled to watch the scene. Another time seven Jews were executed there. It was ghastly, and a woman behind me, who couldn't stand the spectacle, fled crying hysterically. But we were young kids of 12, 13, and 14 years of age, and we stood there with wide-open eyes and looked upon it all as a game. Only much later did we actually comprehend what had really taken place.

The Nazis attempted to put their stamp on everything in this newly occupied area. We children and our teachers had to wear Nazi uniforms. Once a week we had to serve in the Hitler Youth. We had mixed feelings about it. I was in the mounted branch of the organization, and I did love to ride horseback. On the other hand, I had a negative experience with the Hitler Youth when I was confirmed. Members of the Hitler Youth played a loud fanfare in front of the church in order to disturb the ceremony.

The Nazis didn't trust the Baltic Germans. They considered them too liberal and too subject to foreign influences. During the war there were many court cases against Baltic Germans, and this helped foster Baltic resentment against the Nazis. It is no coincidence that Baltic Germans were involved in the assassination attempt against Hitler on July 20, 1944.

We had basic Christian values. They dictated resistance to, or at least distance from, Nazism. And yet we, as Germans living in a foreign country, were greatly impressed by that which Hitler had created. We looked to Germany as a fascinating homeland in the distance. When the Nazis came to power, we suddenly had money for schools, for example. This is also the reason why we initially welcomed the idea of resettling. We had not yet learned what was happening to the Jews.

It is also interesting to note that the young people among us who were old enough to do so volunteered for military service immediately after resettling. This enthusiasm counterbalanced resentment at not living in a country they could call their own.

In my parents' circle there was great confidence that Germany would win the war. We heard about the Jews not being allowed to walk on the sidewalk—they had to use the gutter—but such stories were played down, and we felt that what was good in the Germans would come out in the end. We thought that such events were the evil, natural byproducts of war, and that they would stop soon enough. We thought everything would be different as soon as there was a successor to Hitler.

PETER SCHOBER

*Born 1921; a Sudeten German; served as an
infantry officer until war's end; later worked as
a news editor at the First German radio and
television network; lives in Berlin.*

"They beat it into me that I was German."

I was born in Morava-Ostrava, a Czech city with, at most, a 10
percent German population. I learned Czech as a child on the streets.
I went to a Czech kindergarten where my accent and intonation were
so perfected that even the Czechs couldn't tell whether I was Czech or
German. At home we spoke German, and later I attended a German
school.

That experience had a major impact on my life. At kindergarten I
was a kid just like any other. Then I entered the first grade at the
German school. The day I started first grade, a mob of about 150
Czech kids were waiting for us when we left the building. What
happened on that day is something I will never forget. They yelled,
"Njemcy, Njemcy, Njemcy." That means "Germans, Germans, Germans," but it was intended as an insult. They had sticks in their
hands and started beating us up. And—contrary to my experience in
kindergarten—it was the first time I noticed I wasn't like other Czech
kids. They beat it into me that I was German.

This incident was repeated often. Sometimes our parents picked us
up from school; sometimes we carried weapons, arming ourselves
with sticks to get home. As we got older, we began to beat up Czechs.
Three of us 15-year-olds would jump an adult man and beat him up.
While we were beating him we thought of the times we had been
beaten.

The Czechs always tried to gain footholds in the German areas. For example, they would move a policeman or a post office worker with a big family of six children into a German village. Then they would claim that a school was needed for these children, and a Czech school was established. Of course there was resistance to this, and there was trouble. The Czechs usually left of their own accord. It just would not work out. These were German areas, populated exclusively by Germans.

I remember when German troops entered the Sudetenland. They were welcomed and greeted as Germans, and that was a big thing for us. We felt that we belonged more to a German-speaking country than to one where the national tongue was Czech. We thought that this was the right solution. We thought that there should actually have been a referendum in 1918–19 to decide where the three-and-a-half million Germans living in the newly created state of Czechoslovakia should belong.

SIEGFRIED FISCHER

Born in 1918 in the Sudetenland (Czechoslovakia); dive-bomber pilot; shot down 13 times; totally disabled; highly decorated; after the war was unable to work; currently lives in the Rhineland.

"This was the greatest day of my life."

I was born in the Sudetenland. The Sudeten Germans are a Germanic people who settled in the Bohemia-Moravia-Silesia area 800 years ago. The Slavs later followed them and settled in inner Bohemia and Moravia. Until 1918, we were part of the Austro-Hungarian Empire.

Then we were taken over by the Czechs. Three-and-a-half million Sudeten Germans, almost as many inhabitants as Norway has today, were oppressed by a Czech majority in the so-called democratic state of Czechoslovakia. Sudeten German civil servants were replaced by Czechs, and those who couldn't be fired were sent into Czech districts. Their children, of course, automatically went to Czech schools and quickly became "Czechized."

With the beginning of the Third Reich we began to hope that our situation in the Sudetenland would improve. The German occupation in 1938 was not felt to be an occupation at all. Rather, we waited in happy anticipation for the German troops finally to liberate us. The soldiers were received with flowers and great hospitality. This was, then as now, the greatest day of my life. It made me a German citizen.

LOTHAR VON STERNBACH

Born in 1905 in the South Tyrol; active before 1939 in the movement for an independent Tyrol; retired professor; lives in Bruneck, South Tyrol.

"We in the South Tyrol had never seen Hitler."

In the First World War the South Tyrolians fought as part of Austria. After the war the Italian fascists came. And then in 1939, the terrible Option Treaty came about. The option: we could either retain the Italian citizenship we'd all had since 1920, or we could ask for German citizenship and have to leave the country. As South Tyrolians, we knew we had no future here. And as a primarily agricultural people, the greatest sacrifice was having to leave our

ancestral land, leaving the soil that had been worked by our forefathers for hundreds of years.

It's almost impossible for an outsider to comprehend that, after an
initial vote against emigration by the entire population, the option
result ended with 86 percent for emigration to Germany and 14
percent against. Approximately 240,000 people opted for Germany.
For the most part, only the heads of families made the decision.

Today our people are accused of supporting Hitler by 86 percent.
That's not true; it was simply an option for Germany. We didn't know
about the whole Nazi racket. We in the South Tyrol had never seen
Hitler. As an oppressed minority, we saw him only as an exponent of
a strong, self-confident German policy, which wanted to do right by
its people, and set right the injustices of Versailles.

The emigration was planned for 1940, but then the war got in the
way. Only about 70,000 to 75,000 people actually emigrated, people
without land who could find immediate work on the outside. And of
these 75,000 people, only about 12,000 ever returned to the South
Tyrol.

PAUL TASSER

*Born 1927; as a South Tyrolian, was drafted
into the SS; a lawyer, he still lives in the South
Tyrol.*

"Thank God the war broke out."

I am a so-called "squatter." In other words, when Mussolini and
Hitler agreed in 1939 that the South Tyrolians could opt either for
Italy or the German Reich, my family opted for Italy. We didn't want
to leave the land we'd farmed for hundreds of years, no matter what.

Eighty-six percent of the South Tyrolians opted for Germany back then, only 14 percent for Italy. Thank God the war broke out, otherwise most South Tyrolians would have been sent to Germany. I was too young to be drafted at the time. But after the King of Italy and Marshal Badoglio went over to the Allies in the summer of 1943, the South Tyrol became a *Gau* of the Third Reich. I was drafted into an SS police regiment when I was 17. I got three months of training with Italian weapons. We were originally designated for partisan combat. In my service record book it says "volunteer." But if you didn't "volunteer," they took away your mother, sister, or other relatives and shot them or sent them to concentration camps.

After our training they put us on an express transport to Silesia. The Russians had killed people there like barbarians—horrors one can't even begin to imagine, women torn limb from limb and all kinds of things. They disbanded our regiment and suddenly we were SS grenadiers in the Prince Eugen Division. I was at the front until May 1 or 2, 1945, when I was sent back on a gas training course. I was in the adjutant's room, where the radio was on. An Italian station happened to be crackling out a broadcast, and they didn't know I could speak Italian. Right then and there I heard that the South and West fronts had surrendered.

When I heard how disastrous the situation really was, I decided to desert. I walked about seven miles to the next village. At the village entrance there were two hanged soldiers with signs around their necks which read, "I am a deserter, a traitor." Naturally I changed my mind and marched right back to camp like a good boy.

JOSEF RAMPOLD

Born 1925; grew up in the South Tyrol; drafted into the Wehrmacht in 1943; now the editor of a newspaper; lives in Bolzano, Italy.

"Joining the Wehrmacht was an inner emigration to Germany."

The Nazi Party did not officially exist in the South Tyrol under Italian rule. One could not become a party member, and no one thought of doing so. Joining the Wehrmacht was—I don't mind saying this—an inner emigration to Germany. One was among respectable people.

I loved freedom, so life in a barracks was horrid. I would much rather have studied at the university, enjoyed the mountains, and led a free life. I had had a very close circle of friends interested in literature and music. And there I was in this monotonous, intellectually deadening boot camp, with all of its ridiculous drills. It was only much, much later, at the front, that it slowly dawned on me that these drills had been far from silly. Rather, they had conditioned us to throw ourselves under cover within a tenth of a second, to react quickly without regard to dirt or deprivation. However, after the freedom of student life, boot camp was sheer hell for me.

On September 8, 1943, after the Italian King and Marshal Badoglio went over to the Allies, I marched into my homeland of South Tyrol over the Brenner Pass with a mountain infantry company. It was an unforgettable day. Only someone who was there can know the boundless rejoicing with which we were received. The simple people were especially generous—our rations didn't exactly fatten us up—and they celebrated our arrival. It was a campaign of flowers; people drenched us in wine and fruit.

Later, while staying with some of my relatives who were "squatters," I saw the other side of the coin. For some people it was far from a night of rejoicing. Some tried to escape, and some were arrested and sent to concentration camps. But to us, the picture was one of jubilation.

South Tyrolian children had not been allowed to speak German in the street. Their parents forbade it because they were intimidated by the Italians. Finally they were able to speak German in public again and go to German schools. Music and folk groups formed immediately. The entire population breathed a sigh of relief: We were again permitted to be what we had been for centuries. The people who experienced this will never forget it.

EDUARD STEINBERGER

Born in 1919 in the South Tyrol; served with the German Special Forces, the Brandenburg Division; lives in the South Tyrol.

"We were totally convinced we were doing the right thing."

The older we got, and the bigger and stronger Germany grew, the more we felt ourselves drawn to Germany. We were oppressed by the Italians. We wanted to get away from them, by any means, and our parents had to give in to the pressure of the young people, even though they were still hesitant. We wanted out; we wanted to do something to finally be free. We wanted to be Germans among Germans.

We South Tyrolians firmly believed that after the war was won, Hitler would take back the South Tyrol, and that all this business with Mussolini had just been an emergency solution. That's why we believed the few newspaper articles published on the subject, and the books that also described it that way.

As soldiers, we were totally convinced we were doing the right thing. We didn't have time to politicize. We were at war, and when we got leave we tried to have fun for a few days. Politics was the last thing on our minds. We did our duty, and we did it with enthusiasm. To us there were no two ways about it: We had to protect our home, our people, our Europe.

I was drafted into the famous Brandenburg Division. This was a special unit directly subordinate to the Headquarters of Military Intelligence, Supreme Command Armed Forces. It was supposed to capture objectives behind enemy lines and prevent bridge and tunnel demolitions by the enemy during his retreat. It was called the Brandenburg Division because that's the town where it was founded.

Originally, the Brandenburg Division mostly consisted of non-Reich Germans—Sudeten Germans who spoke Czech, a few Palestinian Germans, and volunteer Ukrainians. There were people from all over, mostly people who spoke other languages, but all units were under German command. Of course we were crack troops, and fantastically equipped. When the commanders of the divisions we were assigned to saw they'd gotten a company of Brandenburgers, they immediately put us with the advance units who would be the first to make contact with the enemy.

We always operated in decoy uniforms. We wore all kinds of uniforms, Russian ones for example, over our Wehrmacht uniforms. We had to be able to get rid of the top uniform quickly.[1] Of course, decoy uniforms were a prerequisite for getting behind enemy lines. If a bridge had to be taken by infantry assault, it could cost thousands of lives, so we prevented that with commando operations. The Americans did it; the British did it too; everybody did it.

My company's first assignment was to go to Gibraltar, where we were supposed to prevent shipwrecked English sailors from landing. Although we were mountain troops, we were transferred to the Bay

---

[1] In World War II, the laws of war forbade "improper use" of enemy uniforms and insignia, but did not prohibit "ruses of war," including camouflage and decoys. This was commonly interpreted as allowing the wearing of enemy uniforms to infiltrate positions or approach objectives, so long as they were discarded before actually beginning hostilities.

of Biscay where we chased around the surf in lifeboats and had to learn a little English. But the operation, which was code-named "Felix," was called off because Franco didn't approve it. My next mission was in Yugoslavia, and then Russia, all the way to the Caucasus. We saw a lot of action around the area of Maikop.

Our missions could be up to half a company strong, about 60 to 70 troops. But usually they were just platoon strength, which meant 20 to 30. We generally played a situation by ear. We always drove over the bridges in captured Russian trucks, with one of us sitting on top while someone who spoke Russian, a Latvian or an Estonian, for instance, sat in the cab. The instant fighting broke out, we always tried to get rid of the decoy uniform fast. Otherwise nobody could tell whether we were friend or foe, and the tanks that followed often shot at their own people in the chaos. If a mission succeeded, we usually had very few casualties. But some missions went wrong, when our people were recognized by the enemy, for example. Then almost everybody was wiped out.

BERNARD SCHMITT

Born 1923; Alsatian, escaped from Germany in 1944 and joined de Gaulle's Free French as a doctor; today is the head of a hospital in Metz, France.

"Hitler came to power like a knight to the rescue."

On my father's side, I come from an old Alsatian family. My great-great grandfather was killed in Spain as a major in the Third Hussars Regiment in Napoleon's army. My great-grandfather was a Grenadiers lieutenant in the Crimean War under Napoleon III.

My grandfather was born during the French time, before 1871, but he grew up when Alsace-Lorraine was a German state. He saw himself primarily as a German who was loyal to the Kaiser. He was enthralled by German culture and civilization. Above all, he worshipped Goethe. My grandfather was well-known in Alsace as a German poet. He never wrote poems in dialect, only in high German. In fact, he was so captivated by Goethe, German civilization, and German culture, that in 1918 he couldn't bear the idea of becoming French. So he went to Karlsruhe and became director of the public library until his death.

In 1913, my father was drafted into the German army. He was sent to Russia during World War I. When he was discharged in 1918, he felt very attracted to French civilization. Therefore he decided to stay in France with his younger brother, and they both became reserve officers in the French army. As such, they had to serve in Syria for two years after the war was over.

I was the only child of an older couple. I was brought up as a European in every sense of the word. I loved my grandfather terribly and found it completely natural that he lived in Germany and considered himself to be German. On the other hand, I considered myself absolutely French.

In 1933–34, Hitler came to power like a knight to the rescue; we thought nothing better could happen to Germany once we saw what he was doing to fight unemployment, corruption, etc. But when the first news of persecutions and pogroms reached us, we began to get worried. We thought to ourselves: My God, how far is this going to go? At this point I'd like to emphasize that my grandmother on my father's side was of Jewish descent. We kept close ties to all our Jewish relatives through her. When my father visited his mother in Germany, he was held at the border at Kehl and pushed around by a border guard who called him "Jew-boy." My father came home horrified.

I began to study medicine in 1940. When the Germans came, I was given permission to continue with my studies in Germany. I went to Heidelberg and studied philology, psychology, philosophy, German, and medicine, all at the same time. Everything went fine for the first three or four semesters. I joined a student fraternity and found everything in it but Nazis. In other words, I found goodness, honor, love, friendship, and comrades, people who protected me as the son of a man "tainted" with Jewishness.

I went from Heidelberg to Leipzig to finish my studies. I never suffered so much from hunger in my life as I did in Leipzig! While there I lived with a real Saxon family. They weren't bad people; they were simply narrow-minded: adamant Nazis. They were totally convinced of it all, and I think they would rather have starved to death than have gotten a single ounce of food on the black market.

I received my psychology degree in Leipzig, where I also completed my medical internship. Suddenly, I didn't have even the tiniest drop of Jewish blood in me; the authorities designated me pure Aryan. My father and I both got *Ahnenpässe* in which it was clearly stated that, though my grandmother may have been named Sarah Mühlenberger, she was nonetheless fully Aryan.

I was told that I would probably be drafted into the German army quickly. Though I was only an ethnic German, a kind of a second-class German citizen, I was told that the minute I took my soldier's oath I would become a full-fledged German citizen and receive a German passport. Naturally, I didn't want any of that. I preferred, as they say, to make tracks.

At the beginning of 1944, I was smuggled out of Germany by German resistance groups. I had been a member of one of these groups myself, and we had already managed to smuggle nearly four hundred French prisoners from northern Germany to the Free French. This was another reason why it was better for me to disappear. I got out through the same channels we had used. Then I volunteered for the French army.

ALBERT SCHOEB

*Born in 1924 in Lorraine; French citizen until
1940; drafted into the Wehrmacht and captured by the Russians in 1945; after the war a
farmer; today lives in Metz, France.*

"World War II took us by surprise."

My native tongue is a German dialect considerably different from
Alsatian. It's a dialect from the Moselle area, which is part of
Lorraine. The Moselle district became separated from France in
1871, when it was integrated into the German Empire after the
Franco-German War.

I was born in 1924, after the Moselle had been re-attached to
France in accordance with the Treaty of Versailles of May 1919. So,
legally, I was born French. I went to a French school where we had
one or two hours of German every week, which was enough to enable
me to write and speak the language fluently.

World War II took us by surprise. From June 15, 1940, onwards,
Alsace-Lorraine was once again Reich territory, thanks to a uni-
lateral decree of the Führer. It was against international law, and not a
word about it was mentioned in the June 22nd armistice agreement
between France and Germany. But now we were eligible to serve in
the Wehrmacht.

Of course, not everybody was willing to join. Some tried to escape
across the border; some just ignored their mobilization orders; many
hid. It's an established fact that about 6,000 of the 30,000 drafted
from Lorraine didn't go. And it had some consequences. In Pan-
nersdorf, in upper Alsace, a memorial was later dedicated to the 26
boys who were supposed to report for service and instead tried to get
across the Swiss border. Only one of the 26 got through; the others

were caught and shot on the spot. The German authorities also resorted to *Sippenhaft* in such cases. They punished whole families.

OTTO KUMM*

"So many young Dutch wanted to join."

At first, the Waffen-SS consisted solely of volunteers. We got our first real draftees only in 1943, but for the ethnic Germans the draft into the SS had begun a year earlier, in 1942. The entire Prince Eugen Division was made up of ethnic Germans who were supposed to be volunteers. But only about 1,500 signed up. You can't set up a division with that. So Himmler had the idea of introducing conscription in areas settled by ethnic Germans, which meant that all men between the ages of 15 and 50 were registered. That included Alsace, the South Tyrol, and all of southeastern Europe.

The SS Viking Division was still made up of actual volunteers, as was our *Das Reich* Division. When we were stationed in Holland as an occupation force after the Western campaign, so many young Dutch wanted to join us that it was decided to set up a separate division with these foreign volunteers. And these were genuine volunteers. The Dutch made up the *Westland* regiment; the Norwegians, Danes, and Swedes made up the *Nordland* regiment. They were joined by the *Germania* regiment, and together, they all made up the Viking Division.

---

* Biography on page xxvii.

HANS GUNTHER SERAPHIN

Born in 1903 in Königsberg; commanded Russian volunteers—a Moslem battalion—in the German army; served as expert witness at the Nuremberg trials; later worked as an interpreter; lives in Göttingen, Lower Saxony.

"*Kapitän*, give them to us—we'll finish them off."

I never fought for Adolf in the last war. When it broke out, it was a matter of preserving the nation and its people; it was a matter of preserving the Reich—no ifs, ands, or buts. At the front we had a saying: "Let peace come so we can go home and straighten things out."

After I fought in the French campaign and in northern Russia, I was sent to the Armenian Legion, which was only inches from revolt. This legion was composed of volunteer POWs who had previously served in the Red Army. Among them were idealists who truly believed they could retrieve Armenia's honor with the help of the Germans.

However, Communist cells had formed in two or three battalions. Because I spoke Russian, the men were not suspicious of me. They made me their confidant, and I discovered the details. The plan involved waiting for some entertainment—movies or something—leaping up on stage, and shooting down the German officers and NCOs with machine guns. So we said, "Let's get them before they get us!" We disarmed the battalions one morning and put the sixteen ringleaders of the revolt on court-martial. And I'm fairly certain those sixteen and more were shot.

I was sent to Italy with volunteers from Soviet Turkestan. These boys were great. Of course, at times it was somewhat funny. Once we were marching through an Italian village when my orderly came up to me. "What's the matter, Kolja?" I asked. He jerked his thumb at the civilians standing in front of their houses and said with disgust in Russian, "What a cultureless people!" Turkestanis were very proud of their own culture.

We were then transferred to the Mediterranean to guard the coast. This was close to the island of Elba. Field Marshal Kesselring arrived for inspection and said he wanted to see the gun positions. After a while he got impatient and asked, "Where exactly are your guns?" And I said: "Well, *Herr Feldmarschall,* three more steps and you'll trip over one." That's how well camouflaged the emplacements were. The Turkestani soldiers were masters at utilizing terrain.

They were also reliable. One time when we were stationed at the fortress at Pola, one of my volunteers came to me and said: "*Kapitän,* we have received replacements. Two of them are in our platoon. Get rid of them. They're subversives; they're stirring things up." So I had them arrested, and he was right; they were Bolsheviks. When this came out, the men came to me and said: "*Kapitän,* give them to us—we'll finish them off." And they did.

The Turkestanis were extremely sensitive when it came to honor. When they believed they were treated unjustly, they killed the Germans involved and went over to join the partisans.

Before I was wounded, my regimental commander said, "Since your men don't have any guns left, prepare them for infantry action." I told him, "That won't work, sir. These men are gunners; they feel superior to the infantry." Then I was wounded. The lieutenant who took my place told the men, "Okay, we are joining the infantry." They answered, "No, we won't do that. And if the *Kapitän* was still here, we would never be asked to do such a thing." The lieutenant said, "Yes we are, and I am going to go with you myself. But first we should all catch a little shut-eye." He lay down and fell asleep under the impression that his men were doing the same. When he awoke, they were gone. They had gone over to the partisans.

PART II

TURNING
POINTS

CHAPTER 5

Barbarossa

The Nazi invasion of Russia reflected more than ideological principles. The destruction of Bolshevism and its Jewish supporters would also secure the territory and the resources necessary to create a true "Thousand-Year Reich." Men like Heinrich Himmler were already planning the resettlement of "Germanic peoples," Dutch and Scandinavians, on the new frontiers. Western Russia would become a network of landed estates linked by autobahns, with "Aryan" colonists ruling a labor force of helots who would need to know no more than how to count to one hundred and take their caps off to a German.

More prosaically, for Hitler and most of his generals, Russia seemed a more vulnerable target than Britain. Their confidence was based on more than the arrogance of victory. In the 1930s, Stalin's purges had emasculated the Red Army's officer corps. Most of the general officers had been shot or sent to labor camps. An ineffective combat performance during the Winter War of 1939–40 against Finland only seemed to confirm Russia's weakness. The German General Staff was well aware of Russia's immense human and natural resources. But the military experts were also convinced that they had perfected a style of warfare making Russia's material potential irrelevant. The air battle over Britain had been lost because it was fought on the enemy's terms. The Luftwaffe still lacked the resources for a strategic air offensive. But the land battle in Russia would have a pace and tone determined by the Wehrmacht. The Soviets would be in the position of a chess player forced into a game of blackjack. Their very abilities would become handicaps.

As in France, the initial work would be done by the mobile forces. The decision to double the armored divisions by reducing the number of tanks in each one did not merely reflect Hitler's fondness for large orders of battle. The German approach to mobile war depended less on strength than on timing: a dozen tanks on the spot were better than fifty an hour later. But Germany's industry was unable to provide the vehicles needed by the new divisions. Occupied Europe was stripped of everything with four wheels and an engine—a process that did as much as the Balkan campaign to delay the attack. Nor did vehicles designed for the city streets of France or Belgium have much life expectancy in a land where paved roads were a rarity.

Even more serious was the condition of the infantry. They were by no means regarded as mere mop-up troops for the tankers. The armored divisions were supposed to penetrate and dislocate Russian positions, but the infantry was expected to bear the brunt of the actual fighting against an enemy with an historic image of resisting to the last man. Unlike their counterparts in the West, German divisions were raised in "waves" (*Wellen*), each with a different level of armament and equipment, depending on what was available at the time. They marched into Russia in 1941 with an assortment of rifles and guns that included booty from a half-dozen armies. The soldier's only mobility was his legs. Thirty-mile marches with a battle at the end became so routine that few veterans of Barbarossa bother to mention them. Supply and transport depended to a great extent on horses. Even most of the artillery was horse-drawn. Western horses, drafted from Belgium or Holland, were no better suited than western trucks to the conditions of the Soviet Union.

The Wehrmacht, in short, had no real reserves. If anything at all went wrong, solutions would have to be improvised. And the strategic planning for Operation Barbarossa virtually guaranteed problems. Instead of concentrating already-thin resources, Hitler's final plan called for an advance along a broad front, in the north toward Leningrad, in the center toward Moscow, and in the south into the Ukraine, toward the Black Sea and its oil fields. Most of his generals, far from challenging the wisdom of "The Greatest Warlord of All

Time," accepted the principle that German soldiers could do anything as long as their wills held firm.

Geography alone indicated that the three major axes of advance
would draw further apart, out of supporting range, as the campaign
progressed. Within six weeks, each sector had its own separate
problems. France or Belgium might be digested in one or two bites by
the blitzkrieg. Russia was simply too big, her armies too large, to be
swallowed at a gulp. The friction of war, from breakdowns to blisters,
gnawed at the strength of a Wehrmacht able to replace neither men
nor equipment. Initial victories, with hundreds of thousands surrendering in confusion, gave way to stiffer fighting as the Germans
penetrated the Russian heartland. Even Red Army soldiers hostile to
the regime could see the truth of Stalin's repeated insistence that this
was a war not for Communism, but for Mother Russia.

Russian resistance was increased by German behavior. Particularly in the Ukraine and White Russia, the Wehrmacht was greeted
with bread and salt, as liberators. But behind the tanks came the
Action Groups (*Einsatzgruppen*) of the SS, and Nazi bureaucrats
determined to exploit the occupied lands without mercy.

Hitler's notorious order to shoot commissars and other party officials out of hand was suppressed in many headquarters. But enough
senior officers welcomed it, enough others passed it on without
comment, to establish a dangerous precedent. The Wehrmacht was
by no means immune to racism. Sharpened by Nazi ideology, it could
encourage indifference to the fate of prisoners and civilians. At best,
war is a dirty business whose rules and conventions are easily forgotten. As partisan activity increased, German wounded were shot and
German dead mutilated. A pattern of mutual retaliation and mutual
escalation brought an end by the winter of 1941 to an era of easy
surrenders that had put over three million Soviet soldiers behind
German barbed wire.

As early as August, the consequences of German overcommitment
became clear. While the General Staff insisted on continuing the
attack on Moscow, Hitler was equally convinced of the need to
control the Ukraine, particularly the Donetz basin. The Panzer divisions were shifted from one sector to the other like chess pieces, with
no concern for the logistical impact of the moves. By this time,

infantry companies had been reduced to platoons and squads. Panzer regiments which began the campaign with 180 tanks could muster only fifteen or twenty. In the air, too, Germany was fighting a poor man's war. In the first days of the campaign the Luftwaffe established complete air superiority against a badly equipped enemy. But weeks of flying from improvised fields took their toll. As the ground forces grew weaker, the Luftwaffe further exhausted itself in a desperate effort to provide close support in place of missing tanks and guns.

With the beginning of the rainy season in late October, the Wehrmacht became stuck in mud that seemed bottomless. Then came the frost. Within sight and sound of Moscow, the last attacks ground to a halt in November—not least because the frontline units had no food, no ammunition, and almost no one left in the ranks to pull a trigger.

Against all expectations, the Russians had held. The failure of their December counteroffensive owed less to Hitler's refusal to allow retreat than to the Red Army's operational clumsiness, and to the ferocity of the Russian winter. Overnight exposure meant death or amputation. The Reich leadership had not concerned itself with providing winter clothing for a campaign expected to be over by autumn. Now fur coats, gloves, and scarves haphazardly collected from the civilian economy were distributed almost at random, sometimes dropped from aircraft to the frontline units. Eventually the Wehrmacht would issue a service medal to survivors of the winter of 1941–42. Its wearers dubbed it *"Gefrierfleischorden"*—the frozen meat medal.

KARL RUPP

---

*Born 1908; served in an armored division in
Russia; after the war became a salesman and
now lives in Ulm, Wuerttemberg.*

"The word fatherland has seen too much abuse."

It looked as if we would see action soon; there was talk of our going to
Africa. This rumor was confirmed the day we were issued tropical
uniforms, helmets, and tents. Our tanks got tropical paint jobs and
new cooling systems. But then, one fine day in June 1941, we got
news on the radio that Germany was taking on the Russians too. I
remember it well: an icy chill went down my spine. The others didn't
seem to be troubled at all. On average, the privates were ten or twelve
years younger than I; the NCOs were only about five to eight years
older than they.

Then—I think it was early September 1941—we were given three
days to get ready to go to Russia. As we found out later, a few fresh
armored divisions were supposed to break through to Moscow after
the initial offensive had slowed down. We were detrained at Vitebsk
and took part in the battle of the Vyazma/Bryansk pocket. But by the
end of October 1941, the new German offensive on Moscow was
stuck in the mud. Our 5th Panzer Division had taken heavy casualties. On that day our so-called Führer shouted out to a mass rally,
"We have the best weapons in the world!" Our 2nd Battalion lost,
would you believe it, a sum total of twenty tanks during *one* attack.
We said to each other, "Somehow we idiots still haven't caught on
that we have such good hardware."

We hadn't been deployed as regiments or companies for quite
awhile; we were now battle groups: a couple of tanks, a few riflemen

and, most important, one or two 88mm anti-aircraft guns. These alone could measure up to the Russian T-34 tanks, which were shooting up our tanks like rabbits. We were powerless to do anything about it with our light guns. At one point, deployed under good cover, we let the T-34s approach to within 40 yards before opening fire, and our shells just bounced off them.

My battle group consisted of two Mk. III medium tanks, three Mk. II light tanks, about forty or fifty riflemen, and one 88. We were all dog-tired. The young guys slept in any position whenever they got a chance. For weeks, we only got out of the tank for minutes at a time. Our breath condensed on the metal, so that everything you touched inside the tank was covered with ice. It was 40 to 50 degrees below outside. Most of the time even the rations were frozen. At night, we had to start the tanks every two hours to keep the engines from freezing up. So even if Ivan did leave us alone for awhile, the tank demanded our attention.

I'd become commander of a light tank, and usually had to start it up from time to time when my driver was asleep. One night the riflemen noticed with horror that, on top of everything else, our machine guns had frozen up. If the Russians had attacked, they could have finished us without the least problem. Fortunately, somebody realized that you could defrost machine guns by rubbing gasoline onto them. Incidentally, the Russian machine guns never jammed, and the Russian infantry was equipped with superior rifles.

We were fifteen to twenty miles from Moscow at that point. There was a streetcar stop nearby, and at night we could see the Moscow flak shooting at our planes.

Our last push was through wooded terrain. The spearhead was formed out of two Mk. IIs and two Mk. IIIs. At the end came another Mk. II, and riflemen were in between. The lead tank was knocked out with no survivors. I was in the second tank. There was no way to get through; we had to retreat.

That was when I became familiar with the crack Siberian troops, who'd been thrown into action on the Moscow front after the Russians had been informed by their German agent Richard Sorge that the Japanese would not attack in the East. These troops were excellently equipped: fur coats, fur caps, fur-lined boots and gloves. Our

Landser were a pitiful sight in comparison: light coats, rags wrapped around feet or shoes. I myself had managed to get some Russian felt boots; I'd taken them off a dead Russian. You had to do this right away, because rigor mortis set in very quickly in that cold.

The first time I got the idea that things might go wrong was during my leave from the front, after the battle of Moscow. The German people were being told that only the cold winter was to blame for the disaster, and not the Russian army. Well, it was just as cold on the other side. The Russians were better and more thoroughly prepared to deal with the severe conditions. They knew what was at stake: their homeland. We, on the other hand, had not only heard so many lies, but we also saw the rear-echelon and home troops taking it easy. We felt like we'd already been written off.

HANS HERWARTH VON BITTENFELD*

"The party succeeded in driving people back into the arms of Stalin."

We soldiers already had an eerie feeling when we first marched into the Soviet Union. I was with a regiment that was half East Prussian and half Bavarian. Prussians and Bavarians alike were in awe of the size of Russia; it reached all the way to the Pacific Ocean. The troops were not at all enthusiastic about the prospects of fighting in the Soviet Union.

Once, a representative from the Propaganda Ministry visited us and gave a speech that was, in fact, quite excellent. In an attempt to prepare us for what lay ahead, he reminded us that in the Middle Ages German knights had also ridden east. We listened silently, and

* Biography on page xxxix.

there was no applause. Afterwards we stood around, and the speaker said to my divisional commander, "I am actually rather disappointed. I don't see any enthusiasm here." A captain responded, "Sir, enthusiasm is not the point. But when we are ordered to fight, we do it extremely well." In a sense, this explains the tragic situation of the German front officer. We did our damned duty, but we never believed in ultimate victory over the Soviet Union.

When we marched into the Soviet Union we were initially looked upon as liberators and greeted with bread and salt. The farmers shared the little they had with us. They hoped finally to be treated as Europeans and as human beings. They expected the end of collective farming. Hitler, on the other hand, claimed this to be the best system for requisitioning grain. Thus Hitler thought the same as Stalin on the subject of collectivization. That was the disaster. The party functionaries succeeded in driving people who were willing to cooperate with us back into the arms of Stalin.

They managed to achieve this through a reign of terror and the behavior of the SS. The SS dealt with the minorities first by murdering Jews and many Muslims. Because Muslims were circumcised, they were thought to be Jews, considered subhuman. Naturally this stupid, inhuman treatment of the population slowly eroded the good will of the people.

Interestingly enough, it was different in the southern part of the Soviet Union. There, because the North Caucasus region was under military administration, people were treated properly. The troops were ordered to behave as if they were on maneuvers in their own country. General von Köstring, the former military attaché in Moscow who was half German and half Russian, was sent to the region to ensure that a situation similar to the one in the Ukraine—where the people were driven back to Stalin—did not arise. In the North Caucasus, the collective farms were dissolved, and the troops behaved properly. The result: no partisans whatsoever.

We realized that the idea of transforming the war against the Soviet Union into a civil war could only succeed without Hitler. That was a tragedy. After all, at the end of the war we had 800,000 Soviet volunteers in the German army. Sometimes people maintain that all these volunteers were pressed into service. That, of course, is incorrect. Granted, there were surely a few who enlisted because they wanted out of the POW camps. But I myself saw how Russian soldiers deserted, came over to us, and said they wanted to fight on our side. Once, a Russian captain we had captured asked me where our artillery positions were. Since I can speak Russian I told him: "That is none of your business." "It is," he answered, "because your artillery has consistently been off target. I want to show your gunners how to aim the guns better." This best illustrates how much hatred there was toward the Soviet Union, and it was justified hatred. There was no family in the Soviet Union which had not suffered under Stalin.

PETER PECHEL

Born 1920; artilleryman in an armored division, fought in Poland, Greece, the Soviet Union, Normandy; battalion leader, captain; after the war became a journalist; radio and television correspondent in London and Washington; vice president of radio and television news for SFB, the Berlin affiliate of the German television network ARD; lives in Berlin and Bonn.

"I don't want to die!"

October 25, 1941: the central sector of the Eastern front is 50 miles from Moscow, an almost ridiculous distance considering the thousands of miles we have behind us. Not only are there Soviet defense forces situated this side of Moscow, there also is mud. The entire country has turned into a thick, dark gravy, frozen at the surface.

Above the black-brown mud hangs a heavy, low sky; everything is gray on gray. A few trees, some shabby, dirty huts. The road is deeply rutted. German army vehicles are bogged down bumper to bumper. The order that morning: "We're going to attack. The objective is Wolokolamsk." There is a strong Russian barricade just beyond the woods in front of us. The 5th Company has to outflank it and attack from the rear. The main thrust will come from other companies in front. "Pechel, you go with the 5th as forward artillery observer and provide them with the necessary support," ordered my commander.

We push forward, a small column of nine tanks. Although we are under fire at times, we continue to advance. I have an uneasy feeling. My assistant observer and radio operator tell me they feel the same way—queasy stomachs and difficulty breathing. Is today the day we are going to get it?

We pass through a quiet forest. When we exit on the other side, all hell breaks loose. We are under fire from all directions. We went the wrong way and are not behind the enemy, but directly in front of his main anti-tank barrier. There is no time to think about what went wrong. The lead tank is on fire. The tank in front of me takes a direct hit on the turret hatch. Before I even have a chance to return fire, there is a brief roaring sound. I can't see. Blue stars dance in front of my eyes. Then I feel two quick blows to my right arm and left thigh. My radio operator cries out, "I'm hit!" Suddenly everything turns quiet inside our tank—horribly quiet. I squeeze my way up, shouting, "Out, quick, get out!"

I jump out of the tank, but only two men follow me. The radio operator didn't make it. Everything is concentrated on this corner of the forest: artillery, anti-tank guns, grenades, machine guns. The noise, the whining, the whistling, the hissing, the whizzing—it's like the beginning of the end of the world. All we have left are five shot-up tanks; scattered around them are the wounded and the dead. My radio operator is dead, shrapnel through the heart. My assistant observer is lying on the ground bleeding from a chest wound. The driver is best off; he just can't hear anything. The entire right front side of our tank is missing. My arm and thigh start to hurt. There is blood on my face. It sticks to my eyes. Most likely, my head caught something too. I feel my right hand and am able to turn it completely around on my wrist. The bone is shattered. The hand turns cold and blue, and there is nothing I can do to protect or cover it. It's 14 degrees Fahrenheit outside.

We are lying flat on the ground. All around us is a raging inferno. Those who have already been wounded once are being hit a second and third time. You can hear their whimpering. The commander of the tank in front of me has taken a bullet in the head, and his brains are running down his face. He's running around in grotesque circles crying, "Mother, Mother." Finally, and almost mercifully, he is hit again by shrapnel and falls to the ground. Suddenly there are Russians all around us counter-attacking. They swarm through the woods. And here we lie, defenseless: the wounded, the dying, the dead.

Oh God, only four days ago I saw the dead of another one of our companies. I saw the poked out eyes, the severed genitals, the horrible, tortured, distorted faces. Anything but that. The Russians don't differentiate between SS and tank troops yet. To them, those of us wearing the black tank uniforms and the death's head insignia belong to the SS. I get my pistol out of the tank, place it in my still-sound left hand, and say to my assistant observer, "Fritz, you first, then me." He nodded. But could I take my own life using my left hand? I'm right-handed and would probably only succeed in shooting my eyes out, not killing myself. On the other hand, did I want to end up in a Russian prison camp at best?

But is there any other way out? There are eight bullets in the clip. Six for the Russians, two for us. But is it that simple? After all, I'm only 21 years old. You just can't go and kill yourself; you're just beginning to live. When you're so young and have been at war since the age of 19, you really haven't had much of a life. I *don't* want to die! I look down at the little dark hole, the muzzle of the gun. I release the safety catch and pray. I pray fervently to a God who possibly exists.

The area is crawling with Russians. Why aren't they closing in on us? Do they actually think we could offer some kind of resistance? My driver suddenly has a seizure. He jumps up and, screaming senselessly, staggers towards the Russians. I run after him and brutally drag him to the ground. He moans, then is finally quiet.

Suddenly the firing stops. The silence is deafening. Then the noise of combat begins again to our left, gets louder, and quickly comes closer. We listen intently. The terrorizing thought of death gradually turns into raging hope of survival. Could it possibly be that we were about to be rescued? Was the return from that far place we had already come to terms with in our minds still conceivable? And then, breaking through the woods are, yes, German tanks. It's the other companies, the ones responsible for the main thrust. Suddenly one of the wounded lets out a shout, a shout of joy, "Germans! German tanks! Our comrades!" We finally realize we have been rescued.

The next day, the division's combat order read, "In a boldly led envelopment attack on Spasskoje, Combat Group Back's forward elements were successful in fighting their way to the train station in Wolokolamsk, 35 miles from Moscow."

JOSEF HÜHNERBACH

Born 1913; an infantry NCO in Russia, the Balkans, and Italy; captured, he was sent as a POW to the United States; a retired city employee, he lives near Bonn.

"We got our winter uniforms in the spring."

There'll never be anything like the German infantry again. The fighting was really bad. At times it was so heavy that the soup boys and the field kitchen couldn't get to us. So sometimes we didn't get food for two or three days.

I was on the Russian front in 1941, when the great cold came. We were fighting near the town of Klin, thirty-odd miles from Moscow. The cold was terrible, and we got our winter uniforms in the spring.

I'll never forget it. It was March 15 when the real winter clothes came. Up to then we had just had regular clothing: an overcoat, a pair of gloves, and headgear. And Hitler said—I'll never forget this— "The Russians will lay down their arms within the next eight weeks. I'm sure of it." After that he didn't say anything. After that came the end, and we were the ones laying down the arms.

One day, while we were stationed in a fortified position between Kalinin and Vyasma, our lieutenant came in wearing a nice fur coat and clapped me on the shoulder: "Hühnerbach, how's it look?" I replied, "What does the *Herr Leutnant* desire?" "Hühnerbach, put on this fur coat," he said. "You're coming a little late with warm clothes, *Herr Leutnant.*" The fur coat was his. I put it on. The arms were so long you couldn't see my hands. I said, "But it doesn't fit, it's too big." "So what?" said the lieutenant. "Put it on. The Führer is on his way, and I don't know whether he'll stop at our sector or not."

Hitler must really have blown up when he visited a neighboring battalion and saw simple soldiers standing in the bitter cold in their summer cotton uniforms. He told the officers "Gentlemen, an ordinary soldier in the front line cannot do his duty in a cotton coat. I order you all to remove your fur coats; they belong in the forward line." "Yes sir, *mein Führer,*" and so on. That's a true story.[1]

The first time I was wounded was during trench fighting. The Russians broke through, and we were pretty thinly manned in the trenches. They began attacking by the thousands, wave after wave, and my gun jammed. By that time the Russians were already in our trenches bayonetting and bashing heads with their rifle butts. I got a grazing wound on the head, my first wound.

On August 28, 1942, I was wounded for a second time near Rzhev, in the battle of the Vyasma pocket. I got it in my left thigh. A Russian tank detachment attacked when it was just starting to get dark. Behind the tanks came infantry. It was a ricochet; I still have the bullet. It was stuck in the bone. I was sent to the hospital, and that was the end of the Russian campaign for me. I was transported out in a horse cart between dead German soldiers and the badly wounded.

---

[1] Hitler never visited the front line in Russia. Hühnerbach's story shows the force of Hitler's image at this stage of the war, and the power of rumor in all armies.

WOLFGANG SCHÖLER

Born 1921; served in the Ukraine on the military railroad; POW in Russia; joined the Bundeswehr after the war; lives near Paderborn, Westphalia.

"The soldiers showed the villagers their photos."

In June 1941, we advanced deep into the Ukraine. And I must admit one thing: I really learned to appreciate the Russians, especially the Ukrainians.

I met a nineteen-year-old Ukrainian girl, a teacher, with whom I became very close. In fact, I was head over heels in love, and I never would have let her go if fate had allowed it to be different. I was at her parents' home often, and that's where I got to know Ukrainian family life.

When the German army first occupied her village, all the young girls were hidden by their parents. They had to wear their oldest dresses and weren't allowed to bathe. When the first tanks arrived and the German soldiers climbed out, the first thing they asked for was water so they could wash. Then the first conversations began, and the soldiers showed the villagers their photos—every soldier carried a picture of his sweetheart! The villagers saw that these Germans didn't fit the images that the Communist leaders had propagated about them. Then the young girls' good dresses came back out of the closets, and they were allowed to wash again.

My Russian got pretty good. I saw, for instance, that the young people there read good books, and were very interested in music. They always played the *"Lied der Moorsoldaten"* by Brecht, because it was the only phonograph record they had in German. I also learned to do some Russian dances. Even though I was a young soldier fighting in a war, I still felt the need to be part of a family. The Ukrainians gave me the opportunity to do that. That's why I still remember those people so fondly.

When we were ready to move on, I had a very bad throat infection, with a fever of over 103 degrees. I was taken to a private home where there were two women. When they saw how seriously ill I was, they offered their help. Even though I was half-delirious, I know those women stayed by my bed all night. They put hot compresses—made of oats stuffed in a wool stocking—on my throat, and they wiped the sweat from my forehead. And most of all, I knew those two women were praying for me at my bedside.

These people were later terribly disappointed by the behavior of certain German administrators, whom we called "*Goldfasanen.*" We saw how Ukrainians there were recruited for work in the Reich, for arms production, including the prisoners who'd surrendered to the Wehrmacht. They were deported and shunted west, their situation getting steadily worse. Many died a miserable death, starving in labor camps. To me and my comrades at the front, this was just as depressing a disgrace in the history of our people as the systematic gassing of the Jews in the concentration camps.

SIEGFRIED FISCHER*

"I was shot down 13 times."

I became a pilot and was sent to dive-bomber training school. I flew throughout the war, only missing half a year when I came down with jaundice. I was seriously wounded three times. Our Stuka unit specialized in the destruction of bridges behind enemy lines. On the Eastern front we were deployed from Stalingrad to Finland as a "fire brigade"; we went wherever we were most needed.

* Biography on page 106.

One of the many bridges I destroyed was at Smolensk in 1941. Our troops were advancing to seal the pocket of Smolensk at this spot, and Russian troops had been fleeing eastward over this bridge. Late one night I took off with seven other planes to knock it out. I had the dubious luck to fly the last plane. I dived, and saw that all the other bombs had missed. So I risked everything: I actually flew lower than the flak, so low that I had to delay the explosion of the bombs to avoid getting hit by the blast myself. It was a full thirteen seconds before the bridge blew to pieces. After that, the Russians were cut off and encircled.

From there, I was transferred to the Mediterranean. I fought in Malta later in 1941, with the first German Stuka unit in that theater. Our assignment was to close off the Mediterranean by destroying the Maltese naval base.

Once we were sent out against a naval unit in the port of La Valetta. The weather was bad and we had to fly under the clouds because we could only attack in visual conditions. When we finally came out into the clear we discovered that the ships weren't below us, but that we were actually alongside them! All hell broke loose. The defensive fire we got from the ships and the mainland was terrifying. I saw the shells of the light flak and bursts of machine gun fire spraying through the water, and shrapnel falling into the sea. At that moment we saw a submarine start to dive. We dropped our bombs on it and pulled out. Our unit scattered, with every pilot having to make it back to the base on his own.

Then we were transferred back to Russia. There we flew the Focke-Wulf 190 equipped with hollow-charge ammunition, and were trained as anti-tank specialists. I destroyed about 80 tanks. We attacked at such low altitudes that even the trees got in our way. The Russians by this time were advancing with an unbelievable number of tanks. When we scored a hit the tanks would usually burn, and then explode.

Altogether, I was shot down 13 times. I bailed out twice. The second time, my head and legs hit the fuselage, leaving a hole in the back of my head and my legs shattered. There was no time to amputate; the Russians were advancing too quickly. My legs were put in makeshift splints, and I fell into the hands of the Russians just south of Berlin. Nothing at all was done for my wounds, there were just no facilities.

Every time I was shot down behind Russian lines I was always prepared to shoot myself, because I never would have let them take me alive. I had seen the remains of Stuka fliers who had been massacred by Russian soldiers, their stomachs slit open, and so on. The Russians really hated Stuka crews.

KURT MEYER-GRELL

Born 1921; as a pilot in the Luftwaffe Special Operations Wing, dropped agents over enemy territory; after the war became a civil servant; lives near Cologne.

"We had strict orders not to bring any agents back."

The Test Formation of the Luftwaffe High Command, later renamed Bomber Wing 200, was a special unit that flew commando operations, as they'd be called today, and dropped agents and sabotage troops behind enemy lines. As far as I can remember, there were fifteen to twenty such commando units in the entire European theater of operations. I flew quite a few missions in Russia dropping agents in Russian uniforms.

We flew a modified Heinkel 111 bomber back then. They were equipped with a special floor mount where the agents would sit and later slide down into the open. Before a mission we never knew where we were going, and we had absolutely no idea what the agents' assignments were. Only after boarding the plane were we informed of our destination by instructions delivered in a sealed envelope. The pilot would break the seal and find out location, drop elevation, and identification signals set up in the drop zone—if any. Most of the time we dropped blind at the assigned map coordinates without even knowing if the ground was suitable for parachute landing.

The agents were always driven up in a closed truck accompanied by counterespionage or security people who wore gray uniforms, not the black SS ones. The agents, carrying their weapons and wearing Russian uniforms, were quickly shunted into the fuselage. Most of them were drunk, a deliberate attempt to numb the fear of these men and women. Yes, sometimes I flew women too.

We took off after we'd plotted our course, the target area was set, and the agents were belted in. It was really bad. German anti-aircraft units were never informed, so we were often shot at by our own guns. The agents in the back would sing patriotic songs in broken German. We had no idea where they came from or what kind of assignment they had. The longer the flight lasted—often we were in the air for up to four hours—the quieter it would get in back, and the more you could sense the fear. The minute we throttled back and went into the gliding run, the crew in the back would start having trouble with the agents. The man who readied them for the jump was prepared to use force if necessary; we had strict orders not to bring any agents back. We excused our actions by telling ourselves that once they were hanging from their chutes, self-preservation would take over, and they'd complete their missions. After all, it wasn't our job.

The less we knew, the better off we were in the event we were taken prisoner. I remember in 1944 we were issued so-called KO pills, little red poison pills. We were required to sign a statement promising we would take them if captured.

HELMUT SCHMIDT*

"Schmidtchen, shut up!"

We soldiers were not Nazis. In fact, many were actually anti-Nazis. I had just turned 21 years old. We all believed that we had to do our duty for our country, just as people had done before us. That is how we continued to think during the first Russian winter, and even after that.

While on staff duty in Berlin, I never met a Nazi that I knew of with one single exception. My commanding generals were the conservative type, and had nothing in common with the Nazis. They spoke their minds openly, but we young officers often failed to recognize to whom and in what situation we could air our opinions. On one occasion, I spoke thoughtlessly, and received a warning from my general. He simply said, "Schmidtchen, shut up! That's no way to behave!"

Everyone knew I wasn't a Nazi. I even received the nickname, "The Red Lieutenant." I wasn't "red"—I didn't even know what that meant.

We were very careful not to come too close to the Russians. We were as afraid of them as they were of us. We didn't even want to take any Russians as prisoners. In fact, we were more relieved than anything else when they escaped.

Only once did I come into contact with actual prisoners of war. It was in a rear area. I saw a freight train loaded with Russian prisoners. They were all in pitiful condition. It wasn't that they had been mistreated; it was more that they obviously hadn't been given anything to eat. They stretched out their arms and shouted something I could not understand. I assumed that they were asking for food.

---

* Biography on page 24.

WILLI NOLDEN

Born 1914; anti-tank gunner in Russia and on the Western front; became a hairdresser after the war; lives in the Rhineland.

"I'll give you a thousand marks for your hand!"

I did my two years' compulsory service in 1936–37, and was called again on August 26, 1939. So I was a soldier for the whole war, and always at the front. I was wounded eight times, three times badly enough to be sent back from Russia to a hospital in Germany.

My division was stationed in France when Hitler attacked Russia. But at Christmas 1941, we were sent east—into that first Russian winter! We had only regular winter clothes, a thin coat and nothing else. We got some civilian stuff, mufflers and a few gloves. But the worst thing was that we didn't have any felt boots.

When we unloaded our equipment, everything was frozen solid, covered with ice. Every battery was dead. So we put all of our trucks and half-tracks in an open field and built fires around them. It was the only way we could get moving again.

Not that it did us much good. I was driver for an anti-tank gun. We had little 3.7cm guns that were almost useless. We could knock out the light Russian tanks, but our shells just bounced off the big ones, the T-34s. There were snow drifts six feet deep. Nothing could move. We had heavy casualties from frostbite—fingers, toes, sometimes whole arms and legs. And then came the Russian counterattack: Siberians, with padded uniforms, felt boots, and white camouflage suits. They used a really interesting vehicle, an armored sled with a propeller to move it over the snow. It had two men and a machine-gun up front. We could knock out the sleds with our little guns, but we couldn't stop the Russians. We had to blow up the tanks we couldn't move. I saw over 200 of our tanks in one small area, destroyed by our own side!

Landser on the Russian front didn't mark time by dates. They remembered the seasons, and when they were wounded badly enough to be sent home. When spring came, the mud came—mud like nobody had ever seen. We built corduroy roads out of tree trunks, sometimes twenty miles back to the rear areas, so supplies and ammunition could get forward.

When you picture the Russian front, you shouldn't think of one long line of trenches. Most of the time the front line was a chain of strong points—bunkers, fortified villages, and so on. One morning I brought my gun into a village like that, then drove my half-track back under the cover in the woods. The Russians attacked, and around noon we saw Germans running back out of the village. On my own, I drove my half-track through the back yards, knocking down sheds and barns, till I got to the crossroads where my gun was dug in. "Toni," I yelled to the sergeant. "I'm coming! I'll get you out of there!" I went across the road full speed. The Russians were maybe a hundred yards away, but they stayed put. I spun the half-track around, we hitched up the gun, everybody jumped on, and we went back the same way I'd come.

There was another gun left behind, from the company we were attached to. So I volunteered: "Lieutenant, I'll bring your crew back too!" I did it the same way, and got the Iron Cross on the spot.

We were nowhere near Stalingrad, but the summer of 1942 was bad everywhere. Finally we'd lost all of our guns, so they used us as infantry. We did a lot of raiding and patrolling. I remember once, we took a bunker. I was lying on the roof watching the Russians run, but there was one Russian I didn't see. He threw a grenade at me and my shoulder was torn open. The Russians took a few more shots at me, but they missed. I got back to our main positions with a finger-sized stream of blood running out of my sleeve. The medics bandaged me up, and they sent me to Germany to recover. I was out of the war at least for a while.

I was back in Russia in time for the winter of 1942, but it was summer before I was hit again. By this time we had heavier guns,

7.5cm, big enough to stop anything the Russians had. But they could be too big. The Wehrmacht was already retreating. We had to cross a river, and the only way was a blown-up railroad bridge. Our engineers laid some boards across the pilings, so a man could make it, but we had to leave the guns. The Russians had us under rifle and mortar fire. They could drop a mortar shell in your pants pocket. I started onto the bridge, and shrapnel caught me in the hand. One of my buddies joked, "I'll give you a thousand marks for your hand!" You wanted to get hit—anything to get away from the front and out of Russia.

I was back by April 1944. We were guarding the battalion command post of bunkers and two-man foxholes. I had a submachine gun and a hole by myself; I was an old soldier and they trusted me not to get jumpy. It was sometime just after midnight. It starts to get light early in north Russia at that time of year, and I just knew something was wrong. All of a sudden, two Russians came toward me. They had submachine guns, but they weren't carrying them ready to use. They looked like they were out for a walk. I was in good shape. I'd camouflaged my hole and scooped out a little shelf for my grenades; and I didn't want to shoot them. I wanted to take them prisoner. So when they were about six feet away, I jumped up, pointed my submachine gun, and said, "Pan!" I didn't really know what it meant—"mister" or "soldier," something like that.

They were so taken by surprise they just stood still. Then they tried to run. As soon as they moved, I brought my gun up. I shouted to my buddy in the next hole to go out and get their guns, but he didn't feel like playing hero. So for five minutes everybody just stood there. The Russians made signs that *we* should go with *them*. I said, "Cut it out. You'll get cigarettes, chocolate." I offered everything I could think of. I didn't want to shoot them down in cold blood. But then a half-dozen more Russians came toward us. And they saw something was wrong. One of them dropped off to the side and brought up his gun. I emptied three magazines one after the other, as fast as I could reload, until nothing was moving. I had no choice. When I checked, they were all dead.

Everybody said without me the command post would have been overrun. They gave me another Iron Cross. We used to joke that a wooden cross was easier to get than an Iron Cross.

When the Russians started their big offensive in 1944, my gun crew and I were in a bunker we'd built ourselves. We dug a hole, laid tree trunks crossways, filled the spaces between them with dirt. Inside it was almost homelike. We'd even dug a little hole for a pantry. Then the Russian artillery opened up for two hours without a break. The shells literally pounded on our bunker like a drum.

We'd put on our gear and our helmets, and lay down under our bunks. We could see the sky. The tree trunks were smashed to splinters, thrown around like toothpicks. More and more red-hot shrapnel came in. The smoke was so thick you could hardly breathe. We were terrified.

By chance, none of us was hurt. Suddenly the shelling stopped and I shouted "Outside, on the double!" The whole woods was a tangle of uprooted trees and shell holes. Our own artillery had started to lay down a barrage to keep the Russians from attacking. I'd never seen anything like it, a real wall of steel. But it didn't stop them. We tried to get to our gun, but it was no use; a shell had dropped a tree right on top of it. I said "Get saws and hatchets," but the saw had been smashed too. So we took spades and picks and, panting like dogs, dug the gun out from under the tree.

That was some job! And the Russians kept coming. For three days we shot them down as fast as they came. Then they found a weak spot and broke through. All of a sudden it got real quiet in our sector. The infantry pulled out. We and the gun stayed till it got dark. Then we pulled out too.

We drove toward the next village. Suddenly a voice shouted: "Halt! Password!" I answered, "We don't know the password, but we're from the Anti-tank Company, Captain Soandso." "Advance and be recognized." They saw we were Germans, and a captain told us, "You can't go on. The Russians have cut us off; we're surrounded and waiting to be relieved. We've got to dig in right here." Me and my crew were sent to cover a gully. If the Russians came through, we were supposed to stop them.

That night, the Russians hit us and I never saw a thing. "Willi, let's get out!" one of my men yelled all of a sudden. I jumped into the tall grass, crawled about 50 yards, and listened. And the Russians were there! They'd infiltrated our main positions without much shooting. All of a sudden it was hand to hand—they were beating the *Landser* to death with their rifle butts. And I heard the captain shout: "Throw away your guns; it's over."

I thought, "My God!" I knew the area pretty well, and me and my men sneaked through the woods. Once a whole Russian company marched past us while we were lying flat on the edge of some woods about a hundred yards away. We didn't have anything to eat or drink. Five days later we ran into a German patrol. The first thing *they* asked for was the password! They told us a truck had driven up to our old position and not returned. I said, "Yeah, and it's not coming back, either."

HUGO VOLKHEIMER

Born 1918; an infantry private and a junior officer in Russia; worked as a salesman after the war; resides in the Rhineland.

"The Red Army fought like men possessed."

In January 1942, elements of the Second Army Corps had been encircled near Demyansk in northern Russia. We stood by to fly in reinforcements and material with Ju-52s.

That was during the first Russian winter, when the *Landser* had nothing to wear. The fur collection drive at home only began later on. And when the furs did finally arrive at the front, they turned out to be ladies' fur coats. We only had summer clothing, and worst of all, no felt boots. The regulation army boots were totally inadequate for this kind of winter. When your feet swelled and the boots were frozen, your toes were gone—frozen off.

I was flown to a landing strip in the pocket. It'd been prepared in a hurry, so of course it was rather primitive. It was maybe eighteen yards wide, no concrete, no hangars, nothing, not even a shelter. There was a trench dug about 10 feet deep beside the landing strip. I'd hardly gotten out of the plane when I discovered strange heaps under an iced-up tarpaulin. Out of curiosity I lifted up a corner, and part of a human body came rolling toward me. It was a leg, with the hip section attached. The rest of the body was gone. It must have been a soldier who'd been torn apart by an explosion. This tarp covered an entire heap of dead soldiers who couldn't be buried because the ground was frozen rock-solid.

The Red Army fought like men possessed. They used mine dogs that were trained to crawl under tanks. The dogs wore a bomb harness with a primer that stuck up vertically and would detonate the explosive as they crawled under the tank. This made short work of our tanks.

MARTIN KOLLER*

"The greater the pressure on a unit, the more it held together."

I learned to fly in Dresden. An elderly lawyer in uniform who called himself *"Kriegsgerichtsrat"* gave lectures on international law. I heard about things like the Hague Convention for the first time, but we were bored and didn't like this old guy who couldn't relate to us. Then a young lieutenant took over as lecturer. He had been at the front, had taken part in the Battle of Britain, and had been wounded while piloting a bomber.

He taught us things that were quite different. He asked us: "What do you do if you get hit over London and you haven't dropped your bombs yet?" "Jettison," we answered. "Right. Is this drop blind or aimed?" "Blind," we said, "because we don't have a military target

* Biography on page xxxvii.

beneath us." "Wrong," he said, "aimed, because you're over enemy territory and it can't hurt." This impressed us, totally impressed us. It was that simple: "It can't hurt."

We were really pushing to go to the front; it couldn't happen soon enough for us. I became a tactical reconnaissance pilot. I got to know the fastest and best aircraft like the Me-109 and the Focke-Wulf 190. I learned flying, diving, photo reconnaissance and everything that goes with it, shooting and bombing.

I applied for the Russian front and was sent to Odessa shortly afterwards. From there, I flew with a Messerschmitt "Giant" over to the Crimea. That was at the turn of 1942–43. We often saw a lot of action over the Kuban bridgehead. The Russian pilots were very brave, and in the beginning, their planes were inferior to ours, but that changed pretty quickly. They got new models that were equal to ours, and then, of course, the Americans delivered the Airacobras in accordance with the Lend-Lease agreement. The Airacobras were far superior to anything we had in the reconnaissance squadron.

I had to reconnoiter an artillery emplacement which our own guns couldn't range on because it was so well camouflaged and set behind a hill. I planned my flight path so that I'd come from the east toward our own lines. I found the battery, but was down so low that I was hit by an anti-tank shell! Whenever a German plane came in low, the Russians expected to be strafed so they opened fire with pistols and anything else they had. I was hit by a chance shot right in the front of the cockpit. Only the plane's elevator responded. The engines were on fire, and I went down. I crashed into the ground between the German and the Russian lines at about 150 mph. Nothing happened to my radio operator, but I was stuck, and I roasted for a while in the flames. German infantrymen pulled me out.

If it hadn't been for those *Landser*, I wouldn't be alive today. A Russian patrol arrived simultaneously; it must have been quite an event for them to see a big bird come down between the lines like that. In spite of the ensuing firefight, the *Landsers* pulled us out of the plane, dragged us back to their trenches, and administered first aid as if they'd been trained and did it every day. Later, in the hospital, I had one leg amputated at the hip.

Soldiers at the front had an especially close relationship. Your outfit was almost like a family. The greater the pressure on a unit, the more it stuck together. I believe that even if there were no more goals, even if you saw that it was pointless and that everything was over, you would have kept on fighting so as not to shame yourself in front of your comrades. You had to stick together to survive. And I think this made these small units as strong as they were, even in a catastrophe.

CHAPTER 6

"You are talking to dead men."

The arrogance of the German high command remained unshaken by the losses of Barbarossa. Hitler and his generals viewed the winter fighting as a temporary setback, a fluke generated by German over-confidence and Russian good luck. A hundred thousand men, cut off in the Demyansk pocket southeast of Leningrad, had been successfully supplied by air from January to the end of April. There seemed no reason why, by repeating the successes of 1941, the Reich could not wrap up this part of the war in 1942. On December 19, 1941, Hitler assumed personal command of the Eastern front. Many key figures of Operation Barbarossa—Guderian, Rundstedt, Bock—were relieved or transferred. In their places stood new men, with reputations and careers still to make. Their perceptions were restricted to the battlefield; their shortsightedness was fostered by pride in the men they led.

The Wehrmacht by the late winter of 1941–42 was a superbly tempered instrument combining the best features of a national army and a seasoned professional force. Eight months in Russia had piti-lessly exposed weak links, human and material. New vehicles and weapons were still on the drawing boards, but officers and men knew how to use what they possessed to best advantage: tanks, assault guns, and anti-tank guns. Respect for "Ivan's" toughness and deter-mination blended with conviction that as a soldier the *Landser* remained far superior. Mobility, communications, shock power, and above all, disciplined initiative—these, resting on the base of comradeship and mutual confidence that had grown out of the bitter fighting of 1941, would bring victory to German arms in the coming campaign.

Operational planning too had improved. Instead of three offensives moving in different directions, as in 1941, the Führer Directive of April 3, 1942, provided for the concentration of all available German resources in the south. Their mission was to destroy the enemy in that sector and secure the Caucasian oil fields and the passes through the mountains into the Middle East.

On June 28, 1942, the great offensive began. For the first few weeks it was Barbarossa all over again as German armored columns rolled across the steppe under a Luftwaffe umbrella that provided both safety and support for the men on the ground. During its year in Russia, the German air force had become increasingly a tactical instrument, geared to clearing obstacles for the tanks and infantry. The relatively light Russian resistance had other causes as well. The Soviet high command had prudently withdrawn its forces rather than risk destruction in place by the German juggernaut. But Stalin and his generals remained puzzled about the Germans' intentions. Did Hitler propose to drive toward the Caucasus, or would the Panzer divisions swing left and threaten Moscow from the south?

Hitler himself was uncertain. His original directive appreciated the possible threat to the Caucasus offensive posed by the city of Stalingrad, on the left of the German axis of advance. But that document also recognized Stalingrad's secondary importance. Then, on July 30, the Führer proclaimed Stalingrad the campaign's key objective.

The prestige of conquering the city bearing Stalin's name may have blinded Hitler to the folly of dividing forces already stretched dangerously thin. But his generals had their own form of *hubris*. Chief of Staff Franz Halder confined his outrage to the pages of his diary. Army and corps commanders gritted their teeth and pinned their faith on the "boys up front." Surely the *Landser* could work one more miracle.

In Stalingrad there was no room for flexibility, for maneuver, for the art of command. Instead, the men of 6th Army clawed their way from house to house, from floor to floor and room to room. Two hundred miles short of Baku, the German attack into the Caucasus stalled. In October, Hitler closed down offensive operations everywhere but in the Stalingrad sector. But by this time German reserves were exhausted. Crucial sectors of the front had been turned over to allies and clients—Italians, Rumanians, and Hungarians, poorly equipped and poorly motivated. On November 19, 1942, the Russians struck, not at Stalingrad itself, but on the flanks, in the open steppe. Axis defenses collapsed; by November 23, the Germans in Stalingrad were surrounded.

At this stage a fighting retreat was clearly feasible. Instead, Hitler ordered the 6th Army to stand its ground. Göring carelessly promised to supply Stalingrad from the air, despite repeated warnings that the task was impossible. The Luftwaffe lost 488 aircraft to bad weather and Russian defenses. It delivered no more than a fraction of the garrison's requirements.

Hitler summoned Erich von Manstein. As a field commander in Russia he had added to the laurels he had won as a planner in France. Now he hoped for command of the entire Eastern front. By December 21, spearheads of a German counterattack were within 30 miles of the Stalingrad perimeter. Manstein recommended preparations for the 6th Army to attempt a breakout, but issued no orders. Army Commander Friedrich Paulus hesitated. His men were too weak to march. He no longer had enough gasoline and ammunition. Behind these excuses were Hitler's repeated orders to hold the line of the Volga. Manstein too bowed to the Führer's will. The proposed breakout was abandoned. To a Luftwaffe officer sent to Stalingrad as Hitler's emissary Paulus only said, "You are talking to dead men here."

On February 2, 1943, the 200,000 men of the 6th Army surrendered. More than men and weapons had been lost. Never in the history of the Prussian/German army had its generals abandoned their soldiers at the word of a politician. As Stalingrad's fate was sealed, no senior officer of the Wehrmacht found the courage to confront Hitler. No one resigned. No one shot himself in protest.

Officers captured at Stalingrad formed the nucleus of the anti-Nazi National Committee for a Free Germany and the League of German Officers, organized in 1943. Relatively few were Communists or

Communist sympathizers. Hoping to save what could be saved, they accepted Soviet hints that Russia was fighting against the Nazi system, not the German people. And in Germany, Propaganda Minister Josef Goebbels called for total war.

HEINZ PFENNIG

Born 1921; captured at Stalingrad in 1943 and remained in Russian captivity until 1955; back in Germany he joined the Bundeswehr; retired, he lives in Bad Pyrmont, Lower Saxony.

"A half-loaf of bread—what more could my heart desire?"

I arrived in Kharkov in July 1942 as a young lieutenant with the 8th Company of the 4th Railroad Engineer Regiment. That's when the march toward Stalingrad began. Our first job was to change the tracks to a wider gauge. The Russian method of construction was simple; the metal track was nailed right onto the railroad ties. Then we were assigned to keep the railroad open between the Don and the Volga Rivers. Three of our company's platoons were quartered in the train station at Karpova, southwest of Stalingrad.

Night after night, small Soviet planes, nicknamed "sewing machines," tried to demolish the Karpova station. It was tough going. Night after night we tried to patch up the damage in the dark. We even had to use chisels and sledgehammers because a blow torch would have given our position away. The calm, the diligence, and the composure of our soldiers were amazing. Not a single night went by that they weren't confronted with death and injury, but they kept doing their duty.

Our real trouble began as soon as we were encircled. We were placed on short rations sometime during December. Bread was doled out. There was rarely any extra food. Our potatoes were just dried potato flakes. At this point all of our supplies were flown in. Then the first snow came, and that was the big problem.

At Christmas, each one of us got a tablespoon of peas, two tablespoons of a soup made of dried potatoes, and two squares of chocolate. We had no winter clothes, and the only thing we could do was to bundle up in the snow and wait for the enemy to come and get us.

The Russians knew that time and the cold weather were on their side. Naturally, we saw that planes were supplying us. But what gave us the greatest lift were the beloved latrine rumors. There were always new ones. We heard that an army was supposed to come up from the south and cut our way out of there. Another day someone said Sepp Dietrich had already reached the Don with an SS tank army, and was going to get us out.

Things came to a head in January. The Russians broke through and our time as railroad engineers was over. From then on we were infantry. On the night of January 10, both my hands and feet froze. I got shrapnel in my right thigh, and my circulation was so bad that months later my toes had to be amputated. My fingers were so swollen that they looked like blood oranges. After two days, my fingernails and my skin came off with my gloves. My CO convinced me to go to the medical tent.

I was lying in the field hospital one morning when the bad news came that the Russians had broken through again, and that my company commander had been killed. We were moved to the center of Stalingrad. I could still walk, but though I had some energy left, I became more and more apathetic.

We entered the city and reached the so-called barricades. A street-car line cut through Stalingrad, and from there the entrance to all roads leading east, to Red Square, were blocked with old trucks and other vehicles, as well as rubble which had been blown into the streets. It was set up so that we could easily occupy the houses along this streetcar line and see when the enemy was coming. In the meantime, I had two thickly bandaged hands, a boot on my left foot, and a bandage on the other.

We developed a system at the barricades. It was a little warmer in the basements of these houses, and, while one or two soldiers sat watch upstairs, all the rest huddled downstairs with their weapons. The guys on watch could see as far as the railroad bridge, and they gave us a signal if anything was up. They put me up there on guard duty. Since I had pieces of cloth wrapped around my hands and wrists and couldn't hold on to anything, they hung a bag of nails from the ceiling. If I shook that bag it was the signal that the Russians were coming, and my comrades should charge up the basement stairs and open fire.

After a short time I was sent into Stalingrad as a runner. I was to go to a department store that had been turned into the headquarters of General Paulus. This was very painful for me because I could hardly walk. By this time the pocket was so small that we were constantly being shelled from all sides. You could really only see dust, dry mortar which fell like fine, powdery snow, and the swaying walls of houses. I made it to the department store and delivered the message. When they gave me a cup of coffee and a piece of salami, I thought my eyes were deceiving me!

On January 30, the slogan went around: "We will not surrender on the tenth anniversary of the national revolution (January 30, 1933)." Big words in a shitty situation. The Russians were already on Red Square and were shelling us. January 31 was the day.

A lieutenant of a different division, an Austrian aristocrat, was beside himself and moaned, "What am I going to do in imprisonment, I'll put a bullet through my head. I have to. What would my forefathers think of me? I would be the first in our family to surrender."

The Russians came on January 31. The first soldiers who reached us behaved very correctly. They asked us if we had cameras, watches, and things like that. But they never took our stuff without giving us something in return. I gave away a fountain pen and got a half loaf of bread for it. What more could my heart desire?

All 26 of us were pulled out of the basement of the department store. The lieutenant, that Austrian, shot himself. They took the rest of us into Stalingrad. There was an enormous pile of rubble where the opera house had been, with a yawning hole in the middle. We went into the hole and found ourselves in a huge, empty cellar with stones and wreckage lying around.

This place was referred to as Collection Hospital 6. There was a doctor, a medic, whose name I remember because it was a simple one, Meier. He was an optimistic and persuasive person, but he couldn't do much for us because the Russian soldiers we met there were less pleasant than those who had captured us. They took our coats, our blankets, and even our first-aid kits. We didn't have a thing left. They made us take off our undershirts, which were full of lice anyway. All of our clothes were infested with lice. This is when the first cases of typhus broke out amongst us. If someone died during the night, he was carried out in the morning, and sometime during the day another soldier or two was brought in to replace him. There were more or less always 26 of us.

Every second or third day they brought in a pail of soup, hot water with semolina or barley in it. And then we got nothing for a few days again. Sometimes we got one loaf of bread for 26 men, half a slice for each, and then nothing. We watched our comrades die. A sergeant by the name of Karl Richter was beside me. He kept staring out into space with big eyes, as if he wasn't part of this world anymore. You could have said he'd gone crazy, but when he spoke he sounded completely normal. He started to tell me something, and suddenly he stopped right in the middle. When I looked over at him, he was dead.

I also got typhus. I lost consciousness for two weeks; the only thing I remember is that I thought I saw lice as large as turtles. And when I came to 14 days later, and I could see and feel again, I noticed that my thigh and my lower arms were in horrible shape. But the will to live came back immediately. It was the instinct to survive.

After weeks, I felt that I had to get out of this cellar. I hobbled up the broken stairs, and saw the light of day for the first time in months. Unfortunately, I also saw a Russian guard standing there with his "mandolin," his machine pistol. Ivan put out his hand and stopped me. I said that I just wanted some sun, and he told me to sit down. Then he reached into his pocket and pulled out some Machorka tobacco, lit two cigarettes, and gave me one. I have met a lot of good Russians, and the first really good one I met was this guy. I quickly got sick from the Machorka, but my soul clung to this little gesture.

There were lifesavers like this here and there. You just had to keep your eyes open for them and take them. I don't mean take in the sense that I took a cigarette, I mean to take the signs that there are good people everywhere in the world. It gave me new courage to face life.

The next important day was April 20, 1943. We were taken out of the basement—on the day of the Führer's birthday, strangely enough—and were brought to a real hospital, an intact building. It had no windows, but it did have plank beds.

This was still in Stalingrad. I met our company's doctor there, and we were very happy to see each other. I weighed only 80 pounds by this time, and walking was more like crawling. He told me I was a pretty sight, and then began to treat my frostbite. He told me that part of my right foot would have to be amputated. As far as my left foot was concerned, he said he thought he could save it, but it would hurt like hell. He said that if he took a sharp spoon and dug out all of the rotten bone splinters, he could save my toes. I told him to try. He was right, it did hurt like hell, but it worked.

Then we were transported to an enormous POW hospital where there was a surgeon. He spoke fluent German and told me he'd have to amputate my right foot. "I don't have any injections for a local anaesthesia, and a general anaesthetic—well, you wouldn't survive that anyway."

I was brought to the operating table and a large cloth was put over me. Then four strong nurses were stationed around me, and they pulled down the sheet so that only my foot poked out. Then he operated and explained what he was doing as he went along. I held out for just about a half an hour, and then I passed out.

On December 30, 1943, we were taken away in groups of five. There were three Germans and two Rumanians in my group. We were taken to Vladimir in a train car with barred windows and a large heating furnace. Five prisoners, miserable creatures, with 3 guards and two watchdogs. So it was five to five. The snow was about three feet deep and we had to march on foot when we got out.

I don't know how we survived that. We only knew that whoever fell and stayed down would be shot. And whoever fell behind would be torn apart by the dogs. So we marched. It was 50 miles and we covered it in one day. A person can do so much when his life depends on it. One of the most puzzling things to me today is how I ever managed it. I only know that death was the alternative.

Like many other POWs, I was held in Russia after the war ended. In December 1949, I was sentenced for alleged war crimes in Stalingrad. At first I was given the death penalty, but on Christmas Eve I was told that the sentence had been reduced to 25 years in a "work and rehabilitation camp."

After Adenauer's visit to Russia in 1954, we learned that we were going to be sent home. At the train station, the local authority, a Russian general, had the audacity to give a speech. They had a band set up there, and we were supposed to tell them something we wanted played. The majority of us wanted them to play the *Badenweiler,* one of Hitler's favorite marching tunes. And the Russians actually played it.

We arrived in West Germany on October 15, 1955. Every town that our train stopped in rang church bells for us.

COUNT HEINRICH VON EINSIEDEL

Born 1921; great-grandson of Chancellor Otto von Bismarck; fighter pilot; shot down near Stalingrad; Russian POW; active in the National Committee for a Free Germany; a businessman, he makes his home near Munich.

"Their monocles and medals sparkled."

I completed fighter-pilot training in 1941, and was sent to France. In the meantime, Hitler had declared war on the United States. I was thoroughly convinced that declaring war on the United States, when we were getting our pants beaten off in front of Moscow, was totally mad. The whole idea was insane. One didn't necessarily have to have the mind of a genius to figure out that the course we were taking was nothing less than suicidal.

In the summer of 1942, I was in a fighter squadron on the Russian front. Suddenly our wing commander told us, "The Führer has scrapped all existing plans. Our new strategy is to take Stalingrad." Only a few more days passed before I ended up in a Russian POW camp. While flying along the outskirts of Stalingrad on August 30, 1942, I was hit and had to crash land on the edge of a Russian air field.

Soon after I was taken prisoner, I met a college teacher from Kassel. He was the founder of an anti-fascist group of POW officers. I became a member of this group shortly after arriving in the prison camp near Moscow.

This anti-fascist group attempted to get captured generals to join the anti-Hitler organization. This was obviously a long-range plan because only weeks prior to the battle in Stalingrad, on November 7, 1942, the day the so-called Russian Revolution was celebrated, Stalin said in a speech to the Supreme Soviet: "Hitler and his gang want to destroy the Soviet Union and the Red Army. They will not succeed. It has been said that we intend to destroy both Germany and its army. This hasn't even crossed our mind. A totally destroyed Germany would be of no use to the victor. But we intend to and will succeed in destroying Hitler's Germany and Hitler's Army."

In reading Stalin's words today, one must conclude that they were an outright offer to those who had become so disillusioned with the Wehrmacht that they would choose instead to work closely with the Red Army. The National Committee for a Free Germany was eventually founded.

I have to admit that we had a better understanding and communication with the Russians than we had with the majority of the German Communists. We had access to Russian newspapers. We regularly read the Russian army report, but it was always full of propaganda and written in a manner that did nothing to improve its credibility. One day it said that 22 German divisions had been surrounded by the Russian army. Initially, we found this hard to believe. By the end of January 1943, we received the news that the 6th Army had capitulated, and 90,000 men, including 24 generals, had been taken prisoner. The Russian camp commander asked, "What do you have to say about that, Graf Einsiedel?" I told him I would believe it only after the first prisoners arrived in our camp. It was out of the question that a German army consisting of 300,000 men could be destroyed, and that 24 of its generals could be taken prisoner alive. Hearing that, the Russian merely laughed and said, "You are still a Fascist!"

In the meantime, I became seriously ill with severe attacks of fever. I faintly recall the white-haired camp doctor, a woman, leaning over me during my brief moments of consciousness, and asking, "What you have, Einsiedel? I want that you get better." This Jewish woman, who lost her only son during the first year of the war, did her utmost to care for us. She had no medicine and no fuel. She had no instruments to help her conduct thorough examinations or make accurate diagnoses. But her kindness and never-failing encouragement saved many of us.

One day the medical NCO in charge of sick call walked in and informed us that the German generals from Stalingrad had arrived. I was conscious, but extremely weak. Some of the other prisoners helped me up. They had to scrape thick sheets of ice off the window panes in order to see anything. What we saw then was like a grotesque nightmare. The generals were on their way to their quarters. Their monocles and medals sparkled. They were wearing heavy fur coats and had walking-sticks in their hands. We saw the bright red trimmings on their uniforms, and their marvelous fur-lined leather boots. Their energetic gestures and bright smiles were difficult to overlook. In the midst of this colorful and elegant picture, there appeared only occasionally a gray spot: the bent figure of older POWs, dressed in a tattered Russian wadded cotton jacket or a ragged German uniform; wearing rags tied with strings around their feet in place of shoes; their exhausted, emaciated faces always bent low, looking at the ground.

Shortly after that, I received another visit from the camp commander. He called upon me to ask that I write a declaration committing myself to collaborate with the Soviet Union in its fight against Hitler. I saw no reason at all to hesitate in making such a statement. Being honest with myself, I must admit that I had totally succumbed to the Communist ideology.

In mid-June 1943, two Communist emigrants, one of them Walter Ulbricht, arrived in our camp and invited a few officers to a meeting. These were essentially all individuals who were able to make dispassionate assessments of Germany's situation without officially being acknowledged anti-fascists. They often took part in discussions and meetings. At this particular meeting, the Communists revealed to us their conception of a National Committee.

We, of course, the officers of the National Committee, were condemned by our countrymen as traitors. One must not forget that the entire free, democratic world was siding with the Bolsheviks against Hitler. We simply told the Germans, "If the power of the Allies is the only way Hitler can be stopped, then that is the end of the Reich. Our fatherland will fall to pieces, and we can't blame anyone but ourselves. The only chance we have to preserve any influence on our fate after the war is to take the initiative and get rid of Hitler ourselves." We had people from the National Committee on all fronts who used loud-speakers so their propaganda messages could be heard even in the trenches.

Naturally, the Communists made sure that the National Committee followed their general line of philosophy. There were those in the National Committee, myself included, who were truly fascinated by Communist ideology. Speaking for myself, I would say that because of my personal intellectual insufficiency, I was not able to recognize immediately the misleading and erroneous ideas in Marxist ideology. One must also not forget that, at the time, I was only 21 years old.

On January 1, 1945, I left Moscow to go to Germany with the Red Army. I witnessed some horrendous crimes committed by the Red Army. As it marched into Germany I was ordered to tell the German members of the National Committee that what I saw were really German soldiers dressed in Russian uniforms committing the atrocities. Of course, I didn't give in to such madness, which resulted in my falling out of grace in the Soviet Union. I was ordered to return to the Committee's headquarters. This is why I wasn't released from Russian imprisonment until 1947.

GERHARD KERSCHER

Born 1916; served in the Luftwaffe as an air supply specialist; involved in the attempt to keep Stalingrad supplied by transport planes; after the war, was a major general in the Bundeswehr; presently makes his home near Siegburg, Rhineland.

"Flying transport aircraft into the Stalingrad pocket was suicidal."

Prior to Stalingrad, I had seen action in the Demyansk pocket. Around the middle of January 1942, parts of two army corps were trapped southeast of Leningrad. For four months we supplied almost 100,000 soldiers with about 350 transport aircraft, Ju-52s and a small number of bombers. We managed to transport up to 1,500 tons of supplies into the pocket to maintain the combat capability of the troops. That earned the transport pilots a certain amount of fame. By spring it was possible to re-establish contact between the pocket and the front.

We were confronted with a completely different task in air supply when the 6th Army was in danger of being cut off at Stalingrad. With winter approaching, our planes could expect to operate at only 40 to 50 percent of capacity. At the same time, we were dealing with an entire army; there were about 350 different units down there.

The 6th Army was encircled at the beginning of November. The Russians broke through its position, and with that the ring was closed. It was the beginning of the end.

According to our Chief Quartermaster of the Air Fleet, a breakout would have been possible. Mind you, that was the Luftwaffe's opinion. Based on our own experiences, we knew that all these units had reserves—especially of fuel—that weren't registered. These could have been used to get them out.

It became apparent that the order to break out was not going to be given. If I remember correctly, even General Viebig of the 8th Air Corps and the Air Fleet Commander, von Richthofen, declared that it was not possible to supply by air. This was reported to the Chief of the General Staff of the Luftwaffe who, for his part, demanded a report by the General Quartermaster. Along with other officers, I was ordered to attend a briefing. According to our assessment of the situation, the number of transport aircraft was insufficient and the ground organization appeared to be too weak. We did not know how long the advanced airfields could be held. Winter was near; the transport units were already exhausted; and the amounts we would have to transport far exceeded our capabilities.

This was quite easy to calculate. Supplying Stalingrad required 1,000 tons daily. This number was then reduced to approximately 600 tons; 300 tons would have been possible. Göring decided that we were to work to the last man, no matter what. All the transport planes at home were scraped together; all available planes were to be sent to the front. This was utter nonsense. It was technically impossible.

We had to report the tonnage flown into Stalingrad to the Führer on a daily basis. And then along came "General Winter," and with it came a new Russian breakthrough. On December 24, the Russians reached the airfield where all the flights to Stalingrad started. They destroyed 70 aircraft. The weather was miserable, with driving snow. Panic broke out.

When the Russian tanks rolled through, a large number of planes were lost, planes sent in from home that were neither equipped for winter flying nor for front action. We also lost 250 crew members who were simply irreplaceable. I believe about 180 planes managed to get away during the attack. I recall a corporal from the ground crews climbing into a plane, a Ju-52 I believe, and flying it home himself. He had never piloted a plane before in his life, but somehow he managed to bring it down in one piece. That was really quiet heroism of the first order.

The transport crews also proved very heroic. They were partly reserve and partly active crews, old men and very young NCOs. In

my opinion, these crews achieved excellent marks for comradeship and for putting their lives on the line for others. I flew as a transport pilot often enough myself, and I know how difficult it is to be sitting up there in an almost unarmed machine. We flew at tree-top height so that no one could spot us. Flying transport aircraft on runs like that into the Stalingrad pocket, surrounded by the strongest Russian units, was actually suicidal.

At this point, our only hope was that someone inside the pocket would be clever enough to think of a way to break out. Once in a while we received radio messages from Paulus, until the last one in which he bade farewell.

MSGR. JOSEF KAYSER

Born 1895; veteran of World War I; in World War II, a Catholic chaplain in the German army; captured at Stalingrad; as a POW in Russia joined the National Committee for a Free Germany; continued in priesthood after returning to Westphalia, where he lives today.

"In November, I closed the eyes of about 1,000 young German soldiers."

I was the Catholic priest of the 96th Infantry Division in Stalingrad. On November 22, 1942, the encirclement was completed. It was a month during which I closed the eyes of about 1,000 young German soldiers. We had fixed up an aid station in a place that had previously been a pig-farming collective. One morning I woke up surrounded by 25 to 30 corpses.

A young German—from Westphalia judging by his accent—kept

reaching in his pants pocket, as if he wanted to take something out. Assuming he wanted to take out his rosary, I guided his weak hand with mine. I reached into an open hole in his stomach and withdrew my hand, red with fresh blood. The boy looked at me with his blue eyes like a small child. "Father," he said, "now I can't fight anymore!" "You no longer need to, my boy," I said. At that moment his eyes glazed over, and he was dead.

November 22 was also my birthday. I had planned to hold four Masses on that day, but only held two. With a temperature of −40 degrees Fahrenheit, there were chips of ice in the Communion cup. Then I packed my Mass kit on a little sled and started for the nearby village where the army corps hospital was set up. On the way, I saw Red Cross nurses and Rumanians fleeing from Russian soldiers that had broken through the German positions. There were about 20 ambulances at the corps hospital, and I helped load out the wounded. I opened the back door of one, and a dead soldier rolled out. "It's good that you're here, Father," said a voice from the dark interior, "that man crowded me so much!" "Well, he was already long dead," I said.

Instead of saying Mass, I held heads and gave shots. One time I left the operating table to get some fresh air. When I got outside I saw a dog running around with a man's arm in its mouth—a wedding band was still on the ring finger. The last two Masses were, of course, cancelled.

Right before the end of February 1943, I stayed behind with the dying, while everyone else ran toward Stalingrad. I still had Communion hosts, and as I walked through the shelters of the collective farm, everyone yelled: "The Russians are coming, the Russians are coming!" And then I saw them. Suddenly I was standing just 20 yards away from five young Siberians.

I knew Siberians from the First World War. They aimed their guns at me, and I knew they were quick to shoot. All the soldiers who tried to run away got a bullet in the back and died in their own blood. Then I suppose they recognized the clerical cross chaplains wore on their uniform. I pointed to it and called to them, "I am a priest! Christ is resurrected in war!" I made the sign of the cross. I thought they would give me a volley and that would be it. My last thoughts would actually have been, "If you had a machine pistol, one burst and you would have layed them flat, those dumb kids." When I made one sign of the cross, they made three, and took me back to Stalingrad in triumph. An officer in a fur cap stood on a small hill and said, "You will live." It was Marshal Rokossovsky, the conqueror of Stalingrad.

Then we were taken north in a series of 12 to 15 mile marches. At night the wolves howled in the distance. Someone dropped every 40 yards. Those last few days were unbearable. One morning I awoke among 29 corpses. I counted the number exactly. I buried 84 men in one day.

RICHARD BLINZIG

Born 1908; salesman; during the war was an artilleryman serving in Russia and on the Atlantic Wall; after the war was a civil servant; lives in Frankfurt.

"Prisoners presented a burden and were often liquidated on the spot."

Winter 1942–43 in Russia! The Russians began their great counter-offensive, and a wide arc of the front at Stalingrad was broken. The artillery unit I belonged to was ordered to blow up the guns and clear out. This was easier said than done because it was mid-winter and the snow was very deep. On the third day of our retreat six Russian T-34s loaded with infantry overran our group and caused such a terrible slaughter that the whole bunch of us saw only one alternative: run!

I stomped through the deep snow handicapped by all the equipment I was carrying: rifle, gas mask, mess kit, bread bag, ammunition belts, steel helmet, and on top of all that, a camouflage suit!

Well, the gas mask and the helmet were the first to go. I ploughed through the snow for about a half hour—where to, I didn't even know—but behind me the bloodbath continued with no sign of stopping. A big ambulance sleigh drawn by horses went by me, loaded with wounded. There was an empty "life boat" trundling after it, a flat oval saucer used to transport wounded over the snow. I climbed into this, losing my mess kit in the process, and after a half hour's ride we reached another *Rollbahn*. There were a couple of huts nearby. But just then some tanks appeared. The tanks had no more ammunition, so they simply crushed the wagons, sleighs, horses, and people beneath them. I flew out of my little "boat" right in front of a deserted field kitchen, with two horses rearing wildly in their harnesses. I managed to unhitch one of the horses, calm the frightened animal, and—wonders never cease—mount without a stirrup or a saddle. And that beast ran like a house afire.

The front didn't exist anymore. For the Russians, operating sometimes only in small groups, prisoners presented a burden and were often liquidated on the spot. This of course doesn't mean that German soldiers were exactly saints in this respect either.

During the night I met up with several exhausted, apathetic, retreating columns, but I didn't run into anyone from my unit except for one young soldier. I stopped in front of an overcrowded Russian hut and found a half sack of oats for my horse. I tried to thaw a can of meat I'd picked up along the way at the little fire that was burning in the hut. It was frozen solid, and I only partially succeeded. Then I heard the word "Kamerad" for the first time from the mouth of an officer, a captain. He was asking for a bite! Afterwards, I brushed off my horse, lifted my buddy up—his toes were frozen—and off we went again.

Toward morning I stopped at a hut that was so full the soldiers literally slept standing up. It was strange to see the mass of sleeping bodies swaying back and forth. Later it cleared out a little and we both were able to lie down for a while. I'd loosely tethered the horse outside. It was bright daylight when I woke up. Apart from the two of us, there was no one left in the hut. I ran out and saw Russian infantry about 200 to 300 yards away. My horse stood between the Russians and me. So with a heavy heart I had to leave the horse to its fate, because I would have brought attention to myself if I'd gone to get it. The two of us quickly crawled down a slope which led to a river. A short while later we reached a good-size town. But everyone was running toward the only bridge across the river. I managed to get my comrade onto an ambulance. I squirmed into a tank trailer which was one of the last vehicles to cross the bridge.

Eight hours later I was lucky enough to find three more men from my unit in a hut, and the four of us "hitchhiked" down the *Rollbahn.* We had virtually nothing to eat. After two days we reached a town with hunger gnawing in our bellies.

There was supposed to be a main field-kitchen there. There was also supposed to be a collecting point for stragglers. Everyone coming through town on the *Rollbahn* who wasn't part of an intact unit was snatched up immediately and put into one of the "provisional battalions" which were supposed to cover the retreat. The "body snatchers" had thought it out pretty cleverly. Those who weren't grabbed as they marched along the *Rollbahn* were caught when they walked into the depot to get something to eat.

The four of us settled into a hut a little way outside of town and thought about what to do next. We had to get food at all cost, so we decided that an experienced corporal and I would see to it. We crept through back yards and gardens to the ration depot, a former makeshift cinema erected by the Wehrmacht with one large room, tables where the screen had been, and the kitchen behind that. My comrade joined the long line in front of the tables while I stood observing the room. Something seemed fishy to me, and I was right. In less than ten minutes the entrance, which was the only exit, was barred. NCOs posted themselves left and right and a "reception committee" stood at the door. All the *Landser* in the room had to present their passbooks and go outside. I saw my buddy disappear through the kitchen, but I was in a tight spot.

And then a small miracle occurred, one like others I had experienced a couple of times in this war. Most of the *Landser* were already outside, and I was ordered to leave for the third time by a sergeant. So I pulled myself together, and with head held high I walked past the line of officers. For some strange reason nobody took any notice of me, even at the door. Outside, I marched past the three rows of "victims" who'd had their passbooks taken from them, and disappeared the way I'd come.

JESCO VON PUTTKAMER

Born 1919; was an army general staff officer in Stalingrad, captured in 1943; POW in Russia until 1947; leading member of the National Committee for a Free Germany; after the war, served as ambassador to Israel, Yugoslavia, Portugal, and Sweden; deceased 1987.

"We walked into total annihilation with our eyes wide open."

I first began to have doubts about final victory when we crossed the Soviet border in 1941. Whether the army would manage this became increasingly doubtful. Although we advanced quickly, the battles were tough; they were nothing like anything we had ever experienced. Poland was a walkover compared to this. Even though breaking through the Maginot Line was initially difficult, France was a walkover too.

A year and a half later we were in Stalingrad. Working in headquarters, I could overhear the commanders' official conversations. I remember that a few hours after the trap closed, my divisional commander, Arno von Lenski, phoned the corps commander, General von Seydlitz, and Seydlitz told Lenski, "If we don't get out of this right now, the shit's going to hit the fan." That's just the way he put it.

Three days later, Seydlitz wrote a memorandum to Paulus saying we had to break out. From that moment on it went back and forth, back and forth among the besieged generals: "What do we do, what can we do, and how can we do it?" But "Schweine-Schmidt"—Chief of Staff of the 6th Army, so nicknamed because of his liking for dirty jokes—stopped them all. He talked them all down. The army stayed where it was.

After a while—it was around Christmas of 1942—it became apparent that the relief offensive wasn't going to succeed, and this led to total resignation. The Stalingrad experience was what befell the entire Reich two and a half years later. We were betrayed and used as cannon fodder. Of the 300,000 men that were surrounded, only 90,000 survived to be POWs, and of those 90,000 maybe only 5,000 ever came back.

Although we were resigned, we kept on fighting. There wasn't any other alternative. I was in the isolated northern pocket. There was nothing left—no ammunition, no rations, nothing at all. We walked into total annihilation with our eyes wide open.

There was a division commander who, wearing his trousers with the general's stripes on the sides, stepped up on a railway embankment and just stood there until a bullet hit him. That was General von Hartmann. Others, like Paulus, just waited in their bunkers until the Russians walked through the door. There was no more heroism, there was hardly even suffering, there was just the inferno.

Naturally, the question of guilt was discussed during the siege. Among themselves, the generals tended to concentrate particularly on Göring and Manstein; Hitler was hardly even worth discussing anymore. All of them knew by then that Hitler didn't understand what he was doing. Most of all, the generals reproached Manstein for his failure to relieve the garrison. And then there were the discussions among ourselves about whether to be taken prisoner or shoot ourselves. The feeling was that you couldn't shoot yourself, if not for Christian reasons, then because you couldn't leave the troops to their fate.

Afterwards it was really grotesque. The generals were given kid glove treatment—put onto trains to Moscow with their orderlies and suitcases, while the soldiers trudged through the snow and died by the thousands on their march to prison camps. The initial months were the worst; our men died like flies. But the Russians themselves in the Stalingrad sector had nothing to eat either.

We were rounded up in long columns and marched through the steppes around Stalingrad to provisional camps. Many were left lying on the ground from sheer exhaustion. Sometimes they were shot by guards, otherwise they just lay there until they froze to death. There were no camp regulations to speak of in these provisional camps near Stalingrad. They were nothing more than unheated corrals. And if there were beds, five people had to share a plank bed made for one or two. There was nothing to eat.

Then came the diphtheria, typhoid, hunger sores—even cannibalism went on in these camps. I avoided death by a hair's breadth because the divisional doctor happened to be with me. He still had his doctor's kit, and was healthy enough himself. He said to me, "There are five to six thousand poor swine in this camp and I have medication for one. Here, take what I have." There were glucose preparations and a few other things in it that picked me up a little. That's basically the reason I survived, even though I also had diphtheria and typhoid.

The Russians found out pretty quickly that I'd worked in headquarters. So I was taken out with many others and sent to Moscow. In captivity I joined the anti-Nazi League of German Officers because I believed it would be the best way to end the war quickly, while something could still be saved.

In the summer of 1943, I was sent to the Lunovo camp, which was the center of the League of German Officers. The National Committee for a Free Germany was already in existence, but had very few members—mostly people who had been POWs for quite a while and German Communists who had emigrated to the Soviet Union. There weren't any members from Stalingrad yet. But the core of the League of German Officers were Stalingrad veterans. We were so deeply influenced and so greatly shocked by what had happened in Stalingrad that we felt we had to share it.

The first step was to break the military oath. The second was to try to share our experiences with our compatriots on the other side of the front, to tell them that what had happened to us was in store for them, too. The realization that we were actually being used as a political instrument by the Russians only became apparent at the very end of the war.

The oath played a role for many men, but not for me. For the older ones, let's say for majors on up, loyalty to their oaths was a major point of debate in the decision to join the League. People like Seydlitz, who finally made up their minds to join after all-night discussions, used this exact argument time and again with their colleagues: The oath is no longer binding because it was sworn to a criminal. This was the major point of dissension in the camp. Not all officers joined the League—maybe a quarter to a third. Those from Stalingrad made up the largest portion. But the others, particularly those captured and imprisoned later, didn't join. Either they were real Nazis—they used to celebrate Hitler's birthday in camp—or the oath was simply an obstacle they couldn't overcome. For the Stalingrad veterans, the oath usually wasn't important.

COUNT FRIEDRICH ERNST VON SOLMS

Born 1911; cavalryman, later tanker; captured at Stalingrad; worked as a salesman after the war and resides in Wesseling, Rhineland.

"To me, it was mostly a matter of betraying our country."

In 1941, I marched into Russia with the 1st Cavalry Division, part of Army Group Center. This cost us an incredible number of horses. In 1942, we were reorganized into the 24th Panzer Division.

We were part of the summer offensive on Stalingrad. We took an unbelievable number of casualties even before we reached the city in August. After that, our losses got even heavier. I was a battalion commander at the time. I went on leave, and when I came back in December, the Russians had surrounded the city. The only way into the pocket was by air; I flew in with a Heinkel 111. There was already snow on the ground. My battalion was in the northern part of the pocket. The Russians drove us back into some high-rise buildings, and there we stayed.

Christmas was miserable. We ate cats and dogs, we had only a little bread. Even the horsemeat had run out. Our morale was bad. Russian broadcasts kept giving the number of Germans killed in Stalingrad. They talked about officers from our division who tried to escape in Russian uniforms. The soldiers didn't want to fight anymore, and the Russians weren't attacking. They let us wait and starve.

Finally, on February 2, Paulus surrendered. We sent someone over to the Russian lines with the message that after 3:00 A.M. we wouldn't shoot anymore. Then the Soviets just walked through our positions. Our division commander was asleep; they woke him up and took him prisoner. They took the generals away separately. We soldiers set off on a two-day march to a camp up north. It was a death march. It was extremely cold, and we had to march about 50 miles. We slept out in the open. When we started off the next morning many men couldn't make it. They just couldn't get up. Then a Russian started out, and we all followed him. Anyone left behind was shot.

We had felt boots, and some of us even had leather boots. The Russians wanted these boots, and they searched us for other valuables too. After about ten days without a thing to eat, they sent us back to Stalingrad. We had to make the whole trip over again. In Stalingrad there were already about 50,000 or 60,000 German soldiers, if not more. Two hundred to three hundred men died there every day. Then the Russians sorted out a group of officers and took us to Oranki, a special camp. Jesco von Puttkamer was with us. He was so weak he couldn't even crawl; we dragged him into our boxcar. Many died on the way into Russia, but I pulled through until we reached Oranki. After that, I went down with a bout of typhus.

When I recovered, Jesco von Puttkamer was a convinced anti-fascist. Word was going around then that he had joined a "League of German Officers" founded in Moscow, which was supposed to work together with the Russians against Hitler and the Nazis. I was invited to a meeting with a Russian colonel who wanted me to go to Moscow with some other "promising" Germans. I said I was too sick to go. He told me I would get a sleeping compartment for the trip there, along with other preferential treatment like better rations. He gave me 12 hours to think it over. I still said no. He threw me out, and that was it.

The League question came back later, though. By then, they'd been to special "anti-fascist schools." There was constant conflict between men who participated in the League with the Russians—like Graf Einsiedel, for instance—and those who didn't. They constantly shoved resolutions in your face, saying, "Sign this if you're in favor of working with the Russians." After I had refused to sign the fifth one, they gave up. They sent me to a different camp, and I didn't get special treatment anymore. To us, it was purely a matter of betraying your country; it was treason.

I had also gotten to know Walter Ulbricht, who later became party leader and head of state in East Germany. He gave speeches about the annihilation of the Jews and concentration camps. Back then we just laughed; we didn't believe him.

After 1945, things changed drastically. The dream was over for the soldiers and officers who had worked together with the Russians. They weren't useful anymore. The anti-fascists and the League people became normal prisoners, and had to work as hard as we did.

I was sent to work as a POW in Moscow, where I got to know Russian people. They were unbelievably kind, and always brought us fruit or bread. They really got us back in shape again. You can't say a word against the Russians.

We finally made it home in 1949.

CHAPTER 7

Battle of the Atlantic

The Battle of the Atlantic had its roots in an internal strategic debate between advocates of a strong surface navy and supporters of the sort of undersea campaign that had almost brought England to her knees during World War I. In the heady days of rearmament, the blue-water school carried the day. Navy Commander Erich Raeder was more concerned with enhancing the navy's position in the new Reich than with contributing to a rational grand strategy. His limited vision fitted nicely into Hitler's dreams of world empire.

The so-called Z-plan, adopted in January 1939, provided for the construction of a battle fleet large enough not merely to challenge Great Britain directly, but to project Germany's power around the globe. Submarines played a secondary role, to the anger of Karl Dönitz, commander of the *Kriegsmarine's* U-boats. Dönitz believed the Reich's clock stood at five minutes to midnight. The Z-plan was scheduled for completion in 1946. Should war come earlier, as was almost certain under the Führer, Germany would once more have to depend on its submarines.

Dönitz's logic was vindicated by the Luftwaffe's failure in the skies over Britain. Germany's surface fleet may have been crippled by its losses, but its submarine force was efficient and active. Dönitz was unique among German senior officers in accepting a war of attrition. A successful U-boat commander was defined by the total tonnage he sank, not how many ships, or what kind. Dönitz wanted 300 boats. In August 1940, he had fewer than fifty. They were enough to squeeze

Britain's throat, but they were too few to complete the process of strangulation, particularly with increasing U.S. support of the British.

Since before Dunkirk, Franklin D. Roosevelt had determined that America's vital interests required a Nazi defeat. An initial policy of cash and carry gave way to lend-lease, to the exchange of U.S. destroyers for British naval bases, and ultimately to convoying British ships halfway across the Atlantic. Six months before Pearl Harbor, the U.S. was waging an undeclared shooting war against the *Kriegsmarine's* U-boats.

On December 11, 1941, Hitler declared war on the U.S. His reasons remain obscure. He may have miscalculated America's capacity to produce anything but refrigerators and razor blades. Or he may have realized that his war had been lost in front of Moscow and that by declaring war on America and planning the elimination of Europe's Jews he set the stage for a truly Wagnerian finale. Either the Reich would achieve Hitler's dreams or it would be destroyed: all or nothing.

To Dönitz and his captains, the Führer's decision meant they could strike their enemies openly. The U.S. was completely unprepared for a submarine offensive: no convoy system, no radio silence, no coastal blackout. From the St. Lawrence to Cape Hatteras, U-boats sank Allied ships as fast as they could reload their torpedo tubes. Not until August 1942 did the "Happy Time" come to an end.

The tactics of the U-boat war were determined by the fact that the German boats were submersibles rather than true submarines. They were considerably faster above water than below. A merchant convoy, even one dominated by slow ships, could outpace a submerged boat with little effort. And a single boat could seldom expect to make more than one attack in the face of escorts that, if they did not sink the intruder outright, forced her to concentrate on surviving. Even before the war, Dönitz had concluded that the best response to the convoy system was to use groups of boats operating on the surface— the famous wolf packs. These packs, anywhere from six to twenty boats, deployed on patrol lines about ten miles apart. When a boat sighted a convoy, it would report to U-boat headquarters in occupied France. Dönitz then directed the rest of the pack to the target. This seemingly cumbersome process was meant to avoid exposure to Allied radio interception.

The efficiency of the system became grimly apparent in the second half of 1942, when Dönitz shifted his focus back to the Atlantic. The airplane was the submarine's greatest enemy. But with long-range aircraft drawn off for the bomber offensive, air cover was available only at the beginning and the end of a voyage. It was in the "black pit" of the mid-Atlantic that the wolf packs flourished and the sinkings multiplied. Yet here, as in so many other areas, victory remained just beyond Nazi reach.

Twenty million tons of merchant shipping left American yards in 1943, double the figure expected by the Germans. Radio intelligence laid bare Dönitz's plans and orders. Long-range aircraft and escort carriers closed the Atlantic gap. Hunter-killer groups began stalking the U-boats on their own ground. Losses multiplied while the rate of sinkings fell. In March, more than 600,000 tons of Allied shipping went to the bottom. In April, that figure dropped by almost half. Fifteen U-boats were sunk in April, a 10 percent loss ratio. In May, 41 failed to return from patrol. This represented a quarter of the operational strength.

A more flexible commander might have reappraised his situation. Dönitz called instead for more U-boats, for improved designs, for greater dedication. Hitler was sufficiently impressed to keep the boats at sea, if only for their nuisance value. By 1945, 785 German submarines had been sunk. Three-fourths of the 40,000 men who wore the submariners' badge did not return—the highest loss ratio of any specialized service in World War II. Dönitz, rewarded for his fanaticism by being named Hitler's successor, was tried and sentenced as a war criminal.

ROLF JOHANNESSON*

"We had hundreds of admirals on land, and only one at sea."

On April 6, 1943, I took command of the 4th Destroyer Flotilla. I arrived at my new station, Alta-Fjord in northern Norway, on July 18. The task force was composed of the *Tirpitz, Scharnhorst, Lützow,* and several destroyers. I made no secret of my concern about the ultimate fate of this impressive force, the last of Germany's surface fleet. Luckily, I didn't suspect how bad it was really going to be.

On September 21, British midget submarines damaged the *Tirpitz* so badly that it was disabled until March 1944. As far as I know, the British owed their unlikely success to the fact that the gate of the anti-submarine net surrounding the ship was negligently left open.

We had hundreds of admirals on land, and only one at sea. Soon we lost him. Shortly after the *Tirpitz* disaster there were rumors in Alta that our task force commander had no desire to spend the long winter nights up there, and was to embark on an extended furlough. I invited the admiral to dinner aboard my ship, and tried to convince him to remain, but without success.

When his temporary replacement, Rear Admiral Bey, arrived in Alta, he told me that this command was a sort of disciplinary transfer because nothing was happening up here. Then on December 22, 1943, our reconnaissance aircraft sighted a convoy. There were approximately 40 ships headed for Murmansk. Initially the thought of the task force taking action didn't even occur to Bey. It was Dönitz who ordered the sortie. He knew that our force wasn't up to scratch because of inadequate oil supplies. Moreover, some of our crews had little sea experience and, above all, Dönitz had allowed many of the senior officers and their staffs to go on leave.

---

* Biography on page xxx.

Bey wrote his operation orders so hastily that they were thrown aboard the destroyers in waterproof bags. The basis of our peacetime training was to discuss thoroughly each operation prior to its execution. This was ignored in planning this difficult, foolhardy undertaking. It was a marvelous beginning!

As we crept out of the fjords into the open sea, we were met with a southwesterly gale at force 8, with a running sea. According to Bey's plan, we were supposed to bear east and attack the convoy head on, with the destroyers as a screen 10 sea miles in front of the *Scharnhorst.*

At 11:40 P.M., we received the following radio message: "Use tactical advantage boldly. Do not break off a battle half won. Your greatest chance is in the superior gun power of the *Scharnhorst.* Abort mission at own discretion. Abort mission immediately in presence of heavy [British] ships."

On a stormy night amidst heavy breakers and with a seasick crew, I had little inclination to attach special importance to a radio message from Berlin. Aside from that, it was odd to receive detailed tactical instructions from land for a battle at sea. Something like that has to be practiced many times in order to work.

By morning our problems were the wind and the sea. The destroyers, especially the larger ones, pitched heavily and began taking water. Around noon we were ordered to attack the convoy instead of screening the *Scharnhorst.* "Thank God!" I wrote in the log.

Then at 1:43 P.M., we got a new signal: "4th Destroyer Flotilla abort." This order surprised me. Did I have to obey it? At first I played for time. In the Mediterranean, I had seen how the British had transmitted false radio messages to confuse the Germans. So I had this message checked to be sure that it had come from the *Scharnhorst.* They confirmed it. The order was crystal clear to me, but to gain still more time, I requested clarification. The response, which came in at 2:20 P.M., was a categorical: "Go home."

I set a course for the Alta-Fjord. Bey and the *Scharnhorst* never returned. The ship was sunk that evening in a hopeless battle with superior British forces. The British had radar; the *Scharnhorst* fired blind after the first few minutes. It was a suicide mission. Ever since, I have wondered whether I should have obeyed Bey's last order.

The following days were depressing. But there was a small glimmer of light, nothing heroic, only human: I had brought all of my men back home. I do not accuse myself of lacking courage. But tactically, had I done everything possible? This question remains open.

Then came July 20, 1944, and the attempt to assassinate Hitler. The next day, Dönitz's order of the day read, "The treacherous assassination attempt on Hitler fills us with righteous anger and embittered fury against our criminal enemies and their mindless accomplices." I found the last words an unnecessary insult to the men of the July 20 plot. What could I do? In a letter to the Chief of the Naval Personnel Bureau, Vice-Admiral Baltzer, I wrote, "The force of arms will decide whether Hitler is a blessing or a curse for Germany." Baltzer sent my letter back to me. I quote his answer: "Dear Johannesson: we can only win this war by National Socialism. Any deviation from this position is stupid or criminal."

In August 1944, the Wehrmacht distributed a handbook to its troops that included a speech by Himmler: "It is quite clear that, once in a while, a racially sound strain emerges from this mishmash of ethnic groups. I believe we have the task of taking these children in, of removing them from their environment, even if we have to take them by force."

I criticized this statement, which apparently the senior officers had let pass without opposition. I said that our national cause did not justify every means, and particularly not those which flew in the face of divine law and human dignity.

This was passed on to Dönitz. The result? After my relief in November 1944, I was ordered to report to the Navy High Command. My conversation with Dönitz was forty years ago, so my presentation of it should be taken with some reservation.

Dönitz was only interested in my bad attitude toward National Socialism. In spite of my having proven myself at the front in all these years of war, he doubted whether I could train my subordinate officers in the necessary fanatical belief in the Führer. He said that at least I had to acknowledge the marvelous indoctrination of the Hitler Youth. I answered that unfortunately I couldn't agree with him on this point either. Neither of us wanted to press the issue, and I finished the war in a meaningless shore assignment.

HELMUT SCHMOECKEL*

"We were lucky as hell."

At the beginning of the war I was an ensign assigned to the cruiser *Admiral Hipper.* We were lucky as hell. We were always on the move at high speed in the Atlantic as a solitary ship.

Once, between the Azores and Gibraltar, we found a convoy going north and went around it at night with our radar, which was already in use back then. We saw that one ship was standing a little off and thought it would probably be an auxiliary cruiser. We fired torpedoes at it, but they didn't hit. The next morning we attacked it with gunfire, and as it emerged from the mist, we saw that it was the *Berwick,* a heavy cruiser, same class as ours. There was a short duel, and because the *Berwick* had taken nine hits from us, the *Bonaventure,* a light cruiser, took over on the English side. We said to ourselves, "Where there is one heavy cruiser there are bound to be more," and as a lone ship we had no choice but to get out as quickly as possible.

After three years on the *Admiral Hipper,* I thought it was time to do something else. The day of the big ships, of cruiser war in the Atlantic, was over. But I wanted to keep giving all I had for the fatherland. That was the reason I'd immediately reported back to the navy in 1939. So I kept pushing to join the U-boats, and that finally worked out in July 1942.

After my training was completed, I was transferred to the Atlantic. My last U-boat convoy battle was not far from the American coast at Newfoundland. It was a convoy of 40 to 80 ships, of which a large number had already been sunk. In addition, there were 30 to 40 escort ships around this convoy, mostly destroyers, and we were 38 U-boats. The fog got so thick we had to break off the battle. We didn't sink much in the days after, so we went back to Bordeaux, where I went for commander training and got my own submarine.

---

* Biography on page 55.

There I was in my U-boat, going west—France was occupied, July 20 had happened, and I had a zone of operations somewhere off the Canadian coast. It wasn't so great, but I did everything I could for the fatherland. Dönitz himself knew the U-boats couldn't do much anymore, but he kept us going with the argument that defending against us diverted Allied planes from bombing German cities.

Then it was May. Berlin had fallen, Hitler was dead. On May 3, 1945, we got orders to continue operations in the harbor area of New York. Ridiculous!

ERICH TOPP

Born 1914; highly decorated U-boat commander in World War II; later joined the German Federal Navy and retired as a rear admiral; now an architect; lives near Remagen, Palatinate.

"Our lives were reduced to a steel tube."

From the war diary of the U-Boat Command: "On the morning of October 31, 1941, the British convoy HX 156, escorted by five destroyers, was spotted in the middle North Atlantic by U-552. The commander, Lieutenant Topp, sank the American destroyer *Reuben James,* one of the ships belonging to the escort, at 08:34 hrs., at the position 51°59' North/27°05' W. This U.S. destroyer was already functioning as an escort for British convoys prior to American engagement in World War II."

The German Navy command was very cautious toward the United States and Roosevelt's "short of war" politics. Thinking I had hit one of the British escort ships, I sank the *Reuben James* in the early hours of October 31. Only later, after having received radio messages, did I learn that I had sunk a ship belonging to a country with which we were not at war.

According to international law, we hadn't done anything illegal, or committed a criminal act. We had attacked a British convoy protected by warships. Nevertheless, I was still baffled by it all. The thought alone that one can possibly be involved in making history, willingly or not, is overwhelming.

I was ordered back to Berlin immediately afterwards and had to give an extremely detailed report on the events leading up to the attack and the actual sinking of the American destroyer. For Hitler, it was important to underestimate American personnel and economic potential. As if it were yesterday, I can still hear Hitler's derogatory remarks at a meeting in his headquarters about the "cripple" Roosevelt. He later said that the "Liberty" and "Victory" ships were so poorly built that they couldn't survive storms in the Atlantic.

I don't really think the political dimensions of sinking the *Reuben James* were all that clear at the time. I was concerned with getting caught up in important political decisions, which I knew even then, from similar situations in World War I, were irreparable. Already in 1941, music was added to a poem written about the sinking of the *Reuben James* and sung everywhere in America: "Did you have a friend on the good *Reuben James*?" A few lines of the poem: "We watched for the U-boats, and waited for the fight" and "Now our mighty battleships will steam the bounding main."

Years later, in 1962, I had lunch with the man who had been a watch officer on board the USS *Niblack,* the destroyer that rescued the *Reuben James* survivors. His best friend had been an officer on the *Reuben James.* His search for his friend among the survivors was in vain. He talked about the search at twilight, in a sea covered with a thick layer of oil, where bodies and wreckage bobbed up and down in a way that reminded him of Dante's Inferno. I will never forget our conversation. It is still too painful for me to talk about it.

Submarine warfare reached a critical stage toward the end of 1942. The chart curves representing U-boats destroyed and those built began to intersect. By the end of that year, we had more submarines being sunk than manufactured. Allied technical development had advanced rapidly. Apart from their convoy system, they had a total surveillance system over the Atlantic Ocean with the help of high-performance aircraft, but above all with radar equipment. Allied technology had developed so much that we had nothing in comparison.

In addition, something happened at the beginning of the war which caused us grave difficulties. We only found out about this at the end of the war. On May 9, 1941, submarine U-110 was sunk. At first, it was attacked by depth charges. The pressure created by the charges exploding underwater forced the submarine to surface. The crew got out and boarded a British ship. A trained British team went on board the submarine and, among other things, found the coding machine. They took it back to England. It was the so-called Enigma apparatus. The German Navy Command did not know that this device was in the hands of the British until after the end of the war.

With Enigma, the British could not only decode our messages, but also intercept them. They could double-check every message we transmitted. With this knowledge, they could dodge every submarine we had out there.

We based our attacks on the so-called *Rudeltaktik* or submarine wolf-pack tactics. When a submarine made contact with a convoy, it was to remain in contact until the other submarines in the area were able to close in. Thanks to Enigma, all of our transmissions were intercepted by the convoys. Not only did the Allies know that enemy submarines were in the area; they also knew the exact position and direction each boat was heading.

Another interesting figure comes to mind: the relation of freighters sunk to U-boats sunk was 1 to 1!

Ultimately, we employed the snorkel. The Dutch had already developed this back in 1937. When we occupied Holland, we found two submarines under construction which had been equipped with snorkels. But we removed them, thinking they were useless! Not until 1943 did we pursue the idea—after the U-boat war was lost. Later, we also had totally electric boats capable of submerging for days at a time, independent of any outside supply of oxygen. The only drawback was that the battery had to be recharged now and then. They had a tremendous underwater speed of sixteen knots.

The question remains: Could or should the submarine war have ended temporarily in May 1943? At the beginning of 1943, Dönitz held a briefing at Hitler's headquarters. He insisted that the U-boats continue to remain in battle. Hitler also maintained that the only way Europe could be protected was by defending the perimeter of the Atlantic. At this time, as I mentioned earlier, our losses were so high compared to our sinkings, that the question should have been raised whether we should temporarily pull out of the U-boat war to wait for the new boats. This, of course, was not done.

It was maintained that if the Germans had prematurely pulled their submarines out of the Atlantic, the Allies would have been left with approximately 4,000 aircraft which could immediately have been deployed to attack the mainland, the harbors, and the industrial areas. According to my information, this would have been only partially true. These aircraft had a completely different mission profile, and were equipped accordingly. For the most part, they couldn't even have been used as bombers.

Furthermore, the German leadership at that time believed that convoy tactics would have been abandoned and that would have provided additional transport capacity. This belief, again, was only partly right. The British would have never given up their convoy system for the simple reason that they would always have to be prepared for a surprise attack. Finally, we assumed that the escort forces, the destroyers and the frigates, would have been free and could have been used, along with the rest of the fleet, to force a passage into the Baltic Sea. This, in turn, would have resulted in cutting off all supply by sea to the army in the East, and all shipping to Sweden. The shabbiest of excuses was that it also would have been impossible to rescue the two million people who were evacuated from the Baltic at the end of the war.

What was it like on a U-boat mission? When we left our base and closed the hatches, we parted with basically everything that made life worth living; from the sun, moon, and stars; from the smell of the sea; from friends and relatives. We were on our own. Our lives were reduced to a steel tube, and we had very little to look forward to.

One thing we relied on extremely heavily was comradeship. We knew we had to live with one another and to depend on one another.

We all came to know each other's families, neighbors, and problems. We could all replace one another if necessary. I believe that what we had was essential for comradeship in the true sense of the word, a word that I believe today has no meaning.

There was one other thing we had to live for. That was survival! From this arose what we called "the U-boat spirit." Churchill even recognized this and at the end of the war said, "They fought to the bitter end, and would have continued to fight if the political leadership and the war on the eastern front had been more stable." Under no circumstances were any of us going to abandon ship.

We only sporadically received information about what was going on. U-boat headquarters occasionally transmitted messages informing us about what was taking place around us in the Atlantic. We could only be reached by long-wave radio, and even then we only had communication with the high command.

I went to sea for the last time in the war on April 28, 1945, on a Submarine Type XXI. It was a dreadful experience. I reported to my commanding officer, Admiral von Friedeburg. What I am going to tell you now is no exaggeration! Admiral von Friedeburg left me with the words, "Topp, if the day should come when we can no longer defend our homeland, then we will defend our foothold in Norway. And when we can no longer defend Norway, I want you to take your boat out until you run out of fuel. Then I want you to go on land and continue to fight the enemy with whatever you have left to fight with." I must say that I always admired von Friedeburg. At that moment, he had tears in his eyes.

We started out with five boats. Three were sunk by British fighter bombers. Two got as far as the base in Horten. The snorkel on my boat, which was not functioning properly, was supposed to be repaired there. Then we were to continue our voyage. In the meantime, the war came to an end.

HORST ELFE

Born 1917; professional naval officer; submarine commander captured by the British; after the war became president of the Berlin Chamber of Commerce; lives in Berlin.

"Damned war!"

We surfaced on January 15, 1942, at approximately 0100 hours; it was dark, the wind was at 3 West, no lights to be seen, long, rolling waves. After approximately two hours we spotted a destroyer ahead and to starboard.

The destroyer suddenly turned and, at a high speed, headed directly toward my U-93. Its searchlights were on. Its guns bracketed us, but made no direct hits. My U-93 turned into firing position. The range shortened rapidly. Both engines running full speed, I turned hard to starboard to avoid being rammed. The muzzle covers were still off, and there were still torpedoes in the tubes. The British destroyer, H.M.S. *Hesperus,* was faster, and rammed us from a sharp angle at high speed. My U-93 was severely damaged. I gave the order to abandon ship. I ordered the conning tower lookouts to jump overboard so they would be clear when our own torpedoes exploded.

The crewmen standing on the conning tower, including myself, were thrown overboard as the boat sank. We lost six men. The *Hesperus* turned around, switched on her searchlights, threw out nets aft, and moved slowly through the swimmers. The Royal Navy always did this when attempting to rescue their own people. They could not risk halting and lowering rescue boats.

The British commander's orderly took me aboard, wrapped me in a woolen blanket, poured me a glass of strong rum, lit me a "Players Navy Cut" cigarette, and stuck it between my lips. He tried to console me by saying, "You take it easy, sir," instead of something like, "You bloody German Nazi!"

The next morning the British commander, Lt. Commander R. Tait, R.N., had me come to the bridge. He returned my salute, shook my hand, and said, "I'm sorry for you, sir." Tears came to my eyes, and I told him that I had been planning to sink him with a spread of four torpedoes. Commander Tait laughed and said that he had known about us for hours. He had located my boat with his new radar, and he pointed to the bow of the ship.

I recognized the radar. I said, "This is the easy way of doing it, sir!" The British commander replied, "Oh yes, but a most successful one, sir!" He added that the Royal Navy had a great deal of respect for the German U-boats.

In the summer of 1943, the Royal Navy announced: "Comm. Tait, D.S.O., R.N., Commander of a U-Boat Hunter Group, mentioned in dispatches, was killed in action." Torpedoed in the North Atlantic! Damned war!

HELMUT BERND

Born 1914; naval war correspondent; served on submarines; continued to work as a journalist after the war and currently lives in Rheinbreitbach, Palatinate.

"Our patrol area was between Europe and Rio de Janeiro."

After I was drafted into the army I was made a war correspondent and sent to Potsdam. One day we were asked to volunteer for the navy. Only two of us did. Thus it was that I came to be a correspondent in the navy.

I was afraid to climb aboard a submarine. I found it eerie to go down there and travel for long distances underwater. But at some point I overcame my anxiety. In the beginning I wrote reports about submarines and commanders who had been out and back. I lived with crew members. When you spent the entire day with the crew, you felt a very strong group atmosphere which made you almost ashamed to sit on land and write. When I look back, I see that it was crazy to join such small-scale combat units. Their operations required a great deal of effort, but they produced few results and the chances for survival were minimal at best.

One time I checked in on board, but found that a doctor had taken my place. That saved my life; the boat was sunk just after it went to sea. The worst time for submarines was the summer of 1943, when the Allies got radar. I found out later that the problem was not only radar; our code had also been broken.

To my knowledge, Dönitz was never willing to believe that the code had been compromised. I was a common sailor, but even I knew in 1943 what had happened. We went out in May 1943. We had suffered so many losses that submarines were taken out of the usual patrol areas; for example, we were sent to South America. That was a completely new area of operation. We had six submarines in the South Atlantic. Our type VII C submarines, the sort I was on, were not actually suited for such a mission, since they did not have the necessary range. They displaced 750 tons and carried a crew of 55. On the way, we had to be refueled by so-called "sea cows," large submarines that supplied us with diesel fuel. These supply boats were sunk one after the other. So we received fuel from combat submarines instead. We were out for about 100 days.

Normally, the U-boats travelled on the surface, since they were then far more maneuverable and much faster than when submerged. We sailed and sailed across the Atlantic and nothing happened. Three times during this trip we had arranged to meet with another one of our supply ships. Each time we had planned such a rendezvous, at map quadrangle so and so, "enemy air," as we called it, was already there to welcome us. When we radioed back to Berlin, our radio signal was surely picked up in London and most likely decoded within a short time. This happened three times: the enemy was there, in the middle of the Atlantic, and it surely wasn't coincidental. Dönitz refused to believe this. It appeared that the ordinary seamen sometimes knew more than the top leadership.

In the time we were out, we had six boats off the coast of South America, and the only one to return was ours.

In spite of great difficulties, we succeeded in sinking four merchant ships on this trip. Our patrol area was between Europe and Rio de Janeiro. One of the ships we sank was the *African Star,* a U.S. ship.

Since I was a reporter, I was up in the conning tower during the attacks. Once when we were closing in I asked the commander, "Aren't we getting too close?" (Some of the merchant ships were also armed.) "No," he said, "we've got even closer." We approached to within 800 to 600 meters. The enemy ships looked enormous at that range. Then came the order, "Torpedo!" followed by "Torpedo running!" and then "Hit!" The ships' crews climbed into lifeboats and tried to reach the coast. In most cases they succeeded, since we were operating near the coast.

After we sank the *African Star,* I called out to one of the crew members down in the lifeboat, "Hello, how are you?" He came on board with some others. It was very dark out. It was very frightening for them, especially when they saw our fullbearded men armed with machine guns. For me this was only a man from America, so why not talk to him? In fact, we had a rather pleasant conversation. Years later, when we met in the U.S., he told me, "It wasn't very nice of you to sink us. We were right in the middle of eating our turkey dinner."

On another patrol, I remember a grisly experience in the Bay of Biscay, and this sort of thing happened more than once. A tanker was hit and the crew members were floating in the water with their life jackets on. The oil spilled out, caught fire, and spread over the water, covering the survivors in flames.

At one point on this patrol, we took on half of a crew that had escaped from a U-boat that had been hit. Another boat took the other half of the crew. Now we had an additional 25 men on board a submarine with 25 bunks for 55 crew members. We were kept cramped together for 100 days with an extra 25 people for whom there was absolutely no room. The smells of the people on board, the heat, and the moisture made one man go completely crazy.

There is one thing that differentiates the life of a submariner from that of a soldier. A soldier has long pauses between periods of fighting; there may be weeks during which nothing happens. The submarine crew, on the other hand, has to reckon with being attacked any minute. This means that for 100 days we were subjected to continual stress.

Such stress has a strong effect on a human being unless he has nerves of steel. Most people don't. I remember thinking, "It isn't likely that we will come back. Therefore accept the situation and make the best of it, but don't dwell on the thought of making it back alive." This attitude gave me a certain strength and support.

The most important person was the commander. Everything depended on him—the fate of the ship and the fate of 55 men. He had to have a tremendous ability to react. Fractions of seconds could make the difference. Surely most of the commanders were inwardly ill at ease under the stress and had a difficult time coping with it, but they were not allowed to show their feelings. As soon as the commander showed signs of uncertainty, the entire crew became nervous and began to fall apart. Some COs also had a "sore throat," that is, the desire to have the Knight's Cross hanging around their necks. That was another psychological problem.

The most important thing about reaching land was not that we were received with music and crowds of people, but that we were able to walk 50 meters straight ahead, and then 50 more, and then 100, and then 300! It was an unimaginable experience going from the cramped existence on a submarine to the normal freedom of motion one has on land!

CHAPTER 8

"Fortress Europe"— Without a Roof

Strategic bombardment, the concept of defeating a state by destroying its industry and breaking its will, originated in World War I. After the war it was advocated by theorists like Giulio Douhet and Alexander de Seversky, and used by publicists as a means of enhancing the horror of future wars. It was institutionalized, however, only in Great Britain. There an independent air force sought a mission. There a government and a population recoiling from the horrors of the trenches sought to wage war at limited cost and with limited losses. The heavy bomber, used already by the Germans toward the end of World War I against London, seemed an ideal instrument for realizing these visions.

Practice did not match theory in the war's early years. Attempts to fly unescorted missions against military targets in daylight proved consistently disastrous. The shift to night operations was a product of necessity, handicapped by inadequate training and equipment. Well after the fall of France, the RAF continued to suffer unbearable losses in raids which had little more than nuisance value. This, despite the weakness of a German defense initially relying on anti-aircraft guns and searchlights, and having only two squadrons of night fighters.

The first attack on a German city came on August 26, 1940. Announced as retaliation for a previous raid on London, it was also a logical result of Britain's expulsion from the continent. The RAF's bombers were the only means remaining to conduct offensive operations. The RAF's generals insisted that they could bring Germany to her knees with enough of the right equipment. Throughout 1941 the air offensive increased in intensity, despite the demands of the Mediterranean and Atlantic theaters on British air resources, and despite an increasingly sophisticated German air defense. At the same time, the RAF's targets began to change. Photo intelligence demonstrated beyond a doubt that the bombers could do no better than hit a general area. In February 1942, Churchill's government announced that henceforth the bombers would seek to break the morale of Germany's civilian population.

The assignment of Air Marshal Arthur Harris as chief of Bomber Command reinforced the decision. Harris was a firm disciple not only of strategic bombardment, but of targeting civilians. Their morale, he argued, was inevitably more fragile than that of uniformed soldiers. Like many Allied leaders, Harris exaggerated the unpopularity of National Socialism. Enough of the right kind of pressure, he said, and Germany might collapse internally.

On the night of March 28, 1942, more than 200 bombers attacked the old Hanseatic city of Lübeck. Lübeck was selected as a target not for any military reason, but for its vulnerability, particularly to incendiary bombs. The result was a spectacular success in Harris's terms. The fires burned for a day and a half, gutting the city center. The RAF moved on to bigger cities. On May 30, the first thousand-bomber raid struck the city of Cologne. Up and down the Ruhr, British bombers hammered the Reich's industrial centers: Düsseldorf, Essen, Hamm. And in mid-1942 they received reinforcements.

The U.S. Army Air Force was as committed as its British counterpart to the concept of strategic bombing, and for many of the same reasons. It sought independence from army control by developing a separate mission. Its generals, mostly young men, believed in their technology with the fervor of acolytes. The Americans, however, retained their faith in daylight, precision bombing. Their principal aircraft were the B-17 and the B-24. Crews trained in the clear skies of America's Southwest were not well prepared for instrument flying in European conditions. The result was a compromise: the British would continue to attack by night. The Americans, as their forces increased, would assume the burdens of the day.

The combined bomber offensive struck its first major blow against Hamburg. Operation Gomorrah began on July 24–25, 1943. More than 30,000 people died in a series of raids then unmatched in scope and destruction. For the first time, a German city experienced firestorms: heat from burning buildings so intense that it created a tornado effect, sucking up oxygen with a force that dragged people alive into the flames.

Hamburg was a benchmark. The attacks continued, growing in intensity. By November, the RAF embarked on the "Battle of Berlin," and Harris spoke of forcing a German surrender by April 1944. Night after night the sirens screamed. Yet in Berlin, as throughout the Reich, morale did not break, nor did factories cease operating. In part, this reflected the Reich's incomplete mobilization. Even after Stalingrad, a significant amount of industrial capacity remained to compensate for the destruction of plants from the air. The Nazi system also showed itself capable of coping with the results of the raids. Local authorities provided food, shelter, and, most of all, a social structure for the shocked and the homeless.

Nor were the Germans entirely passive. Night fighters and antiaircraft guns took an increasing toll on the RAF. The Americans, too, faced heavier casualties as their unescorted formations flew deeper into the Reich. On August 17, 1943, the 8th Air Force lost at least 60 of the 375 bombers committed to an attack on Schweinfurt and Regensburg. Another hundred planes were damaged, and the Americans temporarily ceased missions over Germany. When they returned in force, it was with a new weapon: the P-51 Mustang. With auxiliary fuel tanks, it could fly missions anywhere over the Reich, and was able to challenge the Messerschmitts and Focke-Wulfs on better than even terms.

In preparation for D-Day, the combined bomber offensive adjusted its priorities. Now the bombers concentrated on oil, ball bearings, and aircraft factories. They also devoted special attention to the V-weapons, the pilotless rockets Hitler promised would bring victory from defeat. Since August 1943, the research center at Peenemünde had been a target. Now launching sites came under attack as well.

The new offensive met limited opposition. The German fighter arm, checked by the Mustangs, was mated when it could no longer fuel its planes or train its replacement pilots. The one aircraft capable of restoring the balance, the new Me-262 jet, was denied Germany's airmen by Hitler's insistence that this aircraft was an ideal "blitz bomber" for the counter-offensives he was planning. By the end of 1944, the Allied bomber forces had virtually completed the destruction of Germany's cities. The raids might be heavier than ever before, but all they could do was pulverize the ruins. That fact did not deter the British and Americans from striking one final blow. Dresden had thus far been spared. Its bombing could be seen as a goodwill gesture toward Stalin. It also reflected the fact that the Allied strategic air forces had run out of targets.

On the night of February 13, RAF Lancasters launched the first attack. The next day, U.S. B-17s added another 800 tons of bombs to a city already in flames. Dresden may not have been the war's most destructive raid. It was certainly the most shocking. In Hamburg, Berlin, or the Ruhr, people fought and suffered in familiar surroundings. But Dresden had become a magnet for refugees from everywhere in eastern Germany. Terrified strangers wandered the unfamiliar streets of the blazing city. To people from farms and small towns, who had never seen an Allied airplane, it seemed like the end of the world. Stories of a quarter-million dead developed, circulated, and became accepted in both Germanies. Later calculations have reduced that number by three-fourths. Even at the lower figure, Dresden remains for many Germans a symbol of the terror that stalked the Reich from above.

GUSTAV RÖDEL

*Born 1915; fought the Allied bomber offensive
and flew more than 1,000 fighter missions as a
wing commander; joined the Bundeswehr as a
general; today is a company manager; lives in
Bonn.*

"We shot down nearly 60 Flying Fortresses that day."

The first four-engined planes I ever saw were in North Africa; they were B-17 Flying Fortresses. Seeing these huge aircraft was enough to really scare you. Their firepower was incredible. The barrage was so heavy, I never even got a shot at them; I was too far away.

The air war changed radically after the Allies began using Flying Fortresses. The first time I engaged in combat with the four-engined bombers was over Rumania, in 1942, when they attacked the oilfields at Ploesti. We took off from Athens, and were supposed to engage the bombers over the Sofia area. We had orders to stick with them until we ran out of fuel. Later on, this tactic continued when we were defending the Reich. If we got low on fuel and couldn't make it back to our home base, we had to land at an alternative base to refuel. So what we were doing there in Rumania was a rehearsal for what was to come in the defense of the Reich. You were sent out to fight the bomber units, stayed with them as long as you could, found a base where you could refuel, and then went up after them again.

At any rate, when we flew this mission from Athens, I was leading a group of about 30 to 40 Messerschmitt 109s from my units. I was a wing commander at the time, and had planes based at different airfields. After the alarm sounded, we took off and met at a pre-fixed assembly point in the air. It was then my responsibility to lead the entire group to the enemy. The thing was to maneuver in such a way that we could attack the bomber group from behind.

The difficult part about attacking such large formations—which later consisted of up to 1,000 planes—was to lead your fighters right into the middle of the stream of bombers. The wing commander had to fly ahead to determine the best angle of attack. Of course, our opponents were well aware of that. Whoever flew in the lead was probably a very experienced pilot, and he was naturally the one who caught most of the enemy fire first. As wing commander, you could count on incoming fire from 30 to 40 machine guns simultaneously. It was like flying through a blizzard.

In the beginning, I have to admit, I used to fire far too early, which is why I didn't score a victory on the first mission. Later I learned to go at them from below, from the front or the side, and to stay with it—to grit my teeth and swallow my fear until I was within attack range.

I later flew missions over Germany in the so-called Reich defense. The four-engined bombers came from either Italy or Britain. If the weather conditions over the Alps suggested that an attack on Hungary or Austria could be ruled out, we were put in against the formations coming from the west. Our radar guidance accomplished great feats of navigation here, bringing us from Vienna as far north as Cologne in tight formation.

On August 17, 1943, I took part in the defense of Schweinfurt during a daylight bombing raid. We shot down nearly 60 Flying Fortresses that day, and they lost about 600 airmen. It was highly unusual for bomber formations to scatter; they had to stay close together for mutual protection.

One of the hardest things for us pilots was that we were never really aware of the overall situation in the air. We had to wait and see whether the bombers came from Italy or England, and then we'd be deployed accordingly. Schweinfurt was no exception. It just so happened that two of my wing's fighter groups were at the base that day so we were able to send up about 30 to 40 planes. We took off from Vienna and flew right into the middle of the four-engined bombers in tight formation. We could see the flak bursts, which were always a signal to us that the bombers were over their target. We arrived from the northeast, with just enough time to get behind the formation. I personally didn't score any kills that day, but I saw the burning bombers and crash fires, as well as some of our own fighters going down. I was lucky and didn't get shot down over Schweinfurt, but later, on similar missions, I took many hits and had to make either emergency or crash landings.

The Americans lost so many planes that day that there wasn't another daylight raid on the Reich for five weeks. They were so shocked, they couldn't get their pilots to fly; there was almost a mutiny. Things really only started up again when their fighters had enough range to escort their bombers all the way to the target. But in the long run, we couldn't stop the Fortresses. Driving through the bombed cities after the raids was terrible. Seeing the destruction and the wounded, you couldn't help but feel guilty and think that maybe you could have done more.

It got worse and worse. It even got to the point where we couldn't even take off and land without enemy interference. The chances of survival for our pilots were miserable. The only thing they had to rely on was a heart full of patriotism. The enthusiasm of these youngsters helped me put aside my own fears many times.

After the invasion, we were transferred from Vienna to Munich, and we tried to fly missions from there, but we could hardly take off without being attacked. I was giving combat training to a few young pilots, and one time after take-off we were jumped by six or eight Lightnings. I wanted to give them a fight, but my young pilots didn't stay with me; they broke formation. The Lightnings could see how inexperienced they were and zoomed in to pick them off one by one. In order to avoid complete disaster, I flew back into the swarm of Lightnings to try to draw their fire. It worked! Soon I had their full attention, and they beat the hell out of me. They chased me back and forth over my own airfield like a game of cat and mouse, and it was just dumb luck that they didn't shoot me down. Thank God they ran out of fuel. I felt so ashamed in front of my men when I landed. I tried to conceal just how terrified I was, but my knees began to shake as soon as I climbed out of the plane.

JOHANNES STEINHOFF*

"Classic dogfights were becoming rarer."

It was in the last days before we had to evacuate Sicily in August 1943. The sun was mercilessly hot. We had taken off from an airstrip south of Etna. While we were still climbing I heard in my earphones, "Attention Odysseus [that was my call sign], many bombers 30 kilometers south of Catania heading for the Straits of Messina, escorted by Spitfires."

I routinely checked the fit of my oxygen mask. Following a pattern developed in hundreds of sorties, my eyes searched the skies for enemy aircraft. My altimeter showed 25,000 feet. I assumed the bombers would be coming in at that height. Their fighter escorts, the Spitfires, would be covering them from above, at about 28,000 feet.

Meantime, it had gotten incredibly cold in the cockpit. In a wide-sweeping curve, I flew north. Mount Etna's snow-covered crater vanished under my wings. Across the Straits of Messina, Calabria's mountains were visible through the haze. At first I was occupied with routine: checking the instruments, switching the magnetos to test the spark plugs, testing the oil and manifold pressures, and finally, the automatic feeling for the parachute straps and again the oxygen mask.

I flew in formation, comrades on my right and left. At the same time, I was alone—terribly alone with my thoughts and anxieties in a roaring glass cage. "You still have a choice," I thought. "You still can decide whether you'll obey the order, whether you'll keep flying in this attack formation until you can't avoid a fight. You're the formation leader; you're the wing commander. Isn't the engine running a little rough? Aren't the RPMs dropping?" Minutes passed, and suddenly voices screamed at me through the headphones. "Bombers!

---

* Biography on page 7.

Many bombers! Look out! Fighters! Spitfires!" I saw the bomber formation in front of me. Then everything happened at once.

The elegant Spitfires came from the front, and flew right through our formation. For a fraction of a second I saw the RAF bull's-eyes on the Africa-camouflaged fuselages, the pointed wing-tips, and the fish-like blue-white bellies.

I had that bitter taste on my tongue again. My mouth was completely dry. It was fear, the fear that always overcomes you at the start of a dogfight. Out of the corner of my eye I saw the bombers. They looked like they were standing still; we were all flying in the same direction. Apparently undisturbed, masters of the air, they kept their impressive formation.

The British fighters turned around and came back for a second attack. Hell had broken loose in my earphones: reports, warnings, shouts, mixed in such an incomprehensible babble of voices that my ears hurt. Luckily I could see the rest of my flight alongside me. I had an ideal attack position. I was above two Spitfires and coming out of the sun. Almost automatically, I went into a dive. My speed increased enormously. A Spitfire got bigger and bigger in my sights. But all at once, as if the pilot had been warned, he rolled into a vertical dive. Without hesitating, and against all common sense, I accepted the dogfight. I had no time to look back. I didn't know if my wing man would cover me. The G-forces pressed me harder and harder against my parachute. My neck hurt when I tried to move my head to keep the enemy in sight.

Little by little I closed in on the Spitfire. I had him in my sights again. I cocked my guns. One more circle, and he'd be a clear target! Like a man possessed, I flew this merry-go-round, the last phase of the duel. A sudden blow on my fuselage brought my head around. I saw another Spitfire on my tail, a few meters behind. His tracers reached for me like fingers. My motor bucked wildly. Bullets evidently had damaged my engine cooler, and leaking fluid obscured the windshield. Behind my head, bullets bounced off the armor plate with a sickening rattle. This guy was a damn good shot!

Just like in flight school, I rolled out of the merry-go-round into a deep dive. Like a man paralyzed I crouched in my seat and flew the plane in the classic evasive maneuver. At 2,000 meters I suddenly realized I wasn't being shot at any more. The view through the windshield was clearer. What was coming toward me must be the slopes of Mount Etna. I turned off the ignition. The oil and radiator temperatures had gotten dangerously high. The propeller turned slowly as I plunged toward the ground. Already I could see details. It was not an ideal place for a crash landing.

But I succeeded in maneuvering between the tall trees toward a long, narrow field climbing up the mountain. My prop tips were already touching ground when I saw the boulders scattered across the field. Too late now! Just before touching ground I fastened my shoulder belt. The contact was hard! My cockpit plexiglass flew into the air. Clumps of dirt rattled on the fuselage, the windshield, and the wings. My body was thrown forward, but the belts held. Then with a jerk the Messerschmitt stood on its nose, as if it wanted to do a somersault. When I recovered my senses everything was quiet. The last sound was a shattering crash as the fuselage slammed back onto the rocky ground. Then there was only a gentle humming: the radio was still on.

Dazed, I unbuckled the belts and climbed out of the cockpit onto the wings. I took a few steps on solid ground. Only then did I feel the sharp pain in my back. Slowly I slid to the ground, propping myself up with my hands on the rocks.

I don't know why I accepted the Englishman's challenge to a dogfight. But he had offered me the duel even though he could easily have dived away. My risk just didn't pay off. Duelling in the air, the classic dogfights we got accustomed to in the Battle of Britain, were becoming rarer. The demands of the strategic air war were determining events now. There was no more time to match strengths and flying skills. When the bombers flew in streams and the fighters formed a defensive umbrella over them, the only counter was head-down attack, attack until you broke into the bomber formation or were shot down by the escorts.

It was miserably hot, but surely they were looking for me. There were fields, trees, hedges, but not a sign of life. Half-conscious, I heard the clink of metal on metal. I heard men's voices. When I opened my eyes I saw two Sicilians in dirty white shirts and black pants. They were leaning into the cockpit, tugging at the parachute.

"Hello" I called loudly, and when they jerked upright I took my flare pistol and called "hello" again. They looked over as if they heard my voice, but still couldn't see me under the olive trees. They slowly straightened up, and now I saw the long hunting rifles they'd leaned against the fuselage. Guns in hand, they walked toward me and stood silently in front of me. They didn't exactly look frightening. One had friendly eyes. He was skinny, and the veins stood out on his bony arms. The younger might have been 13. "Good morning," I said. "Good morning. German?" "Yes," I answered. Both crouched down beside me in the shadows. For a moment I wondered what they might have done if I had been British or American. Maybe an hour passed. Then a Storch landed on the field. They'd come to pick me up.

ERICH ANDRES

Born 1905; war correspondent and navy photographer; after the war was a photographer/reporter; now lives in Hamburg.

"The night of the firestorm."

I was a navy war correspondent stationed in Wilhelmshaven. I went to Hamburg over the weekend of July 24–25, 1943, to meet my wife who was coming from Dresden by train. She arrived on Friday afternoon and went to the butcher and bought meat to prepare one of my favorite meals. I arrived later that evening. It was really great being together again. Our plans for the weekend included long walks and a quick trip to the suburb of Blankenese. We hoped the weather stayed good.

All in all, we were very content, almost forgetting there was a war going on. We went to bed at 11:30 P.M., and at 1:30 A.M. we were awakened by the wailing of the sirens. We immediately went to the basement, and listened to the distant explosions. Then, because nothing was happening in our part of Hamburg, we went back to our apartment. We slept and slept and slept till noon. Oddly, it was still dark outside when we woke up. Usually the sun rose around 5 A.M. But here it was noontime, and still dark out. Then we found out that Hamburg had been severely bombed; it was dark due to the smoke and dust. The Altona district had been particularly hard hit.

I returned to my duty station on Monday, July 26. On Tuesday, we heard that targets of the second attack were residential, with little or no industry hit. Then on Friday morning, July 30, Hamburg was under heavy attack again. A couple of the other men in my unit were from Hamburg as well, and our commander let us go to the city. We were certain that we could help out one way or another. I wondered what condition my house was in. Though I had been in Hamburg only the Sunday before, after the first attack, this was different. Not one house was standing. The entire place was one huge pile of bricks. They had been bombed Monday night, and I didn't get there until Saturday. But the heat was still intense, the walls of the houses still burning hot.

I finally reached my house. There it was, in terrible condition—black, scorched holes in place of the windows. Once inside the house, I was able to make my way through the wreckage in the hallway to the basement stairs. The heat coming from downstairs was so intense it was going to be difficult getting down the stairs at all. I walked past a glowing furnace, the reason for all the heat in the basement. The beds hadn't been burned, and there were people lying on all of them. I couldn't stand the heat and the awful smell any longer, and went back upstairs.

After catching my breath, I went back down to see if I could recognize anyone. During the three days since the bombing, their skin had been roasted dark brown, and their faces and bodies were bloated beyond recognition from the intense heat. Gasping for air, I was extremely relieved to finally get back up to the ground floor again.

I could accept the fact that 30 or 40 people could perish in the event that such a large house somehow caught fire. But I never thought it conceivable that people could be deliberately killed this way, thousands of times over. Perhaps out on the front, yes—but not at home. At the front, you could defend yourself. There was no way those people in the cities could have defended themselves against the bombs dropped on them.

I left the house, and stood outside looking at what was left. I couldn't see any dead in the yard. They were all in the basement. Each air raid shelter warden had had strict orders not to let anyone out until the bombing had subsided. That had been their doom. At least a third or a half of those trapped in the basement could have perhaps survived had they been allowed to run out onto the streets. Even though there was the possibility that they would have been hit by a bomb or buried under falling buildings, they would have still had a greater chance of surviving, compared to certain death by suffocating down in the basement.

I passed a number of dead bodies lying close together, mostly only half-dressed. It looked like the women had ripped their clothes off, either because they were on fire or they just couldn't stand the heat. Perhaps their clothes had caught fire after they had become unconscious, which would also explain why they were half or totally naked. In the middle of the group, I noticed a 10-year-old boy lying there, clinging to one of the air-raid wardens. The boy must have crawled along the floor with the last little bit of life that was left in him, over to the warden who had probably already suffocated and was dead.

I took pictures of what I saw. Later, I was often condemned: "Why did you take those pictures? Wasn't it enough that they were all dead?" I always answered, "Future generations must know about the catastrophe, the crimes committed against literally millions of defenseless and helpless people as a result of the big-time politics determined in Berlin and elsewhere."

One afternoon in the fall, I met my neighbor in front of what had once been our home. His first words to me were: "Well, Mr. Andres, only a year ago, we were all a lot better off, weren't we?"

He began to tell me what had happened during the terrible night of July 27, 1943, the night of the firestorm:

"I left my house that Tuesday night at about 11:30 P.M., just as the sirens began to wail. It was my turn to pull duty at our factory's air raid shelter. I had barely reached the plant when the first bombs began to explode. You could hear them getting closer and closer all the time. By the sound of it, huge bomber formations were circling over Hamburg, flying in from all directions. The entire sky was lit with hundreds of flares, so-called 'Christmas Trees,' which glistened brightly as they slowly made their way to the ground. Amid this, the roaring and rumbling, the whizzing and whistling of the falling bombs passing through the air seemed never to end.

"I ran out of the shelter and headed home. The city was an inferno. Because of the unbearable heat, I wasn't able to take the usual route. Getting to the river and swimming was the only alternative I had.

"Up above, the sky had turned a deep red. I could not see one single house in the entire area that was not ablaze. People were running crazily back and forth in all directions, crying out names, throwing themselves down onto the asphalt, and slapping themselves with towels. Some were already lying totally still on the street, not moving, even when someone else tried to get them up. Was this the end? For all of us? When would I be caught? Why were we being punished like this? Why?

"Continuing to crawl, I finally reached our street. Our house, number 43, was also on fire. A few people ran past me in the direction of the Bille River. Despite the intense heat I succeeded in getting to our house on the other side of the street. I crawled on the ground along the side of the house, going from one basement window to the next, yelling out names as I passed.

"I reached the last window and called out more names. My God! There were people still alive down there! Maybe my wife was down there. Although I couldn't recognize any of the voices, I did understand what they were telling me. The fire and heat had closed off all other possible exits, and their only way out was through the small hole on which I was standing. I found an iron rod which I used as a lever to bend the iron bars in the window; slowly but surely the gap widened between them. That took 20 agonizing minutes. My entire body was dripping with sweat.

"In the meantime, the wall of fire had steadily moved closer, and the cellar got hotter and hotter. I heard women sobbing, men scream-ing, and children whimpering. A woman cried out that her child was unconscious. Finally, the opening between the window bars was just large enough to squeeze a person through. Pure heat blasted out from below. At last, one head appeared through the opening. A woman, crying uncontrollably, grabbed for my arm. I reached for her and pulled and tugged until she finally squeezed her way through. Then another head came through. I reached down, and felt a child being pushed up from below. Still crying, the frenzied woman took the child in her arms and ran off in the direction of the river. A man's head appeared next. I pulled and pulled. He was screaming, begging me not to let him fall back. It was difficult, but he finally made it through.

"Suddenly there was a tremendously loud crashing sound that came from inside. Bricks and pieces of concrete of all sizes were flying all around me. But with the exception of a few superficial wounds—scrapes, cuts, and burns—I wasn't seriously injured. Dawn broke a few hours later, and you could see heavy clouds passing over the ruins of the burning city. I made my way back to that ill-fated room in the basement. The intensity of the heat still flowing out of the window openings was unbelievable. Later, during the clean-up, 72 bodies were counted. They were residents of 43 Campe Street and 2 Salzmann Street, with a few from Basedow Street. I had been able to rescue three of them."

IRMGARD BURMEISTER

Born 1931; in Hamburg during the war; after the war was employed as a secretary; still lives in Hamburg.

"Although we were living in a suburb, we were still scared to death."

An 8- or 9-year-old child really isn't able to comprehend how mortally dangerous a situation can be. Initially, we were all terribly excited about the bombing attacks. It was all so new to us. Being bombed and shot at gave us the feeling we were like the soldiers fighting at the front. We even invented games to play. After a bombing raid, we would run out on the streets and into the yards to collect the fragments and splinters from the anti-aircraft shells, and trade our newly acquired "treasures" with the other children. We collected and traded fragments of all shapes and sizes. Some glistened while others were dull; it was almost like collecting stamps. But when the raids continued and the bombs kept falling, we soon lost interest and quit playing our game.

All of the commotion caused by the raids naturally affected our school life. I remember, for example, that if there had been an air raid the night before, we didn't have to go to our first-hour class. If the attack had been long and severe, our school hours were changed again. It was all pretty confusing. During the day while in school, there was always an advance warning in the event we were about to be bombed. We had just enough time to run home before the main siren sounded. I remember there was a radio station we could tune in to find out information about where the various bomber formations were. The man who broadcast this information had a particularly calming voice. He was generally referred to as "Mr. Tranquilizer."

During the attacks, we always sought refuge in our basement. Since it wasn't built totally underground, we saw and heard everything. We even had shell fragments on our basement stairs. Although we were living in a suburb and didn't experience the massive bombing of the city, we were still scared to death. We didn't dare move during such raids. My grandmother knew how to tell fortunes with playing cards. Every time the situation became particularly precarious, she would pull out her cards. Reading them, she always said, "No, nothing is going to happen to us. Everything is going to be all right this time." We all knew she was fantasizing a bit, but at times like that we always believed her.

The raids were the worst during 1943. The people of Hamburg still refer to that period as "The Catastrophe." It was really the end of the world for the inner city. At first we didn't know what had happened. We only heard the huge bomber formations in the sky. The attacks were heavier and lasted longer than before. When it was over, the city glowed with fire; the sky was burning red. The next morning, the entire area would be covered with ashes. Even though the weather was good the sun could not break through. The air was thick with ashes and tiny pieces of paper, like fog or clouds.

The bombing was intensified from July 23 to August 3, 1943. During this time, one part of the city after another was systematically wiped out. We became very bitter. Bombs were dropped on the helpless civilian population. Residential areas were their sole targets, and it was obvious that this strategy had nothing to do with any military targets. Simply put, it was sheer terror.

Day by day, we began to realize the extent of the damage. An almost endless number of refugees from the city began to pass by our house. They were either on bicycles or pulling small carts packed with the few belongings they had managed to salvage. Having never seen anything like this before, I was astounded. The thing that impressed me most was the total silence. They just kept passing by, not uttering a word.

An old friend of my grandfather's was living with us at the time. Somehow he managed to get to the city. As though it were only yesterday, I distinctly recall his return: he was covered from head to toe with soot; his suit was filthy dirty; and I will never forget the frightened look in his eyes. He had witnessed the inferno. "It's all in ruins; everything is gone. Hamburg no longer exists," was all he said.

INES LYSS

Born in 1924 of German-Italian parentage; lived in Hamburg during the raids; is a television engineer and resides in Hamburg.

"Oh dear God."

You could already hear the whistling of the bombs. Naturally, we all ran as fast as we could. I remember first sitting on a small wooden bench in the basement. Then everybody jumped up when the first bombs hit. Dust and limestone whirled through the air, the walls cracked. When it didn't seem it was going to stop, people began to pray; some started to scream.

The fear that prevailed as the bombs continued to fall was incredible. We were totally paralyzed. I started to pray too: "Oh dear God. . . ." We were all a little religious, that's why the "Oh dear God." I kept saying, "I'll never see Jupp again, I'll never see Jupp again!" He was my fiancé at that time.

KLAUS KÜHN

Born 1928; a Hitler Youth flak auxiliary during the bomber raids; lives in Hamburg-Bergedorf.

Underground bunkers were built three to six feet below the surface of the earth, and consisted of two to four large tubes about 150 feet in length. The tubes, which were situated pretty far apart from one another, were connected only by fireproof doors.

You got into the bunker by using stairs—like in an underground garage. Once you got downstairs, you had to walk down a long hallway. Depending on the size of the bunker, two or three tubes were connected to this main entrance. These tubes were nothing more than long, narrow hallways. Benches sat on either side of the hall. And each tube was separated from the other by thick concrete walls so that in case one tube got a direct hit, it would be the only one destroyed.

UWE KÖSTER

Born 1930; lived through the air raids as a Hitler Youth in Hamburg.

"The corpses were beyond identification."

I was a Hitler Youth messenger. As such, I was stationed at an air raid bunker built both above ground and underground. When an air raid alarm sounded, we had to be there on time and open the bunker with the "block leader," a party official who was responsible for the street. We had to care for the children, give them milk, and so on, if the alarm lasted a long time.

I cannot remember a single outbreak of panic. I must say that the people responsible back then, the people assigned by the party, like the block and district leaders, were in control of the situation at all times.

It did happen once in awhile that people, especially women who were often alone, showed signs of nervous breakdowns which were apparent in the form of crying jags, but never to the point that you couldn't quiet them again. Of course, from time to time they would take something to calm them down. That happened in our bunker, too. The block leader or the women from the Nazi women's organization went around and handed out toys to the children and light sedatives to adults. And the louder the attack got outside, the quieter it got in the bunker.

The underground shelters were more like "tube bunkers." When you came through the steel door, fitted with rubber around the edges to make it airtight, you entered a diagonal hallway. This hallway was joined by three or four tube-like hallways perpendicular to it. Each of these, in turn, was a separate bunker. Air was pumped through each tube by machines which we Hitler Youth operated. That was one of our jobs. My duties also involved running messages from one bunker to another if the telephones went dead. We were outfitted with gas masks, steel helmets, etc. We had to go out at all times, even when the bombs were falling. I was 13 years old at the time.

Sometimes I was very careless and very tired because we still had to go to school. We had six hours of school a day. Then we were sent out to collect junk that could be recycled. We had a cart, like a huge wheelbarrow, that we pushed and loaded. Earlier these carts were used for delivering coal. In our district we collected old scrap metal, old newspapers, and bones. Oil was made from the bones, which was made into grease for weapons.

So our tasks in school were homework, junk collecting, sports, plus Hitler Youth service twice a week. All that six days a week, including Saturday nights. On Sundays there was usually a field trip or a sports event. So the week was thoroughly organized: every hour of our day was planned.

I heard the alarm on the night of the first attack on July 24, 1943. I got up very slowly and then jumped into my uniform. It was always ready beside the bed so that I could get dressed in the dark. My mother, my sister, and I went down the stairs but could get no further than that. We huddled in a small corner for the entire attack, two hours, standing up. We couldn't go out into the street because the bombs were already falling by the time we had gotten downstairs. They fell in short intervals. It was literally hailing fire bombs, incendiaries with phosphorus canisters.

Afterwards we were called in to clear the streets. We cleared out the corpses, sometimes the burned bodies of people in cellars as well as those on the streets. We saw just how many people had died.

We stacked the bodies in 30 to 35 layers on top of each other. We stacked them all, and if you went past two or three days later you could only go with cellophane over your eyes because everything was smoky. The air was absolutely still. We didn't have any sun at all for three or four days; it was completely dark out. We only saw a blood-red ball in the distance, which didn't penetrate the dark cloud that hovered over Hamburg for days: smoke, cinders, and ashes. The dead were piled in the entrances of houses. And when you went by you just saw a heap of feet, some barefoot, some with burned soles. The corpses were beyond identification. We would dig entire families out of their basements, sometimes two, three weeks later; they'd fit into a bathtub. Even adults were very small. They were completely mummified, burned, and melted together by the heat. Yes, stacking the dead near the house entrances was actually the fastest and best way of getting them off the streets. After a while they were taken away to a mass grave.

GERTRUDE LÖHR

Born 1919; spent the war with her child in Berlin and Hamburg; went on to become a writer; lives near Luebeck, Holstein.

I was terrified during the air raids. I felt like a rat being smoked out of a hole. I remember sitting down in the basement with my 4-year-old son on my lap, clinging to him for dear life. I had wrapped the blanket from his bed around his head. The minute he made a noise, I told him to be quiet! I mean I really hissed at him. All of us were just sitting there on edge, trying to hear anything we could from the outside. We wanted to know what was coming—why, I don't know.

HERIBERT SUNTROP*

The morning after one attack, I was going to work. On the way, I found the corpse of a British pilot who had come down without a parachute. Next to him lay a tree branch from the tree above us. I still wonder today with what coldness I stood there and looked at the dead man. I kicked him with my foot. Another British airman was lying a bit farther down the street. His body had been cut in half at the navel. Only the upper part was there, completely naked. And this sight left me completely cold as well.

* Biography on page 13.

KAETHE BREUER

Housewife in Cologne during the air raids;
lives in Leverkusen, Rhineland.

"He shot himself; he couldn't bear it any longer."

Then there was another alarm and we went into the cellar. A man who lived above us—he must have been strong as an ox at one time—had a bad case of asthma, and he said, "I'm not going with you into the cellar." Then he sat down in the courtyard. He did that twice. One day when we climbed out he was dead. We did not always agree with his family on certain issues, but we were still fairly good friends. My husband went up to their apartment and saw that he had been shot through the temple and that the pistol was lying on the ground. He had shot himself; he couldn't bear it any longer. My husband immediately took the pistol with him. The man's wife went to get the doctor, since the cause of death had to be determined. The man's wife said later, "Thank you, Mr. Breuer, for taking the pistol away. The doctor said it was a bomb fragment—otherwise I would have had no claim to supplementary insurance."

WOLF SOHÈGE

Born 1926; a teenager when Hamburg burned; a physician after the war; lives in Hamburg.

"The people sat totally still against the wall . . . they were all dead."

After the air raids, everything was really well organized. It was very surprising; all of a sudden everything was there, food and so on. I was young, a bit big for my age, and had a hearty appetite. The cellar of the district party organization was nearby. There were cans of fish, and bread, everything imaginable. Suddenly everything the Nazis had hidden for their personal reserve was available to us. We didn't think it was right for them to hoard like that; it was, after all, food that belonged to all of us. Food was also made available from the mobile kitchens, the Red Cross, and so on. Hot meals were distributed in the fields outside the city.

Care for the wounded was also well organized. They had to be carried; some were so badly burned that we had to put them on stretchers. When the phosphorous canisters hit the houses, this phosphorous stuff ran down the stairs and out into the street. It set an entire house on fire in one go. The people ran out of these houses like living torches, and the flames on their bodies were put out by whoever could help them. The badly burned had to be taken away in trucks or ambulances. Sometimes people carried them short distances to a place where they could be picked up by ambulances. But the drivers had to be careful that the phosphorous didn't get under their tires—the rubber burned immediately.

Those who already had phosphorous on their bodies were wrapped in wool blankets to extinguish the flames. Water was scarce; the water supply completely collapsed. First the fires were put out, then the burn victims were bandaged.

The hospitals were already overcrowded in the central area. Therefore we got orders to pick up five ambulances from here and there. I got on my motorcycle and led the ambulances all the way across Hamburg, out into the suburbs and to hospitals in rural areas.

The corpses were transported by other work teams, mostly made up of POWs. Lime was spread because there was a danger of epidemics. Some streets were simply closed off with barriers. The police shot to kill if they caught anyone looting. But there wasn't much left to get; the houses were completely destroyed. Only the skeletons of buildings were left standing, the rest had been destroyed. Naturally there were still some people trapped in their cellars. We had to go out and look for them ourselves. It was extremely difficult finding them; sometimes it was impossible.

The local hospitals were, of course, quickly filled with burn victims. These people had second and third degree burns. There were no special wards for burn victims back then. Most of the people died; it was impossible for so many injured to get the proper treatment. There was no option but to bury them in mass graves.

We had to see to it that the corpses were removed as quickly as possible to prevent epidemics from spreading. The bodies were often so badly mutilated that it was impossible to identify them. Many of them had died under collapsed buildings. We dug out the ones we knew or suspected were still trapped in their cellars. Of course we asked everyone we got out if anyone else was still down there. For the most part, we were able to get them out through trap doors that could be opened from the outside. Other times they went through the neighboring houses to get out.

Although we did all we could, many people suffocated from smoke inhalation, carbon monoxide poisoning. At one point I found a basement shelter that was full of smoke. The people sat totally still against the wall, no one made a peep. I thought my eyes were deceiving me, but they were all dead. We had to get the bodies out quickly, and had to make an opening large enough. After we got the corpses out of the cellar, the entrances were sealed.

FERDINAND SCHUMACHER

Born 1930; lived through Allied bombard-
ments; resides in Cologne.

Only later, when I was a 13-year-old, did hard reality hit. The war took on terrifying forms. There was a shortage of adult men. People remembered the youth, who in part were pressured into filling the gaps on a volunteer basis. They attended short courses and were trained as medics or as security and aid service personnel. Our playground was the Aachen pond near the university. There were ack-ack guns and searchlights set up in that area under the command of experienced officers and crewed by half-grown boys and girls and Russian volunteers. Thousands of coffins were stored in the basements. They were ideal for playing hide and seek. The incendiary bombs were our favorite toys. We threw them down from walls or from ruins. We wanted to be just like grown-ups, putting out fires and recovering the injured. That was our everyday play.

INGE MEYN-KOMMEYER

Born 1925; survived life under the air raids; a
housewife, she lives in Hamburg.

"He couldn't stand the air raids."

One morning at about six o'clock, I woke up and heard some strange noises coming from the kitchen and went to see what it was. I couldn't believe my eyes! There was my brother, who was on leave from Russia marching back and forth, wearing his heavy army boots. I said, "Edi, what on earth are you doing? Are you crazy? And get rid of those boots." He looked at me and said, "Why?" I said, "It's six o'clock in the morning and we all want to get some sleep! If you can't sleep, then get dressed and go out into the yard or go for a walk in the park. Do whatever you want. Just don't keep us awake marching around in those ridiculous noisy boots!" He looked at me with a dazed expression on his face and said, "That's it! I'm going back!" I asked, "Where to? The front?" "Yes!" he replied. He couldn't stand the air raids, because he didn't feel he could defend himself as well as at the front.

HUGO STEHKÄMPER

Born 1929; fought at war's end as a Hitler Youth; at present is the director of the Cologne City Archives.

"You learned to live from one air raid to the next."

The first bombings began in 1941. People gaped at the destruction even though it wasn't serious enough to affect us too terribly at the time. As good-for-nothing boys, we thought that if a bomb hit the school it would make for a nice change in the lesson plan. In 1942, the school was badly damaged, but lessons continued in a building without window panes, while doors hung crookedly from their hinges. None of that affected the functioning of the school.

Many of us were pulled out of class and put into special basic training courses, though I wasn't one of them. The flak helpers received "classroom" instruction right out at the gun positions; the teacher went along with them. What they got out of these lessons, I don't know. In any case, the teachers could count on a bunch of weary students. We were all tired; the air raid alarms sounded regularly every night, and it was impossible to get any sleep before 2 or 3 o'clock in the morning. The school was damaged more and more all the time.

Meanwhile, the older men, who'd been drafted into the so-called security and auxiliary service, had taken up quarters in the school. This wasn't exactly conducive to an orderly school atmosphere. Everything that took place depended on when the alarm went off, how long it lasted, and, of course, which rooms of the school were still usable afterwards. Sometimes we had to move into neighboring rooms which, for the most part, were already in pretty bad shape.

You learned to live from one air raid to the next; it became routine. Of course, many people went out into the country where there was already a severe shortage of housing. A lot of people said they'd rather stay home than have to live under strained circumstances and be given funny looks someplace else. Naturally you knew you risked your life every day by staying in a big city. You simply continued to live from day to day with a certain degree of indifference.

During the actual bombings, this feeling of indifference was replaced by a deathly fear, fear for your life, a fear that still haunts me today. Even after over forty years, I cannot bring myself to watch a film about the bombings; it would rob me of at least three nights' sleep. Those memories are still very real. It would be like rubbing salt into the wound.

WILLI HOFMANN

*Born 1908; top manager of the Bosch Electric
Company during and after the war; now resides in Stuttgart.*

"If the Bosch firm fails, heads will roll."

In January 1942, I returned to Stuttgart and was classified "unavail-
able" for military service. That was because I was responsible for
planning and supervision in the *Lichtwerk,* Bosch's main factory. In
the meantime, the first bombings of the city had begun.

The plant manufactured small starters and dynamos for army
jeeps. For a while it produced starters for airplanes; these were later
manufactured in Berlin. We produced adjusting motors for pro-
pellers, headlights, horns, regulators, and switches. The plant also
manufactured certain items for submarines. In other words, our
products were used on water, air, and land. One day this factory was
bombed, too. In anticipation of the danger, we had, however, moved
part of the production facilities to textile factories in Württemberg.
These factories were shut down and opened their doors not only to
Bosch, but to a number of other armaments firms. All the factories
along the Neckar Valley switched production in this way.

This so-called "pearl necklace" of factories along the river was
also bombed later in the war, but for now my task was to plan the
Bosch factory transfers without interrupting production, while moving machines, tools, and workers. The raid on Stuttgart severely
damaged the main plant. The next day, Field Marshal Milch visited
the executive committee and said, "If the Bosch firm fails, or if the
German Wehrmacht fails because the Bosch firm has failed, heads
will roll!"

Therefore I was assigned to move the factory so that if one part
was damaged or broke down, the entire production line would not

collapse. Among other things, a plant was to be constructed at Langenbielau in Silesia, which was not exactly next door. The freight trains rolled toward Silesia with machines and tools, and if even the smallest part had been missing, nothing would have worked. That sounds exaggerated, but that is exactly how it was.

By 1943, the original factory was operating at sixteen different locations, including two prisons in the Stuttgart area. The government requirements were that production was by no means to be permitted to slack off; on the contrary, we were expected to speed up production all across the board. Everything had to function precisely and punctually.

In February 1944, there was another heavy bombing raid on Stuttgart-Feuerbach. The main plant, a building 350 by 350 feet, was set ablaze. You had to hold on tight to avoid being dragged into the roaring flames by the tremendous air suction. The plant was precision-bombed, no doubt about it, and it broke the old factory's back, so to speak. But fortunately the machinery had already been moved to another location. Catastrophe had once again been averted.

ANNE BREYER

Born 1919; did compulsory labor service during the war; later worked in a department store; lives in Cologne.

"We stood at the window many times to enjoy the show."

Every morning the Allied prisoners of war who worked for our company had to assemble there. They were guarded by Austrians, all born around 1890. In the winter, these old privates wore soldiers' coats that looked like they had been pulled out of the most remote corners of a second hand clothing store. Since these old soldiers were almost all short and squat, the coats reached down to their shoes. They were armed with old rifles at least six feet long.

The best show came when there was an air raid alarm. Since everybody wanted to get to safety, they had to move fast. The prisoners had their own shelter, and after assembling, they had to run as quickly as possible. But, because the old guards weren't as mobile wearing those ridiculous coats and dragging those long rifles, two POWs would run back, grab them under their armpits, lift them up, and carry them off to the bunker. This was quite a sight: the long rifles sticking out at one end, feet sticking out at the other, and the guards' bodies dangling between the two prisoners. We stood at the window many times to enjoy the show, but then we too had to take cover quickly.

GESA HACHMANN

Born 1935; married to a Canadian; now divides her life between Hamburg and Canada.

"Peace is when I can spread butter on both sides of a slice of bread."

I was four when the war started. The ration cards weren't so bad, it was enough to live on. We had butter that was divided up into equal little pieces. Each of us got a slice which had to last four or five days. My sister, who was five years older, and the son of a family living with us because their house had been bombed, each got a little more because they were older. But it wasn't much more, a knife tip, five grams maybe.

It sounds horrible, I know, but at the time, we children didn't know anything different. I didn't know the slightest thing about getting food with anything other than with ration cards. That we were afraid on our way to school, or were given instructions about what to do if the air raid alarm sounded, well, that was normal. In our eyes, the Americans, the Russians, and the British were all enemies without any human qualities. I didn't know a life where you could go into a store and buy things, go on a vacation, or even take a Sunday drive in the car. I didn't know what it was like to get a new dress. We always wore the hand-me-downs from our older brothers and sisters.

One time my sister and I got a pair of brand new shoes. I should say we had to share a pair of brand new shoes. Since we only had the one pair, we took turns going to school—one day she went and the next day I went.

We were bombed while at school. During one raid, a wing of the school was totally destroyed while we children hunched in the basement just 50 yards away. I remember the clouds of dust, the wooden beams crashing, and 300 screaming children. I was eight years old at the time, so I have difficulty recalling just how afraid I was. I still see the beam cracking and everything, but I don't know if a child feels fear as intensely as a grown-up does. As I said, it was nothing unusual for us—just air raids.

What has remained with me to this day, more than any other fear, are the anxieties I feel when I hear the drone of a high-flying airplane. When I hear that, I still get goosebumps.

One time I asked my mother, "What is peace?" "When people like each other again," she said. "And could we," I asked, "could we go to the grocer and say, 'I'd like two eggs, please?' " "No," my mother answered, "in peacetime you can ask for seven or eight eggs, or one for however many of us there are." "And butter," I asked, "could we buy a whole half-pound of butter?" And my mother said, "You could buy two pounds of butter, or as much as you like." And I said, "So peace is when I can spread butter on both sides of a slice of bread."

LISELOTTE KLEMICH

*Born 1916; a housewife living in Dresden with
her two children when the city was destroyed in
1945; lives in Northeim, Lower Saxony.*

"From under a fallen tree, a hand in a white glove was slowly opening and closing."

In 1933, I got married and moved to Dresden. My husband was from
there. He was a lawyer and a reserve officer in the army.

People envied me for living in Dresden; it was a beautiful city. On
the day I was married, my brother took me in his arms and said,
"How I envy you because of Dresden." We called it "Florence on the
Elbe."

We felt safe. The war had been going on for five years. Rumors had
been going around that perhaps Churchill had relatives in Dresden
and that was the reason it hadn't been attacked. Gradually we also
began thinking that Dresden would remain intact because of the
wonderful art treasures and because the city itself was so beautiful.

We had an air raid shelter, but we had become very careless. Most
of the time I didn't even wake my children when there was an alarm.
But on this particular evening, when I turned on the radio—I always
turned on the radio when the sirens began wailing—I was horrified
to hear that large bomber formations were on their way and that we
were to take shelter immediately. I woke and dressed my three small
daughters and helped them into their little rucksacks containing extra
underwear. I took along a briefcase, which held a fireproof box with
family documents, all of my jewelry, and a large sum of money. We
dashed down into the shelter. Most of the others were already there.
They had looks of horror on their faces.

The shelter was very primitive. The exterior protection was a large box filled with gravel that stood directly in front of the window. We had hardly gotten into the shelter when the entire window and the box were blown into the room. This was about ten minutes after we had received the warning—the attack had begun immediately. There was one explosion after the other. This was between 10 and 11 P.M.

The people in the shelter reacted in very different ways. Some screamed every time there was a hit. Some prayed. Some sobbed. I was choked up with emotion. I kept thinking, "My poor, innocent children. They will be taken now." I kept trying to protect them. What's more, I was pregnant.

Finally it stopped and we were all still alive. I couldn't believe it, because no one had thought we could come out of that shelter alive. The air raid warden went into the house to inspect it, came back, and said that our part of the house had been most heavily damaged. The children were then taken into an apartment on the ground floor on the other side of the building. Everyone was very helpful. Then we went into our part of the house and discovered that all of the windows and curtains had been blown into the apartment. I thought it was over, but my poor Annemarie kept crying out, "They're coming back, they're coming back." She was right.

The next attack occurred at around 1:30 A.M. We ran into the shelter again. The children were at the end of their ropes; they cried and clung to me. We stood in the hallway—we couldn't get back into the shelter because the windows had been blown in. We stood crowded together. Some were sitting on the floor. My little Karin, who was five years old, began to pray very loudly, "Dear God protect us, dear God protect us." Her little voice kept getting louder and more penetrating.

And we survived this attack, too. The bombs from the second attack came much closer. Our house was struck by incendiary bombs.

We stood there in the hallway and saw the target markers in the sky. The air raid warden said, "The house will burn fast, we have to get out of here."

We went out into the front yard, but the gate was locked and we couldn't get out. The situation was becoming very dangerous. One of the women took my two oldest children to a large park that was only an eight-minute walk away. Then I took my little Karin by the hand and followed them.

When we got to the park, we couldn't even get in, because thousands of others were already looking for shelter there too. Many were lying or sitting on the ground.

My two other children weren't with me. I couldn't find them in the darkness. Karin fell asleep right away and slept and slept. A tremendous storm had come up. There was a rushing sound in the air, and trees were cracking and falling down. Only later did I realize that this was from the fire. And then something particularly horrible happened. Earlier, while we were leaving our house, a friend had gone by who had on white gloves. The children used to call her "Aunt Nietsch." And from under a fallen tree, a hand in a white glove was slowly opening and closing. No one even tried to lift up the huge tree trunk. People even sat on the tree while she was under it.

My maid said she would go and try to find my children, and after an hour and a great deal of calling she actually did find them.

The oldest of my children suffered a great deal from the experience. Whenever she heard sirens wail, she began crying or trembling or clinging to me. Annemarie says that to this day she is chilled to the bone when she hears sirens. The other children weren't affected as badly.

The fire kept burning for weeks. I wasn't there for the cleaning up of the bodies. We read about that in the newspapers. They swept the bodies together and burned them in the market place.

GÖTZ BERGANDER

Born 1927; lived in Dresden during the bombardment; is a radio journalist; makes his home in Berlin.

"A feeling of utter helplessness and terror."

There had been two American daylight attacks on Dresden, one in October 1944, one in January 1945. The latter was somewhat heavier and we knew that Dresden wasn't going to come out of it untouched. Nevertheless, we had no idea what we were in for; we didn't have the experience they had in Hamburg, Berlin, Kassel, or the Ruhrgebiet.

I got myself a grid map of Germany. You could listen in on a radio channel—we called it the flak channel but it actually came from the headquarters near Berlin—which transmitted coded air intelligence. Whenever I was home I listened to this channel and marked the flight paths on the large map which I'd covered with onionskin paper. I still have this map.

And that's how it was on the evening of February 13, which happened to be Mardi Gras. You could determine the approach of a massive raid far into central Germany, beyond Leipzig. When the alarm sounded, it was approximately 20 minutes before 10:00 P.M.

The city was already filled with refugees; everything was a dull, war gray. The train stations were bursting with people. I had already participated in some so-called refugee aid there. We received refugees from Silesia and tried to get them and their baggage out of the city as quickly as possible. They were taken to old dance halls, ballrooms, and cinemas in the suburbs, but some always remained in the city center—those who'd just arrived and had not yet been accommodated.

According to certain city documents, Dresden had approximately 640,000 inhabitants, and I'd estimate that there were perhaps a million people in the city, so there were about 300,000 refugees. There were no bunkers at all—not one public air raid shelter. At Dresden's main train station, luggage storage rooms and basements had been set up as shelters.

People thought Dresden would be spared. There were rumors that the British thought a great deal of Dresden as a cultural center. The story also went around that an aunt of Churchill's lived in Dresden, and in 1945 the rumor circulated that the Allies intended to use Dresden as their capital. Even by then, we expected partition; we thought the Russians would occupy the eastern half and the others the western half. Finally, people said, Dresden is full of hospitals.

All of this was wrong. All these claims, including the one that Dresden was protected because it was a "hospital" city, were false. Dresden was completely unprotected. The flak had been withdrawn during the winter. Half the guns were sent to the Ruhr to strengthen the air defense there, only to be lost when the Americans overran the area. It was ridiculous. The Dresden anti-aircraft troops weren't killed in Dresden, but died fighting against the Americans.

As I listened to the flak channel, I had a feeling of ever-increasing dread, but layered with excitement. You could compare it to what every soldier feels before he has to leave the trench. You're afraid, yet at the same time very excited, wondering what's going to happen. Talk about butterflies! I took my radio down to the air-raid shelter and tried to tune into the flak channel. Our shelter warden was outside.

While I was still fiddling with the radio dial he came running down into the cellar and called, "It's getting light, it's getting light, it's bright as day outside! They're coming, they're coming, the dive bombers are here!" I told him: "But that's impossible, dive bombers can't fly at night." He said: "I saw them, they came right over the Friedrichstadt hospital." After the war we found out that he had really seen Mosquitos come down with target flares. They dropped the target markers about 500 yards from where we lived, and the markers exploded in the air before they hit the ground. The so-called "Christmas trees" came down by parachute. Everything was quiet for awhile, until we heard the bombers and the first explosions.

It was as if a huge noisy conveyor belt was rolling over us, a noise punctuated with detonations and tremors. It lasted for about 25 minutes before it gradually ceased. Then there was absolute quiet.

I had tuned in to the local air raid broadcasts, and their last announcement had been, "Attention! Attention! This is your local air defense office. Bombs in the city area. Citizens, keep sand and water ready." Then it was cut off.

I went outside after this first attack because our warden told us we had to look for incendiaries. We didn't find any, but coming out of the cellar was unforgettable: the night sky was illuminated with pink and red. The houses were black silhouettes, and a red cloud of smoke hovered over everything. I left our courtyard and climbed onto the roof of the factory next door with my camera. I thought, "You have to take a picture of this."

People ran toward us totally distraught, smeared with ash, and with wet blankets wrapped around their heads. These people made it out of the burning areas without too much difficulty, because the firestorm only developed about half an hour to an hour after the first of the two night attacks. All we heard was, "Everything's gone, everything's on fire."

In the meantime, many people had gathered in our courtyard. They had all come to our house because it was still intact. Everyone talked at once until someone yelled, "They're coming back, they're coming back!" Sure enough, through the general confusion we heard the alarm sirens go off again. The alarm system in the city had ceased to function, but we could hear the sirens from the neighboring villages warning of a second attack. That's when I was overcome with panic, and I'm also speaking for the rest of my family and those who lived in our house. It was sheer panic! We thought this couldn't be possible, that they wouldn't do such a thing. They wouldn't drop more bombs on a city that was already an inferno. We were a target not even the worst shot could miss. We rushed into the cellar, and the second attack began just like the first one.

The first raid was flown by the famous 5th Bomber Group which had been specially preselected for the initial incendiary attack. The rest of the bomber groups came in for the second attack. The British really put everything they had into the air that night, though not all of it was used against Dresden. Approximately 800 planes were deployed against Dresden, and another 300 went against a refinery near Leipzig.

This attack left exhaustion and tension in its wake, a feeling of utter helplessness and terror. Since high-explosive bombs came down in our immediate vicinity, we had no idea of what it looked like outside. Neither did we hear the slapping sound of incendiaries. There was an indescribable roar in the air: the fire. The thundering fire reminded me of the biblical catastrophes I had heard about in my education in the humanities. I was aghast. I can't describe seeing this city burn in any other way. The color had changed as well. It was no longer pinkish-red. The fire had become a furious white and yellow, and the sky was just one massive mountain of cloud. The blaze roared, with intermittent blasts of either delayed-action bombs or unexploded bombs which were engulfed by the flames.

In the morning I turned on my radio and listened to the BBC. On the seven o'clock news, the BBC reported: "Last night, Dresden, one of the few German cities thus far to be spared, was attacked by RAF bombers with great success."

Later, people arrived from the inner city asking if we still had water. We said yes and opened the hydrants. Several of them settled into our house, but many others told us, "Out, out, get out of the city. Get away from here," and went on. Some were speechless with horror. They only said, "My home and everything in it are gone."

Since the factory supplied its own power and water, it could be kept running. My father, who was the manager, had to decide whether work should continue. We produced yeast for baked goods. My father said that food was important, so we'd have to keep operating. And the workers showed up too. I don't know if anyone can work like the Germans. It was amazing. Some even came on their bicycles between the two night raids. I still remember one of them pedalling up and my father asking him, "What are you doing here?" And he replied, "I just had to see if the shop's still in one piece."

The city was absolutely quiet. The sound of the fires had died out. The rising smoke created a dirty, gray pall which hung over the entire city. The wind had calmed, but a slight breeze was blowing westward, away from us. That's how, standing in the courtyard, I suddenly thought I could hear sirens again. And sure enough, there they were. I shouted, and by then we could already hear the distant whine of engines. We rushed down into the cellar. The roar of the engines grew louder and louder, and the daylight attack began. This was the American 8th Air Force, and their attack came right down on our heads.

Normally, there were only 20 to 25 of us down in the cellar. But now, with many people off the street, including those who'd stopped over at our house, there were about 100 of us. Nevertheless, no one panicked—we were too numb and demoralized from the night before. We just sat there. The attack rolled closer, and then a bomb hit. It was like a bowling ball that bounced, or jumped perhaps, and at that moment the lights went out. The whole basement filled with dust. When the bomb carpet reached us, I crouched in a squatting position, my head between my legs. The air pressure was immense, but only for a moment. The rubber seals on the windows and the steel doors probably helped to absorb some of the impact. Someone screamed, and then it was quiet. Then a voice shouted, "It's all right, nothing's happened." It was the shelter warden.

Someone turned on a flashlight. We could see again, and that meant a lot. If it had remained dark, I don't know if the people wouldn't have jumped up and screamed to get out. However, after this flashlight went on everyone relaxed, and in spite of the loud crash that made me think the whole house was caving in on top of us, a loud voice shouted, "Calm down, calm down, nothing's happened." Although the drone of the bombers faded away, we heard another load of bombs explode in the distance. The entire episode lasted about 15 minutes.

We listened for it to become quiet again. The deathly silence that ensued was a stark contrast to the previous minutes. Our house was still standing, a true miracle. There were no more windows and the entire roof had been torn off and strewn about the street. In front of the house there was such an enormous crater that I thought, my God, it's not even 20 yards away, how did this house ever make it through as well as it did?

After a while, we began to clear the rubble out of our apartment. It was one big junk pile. We were so preoccupied with ourselves and the thought that we might be the next to go up in flames, it never occurred to us to go immediately into the city to help dig people out. Compared to those people still trapped in their cellars twelve hours after the night raids, waiting for someone to get them out, our problems were laughable.

PART III

DEFEAT
AND
CRIMES

CHAPTER 9

The Reich Starts Shrinking

In January 1941, the Wehrmacht had dispatched a task force of two understrength divisions to North Africa. Its commander, General Erwin Rommel, was expected to do no more than stave off disaster. Instead, for the next two years the tide of war swept back and forth across the desert. Rommel's tactical skills earned the respect and admiration of all who fought against him. But the movement of men and supplies to North Africa was consistently obstructed by the British-held island of Malta. Italian attempts to neutralize the island from the air failed, as did the best efforts of the Luftwaffe.

Meanwhile, Allied troops and equipment continued to pour into Egypt around the Cape of Good Hope. On May 26, 1942, the Africa Corps began its final offensive. Lack of supplies and stiffening British resistance brought Rommel to a halt in front of El Alamein. On October 23, British general Bernard Montgomery launched his counterattack. In defiance of an order by the Führer to hold El Alamein at all costs, Rommel ordered a general retreat on November 4.

Three days later, an Anglo-American expeditionary force landed in French North Africa. Resources long denied to Rommel to reinforce victory suddenly became available to stave off defeat. But the contest of rapier and broadsword could have only one ending. On May 13, 1943, a quarter-million German and Italian soldiers marched into Allied captivity.

In July, British and American troops landed on the island of

Sicily—the first direct thrust into what Winston Churchill called "the soft underbelly" of the Axis. On July 25, a royalist putsch overthrew Mussolini and took Italy out of the war. Hitler reacted by ordering the occupation of his one-time ally. For the next two years, German forces under the overall command of Luftwaffe Marshal "Smiling Albert" Kesselring conducted a brilliant fighting retreat up the peninsula, pinning down Allied troops from five continents and fifty peoples. Salerno, Anzio, Cassino—epics of heroism, half-forgotten now, filled the military cemeteries but could not decide the war in the West. That was the function of still another set of landings, this time in France.

Within weeks after D-Day, the Germans in Normandy decided their new enemies were less formidable soldiers than the Russians. British and American commanders were less flexible, less willing to take risks, than their German counterparts. But materiel was another story. The Allies dominated the skies and thereby controlled the campaign. Not only were their fighter-bombers everywhere, it sometimes seemed every infantryman had his own radio to call for air support. And if Allied tanks were individually inferior to the Wehrmacht's Tigers and Panthers, there seemed to be an endless supply of them.

On June 25, American troops broke the German lines at St. Lô, trapping 150,000 Germans in the Falaise Pocket. Only 20,000 escaped as the Allies drove toward Paris and Antwerp. Other French and American troops landed on the southern coast of France. By September, German resistance in France was broken. More than 2,000 tanks and assault guns had been lost. Wehrmacht fuel reserves were down to 327,000 tons. Yet with the war on their doorsteps, the Germans rallied. Divisions reformed and re-equipped while Allied generals debated strategy and quarreled over logistics. An Allied airborne attack into Holland was given a bloody nose at Arnhem. U.S. infantrymen walked into a meatgrinder in the Hürtgen Forest. By the end of November, Allied hopes for victory in 1944 had bogged down in the snow and mud.

Then Hitler intervened once more. The Führer ordered the concentration of Germany's entire strategic reserve opposite the Ardennes Forest. A breakthrough might lead to the capture of the port of

Antwerp. It might even encourage the western Allies to consider a separate peace. But after initial successes, German spearheads were slowed, then stopped, by Americans who showed that they could fight and win without aircraft grounded in the bitter December weather. Once the skies cleared, the outcome was no longer in doubt. Western front commander Field Marshal Gerd von Rundstedt spoke of "a second Stalingrad." The loss of 90,000 men and hundreds of irreplaceable tanks gave weight to his words. No less significant was the sacrifice of over 1,000 aircraft, and dozens of the Luftwaffe's best pilots, in a last, futile challenge to Allied dominance of the air.

In the aftermath of Stalingrad, the Germans could count gains as well as losses on the Russian front. The 6th Army was gone. But the Caucasus had been successfully evacuated. A dozen badly worn Panzer divisions had once again taken the measure of the best the Russians could throw at them in the open field. A major German attack now would not bring final victory. It might, however, buy time, and give the Wehrmacht breathing space to cope with the developing threat in the West.

The most favorable site for such an attack was the Russian salient around the city of Kursk. The army General Staff prepared plans for a two-pronged attack on the salient's base. Hitler was less than pleased. Better than his generals, he realized that 1943 was not 1941. But the Führer only postponed the operation, and that gave the Russians time to reinforce their positions. On July 5, 1943, the panzers rolled forward into a buzz saw.

Kursk, the death-ride of the panzer divisions, also marked a moral turning point. Henceforth the scale of the fighting challenged the imagination. Whole divisions vanished without a trace. Individual acts, individual decisions became lost in a collective experience that can be analyzed but remains difficult to assimilate. And yet for the Germans who fought on the Eastern front, it was increasingly the individual who mattered. After Stalingrad, the Wehrmacht was no longer able to match its Russian enemies in materiel. Spirit and skill became ever more important. And these depended on individual men. As the Russo-German war entered its final phase, the Wehrmacht in the East evolved more and more into a military community, a *Gemeinschaft* ruled by its own dynamics. The *Landser* in Russia were indifferent alike to party slogans and patriotic appeals. The "German mission" had been reduced to survival in the face of an enemy determined to exact retribution for a devastated country.

"Keep the Russians out" was the closest thing to a watchword remaining to the men who held the line. They fought because they saw no choice. And if they gave their sacrifices a higher meaning, they did so in terms of a homeland that became more a dream than a reality—not the bombed-out cities, the hungry children, and the exhausted women of 1944, but images of peacetime preserved on worn photographs and in fading memories.

For the remainder of 1943, the Wehrmacht fought desperately to prevent a Soviet breakthrough. In the south, Manstein traded space for time, bloodying the Russians in a series of tactically brilliant ripostes. But the German front moved steadily backwards. Earlier the Red Army was able to mount no more than one grand offensive at a time. Now it struck hammer blows everywhere. In March 1944, three army groups drove into the Ukraine, cutting off and surrounding most of the German 1st Panzer Army. It escaped as a "traveling pocket," fighting its way westward in the pattern of a Gothic migration with the tanks and infantry on the perimeter, wounded men and soft-skinned vehicles at the center. Hitler responded by relieving Manstein of his command.

By the end of April 1944, the Russian armies in the south had advanced almost 350 miles closer to the Reich. Their success put the Germans in north and central Russia in a gigantic salient. Since Hitler was still unwilling to shorten the front, his commanders had virtually no mobile reserves. On the third anniversary of the invasion of Russia, the *Landser* paid the price. Two hundred divisions supported by 6,000 tanks, 45,000 guns and mortars, and 7,000 planes, eviscerated Army Group Center in a week. The German front did not collapse; it disappeared. By July 3, the Russians had crossed the prewar frontier into Poland—200 miles from their lines of departure. Twenty-eight German divisions, 350,000 men, were gone: twice the losses of Stalingrad. Not until autumn did the Soviet offensive stop at the borders of East Prussia and the gates of Warsaw. And then the halt owed as much to lack of supplies, and to Stalin's desire to see the independent Polish resistance crushed in a futile uprising, as to a

German defense conducted with the fury of despair, but without corresponding resources.

GERHARD BECK

Born 1920; tail gunner on a Stuka Aircraft; shot down in Africa; severely wounded; worked as a district attorney after the war and resides in Constance, Wuertemberg.

"To be eaten by vultures was too much."

It was spring of 1942 in North Africa. At the time, there was a lot of fighting around the Libyan port city of Tobruk. Early on the morning of June 4, 1942, my Stuka unit received orders to attack the enemy.

We flew fairly high. I was a rear gunner, sitting behind the pilot. We reached Bir Hakeim and dropped our bombs in the usual dive maneuver, a routine mission. We had already begun to gain altitude when we picked up a radio message from one of our pilots: "*Achtung* Stukas, Indians behind you!" "Indians" was our code word for enemy planes.

The group commander gave the order to dive. At least this maneuver gave us a chance of escaping the enemy fighters. All of a sudden, an enemy plane approached us diagonally from above. It opened fire on the Stuka in the rear of our formation. The gunner fired back, but only for a second. Then his machine gun was silent. The left wing dropped. The plane hit the ground, blew up, and disappeared in a thick, dirty red cloud of fire. The enemy plane zoomed away over our heads and came back for another run. This time my plane was the target.

Our situation was as good as hopeless, but I kept firing. Suddenly, I saw the enemy fighter's muzzle flash. At the same moment there was a blow right in front of my face that ripped the machine gun out of my hand and threw me back in my seat. Again, I heard the enemy plane roar up and away.

It came back for another attack. I looked up, heard shots, and then—in the flash of a second, before I felt a thing—I saw a hole in the pane of reinforced glass in front of me. Only then did I feel a violent blow on my right shoulder. I was hit!

Now it was a matter of saving our lives. Our plane was badly damaged and could begin to burn any moment, so we landed in the desert. The plane had barely rolled to a stop when the pilot opened his cabin door, jumped out, and ran. I looked up and saw the enemy fighter diving toward our plane. It was an execution. I couldn't see the pilot's face as he opened fire. There was a horrible blow to my left calf; it felt as though my leg had been ripped off. The plane roared over us and disappeared. I remember trying to get out of the plane, falling to the ground, and hobbling a few steps. Then, someone grabbed my arm and quickly dragged me away. It was my pilot.

I was hardly out of the danger zone when I collapsed. I told the pilot that he would have to go get help. He set off and was soon out of sight.

The sun gradually rose higher. As time went by, its rays became more and more piercing. There was no shade to be found. As the sun reached its zenith, I wanted to take another tiny sip of water, but the canteen was empty.

But what proved the worst torture was something I hadn't thought of: the flies. Attracted by the smell of my bloody wounds, they came. African flies are different from European ones. They don't fly away when you swat them. At most they crawl a little bit further, or simply allow themselves to be squashed. And they kept coming.

To protect myself from the sun, I spread a handkerchief over my face. There was blood on it from my wounds. The flies crawled underneath it, into my eyes, my nose, and my mouth, wherever they found a trace of moisture. Clumps of flies were in and around my shoulder wound. I had long since given up trying to shoo them away, even though the feeling of these flies crawling all over me was sickening. So I gathered all the strength I had left, gritted my teeth, and managed to prop myself up a bit. I looked around; there was nothing to see but the wreck of the plane and a few tracks in the sand.

It got dark very quickly, and downright cool at the same time. A clear, starry sky unfolded above me. I saw the constellations, Orion and the Big Dipper. Hours passed, and it became colder and colder. I began to shiver uncontrollably. I thought of my dead mother, and of my father; I didn't want to give up.

Even the longest night somehow passes. The next day I was depressed and tired. The heat beat down intensely. I had shut my eyes, but was still awake when I felt something move against my right leg. I jerked my leg away and looked up. I saw a large vulture hopping backwards, wings flapping clumsily. There were two or three more behind him. Apparently, they had sat there a long time until the most daring of them had hopped up to see if I was in a proper state for consumption. Now he squatted about two steps away from me, dirty-white wings folded, bare neck stretched forward, crooked beak half open, staring at me with his black eyes: the picture of greed personified. By then I had figured out that I would probably die of thirst, but to be eaten by vultures was too much.

I pulled out my pistol, which was rather difficult since I was lying on top of it. The vulture just stood there and stared at me the whole time without moving. I took a breath, aimed at the vulture, pulled the trigger, and instantly saw a red spot on the yellowish-brown feathers of its breast. It fell over, and I used the rest of my bullets on the other vultures. Except for one. I wanted to save one shot as a reserve.

The battle against the vultures must have taken a lot out of me, because after that I passed out. In any case, I was startled awake by the sound of a motor. And suddenly, a plane appeared over a sand dune like a ghost; it was a Fieseler Storch.

It was a Red Cross plane tasked with flying over the stretch of ground the Stukas had flown over the day before, the area from where fewer than half of them had returned. Two men got out of the plane and came to me, the pilot and the observer, both of them medics. But they didn't help me right away; they just stood there and stared. Later, they described the situation: "The body that lay before us was barely human. The face was distorted with blisters, shreds of skin, and blood. The hands were torn, burnt, and bloody. The right shoulder was covered with blood and clumps of flies, and the calf, shredded flesh, blood, with flies, flies, and more flies." I was not taken to our airstrip, but flown back to the main hospital at Derna.

JOHANNES STEINHOFF*

"Hitler was totally exhausted."

Our fighter group was transferred to East Prussia in the early summer of 1941. The offensive against the Soviet Union began on June 22. Operation Barbarossa was initiated—the beginning of the end. In the tremendous summer heat, the tank spearheads made their way in a fanned-out formation into a seemingly infinite area. We were employed like a fire brigade to fill the holes where the front line had been broken. We were sent to the central sector near Smolensk and Moscow; we were in the north near Leningrad, in the south on the Crimea. Nevertheless, fighting in Russia was almost a piece of cake for us fighter pilots. The outdated Russian planes were very much inferior to our own.

Hitler's plan to take Moscow before the Russian soil turned to mud and before the severe winter had failed, and the Germans were doomed. My fighter group had no alternative but to destroy the planes and equipment we had on the ground, because our motors would not start at 55 degrees below zero. We continued fighting as an infantry unit. We had to stop the attacking Soviet troops in man-to-man combat. Our losses were severe, because we were not trained as footsoldiers. Our army had no winter uniforms, and at times the temperature fell to −67 degrees Fahrenheit. I had seen pictures portraying the misery and distress of Napoleon's troops retreating across the Beresina River. What the German army had to endure was not much different.

For the first time, people began openly to doubt Hitler was the military genius he was proclaimed to be. What most upset us was the awareness that the leading generals had obviously failed to have any influence on Hitler whatsoever, even though they must have known

* Biography on page 7.

they were dealing with a total military amateur. Had they already become opportunists themselves? Or at a point when something still could have been salvaged, did they perhaps simply lack the courage—the courage responsible military leaders should have—to stand up for their own convictions?

In autumn 1942 I was called back to the Führer's headquarters in East Prussia to receive a medal. The Hitler I saw was confident and high-spirited. With the resonance of the greatest commander-in-chief who had ever lived, he declared, "Now I have their oil!" (I had just come from Maikop, where the Soviets had destroyed the German capacity to produce oil.) "Next I am going to cross the Caucasus and press on to Baku—and the Caspian Sea is not far from there. . . ."

I returned to the front only a few days later to find that my fighter group had been relocated to an air field along the great bend of the Don River. I was met by the adjutant, who had remained behind. "We've got to hurry!" he said. "There's heavy fighting up the line! Our army has reached the Volga River near Stalingrad!"

From October 1942 to the beginning of February 1943, I was to experience the tragedy of Stalingrad from a bird's eye view. Winter came early. I was shot down and landed among the ruins in the northern part of the city. A few days later I was hit again by anti-aircraft artillery while chasing Russian fighters, and was forced to make a belly landing in a huge snow drift. Both times I got out safely.

I will never forget what I saw happen in Stalingrad. The field marshals washed their hands of that tragedy. But the series of tragedies during the Second World War did not end in Stalingrad. I was sent to Africa to help to extinguish the next fire. I was shot down on my very first mission. After Russia, I guess I was a bit rusty when it came to fighting the Americans again.

We were thrown out of Africa on May 8, 1943. I met with my wing, or what was left of it, in Trapani in Sicily. We got new planes, new jeeps, new radio cars, and away we went on our next mission.

Our first encounter with four-engine bombers ended in disaster. We met a formation flying in from North Africa in low-level flight between Sardinia and Sicily. I was the only one who scored a hit. Later that evening a telegram arrived from Göring: "I regard the fighter pilots in the South only with contempt. Each of the participating units in today's disaster is to send one pilot to appear before a court-martial on grounds of cowardice in the face of the enemy."

In each case, it was the respective squadron commander who voluntarily stepped forward in response to Göring's demands. The Commanding General of Fighter Pilots, General Galland, fortunately succeeded in quashing the proceedings.

Our fight against the four-engine bombers was part of a vain attempt to keep the Allies from landing at Salerno, and later at Anzio. We had already arrived in the Po Valley by the fall of 1943. Our daily encounters with the armada of Fortresses and Liberators that came from the Adriatic Sea or over the Balkans were murderous. Our losses were high.

The Allies' proclamation of unconditional surrender made it easy for Nazi propaganda to motivate the soldier to carry on to the end. Rumors about "wonder weapons"—long-range rockets and jet aircraft—were making the rounds.

Ten days after the attempt on Hitler's life in 1944, I was once again ordered to the Führer's headquarters in East Prussia. This time I was to receive the Swords to the Oak Leaf Cluster of the Knight's Cross I already had. Before departing for Berlin, I saw Colonel von Maltzan, a man I admired and who had commanded the German fighters in Italy. His closest relatives had already been thrown into prison. His remarks revealed his bitterness: "Now that the assassination attempt has failed, the outcome of all of this is going to be horrible!"

Galland had failed in his attempt to convince Hitler that the new jet fighter, the Me-262, was essential for our air defense. He asked me to try to persuade Hitler to put this superior aircraft into action against the increasingly destructive bombing attacks. Until that time, Hitler had been strictly against this idea. And Göring, who played the role of Hitler's court jester, had no opinion on this. I met with Hitler in the *Wolfschanze*. He was totally exhausted. He had become an old man. His voice had a monotonous tone to it. But when I changed the subject of conversation to the new jet fighters, he suddenly reverted to his familiar bombastic tone. He insisted that what I was asking was nonsense. This plane was not a fighter, and we should completely forget about it, and so on. Toward the end of such conversations, you could be sure Hitler was going to let you in on "the big things that are yet to come!" And so he said, "I'm going to mobilize the German people in a way the world has never seen before!" The *Volkssturm,* composed of teenagers and men over 60, was created not much later. We referred to the *Volkssturm* as the "casserole"—old meat and green vegetables.

As part of the Luftwaffe's "fire brigade," I was naturally sent to the next fire—the Allied invasion of France. Our showing was brief, but very bloody. Back home, I had the opportunity to meet with Göring once again.

In October 1944, he called for all decorated Luftwaffe officers to meet in Berlin. There were so many Knight's Crosses in the room, it literally sparkled. Göring walked in. He said that he wanted the meeting to be an open discussion. After quite a bit of fruitless debate, the "ideologists" amongst us did actually go so far as to formulate a Creed or Oath for the Luftwaffe: "We are loyal to the Führer," etc., etc.

After the meeting, Galland said he had other plans for me. I was to set up the first jet fighter wing in the German Luftwaffe, certainly a challenge for any young man. But once again, my mission was cut short. Shortly before Christmas, while checking out various air bases in the west, I was simply dismissed from my new position without any further orders or explanation.

HANS-JÜRGEN BRANDT

Born 1919; military surgeon during World War II in North Africa and France; continued to work as a physician after the war; makes his home in Berlin.

"Once we operated for 72 hours in a row."

A tent hospital in Africa had limited means at its disposal, and was often under fire. We were always getting people fresh from the front, some in hopeless condition. As a doctor, you sometimes reached the point of despair.

Especially at El Alamein, I really got to know what triage means. You have to picture it. We had three main dressing stations in El Alamein, and each admitted incoming wounded eight hours a day. The senior surgeons took care of admittance and sorted out the patients. They operated for eight hours, and afterwards voluntarily treated those who had been set aside in triage—for example, stomach wounds. Those with stomach wounds, for the most part, didn't have any chance of survival. Thus they weren't operated on at all; they were just set aside.

Once we operated for 72 hours in a row. How our feet ached! Two doctors collapsed. It was a steady flow of patients; one was treated after the other. Naturally you're exhausted, you're dead tired. And what do you do when, on top of everything else, bullets pass right through the tent? The senior doctor ordered me to lie down. I said, "I'm not the patient." We looked at each other, remained on our feet, and continued with surgery. I would say that what could be done was done, but God, the conditions were primitive! One can't forget what a rare commodity water was in the African desert. The best water was used for infusions. Then it was used to wash and sterilize, then to wash off the operating table, and finally for the floors. It was slowly so degraded that by then it wasn't even water anymore.

KARL SCHULZE*

"Do whatever you want with me."

The political turnover in Italy occurred in the summer of 1943. Mussolini no longer had a majority in the Supreme Fascist Council and was voted out. He went to the King to notify him of these developments. Leaving the palace, he was arrested and disappeared. The King and Marshal Badoglio fled to the Allies.

The Gran Sasso is the highest mountain in the Appennines at 9,000 feet, and there is a hotel at the top. On the pretext of seeing whether this hotel could serve as a recuperation center for paratroops, General Student sent someone to the Gran Sasso. As it turned out, the whole place was sealed off hermetically, which, in turn, led to the assumption that Mussolini was being held there.

General Student had orders from Hitler to free the Duce as soon as he was found, because it was feared that he would be handed over to the approaching Allies. This was a Wehrmacht operation. Otto Skorzeny, already well-known for his commando raids, was allowed to participate although he belonged to the Waffen-SS. There were two possibilities. One was to reach the Gran Sasso overland and take it in mountain-troop fashion. But this would have made a surprise attack impossible. So the second option was chosen. Commandos were to land in gliders right at the hotel, and simultaneously the valley cable car station was to be taken by ground troops to secure the retreat. Mussolini was to leave the Gran Sasso by air, though it was doubtful, judging from the aerial photographs, if this would be possible.

---

* Biography on page 87.

I had orders to reach the valley station by land with my company. We were to take the station at precisely 2:00 P.M., and then establish communications with the part of the battalion that was to land on the mountain top. For support I had been given a tank destroyer company. As we set off on our march, another company of our battalion, which had been disarming Italian army units, joined us. So we were two companies reinforced by tank destroyers and elements of our heavy weapons company.

The plan was put into effect. Cargo gliders which had been towed by bombers landed at the top of the mountain, right in front of the hotel. There were nine or ten paratroopers to a glider. We expected stiff resistance because we knew there had to be a strong force of guards up there.

We—the ground troops—met our first resistance at a roadblock not far from the valley station. This was quickly overcome. Then our motorcycle platoon occupied the cable car station in a surprise attack. According to the plan, the landings and the occupation of the valley station were to take place simultaneously, at 2:00 P.M. And what so seldom happens in war came about: both objectives were reached as planned and precisely on time. We were at the station shortly before two o'clock, and were keeping an anxious lookout for the gliders. They arrived right on the dot, detaching from the tow lines at exactly 2:00 P.M. We had been lucky. The cable car was started up immediately, and we were up on the mountain about a half an hour later.

Meanwhile, the gliders were approaching the mountain top. Then to the horror of my friend who was watching, Skorzeny's glider fell away from the group and dived straight at the hotel. What you have to know is that, with these gliders, we could dive at a target and land at the last instant with the aid of a brake parachute. He pulled it off, but it was very touchy. At this point, there was only one glider landing at a place guarded by 500 hand-picked men. But the surprise effect paralyzed the Italians. Also, they didn't recognize our uniforms and didn't realize, at least at first, that we were German. Not a shot was fired, and we didn't lose a man. One glider had to crash land, but there were only a few broken bones.

After coming up on the cable car, we went straight to the hotel. We were in the lobby when Skorzeny and the Duce came toward us. Mussolini didn't make the impression on us that we were used to from the newsreels, where we had seen him as an active, sparkling, energetic person. We could not believe that this was Mussolini—this sick-looking, unshaven, aging man in a dark coat, looking at us apathetically. We didn't feel that he saw his liberation as any kind of climax. Somebody said to him, "Duce, this is a truly historic moment." With an apathetic gesture, Mussolini replied, "Do whatever you want with me." It wasn't a happy occasion for him. He just let everything happen.

Meanwhile, Captain Gerlach had landed a Fieseler Storch at the mountain top. Against Gerlach's advice, Skorzeny squeezed himself into the plane along with the Duce, and thus put the pilot into a very difficult position. The light plane was now hopelessly overloaded, especially at an altitude of 9,000 feet. They got off the ground thanks to a brilliant feat of flying, even to us laymen. Gerlach had landed on a rock-strewn patch of ground and had asked us to clear away some of the larger debris to make a small airstrip. Taking off was all the more difficult because the runway sloped downward and the plane would have tail wind. At his suggestion, a large group of us held onto the plane until he had it at full throttle. At his signal we all let go, and he started as if from a catapult, roaring over the rocks and, to our horror, disappearing over the cliff. But a short while later, the plane lumbered back into view like a tired crow and flew off in the direction of Rome.

BARTHEL KUCKERTZ

Born 1922; served as a paratrooper at Monte Cassino in Italy; joined the postwar army as a master sergeant; lives near Aachen.

"We will never get out of here alive!"

We were in the lowlands of southern Italy, marching through rain and mud. On February 26–27, 1944, we reached our goal near Cassino, although we had no idea what was in store for us. We had already gotten used to quite a bit—we had been in Russia in 1942–43, and that had been extremely difficult. We were there until the collapse of the central sector, Stalingrad, and afterwards. Then the 3rd Paratroop Regiment was flown to Italy, with stops on the way in Rome and Naples, and continued on along the Mediterranean coast in the direction of Sicily. There we were air-dropped onto the plains and fought until the evacuation.

We had many people on the inactive list, from malaria and fevers—all the after-effects of Sicily. We were thrown from one position to the next, from east to west and back again. Allied troops landed near Taranto, and we had to move in that direction. A short time later the Allies landed near Salerno. We experienced heavy fighting near Naples, and rear-guard actions of every sort.

We ended up at Cassino at the end of February 1944. On March 15, at around 8:30 A.M., the inferno of the Allied bombing of Cassino began. When the first bombs fell, I grabbed my things and ran across the street into our meat cellar. What happened then was something we could not see, something that is very difficult to describe. Continual droning, the strike of bombs, and hits in the immediate vicinity made me think, "We will never get out of here alive!" It is impossible to express what went through our minds. Fear was written all over our faces.

Because the city of Cassino has an entire network of subterranean sewers and waterways, people who didn't want to or who couldn't leave the city sought shelter in these tunnels. Most civilians had been evacuated a long time ago. Mostly it was old people, women, and children, who were near starvation in the sewers. We didn't have orders to drive these people off, and we were not able to care for them with the means we had available. It was sheer misery! There were corpses wrapped in sheets piled meter-high in individual niches. Most of the living were sick with rashes all over their bodies. Children with sunken eyes begged us for something to eat. We left bread and fruit in the entryways; we were afraid to go into these holes in the ground. We saw later that the carpet bombing had reduced the entire city to rubble.

Every day, the enemy tried repeatedly to break into our positions, but he wasn't very successful. Both sides observed ceasefires in order to recover the dead and the wounded, and to have time to bury the dead. A seriously wounded comrade of ours was taken on a stretcher by captured British soldiers to their lines where he was cared for. Only at night were we able to receive ammunition and food. We always lacked everything. The British, the Canadians, the Gurkhas, the Indians, and the Moroccans were all very determined enemies.

Then starting on May 17, battles took place on the slopes and rocks near the abbey, near the so-called nun's cloister, that could have hardly been more grisly. We fought hand to hand with Polish soldiers; at times, with knives among the rocks.

RICHARD BLINZIG*

"We prevented the destruction of the café at the last minute!"

It was in the Spring of 1944. Four of us were stationed as artillery observers at a strong point in a small Brittany port. The "Nissen Hut Café" was located near the base on the harbor road. It got its name

---

* Biography on page 166.

because it was a shack with corrugated iron walls. It was famous throughout the area not only because the proprietress offered soldiers good food and drink at very low prices, but also because she had two very attractive daughters—Jacqueline who was eighteen and Mimi who was twenty. It was no wonder that the café was frequented daily by the German Wehrmacht!

One fine day, it was probably April or May of 1944, the German troops—except for the four of us—were replaced by Russians of the pro-German "Vlassov army." The Russians settled in, and on the very first evening the Russian commander visited the "Nissen Hut Café" with his aide. He found the cuisine, the wine, and, above all, Madame's daughters exquisite. When he got up to go, full of sweet wine, he gruffly demanded that Mimi come with him. Well, the good Mimi immediately refused. The commander was seized by a holy Russian fury. He grabbed the screaming Mimi, intending to carry her off. A great tumult ensued. The German soldiers jumped the Russian commander and his aide who'd rushed to help him. They tore Mimi away from him, beat up the two Russians, and kicked them out the door. The commander and his aide picked themselves up with effort, brushed themselves off, cursed the Germans and the French women in Russian, and, with difficulty, staggered back up to the strong point and—sounded the alarm! The commander had all three of his 5-centimeter anti-tank guns aimed at the "Nissen Hut Café" and was about to blow the place away! We four Germans had "witnessed" the whole thing and had already phoned the regimental commander and the division, and thus prevented the destruction of the café at the last minute!

ROBERT VOGT

*Born 1924; an infantryman when the Allies
landed in Normandy; later became a salesman; makes his home in Zweibrücken, Saarland.*

"Ships as far as the eye could see, and I thought, 'Oh God, we're finished!' "

Before June 6, 1944, the day of the D-Day landings, we were directly
on the coast near Arromanches, planting "Rommel Asparagus." We
did all of this at low tide when the sea retreated for several miles. We
put in a wooden beam and then, at a distance of, I'd say, five yards,
another beam. On top of these, we attached a third beam with
clamps—all of it done by hand—and secured more clamps. We
attached land mines to the tips of the beams, all such that at high tide,
the mines were so close to the water surface that even a flat-bottomed
boat would touch them and be destroyed.

All this construction went on under great pressure because there
were virtually no bunkers at our location, only dugouts. This was the
time when Field Marshal Rommel said the famous words, "You must
stop them here on the first day. If you don't stop them here, it's
over."

We worked in shifts around the clock. I caught some shut-eye that
night. We had built two- and three-story bunk beds in a farmhouse
about 500 yards from the beach. It must have been around 2:30 A.M.
when I jumped out of bed at the sound of a huge crash. At first I had
absolutely no idea what was going on. Of course we had been
expecting something, but we didn't have a clue as to where and when.
We didn't know that this was the invasion. In the distance, we heard
bomb carpets falling all along the coast and in the rear areas. There

were intermittent pauses which lasted anywhere from half an hour to an hour, but the area we were in was a terrible mess. All at once we were under alarm condition three, the highest level. By then, we guessed it must be the invasion, but since it was still dark outside and we couldn't see any ships or anything, we still weren't sure.

In the morning, my platoon leader told me to go to the coast to try and make contact with the other platoons in our company. On the way, I ran into a bomber attack, but I managed to get to our position on the Arromanches cliffs. Guns and machine guns were already firing. Then a voice called, "Enemy landing boats approaching!" I had a good view from the top of the cliffs and looked out at the ocean. What I saw scared the devil out of me. Even though the weather was so bad, we could see a huge number of ships. Ships as far as the eye could see, an entire fleet, and I thought, "Oh God, we're finished! We're done for now!"

During the following days, we were stuck in foxholes along the front. And when these foxholes were shot up—if the Americans were stalled for long enough—other troops came and we were pulled out again.

I last saw action on July 16, 1944. We only had infantry weapons; we didn't even have a bazooka. And to top it off, we were even short of small-arms ammo. The supply columns had not taken the Allies' total air superiority into account. They got caught in heavy fire and were terribly shot up, so we didn't get any supplies. Our company commander sent several men to the shot-up supply units at night to pick up ammunition and bring it back to us at the front. And the Americans were right. They dropped leaflets in German which read, "Attacked from the front, Cut off from behind, Written off by Hitler."

Every day we told ourselves, "Now finally, the Luftwaffe squadrons are going to come and whip them good." They didn't come. I didn't see a single German tank the entire time, either. We only had some light machine guns and the ammunition we had scrounged up, no heavy weapons or anything else. Well, we dug ourselves in at the edge of some woods, and when the Yanks came over the next hedgerow, we shot at them with our machine guns, trying to use our ammunition sparingly. After two or three bursts it usually got quiet, but it didn't take long until mortar and artillery fire set in. What was really bad were the heavy battleship guns. And then came the Marauders, the Lightnings, and the Thunderbolts—that was the worst.

I think we were used as cannon fodder. You know, it was the fifth year of the war, and we just didn't have the means. The Allies could afford to spare their troops, what with their superiority in equipment. They said, "Why should we sacrifice a single GI against German infantry fire; the Germans outdo us there anyway. No, we'll just carpet-bomb them. We'll just use our fliers to drop the sky on their heads. We'll just make use of our superior artillery."

At the time, we had to rely on little apple trees for cover. I could still hug those trees today. The pilots flew 100 feet over our heads and if they saw anything, they didn't only drop bombs, they sent their Thunderbolts to fire rockets at us. It was pretty bad. We made use of every blade of grass and every little tree when we heard the planes coming.

I was scared stiff the entire time, but at the same time, I was incredibly angry that we were even being used against such odds. Still, we wanted to hold the front under any circumstances, and hoped from day to day that the German tanks would finally show up, that some artillery would arrive, and, above all, that the German Luftwaffe would fly in. One single time I saw two German fighter planes, and that was at Arromanches on the morning of June 6. Two Messerschmitts. When we saw them, we all shouted hurrah, but they were the only ones. That was it. It was so terribly depressing.

On the morning of June 16, between 11:00 and 11:30, we came under heavy machine gun fire. And then the monsters came: tanks. They approached our positions through the brush and fired at us. At this point we were in a large meadow surrounded by hedges. I would guess that the tanks were about 250 yards away. I counted 15 of them. They didn't come directly at us. They stopped, practically taunting us. And whenever they spotted any of us, they let loose a barrage of shells. It was horrible.

I looked right and I looked left, and I told myself that shooting any more with a machine gun was pointless. We didn't have any bazookas. They must have thought we did though, otherwise they would have advanced more quickly. As it was, they stopped at a distance slightly out of bazooka range. Then they came forward very slowly. We got tank fright and I saw German *Landser* moving back to my left and right. My comrades and I took off too. We only took our weapons along with us. We left all of our personal belongings—there wasn't much—back in the foxholes.

About 400 yards from the positions we had just left, we came upon a great miracle: an 88mm ack-ack gun. We reported to the commanding officer that tanks were coming up. At nineteen, I was one of the oldest. The officer pulled out his machine pistol and said, "If you don't advance and reinforce our position in a half-circle of at least 200 yards, I'll shoot you!" To say the least, we suddenly got our courage back!

I had advanced about 150 yards when I came under heavy fire again. I hit the dirt behind a tree and then, oh God, I heard our flak gun shooting. I can't tell you what a tremendous lift that gave me! The next moment I saw a tank coming toward me, crushing the shrubbery in its path, and I did exactly what I shouldn't have done: I jumped up and ran away because I thought it was going to crush me flat. I hadn't gone three or four steps when I was hit above the left knee with what felt like a sledgehammer. It hurt, and then again, it didn't. I tried to stand up two or three times, but my leg just wouldn't participate. Uh-oh, I thought, now they've got you. And then my only thought was the hope that I wouldn't be run over by that tank.

Later I heard that the attack was stopped by the German flak gun, and that the Americans drew back again. The unwounded German soldiers were able to hold the position for a few more days.

FRANZ VEITSMEIER

*Born in 1907 in Austria; served in Normandy
as a medical officer; practiced medicine after
the war; lives in Vienna.*

"I'll have to take one of your legs off."

I was assigned to a field hospital in Normandy when an American medic drove in with a funny-looking vehicle that resembled a large tub more than anything else. It was a kind of amphibious truck. He brought wounded to the field hospital with this vehicle every day. I let him get on with this very useful work without bothering to have him taken prisoner. One time he brought 24 soldiers with lung wounds, one right after another. All of them were in critical condition. I stood at the operating table for three days and three nights. My legs were very swollen, and it was only with great difficulty that I could even get my boots off. At one point the company commander stopped by and asked how I was doing. I only said, "You deserve to have your commission revoked for not finding someone to take over here."

One man they brought me was in shock; he had been seriously wounded. I saw that I would have to amputate one of his legs and, in my best fatherly bedside manner, told him, "I'll have to take one of your legs off." He looked at my assistants, and could tell from their expressions that it had to be done, so he agreed. It was a complicated procedure. I had to drain the leg of blood because his heart could not have coped with the loss of even more blood. Afterwards, I amputated. When I was finished, the man was carried out, still under anaesthesia.

All of them were such young men, torn from their normal lives. They brought me another patient, and I saw his bladder lying in front of me. He railed against Hitler, cursed him. My assistants and I listened to this and let it pass. What else could we have done? Just as an illustration: during the winter offensive at Ardennes, the Battle of the Bulge, 3,000 wounded passed through my hospital, and I treated 1,500 of them.

GERALD KELLNER

Born 1902; paratrooper in Normandy; was captured by American troops; became a sales representative after the war; resides in Munich.

"During house-to-house combat at night, you normally didn't take prisoners."

I was a paratrooper in Normandy. As far as I can remember, our tour there began on July 11, 1944, north of St. Lô. We relieved an SS division. We were in our first foxhole with a light machine gun and a mortar. There were six dead SS men lying beside the foxhole. Because of the constant shellings, they couldn't be buried. A bit of dirt had been shoveled over them, you could see their boots sticking out. The first two weeks went okay enough. We improved our positions; there were small skirmishes every day.

The Americans were across from us. I think it was the 2nd Infantry Division, the Indian Head Division. Every day they'd send small raiding parties over to try and unhinge us. They came with tanks almost every day. They also had snipers who climbed the tall trees at night, and shot everything in sight during the day. The fighter bombers flew back and forth every day.

There were three massive attacks in July at St. Lô. The first barrage began at 4:00 A.M. This lasted for exactly five whole hours!

Then they came at us with an unbelievable number of tanks and fighter bombers. We left our positions because they were completely shot up. We made a fighting retreat, maybe a half a mile back. Then we dug in new positions again. They just couldn't get through anymore; we'd shot up a lot of tanks. But our losses were colossal. On the average, our regiment had 40 percent to 50 percent casualties. Of those, half were dead and half were badly wounded. I remember that my unit, a company of approximately 120 men, suffered nearly 60 percent losses. It went on like this every day. Every day, ten dead, eight dead, ten dead, etc., in our unit. But we didn't budge.

The last time they came at us with five tanks and a mass of infantry. First they demolished the houses. Everything was in flames; they went from house to house. We threw our weapons down; we didn't have any more ammunition anyhow.

Two SS men were shot right in front of my eyes—why, I don't know. At any rate, I put my hands up fast and said in English, "I surrender." We had been taught to say that. During house-to-house combat at night, you normally didn't take prisoners, so I expected to be knocked off too. Why they didn't kill me, I still don't know. I only know that an American officer standing on top of a tank ten yards away said something into his radio.

Then they tied me up and took me away. Naturally, they beat me up, beat me senseless. That's what they did, those SOBs. Those were the guys from the 2nd Division, the ones with the Indian Heads.

They sure were brutal, but you didn't feel any pain. You didn't feel anything anymore. Your entire nervous system, as in my case, just shut down. They could have tortured me, cut off my arm, knifed me, whatever, but I wouldn't have felt much—my nerves and soul were totally wrung out, completely exhausted.

If you are in heavy fighting, continually in heavy fighting, you're not a person anymore. After a while, when you begin to come to your senses again in imprisonment, you begin to think, "Well, I'm alive, and they can't take any more away from me than my life." In spite of it all, I had the feeling, after all those weeks of fighting, of a sense of salvation—I somehow felt relieved because I wouldn't have to fight any more.

RUDOLF WÜRSTER

Born 1920; served in the Luftwaffe; later volunteered for the Waffen-SS; worked as a head waiter after the war; lives in Bad Driburg, Westphalia.

"I was in awe of my comrades' show of fearlessness."

I was an orderly in the officers' club in a fighter wing in Poland. One morning our first sergeant received a teleprinted message and announced to us that the Waffen-SS was looking for volunteers. I remember turning to my friend and saying, "Hey, why don't we?" And so we volunteered. We were then split up, a smaller group going to the Division *Das Reich,* while the larger group was sent to the *Leibstandarte,* Adolf Hitler's personal SS armored division.

We never received any special political schooling. This was something we just never talked about. We saw ourselves as elite troops. I was actually in awe of my comrades' show of fearlessness in just about any situation. Their enthusiasm swept us along.

It is debatable whether we were the best-equipped unit in the war. I have read that the armored units of the Wehrmacht were just as well equipped as we were. The myth that our people threw themselves into combat, literally sacrificed themselves, is more or less based on the fact that we did lose one-third of our 900,000 SS soldiers in action. Our number of casualties was the highest in the entire Wehrmacht. I witnessed it with my own eyes. Often the SS soldiers went into battle even though they were severely wounded. Doing otherwise never crossed their minds.

Later, I was transferred to the armored Division *Das Reich.* We also had Dutch, Belgian, French, and Norwegian soldiers in the

Waffen-SS. They had volunteered and fought very well, especially in the Division Charlemagne. Just about all of Europe was represented in our units. The Spanish soldiers, who were part of another outfit, fought very bravely. They were not Nazis. They had no real concept of what a Nazi even was, for that matter. We were all so young. None of us cared for politics.

We saw a lot of action in the East, at Kursk and Orel. Later on we were sent to Normandy to ward off the invasion. By then I was in an SS tank battalion, equipped with Tiger tanks. On July 10 at six o'clock in the morning we retook our positions on Hill 112 from the British. That was where I destroyed my first three tanks. Later that same day, attacking British infantry, I shot over one of our tanks. The crew was surprised, felt threatened, turned their turret around, and fired three armor-piercing rounds point-blank at me. Amazingly, they missed me.

During this period of the invasion, we were gradually being pushed back to the south. Most of the outfit was surrounded, but only one crew was captured. The crews without tanks all got out.

I had one interesting experience on the retreat. My commander and I were relaxing, just enjoying the sun. I was sitting on the tank, when suddenly my commander dove down back into the tank and pulled the turret hatch shut behind him. I thought that was rather peculiar until I turned around and saw two Typhoons loaded with rockets coming straight at us. I instinctively jerked the hatch back open—fortunately he hadn't locked it—and dove head first down through the hatch. I remember thinking at the time, "Your legs can stand to take a hit, but you've got to protect your head!" The driver looked at me and asked what he should do next. I told him to just drive on! The Tiger had eight forward and four reverse gears. In eighth gear, and moving at 40 miles an hour down a country road, the rockets whizzed around us on all sides. But we kept right on moving and made it.

HANS EICHINGER

Born 1920; Austrian citizen; went from recruit
to captain in an armored division; wounded
and captured in Normandy; was a POW in the
United States until 1947; returned to Austria,
where he became a salesman; he lives in Lang
Enzersdorf, near Vienna.

"I made a recruit's mistake . . . and the shrapnel went right through the heel."

I was wounded near Falaise as a company commander. My commander told me to get into defensive positions. The 116th Panzer Division was in front of me, and I was supposed to get an armored car as support. The minute after he finished speaking, a jeep screeched to a halt and an officer from my company jumped out and excitedly told us that the Americans were just down the road.

The CO was terribly excited and started to radio the division, for all the good that was supposed to do. I told him I'd bring up the company on the double, and see to it that the Americans didn't get any farther. He said, "Yes, yes, just get moving." I wanted to set up a blockade on the main road from Falaise to Argentan, but we got into a firefight. Shells were bursting everywhere. American tanks drove straight toward us. I hit the dirt, but I made a recruit's mistake. I forgot to keep my foot down, and the shrapnel went right through the heel. I've still got one of them in there today as a souvenir.

Through the clouds of smoke, I saw everybody running away, and I tried to get away too. Little by little, the firing died down, and I found that I was all by myself. I crawled on my hands and knees about 100 yards down a gravel road because I couldn't stand up. You wouldn't believe how that hurt! I didn't have a first-aid kit, and I was losing a lot of blood. I tried to tourniquet my leg with a handkerchief. After that, I lay down in the middle of the road, unfastened my belt, and threw away my pistol.

The Americans picked me up and laid me in the back of an open jeep. My feet were sticking out on one side, and my head on the other. They picked up some other soldiers, and then we drove on the main road back to the American positions. When we reached towns where the Americans had passed through, there were only French people hanging around; they greeted us warmly. But when we went through towns where there were still Americans, they shook their fists at us, and I was afraid one of them would hit me over the head.

We finally came to a large field hospital with several tents. I was operated on by an American doctor, and in my opinion he did a rotten job. He just cut here and there and picked out the splinters wherever he happened to find any, no anesthesia. Then he stitched me up and slapped on a bandage.

I was sent to England, and then on to the States. I was operated on again in Boston. The doctor told me that he was a Polish Jew and had studied in Vienna. We got to talking about how I hadn't been married long, and that my wife was expecting a baby. Naturally, I was concerned about how things were going at home. The next day a lady from the Red Cross came to my bed and said, "I heard that you wife is expecting. Would you like to send a telegram home?" Well, who wouldn't! She formulated the text for me: it had to have a certain number of words, and so on.

Later, I learned what had been happening at home. My wife had already been evacuated to the countryside. She gave birth to our eldest daughter on October 29. It was a premature birth, and she only had her mother with her. A clerk had brought her the news that I was missing in action three days earlier, which was probably a contributing cause to her going into labor early. Of course, the whole family was very sad. The telegram from the Red Cross arrived the day after my daughter was born. My mother-in-law intercepted it, afraid that it was my death notice, and that it would be too much for my wife, in her condition. The telegram had gone via Geneva to Berlin, and then to Vienna. My family was overjoyed to hear that I was alive.

HERMANN BLOCKSDORFF

---

*Born 1919; infantryman during the Allied
invasion of Normandy; worked as a precision
instrument maker after the war and lives in
Erlangen, Bavaria.*

"Gradually I began to get the jitters."

On July 6 we were headed through Orleans from Lyon, moving by
rail at a pretty good speed. When we finally rolled into the next
station, a French switchman crashed us into another train. The
French resistance was doing its job. Our colonel sent us to get rations
at a nearby barracks. While we waited for a new locomotive and
some new cars, the switchman was hanged from the window of his
little cabin. The war was taking on new dimensions.

As we moved on, the journey was possible only on a stop-and-go
basis. We would come to a standstill and take cover. We jumped out
as soon as the train began to brake. When the strafing began, we were
always a few hundred yards away from the standing train. We jumped
back on when it started moving again. The train started slowly
enough for everybody to catch up and get on. Thus we arrived a few
miles from Caen at midnight on June 7, 1944.

All hell was breaking loose ahead of us. Caen burned and the sky
was bright with fire. We were ordered to march toward it, to our
assembly area. Our regiment was given a big sector of the front to
hold. The air was filled with a roar, and the shells sounded strange.
Later we knew why: 15- and 16-inch naval guns. Toward morning, as
we lay before Caen in our regimental command post, the infantry had
already moved into the city and taken up position in the ruins and
what remained of the cellars. We made a head count first. Thank
God, not one man had been lost in the whole regiment. But we

sustained a complete loss of equipment. Not one motorized vehicle was intact. There was no artillery; we had nothing.

We only had infantry, with the machine guns and mortars they always had with them. A few guns showed up later on. Little by little, we discovered that through re-routing, a couple of train cars had made it. But during the day we couldn't move a thing. Fighter bombers attacked every moving man or vehicle. We learned a new form of warfare.

We sat in and around Caen, confronted with an opponent who had ten times as many troops and 150 times the amount of ammunition and equipment. We held out there for four whole weeks. We couldn't move during the day. There was no transport and no troop movement was possible because the sky was always full of planes.

Once a fully loaded four-engine bomber came down 100 yards from our command post. If the plane hadn't spun because one wing broke off, the whole thing would have fallen right on top of us, bombs and all. That's when I saw my regimental commander totally panic. "Blow it up!" he yelled at me. How was I supposed to get at this burning monstrosity? The ammunition on board detonated. It was an inferno. I couldn't get closer than 20 yards to it because of the heat. Well, I found a solution. The plane had buried itself half-way into the ground. All the bombs were still in the bay. After I'd dug myself in as best I could, I threw a satchel charge at where the bomb bay should have been. I had four seconds. I virtually pressed myself underground. It's indescribable what one is capable of when one knows it's a matter of life and death. The plane flew apart into thousands of pieces, but the whole mess went over our heads. My regimental commander calmed down. I had carried out an insane order.

We held the British and Canadians for four weeks. At the front, the very front line, the casualties grew and grew. There could be no talk of real fighting by the enemy. If they got the slightest infantry fire, they retreated immediately and plowed the ground with bombs for 12 to 20 hours. After that, they came with flamethrower tanks and burned everything down. Once a man was hit with the flame-oil, nobody could help him. These men died a miserable death. Our hatred of the enemy grew from day to day. They only had to march in and overrun us. We were only a handful of soldiers, and it wasn't as if we could have caused them any losses.

After four weeks our regiment was down to one-third combat strength, without heavy weapons. But the British and Canadians didn't get through, even though our regiment was trying to hold a division-sized sector. The Americans broke through in a different sector—from Bayeux to St. Lô—and came at us from behind. So we had to run a race with them. We went along the coast in a delaying action, and they went parallel to us, farther south, marching on Paris.

In the middle of December 1944, we were stationed in the Eifel region. Bomber squadrons flew over us into the homeland every day. Continually. We sat at the radio and heard which cities had been the intended targets. None of us knew whether our families were still alive. The enemy dropped leaflets, copies of intercepted mail in which regards were extended by loved ones, and others which reported their deaths. What was the truth?

The Americans attacked again toward the end of February 1945. The heaviest combat was in the Hürtgen Forest, around Kommerscheid and Schmidt. The Americans suffered their first casualties. Toward the middle of March, we drew back. Before this, the Americans had attacked with heavy bombers. A 1,000 pound bomb was left on the Erft Valley Dam. I had to defuse it. Gradually I began to get the jitters. The colonel poured me a canteen cup of schnapps and said, "Bottoms up." It worked; my hands stopped shaking. And you need steady hands at this kind of job. I had to remove five fuses. Then the thing was rolled away and detonated in a safe place. That was the last one I ever touched; after that, I left the things alone. We retreated daily, fighting delaying actions. Our group became increasingly smaller, but we kept on fighting. I couldn't continue my diary— we were all just too tired.

WILLI NOLDEN*

"The Americans fought with shells instead of men."

I was supposed to go back to Russia. But a buddy at the replacement depot in Aachen pulled some strings, and the captain said, "You're staying here to show the recruits how to handle anti-tank guns." It was no problem for me. I trained young soldiers on 7.5cm guns until the Americans got too close. Then me and my battery of kids were sent to defend the city. My gun was dug in along the Siegfried Line, on a line of low hills. In front of us were the dragons' teeth, concrete blocks that a tank couldn't climb. The road was blocked too. The Americans were in the woods west of us.

They came right at noon, not directly across the fields, but toward the road block. There were five tanks. One had a bulldozer blade in front to shovel dirt on the dragons' teeth so the tanks could get over them. But they didn't see me. By this time I knew how to camouflage a gun! We'd dug in alongside a bunker, and that gave us some courage. But the bunker had no firing slits. We could only use it as cover; we couldn't fight from it.

I let the tanks close to about 200 yards. I was in a good position. I had the high ground, and the tanks were worried about the dragons' teeth, not an anti-tank gun. The only problem was, I had to shoot down at the tanks, and we anti-tank gunners were more used to shooting straight ahead. I sighted and fired. The first round went six feet short. The second was a direct hit, and the tank burst into flames. The third was another direct hit. I'd have got them all if they'd given me a few minutes. But the other crews opened their hatches, jumped out, and ran back to their own lines. They let their tanks sit there. I'd fired only three rounds.

---

* Biography on page 142.

I never got off the fourth. The tanks still in the woods had spotted us and opened fire. Our position took a direct hit, and all of a sudden the gun was on top of us. All four of us were wounded, one was real bad—an artery was cut. So we crawled into the bunker, and found out what American artillery could do! Tank guns, mortars, artillery—they threw everything at us. Every time the bunker took a hit, it was like being hammered ten yards deeper into the ground. I was the sergeant, and looked out to see what was happening. A shell burst right on the bunker, and I got a face full of splinters, nothing special. But the Americans didn't come any closer. They just kept firing till around six o'clock. The only ones who came were German medics. They said, "Come on, let's get outta here." I'd spent the six hours holding my buddy's artery closed.

The Americans fought with shells instead of men. They used a lot of phosphorous. Wherever it hit, the earth burned. Day after day, bombardments and artillery fire, but no infantry. We held our front lines with dummies, but the Americans just kept shooting. It never came to close combat, like in Russia. The Americans came only when they thought no one was left alive. No risks. They advanced step by step, but they advanced.

My war ended on March 18, 1945. We knew everything was finished, but we still wanted to get back across the Rhine; kind of a homing instinct, I suppose. We didn't want to be taken prisoner at this late date. We'd spent the night in a little village. Next morning I woke up and heard firing. I ran into the next house and looked through the curtains. Tanks rolling by, columns of infantry—all Americans. Suddenly they stopped. And a German, an older man, said, "Give yourself up. They're already searching the houses." I said, "Let's go." So we went out, hands up and overcoats unbuttoned, to show we had no hidden weapons. An officer in a jeep—he even spoke German—said, "Just go that way."

We kept walking till we got to the village square. Ten or twelve SS men were already there. We all squatted down with our hands clasped on our heads. We soldiers were OK—a kick in the behind or a rifle butt in the back, all pretty much harmless. But the SS men were taken out one at a time and beaten to a pulp. Later we were loaded into trucks and taken to a POW camp.

JOSEF LÜCKING

*Born 1925; fought partisans in the Balkans
and was captured by the Russians in 1945;
now a farmer living in Paderborn, Westphalia.*

"It was a relentless and merciless way of fighting."

I'd count Yugoslavia among the worst theaters from a soldier's point of view. The partisans used treacherous methods of fighting. As soon as it got dark, every partisan who hadn't volunteered was forced to grab a weapon. They dragged people out of their towns, out of their homes, and—I heard this personally from older women in Yugoslavia who'd witnessed it—young people who didn't cooperate were shot to encourage the others.

I had the impression that the partisans didn't organize because of the pressures or burdens that went along with it. It started out with a few who called themselves Communists and who, under this guise, practiced sabotage, blew up railroad tracks, ambushed German outposts, all just to stimulate repression. As permitted by the Geneva Convention, we carried out reprisals on a 1:10 ratio: ten hostages killed for every German.[1] The whole thing got so out of hand that in the end it was all just a matter of killing as many as possible.

[1] "It cannot be denied that the shooting of hostages or reprisal against prisoners may under certain circumstances be justified as a last resort in procuring peace and tranquility in occupied territory and has the effect of strengthening the position of a law abiding occupant. The fact that the practice has been abused beyond recognition by illegal and inhuman application cannot justify its prohibition by judicial fiat.

"Military necessity (however) does not permit the killing of innocent inhabitants for purposes of revenge or the satisfaction of a lust to kill."

Trials of War Criminals before the Nuremberg Military Tribunals, Vol XI, *The Hostage Case,* (Washington, D.C., 1950), p. 1253.

I remember a particular experience I had after I arrived in Yugoslavia. It happened the first time we cleared out a partisan-infested area. We tried to send wounded back in three ambulances. They got ambushed by partisans. The drivers were overpowered and the ambulances were set on fire, occupants and all. So these badly injured men were burned alive.

It was a relentless and merciless way of fighting, the likes of which I only experienced in Russia on one or two occasions.

WILLI WEISSKIRCH*

"The medic yelled, 'You could have left this one out there!' "

I know that without the help of my comrades, I probably wouldn't be alive today. They risked their necks to get me out of a dangerous situation. In 1944 I was an infantryman in the Balkans fighting Yugoslav partisans. I was wounded at eight o'clock in the morning, just when we were about to retreat. A shell exploded about three feet away from where I was standing. I caught the whole package. I was the last one in the trench; everyone else had left. I remember yelling, "I'm hit! I can't get out of here!"

I lay there until after midnight in a dried-up river bed that was slowly but surely filling up with water. Two of my comrades heard my call for help and went and got a stretcher. They walked the six miles back after dark, hoping to find me still alive. I was only semiconscious, somewhere between life and death, when they found me. I had lost a lot of blood. They gagged my mouth to keep me from screaming. Then they dragged me back with them.

Twenty-four hours later they turned me over to the medics. I'll never forget it. The medic yelled, "You could have left this one out

* Biography on page 22.

there!" Then he said, "Well, give him a tetanus shot as a precaution anyway." He ended up giving me the shot himself. We all had a really solid sense of comradship. We were all in the same boat and we all wanted to survive, any way possible. We were only 19, 20, 21 years old.

OSWALD LAUER

Born 1913; NCO in a rifle battalion; later sentenced to serve in a Wehrmacht penal battalion; printing specialist; lives in Darmstadt.

"Whoever was in Penal Battalion 500 was on death row."

In February 1943, I was sent to Penal Battalion 500, in the Caucasus area, for threatening a Nazi officer with a knife. The thoughts running through my mind on the way were anything but reassuring. But the new company greeted me warmly, and this was comforting to me as an outcast. All branches of the service were represented there: infantry, U-boat men, Luftwaffe, and wearers of the Knight's Cross, not to mention the other decorations. Nobody wore rank insignia because all of them had been demoted. They were all fighting soldiers who had been shunted off by their superiors for serious transgressions such as refusal to obey orders.

The penal battalion was the melting pot for the Wehrmacht's undesirable elements. Now they were supposed to prove their worthiness as cannon fodder at the front. For all of them who fell for the fatherland, the next of kin were always notified with mention of the dead man's previous unit. This was because the public was not supposed to know that penal units existed, and under what conditions these *Landser* had to risk their lives for the Führer's retreat plans. The lives of his front-line soldiers weren't worth a cent to him. Being one of these men, witnessing their individual fates and picturing what was in store for me, I decided to hold on as long as possible. After all that I had lived through up to that point, it seemed to me that my time hadn't run out yet. This restored my courage time and again. Many *Landser* tried to accept their fate lightly, expecting to say goodbye to our club and to be allowed to return to their old units. But this was self-deception. Whoever was in Penal Battalion 500 was on death row, with no end in sight unless you were taken prisoner.

The battalion commanders were SS officers. We were put into action at locations where partisans had been spotted. They were causing the retreating German troops a lot of trouble. The SS units which should actually have been used for these operations were only put in after we had cleared everything out. Then they were the ones who acted as if they'd saved the day. Of course, that caused bad blood between the *Landser* and the SS. But we had to keep our mouths shut, which was pretty hard for some of us. Before combat we were always issued a bottle of wine or champagne to share among three men, so that we would bear our soldier's death more easily.

Once we were in a bad position in front of a slope. The troops on our right flank pulled out the same night, leaving us to our own devices. There were sixty of us. Partisans were supposed to be hiding nearby, and at daybreak they suddenly attacked.

We were sitting ducks for them. I had an inkling that it would be touch-and-go. I didn't have much of a field of fire; there was too much scrub. But I fired bursts at everything that moved. You couldn't see much of the partisans; they were well camouflaged. They had detected me even though I was under cover. I instinctively put on my helmet, something I never did otherwise. I usually kept my cap on so I could hear better in the woods. But the steel helmet gave me better protection when the first bullets began to whistle past my ears.

A sniper had seen me. I was supposed to man the machine gun because I was closest. But as I leaped forward, I got a bullet clean through the left thigh. I pivoted on my stomach and jumped into a gully, but while jumping I was shot from behind through the right hip. I crawled as best as I could to the embankment for cover. Suddenly I felt a dull thud against my helmet. A hand grenade had hit me—but instead of blowing up, it rolled down the incline. The helmet had saved my life. Then I lost consciousness.

I don't now how long I lay there when I felt someone nudge me. I moaned and opened my eyes. Lying on my back, I saw a partisan's face above me—I recognized him by his civilian clothing. He said; "Me partisan" and ordered me to get up. I pointed to my wounds. After he had taken all of my valuables—he overlooked my wedding ring—he called some other Russians over. He looked at the picture of my wife for a long time: "You married? You children?" He pulled a photo of his family out of his quilted jacket and shoved it to me. Two Russians took me under their arms and dragged me through the wooded terrain for hours. Blood streamed down my legs from both wounds. It must have been afternoon by the time we reached a dugout which gave onto a cave in the rocks.

Abandoned by the entire world, I lay there at a Russian partisan regimental headquarters; candles as thick as your arm were burning on a stone table. The interrogations began in the stinking air. I was thoroughly exhausted after the terrible experiences of the day. I recapped: captured badly wounded near Feodotovka, four miles south of Novorossisk on February 17, 1943. Ex-NCO of the 129th Rifle Regiment, 101st Mountain Division—the one with the bow and arrow patch. Last unit: Penal Battalion 500. Age: 30.

OSKAR HUMMEL

*Born 1921; volunteered for the Waffen-SS and
fought in its ranks from 1939 to 1944; lost both
legs in Russia; lives near Aachen.*

"I woke up and one leg was gone."

In 1941, I was in Holland when the SS Division Viking was organized. It was an international volunteer force, formed exclusively of
foreigners who volunteered from the Netherlands, Finland, Norway,
and Latvia, all thrown together. I don't really know why the Scandinavians were so interested in joining the SS. I don't believe that it
was their lust for adventure; it was actually the dream of a united
Europe. I am convinced they joined in good faith.

The Viking Division was sent to Russia, and I ended up in the
Cherkassy pocket in January 1944. The fighting was very tough
there, as it was everywhere. Large parts of the German 8th Army
were surrounded, but it didn't come to a second Stalingrad. The
German troops retreated in good order and then broke out of the
pocket. I was seriously wounded there; my right leg was shattered by
a shell in a counterattack. As soon as I was wounded the counterattack was broken off, and they saw to it that I was brought back. The
whole platoon covered me so that I could even make it to the field
hospital. Ten men would rather have risked their lives than to leave
one lying wounded; we knew that all Waffen-SS soldiers were automatically shot by the Russians.

That's how I got back. They dropped me off at the field hospital,
said good-bye, and went back into the fighting. Then the field hospital had to be cleared out helter-skelter. An artillery unit passed by
with transport vehicles, and they took me to another station. From
there we were supposed to be flown out in a Ju-52 which had arrived

at the airstrip, but it couldn't take off. Everybody looked after themselves in finding a way to get out.

People from the Viking Division came through, put me on a horse cart, and took me along. While they were attempting to break out of the pocket, I was wounded again in the left arm. They put me on a horse, and since I could only hold on with my right arm, there was a man to the right and one to the left to keep me from falling off. A reconnaissance unit always went first, and we had to halt many, many times.

At one point we got word that the path was clear. The soldiers had made a breakthrough in the lines through which we had just been able to escape. We took a deep breath, and all of a sudden we heard, "Halt! Who goes there?" It was our troops. They naturally sent us farther back, because every tent hospital was already overcrowded. They set me up in a farm shed. We woke up the next morning and saw the German tanks coming back. We had gotten out of the pocket now, but the Russians were on our tails again. So, it was back onto the horsecart, with no other thoughts but of getting away.

We found two Ju-52s. They had just dropped fuel and ammunition to the ground troops, and these two pilots were daring enough to land. So we naturally rode out to the planes, where a master sergeant with a submachine gun said, "Wounded only." We boarded the plane, and began to feel very uneasy. "Can you take off again?" I asked. The pilot, a lieutenant, said, "Sure, don't worry; I'll make it up." And he brought the plane out. That's how I got out of the Cherkassy pocket.

My wounds had been left untended for nine or ten days. My shredded clothing was stuck in the wounds, and everything had frozen. Gangrene. And of course it was too late to stitch up my leg. Amputation. The front part of my left foot was amputated along with my right leg. My left leg was full of shrapnel, and my left upper arm was badly damaged. I woke up and one leg was gone. But I came through it, and I'm still alive.

That was the main principle at the front: survival, somehow making it through alive. Just as long as you came out of it alive, even at the cost of a leg. Everyone had to come to terms with it by themselves. But you knew that there were thousands, hundreds of thousands, who weren't any better off, maybe even much worse. There was an army lieutenant next to me who had both arms amputated. When I saw that I thought I should be content with what I had: "You've still got your arms." Better the legs than the arms.

ERICH KERN*

"A comrade next to me had his hand blown off."

We spent a whole day in a Russian forest just waiting. Then they came. The 8.8cm gun to my left knocked out eight T-34 tanks before receiving a direct hit. Two T-34s broke through. One was trying to roll over our holes to crush us. I jumped on it and stopped it. I shoved a hand grenade into the gun-barrel and blew it apart, but the tank didn't burn and the Russians were still inside. I put an adhesive hollow charge on the front of the tank. After that went off, the hatch opened up and two Russians came out. They were sent to the rear.

I was wounded once, in Russia. A salvo hit next to me and I was hit in the arm and the back. A comrade next to me had his hand blown off. He jumped half a meter for joy because it meant that for him the war was over.

I wanted to give up in Russia. I saw no way anything could turn out well and I was in despair. You have to imagine 40 degrees below zero, out in the open, day and night. We were in shallow holes and we couldn't dig any deeper.

Deserting to the other side was never an alternative for us. The grisly fate that awaited us if we fell into Russian hands kept us from deserting. It deterred everyone from taking such a step. The soldier knew very well that in doing so, he would go from the frying pan into the fire. We had no other choice but to keep on fighting.

---

* Biography on page 97.

HANS-ULRICH GREFFRATH

Born 1923; an officer in one of the Wehrmacht's elite divisions; wounded four times, the last time losing a leg; vice president of the largest German veterans' organization: lives in Bonn.

"We saw mutilated soldiers who had fallen into the hands of the Russians."

I first experienced combat in the beginning of the 1942 summer offensive in Russia. I was a PFC and a leader of a machine gun squad in the Grossdeutschland Division. There was a certain arrogance in the army. We were told, for example, that a German infantry soldier was worth ten or twelve Russians.

Then I was sent to an officers' training course, but returned to my division in time for Operation Citadel, the big attack on Kursk. I celebrated my 20th birthday a few days before the beginning of the offensive. Two first lieutenants and twelve second lieutenants were at the party; only two of us were still alive eight days after the beginning of the offensive. Perhaps this characterizes the situation we were in at that time in the Soviet Union.

I was escort officer to a certain general during some of the hardest fighting. He had been in Africa and was familiar with Rommel's battle tactics. He attempted to put them into practice in Russia. I admired his courage. One day while I was sitting behind him in a jeep, Russian planes attacked us and shot his arm off, but he kept on giving orders. Even after one of my other commanding officers had lost his leg, he voluntarily returned to duty and was later decorated with the Knight's Cross for his performance in hand-to-hand combat.

I personally never fought for Hitler. I was a German soldier and I fought for Germany, for my fatherland, and for my homeland. I think all of my comrades did the same. The fact that we fought harder and harder the longer the war dragged on might come as a surprise to many people. We simply did our duty. We fought with ever-increasing defiance and bitterness not because we were Nazis, but because of the terrible experiences we had at the front. We saw mutilated soldiers who had fallen into the hands of the Russians—soldiers without ears, without noses, without eyes. One of them was a very good friend of mine. We knew we had to keep on fighting if we wanted to prevent this sort of thing from happening to our families at home. We acted in good faith, without suspecting the extent to which we were being misused by the regime.

I was wounded for the third time in Russia when a shell fragment lodged in my lungs and three of my ribs were shattered. However, instead of being taken to a hospital, I was sent to a training course in Versailles and recovered there. I was sent back to my division on January 12, 1944.

I was wounded for the fourth time that spring fighting Russian tanks hand-to-hand. We learned later that we had been attacked by 420 Russian tanks. In 3 days we knocked out 382 of them. My leg was smashed right below the knee, and was amputated immediately at the main field dressing station. I was lucky enough to be evacuated to the base hospital in Cracow. It had been real emergency surgery; I was left with a stump of a leg upon which no prosthesis could be fit. There were 14,000 of us amputees in the hospital; about 12,000 walked on crutches, and about 2,000 were bedridden. We didn't take our mutilations too seriously; we were glad to be alive at all. I was two months shy of being 21.

PATER BASILIUS HEINRICH BARTIUS STREITHOFEN

Born 1922; served in the Luftwaffe's Hermann Göring Division; became a Dominican priest after the war; lives in a monastery in Walberberg, Rhineland.

"We were soldiers, not butchers."

Heroes and saints make up only a very small portion of humanity. Most people are opportunists who simply adapt themselves to circumstances. For this reason, I don't believe in collective guilt. There may be such a thing as "collective adaptation." That was certainly my experience during the war. Initially a bunch of my friends and I signed up for the Waffen-SS. I was only 17 and hadn't started to shave—political considerations weren't determining my choice. We were troublemakers, tough kids, and we wanted experience and adventure. Instead, a friend of my mother's pulled some strings, and I wound up in the Hermann Göring Division as a radioman.

I was sent to Holland for training. Next to our barracks was a large concentration camp, and Jews were always being moved in and out. One day we were asked if any of us wished to volunteer for a firing squad. In my room there were 16 or 17 of us, from everywhere in the Reich, and not one of us signed up, even though that would have meant extra rations.

After this, I went to Italy and participated in the retreat from Calabria to Abruzzo, on the Mediterranean coast. Since we were fighting against the Americans, we had no qualms about being taken captive. In 1944, we were sent to Poland, and there we felt completely different. We did not want to fall into Russian hands.

It was a hard war, and the Hermann Göring Division was a tough outfit. During the Warsaw uprising, we were shot at from a row of houses. In the evening we got together a detachment; early the next morning we made short work of the snipers. These are the sorts of things you can't forget. But we were soldiers, not butchers. In East Prussia, some Russians deserted to us. Our commander ordered us to shoot them. We told him, "Lieutenant, shoot them yourself!" And he said, "I insist that you obey my order." We let them go. Collective adaptation.

PETER PECHEL*

"The armored divisions would soon have to get along without any heavy weapons at all."

On June 1, 1942, after having been wounded and spending nine months in the hospital, I was ordered to the Home Army Headquarters in Berlin. At 22, I was surely one of the youngest officers ever to be assigned there.

It was a fascinating experience for me. There I was, a young man, suddenly sitting in one of the centers of power. I had a reinforced safe in my office, and in this safe were top secret documents. This was very exciting, because as a front officer you only came into contact with papers with low security clearances. I spent the first week on my new job studying the material in my safe to get a picture of what I was supposed to do, and what I should watch out for.

What absorbed me most was the report regarding the supply situation. I knew from my own experience just how many tanks and guns we lost on the Eastern front every day. And I expected to see

---

* Biography on page 131.

numbers listed here which would give me hope that the war might end at least short of total defeat. When I looked at the first figures, I felt sick. The newly produced tanks were only a fraction of what we lost at the front every month. For example, for the Mark IV, the backbone of the armored regiments, there was a difference of 233 between the newly produced and the lost tanks—almost enough for two regiments! At first, I didn't believe the figures. I didn't think it possible that in the third year of the war so few tanks and so few guns were being produced. It didn't take long for me to figure out that the armored divisions would soon have to get along without any heavy weapons at all. When I read this, I had to think of my buddies at the front, who I knew trusted the leadership.

That evening, I went to a General Staff major, an Austrian with whom I had become friends and who was later executed in connection with the 20th of July assassination attempt. I asked him, "Major, are the supply figures on tanks and guns accurate, or have they been manipulated?" He looked at me strangely, and must have sensed that I was seething like a volcano. Then he said, "Wait a minute, and we'll go to the Rio Rita for a drink." The Rio Rita was a well-known bar in Berlin. There I asked him again, "Major, are these numbers correct?" And he said, "Yes, right down to the last dab of ink." I said, "So this man Hitler has not only started a war for no reason whatsoever, he hasn't even prepared for it from an armament standpoint." He answered, "You have just presented a fully correct analysis of the situation." I said, "Major, this is a crime, above all against the *Landser* who are sticking their necks out, trusting that they will get the weapons they need to fight." And he replied, "You're absolutely right. It is a crime. Not only has Germany begun a criminal war, but worse, there is no chance of ending it successfully."

It is not necessary to mention that all the other general staff officers, and the generals, must have read these statistics too. Their reactions seemed to be more composed than mine. For a long time the myth had been that "the *Landser* can do the job, even without tanks." That evening, the major and I got completely drunk.

BRUNHILDE POMSEL

Born 1911; a secretary at the German radio network, she was drafted to work in the office of Propaganda Minister Goebbels in 1942; captured by the Soviet army in Berlin in 1945; spent four years in a Russian concentration camp; returned to West Germany and worked for German radio and television; resides in Munich.

"Goebbels didn't believe in final victory after 1942."

In 1942 I was drafted into, of all places, Goebbels' office as a secretary. I saw Goebbels just about every day. When he came, he always walked through the office greeting everyone coolly and politely. I was often called into meetings to take down the minutes and record what was said. Goebbels was very reserved, almost arrogant, when it came to dealing with other people. Nevertheless he was actually quite a nice man, not at all diabolical. He did have a certain charisma. But whether this was natural or whether it had been built up, the fact remains that he was a fascinating individual. Of course, I was a 30-year-old innocent at the time, so I assume working in his main office had something to do with my view of him. I must say, I enjoyed my work there.

I also knew that Goebbels was having a lot of difficulty with Hitler. It happened often that Hitler wouldn't even see Goebbels. Our office made the arrangements for his trips to the Führer's main headquarters. Goebbels always took a special train which was very exclusive and luxurious. Once he arrived at the *Wolfschanze,* he would wait anywhere from three hours to three days to see Hitler, only to be told he wouldn't be let in after all. A few of Hitler's courtiers worked actively against Goebbels. He usually returned from these trips without having accomplished anything.

Personally, I sincerely believe that Goebbels knew just how hopeless the situation was as early as 1942. He also knew that all of the articles he had written and all of the fiery speeches he had made were all totally against his better judgment. It is perhaps true that he still believed in Hitler and in the Third Reich, but he certainly didn't believe in final victory.

KLAUS VON BISMARCK*

"Himmler was like an arrogant, narrow-minded, petty-bourgeois high school teacher."

In December 1944, I was awarded the Oak Leaves to my Knight's Cross by Himmler, who was acting on behalf of Hitler. I was a lieutenant colonel. Before we were brought to Himmler—there were 15 of us—we were told to lay down our pistols. This was, of course, after the July 1944 assassination attempt. I was adamant. "No, I am not going to do that! I'll go back home first!" I protested. One other officer in our group also declined to take off his gun.

Naturally, this caused quite a bit of commotion. It was obvious that Himmler's staff officers didn't quite know what to do. I asked them to understand my position. "I have been fighting in this war for almost six years," I said. "Considering that, your demand that I lay down my weapons to receive a decoration is uncalled for." Ultimately, the two of us were permitted to retain our pistols after all. But in all probability, a couple of guards were ordered to watch every move we made.

---

* Biography on page xxxv.

Then Himmler walked in. Not many people had ever met him. He was a macabre individual. His main headquarters was situated in an extravagant villa that belonged to a *nouveau riche* entrepreneur. These surroundings looked grotesque to a soldier returning from the front. Himmler himself was arrogant, and spoke with a strong Bavarian accent in a very aloof manner. He talked about collecting herbs and living a healthy life. He was extremely didactic, which was bizarre considering how brutal the man could be. The image he projected was that of a narrow-minded, petty-bourgeois high school teacher. Himmler was weak, unpleasant, and slimy.

CHAPTER 10

Genocide

Among history's grotesque ironies is that Adolf Hitler, an Austrian, developed German anti-Semitism into a unique form of mass murder. For the Nazis, hatred of the Jews was an alternate religious ritual, a way of striking back in particular at Christian churches whose doctrines challenged Nazi ideology. The Nordic neo-paganism of men like Heinrich Himmler, dismissed by most Germans as a farrago of nonsense, was a harbinger of National Socialism's ultimate goal: the annihilation of Western civilization's fundamental values. But Aryan racism did not originate with the Nazis. Even before World War I, German cults sought older gods. If the SS was the ultimate incorporation of National Socialist ideology, its leadership and many of its rank and file had begun releasing themselves from the restraints of civilization well before the first extermination camps were erected.

This does not mean the Holocaust was systematically planned. Hitler frequently described Jews as vermin. Ideologically, National Socialism regarded Jews as parasites. Themselves possessing no racial value, Jews could live only by preying secretly on healthy peoples. To a believing Nazi, a rhetoric of segregation and a policy of ostracism were final solutions in their own right. Like any parasites, the Jews would die out once isolated from their hosts.

Separation was the purpose of the Nuremberg Laws, the emigration policies, the systematic persecution. Yet Hitler's foreign policy rendered his Jewish policy self-defeating. The absorption of Austria and the Sudetenland gave Germany more Jews than it had when

Hitler first assumed power. The conquest of western Poland gave the Nazis power over additional hundreds of thousands.

What was to be done with them? Even after the outbreak of war, some Jews were permitted to leave the Reich if they could find anywhere to go. After the fall of France, the island of Madagascar was seriously considered as a Jewish reservation. But these and similar schemes flew in the face of reality. More practical, direct solutions to the problem of exclusion included the ghettoization of Polish Jews and the deportation of Jews from Reich territory. In October 1939, the first shipments began from Hamburg and Vienna.

Germany's Jewish community had survived expropriation, harassment, and discrimination. They had learned to avoid confrontations while slipping through the system's loopholes. Mixed Jewish-Gentile marriages, and the children of such marriages, were cast into a twilight zone. The ambiguous status of those people officially defined as *mischlinge,* or "half-breeds," sometimes generated within them a close identification with their Jewish heritage. Often, however, it led to an even closer identification with Germany, and to a determination to prove oneself as good a German as one's tormentors.

For "full Jews" the choices and the chances were fewer. Even before the deportations began, these men and women had been excluded from virtually every aspect of normal, everyday life. Their driver's licenses were cancelled. They were forbidden to possess radios or telephones. In many communities, Jews were allowed to shop only at certain times, denied access to parks and swimming pools, forbidden to appear on the streets at all on specific days. Under such circumstances survival depended heavily on cleverness, foresight, and plain luck. But it also involved the good will of Gentile Germans.

Anti-Semitism in Germany had always been more abstract than personal. Most Jew-baiters wanted to "teach the Jews their place" rather than put them in their graves. By 1940, that goal had been so obviously achieved that surviving Jews could be treated with a degree of sympathy. In general, this sympathy was passive. But some Germans would take significant risks to aid Jews against a system that, as the war progressed, was becoming anonymous as well as repressive.

More and more German Jews took the corresponding risks of life in a "submarine," "diving" into illegal status rather than taking further chances with the Nazis.

If Jews were parasites, then their segregation should have meant their annihilation. The failure of this approach in the Reich proper might be explained officially as a result of softness and inefficiency. But in Poland the Nazis had a free hand in the midst of a Gentile population overtly anti-Semitic in a way Germans were not. The process of physical isolation was, by 1941, as complete as human ingenuity was likely to make it. Yet the ghettoized Jews continued to survive, to reproduce, to sustain community life.

The failure of the ghettos was highlighted by preparations for Operation Barbarossa. The invasion of Russia promised to bring still more millions of Jews under Nazi rule. Hitler's insistence that the coming war was a struggle to the death between ideologies set the stage. Himmler's Action Groups were ordered to kill every Jew they could find in the rear of the fighting troops. The pretexts given were the prevention of sabotage and the suppression of Communism. They were excuse enough for the army leadership to look the other way as more than a million people were massacred.

Wehrmacht willingness to allow this ideologically based race war against defenseless people was a key factor in Hitler's consideration of extending the "Russian solution" by concentrating the rest of Europe's Jews in the conquered eastern territories, then eliminating them. Conventional methods, however, had shown their limitations. The SS was receiving an increasing number of reports about the adverse psychological effects of shooting down women and children. Even in remote areas, moreover, the sounds of gunfire often attracted Wehrmacht troops who were too shocked by what they saw to be intimidated into silence. Nazi technocrats began work on finding a quick-acting poison gas.

Hitler's uncompromising stand was reflected in the attitudes of his subordinates. There was no reason to put anything in writing. The Führer's wishes were clear enough, and the best way to stand well with him was to take a similar position. On January 20, 1942, key party and administration officials met at Berlin-Wannsee. They were confronted with the Final Solution: the proposed murder of 11 million European Jews. In February 1942, the first deportations began from the Polish ghettos to newly established extermination centers: Chelmno, Belzec, Treblinka. Other camps, notably Auschwitz/ Birkenau, "employed" Jews who were expected to work themselves to death before being fed to the crematoria.

Apologists for Germans of the wartime generation frequently and accurately note that the Reich did its dirtiest work in secret. The extermination camps were built in Poland, and staffed in part by guards recruited from the anti-Semitic populations of the East: Ukrainians, Latvians, Lithuanians. Yet for that generation a key question remains: "What did *you* know about the mass murder of Jews?" The answer varies from individual to individual. A state secretary and a common soldier, an *Abiturient* and a school dropout, an officer on the Russian front and a farmer's wife in the Eifel Mountains, all had their own viewpoints. The regime was determined to preserve secrecy on the subject of the Final Solution. Many soldiers and civilians saw enough to trouble their minds and consciences. But when they unburdened themselves, it was likely to be in a circle of intimates, or to total strangers on trains or in bars.

Verification of the stories was difficult, and accompanied by significant personal risks. In the Third Reich it was not wise to ask questions on any subject outside the sphere of one's direct responsibilities. Some students of German public opinion in the wartime years have described it as indifferent to the fate of the Jews. Others suggest a kind of passive complicity, a conspiracy of silence. Both positions are oversimplified. Even the Holocaust's direct victims often found it difficult to believe what was happening to them. Rumors of executions and other atrocities might be widespread. But for that mass of Germans who were neither wholehearted Nazis nor outright opponents of the regime, crediting these rumors was psychologically difficult, if not impossible. As the war progressed, the personal sacrifices it demanded tended to close off such lines of thought. The war itself was a dubious enough enterprise in the minds of most Germans. If to these doubts was added the question of whether one was fighting for a system capable of genocide, the emotional burden would have become unbearable.

Concentration camps? Their existence was familiar, but it was also believed that their inmates could survive by working hard and obeying orders. For the ordinary German, air raids, food shortages, grief for lost relatives, worry about those at the front, surviving the next action—these personal anxieties left little time for concern about the fate of others, particularly others stamped for years and decades as aliens.

LILO CLEMENS*

"There goes a Jew girl."

All Jewish schools were closed in June 1942: "No more instruction— the Jews don't need to be educated." I was 14 years old and was extremely lucky not to have been sent to a factory. Instead, I became a so-called "young helper" at the Jewish cemetery in Berlin-Weissensee. Even today, I'm not exactly certain who was actually responsible for initiating the program, but, in any case, most of the children from Jewish schools were sent to work in the factories. There weren't that many really young Jewish children my age around any more anyway. Most of them had already been sent with their parents to concentration camps. As far as I was concerned, I considered myself exceptionally lucky to have to work in the cemetery because I'd always had an interest in working with plants and flowers. In fact, I'd always wanted to become a landscape architect, so the work was perfect for me.

I worked at the cemetery until the end of 1944. No one really bothered us at all during that time—no police, no Gestapo. And if they showed up, they never went further than the main office building. It was a wonderful refuge for us. Naturally, we had to go home at night. Later, when the air raids began, we had to run at least half the distance through the burning city, a good six miles by foot.

---

* Biography on page 57.

And then the day came when I took off my Star of David. We had to wear the Star at all times. But we had come up with a hundred different ways of taking it off. For example, we sewed them on snaps or simply used safety pins to attach them to our clothes so that it would be easy to pull them off and hide them in our pockets. I had a raspberry-colored raincoat—something I'll never forget—and the Star was attached to that.

One day after a massive air attack, the transportation system had all but broken down. I had to change streetcars three different times to get home. I had to run through the yards of burning houses. When I ran past one crowd of people, they began yelling, "There goes a Jew girl! This is all their fault!" The headlines they had read that morning in the newspapers began to have an effect. The people picked up stones and gravel and threw them at me, a 15-year-old girl.

I don't remember how I got away. All I know is that I didn't get hurt; I was still wearing my raspberry raincoat when I got home. It must have taken me an hour and a half to make it through the burning city. When I got home I said to my father, "I've had it! I don't care what you do to me, but I'm not going to wear the Star ever again! I'd rather be sent to a camp!" It was unbelievable, but from that day on, my father never wore his Star either.

Even though we were a lot better off than those in the concentration camps, we were living in total warfare. We were continuously in danger, and lived with this danger—man is a creature of habit. We were persecuted 24 hours a day, but we somehow learned to live with it.

I recall one incident having to do with our air raid shelter. It was more of an improvisation than anything else; doors that were allegedly air-tight were installed in the basement. Of course, we Jews were not allowed inside, and had to sit in front of the doors. It was common practice in our area that the house custodian was also the air raid shelter warden. In the winter of 1943, our roof was hit by stick-type incendiary bombs and caught fire. We naturally helped carry buckets of water. You wouldn't believe the number of buckets we carried—hours upon end, heavy buckets or tubs of water up five flights of stairs! In any case, we were not only able to save the roof, but the entire house as well. And the next evening, our custodian announced, "I say, because the Jews here helped to save our house, they can stay in the air raid shelter." No one said anything against the idea. From that moment on, we sat on the other side of those air-tight doors.

In February 1943, a large-scale operation to "free" Berlin of its Jewish citizens began. Jews who were working in armament factories were arrested while they were on the job and, for the most part, were deported to Auschwitz. My father—and this is one of the coincidences which enabled us to survive—was also arrested, but released because he was married to an Aryan. Instead, my father was one of several selected by the Nazis to immediately begin with the packing and storing of the files and documents in the Jewish community house.

It's unbelievable, but it's true! The Nazis wanted to exterminate the Jewish people, and they wanted to be able to say, "Look at these documents. Look how many Jews we used to have, and now we don't have any at all!" They wanted statistics! The Jewish Community Archive in Berlin, the largest in all of Germany, was to be salvaged and stored, an official order from the Gestapo.

My father continued to work there until the end of the war. During that time, he got to know some Gestapo people and had me officially declared "Jewish Half-Breed, First Class." He thought he was doing me a favor, protecting me from being deported. I was forced to leave my wonderful little world at the cemetery and go to work for a street repair firm. As a "Jewish Half-Breed, First Class," I was allowed to pound stones into the ground around Alexander Platz. That's where I got my rheumatism. I was 16 years old.

KLAUS SCHEURENBERG*

"They felt like traitors just because they knew a 16-year-old Jewish boy."

In 1941, when I was 16 years old, I was forced to perform hard labor in a parquet flooring factory. I had to catch the commuter train every morning at 5:20 A.M. I always sat in the same part of the train, and pretty soon I knew all of the other commuters. There was a brick-layer, an Italian, an older man who always wore a coat and tie, a chubby-faced blonde woman who rode five station stops with us, and others. We greeted one another every morning. And then came September 18, 1941. That was the first day I had to wear the Star of David. I was terribly embarrassed. All of a sudden everyone could tell what you were. They could spit on you, beat you to death—you were suddenly totally unprotected. I wanted to hold my lunch bag in front of the Star, but I knew if I was caught, I'd be deported. No, I couldn't do that.

I walked to the train station that first morning as inconspicuously as I could. I even wanted to get into another train car, but everything happened so quickly. I got on the train and ended up in my old compartment. I stood at the door and almost whispered "Good morning." The others looked at me as if they were thinking, "What's the matter with him today?" Then they noticed what I was wearing: the Star. What followed after that really surprised me. Like a chorus, they all sung out loudly and clearly, "Morning." The bricklayer asked, "Why don't you come in and sit down in your seat." I told him that I couldn't and that it wasn't allowed. And he said, "Oh, that's ridiculous! Come on in and sit down!" The person sitting across from me gave me a cigarette, and the old man offered me a light.

---

* Biography on page 53.

Everybody smiled reassuringly at me for a few seconds, then the expression on their faces changed. It was as if they suddenly realized they were betraying the German people. During the last several years, they had been indoctrinated with the idea that the Jews were Public Enemy Number One. They felt like traitors just because they knew a 16-year-old Jewish boy. They never came back to that compartment again. There was so much mistrust, they even avoided one another after that day. Their behavior was typical of how people act under a dictatorship.

ÄNNE SCHEURENBERG

Born 1916; her family was one of the few Jewish families to survive in Stettin by hiding out; she later married Klaus Scheurenberg; a housewife, she lives in Berlin.

"The only way out of Auschwitz is through the chimney."

The Jewish community in Stettin, a rather large one, was deported in February 1940. This was a "Night and Fog" operation throughout Pomerania. For the most part, people were taken to the suburbs of Lublin. These were not the camps yet, rather ghettos.

The ghettos were dissolved in 1943 at the latest. Of course, many died before it came to that, including my grandparents who were both 80 years old. After being unloaded in Lublin, all of them were forced to run. Naturally, there was no way my 80-year-old grandmother could keep up, and they beat her until she couldn't get up anymore. She was the first of the two to die. My grandfather died of natural causes the very next night.

On Hitler's birthday, April 20, 1940, the *Gauleiter* reported, "Mein Führer, Pomerania is free of Jews." That was his birthday present to Hitler. But a few Jewish families had remained behind. The deportation had been rather disorganized and they overlooked a few, including us.

I was 13 years old and had attended the Jewish school in Stettin, but it was closed down. Then people remembered that there was a 13-year-old girl who still had to go to school. Since I was only permitted to go to a Jewish school, they sent me to one in Berlin to finish my education. I lived in a Jewish girls' dormitory and attended this Jewish school in Berlin until I was 14. It was schizophrenic!

Afterwards, I returned to Stettin and was put on a Jewish work gang to do forced labor. I worked in a factory which produced roofing material, really awful work. We worked under very primitive conditions, and the people working there included criminals with life sentences and prostitutes, as well as Russian and French POWs. It was hardly a place for a young girl. I was there until I turned 17, in 1944. This was when the last Jewish families were to be deported.

Someone had noticed that there were still a few of us left. There were, I believe, still five families in Stettin who wore the yellow star. There were also a few mixed marriages; these people were not required to wear the star. The head of the Gestapo phoned my mother and said he had already prevented our deportation a few times, but that he wouldn't be able to postpone it any longer. This Gestapo man had been a fervent Nazi until he lost his son in the war. Then he grew more thoughtful somehow, more reflective. He had then been invited to visit the concentration camp in Auschwitz, and his reaction was opposite to what was expected.

One time, I was told to report to the Gestapo because someone maintained that they had seen me out on the street without my star. Any other Gestapo man wouldn't have even asked me about it, I would have been arrested with no questions asked. But he told me I was free to go. "And I hope," he said, "we will not see each other here again, because the only way out of Auschwitz is through the chimney."

We went into hiding after that. We had the opportunity to live, or rather vegetate, in a cellar under some ruins. It was a miserable way of existing and, of course, we didn't have any ration coupons. But at the factory where I worked, there was also a section where used food coupons were glued to sheets of paper and then destroyed. People would steal these at the risk of their lives. They tried to scrape them off and re-use them.

This was when my father went to the owner of the grocery store. He was terribly afraid, because in unsticking the ration coupons they had become smeared and discolored. My father gave him one of the coupons and the storekeeper said, "Wait until everyone has left the shop." My father was about to run away when the shopkeeper said, "Why bother so much with stealing the coupons? Forget it. We can make a deal. I know somebody at the coupon office. You won't be able to get everything of course, just the surplus, but it will be enough for you to get by." After that, we had enough to eat. We only cooked at night so that no one would see the smoke. The grocery store man was, of course, Aryan, but when he fled, he gave us everything he had left over. We were freed when the Russians came to Stettin.

KARL-HEINZ MAIER

Born 1923; drafted into a Wehrmacht armored unit, later discharged for being a "half-Jew"; after the war served in an Israeli army armored unit as a major and tank battalion commander; returned to Germany to work as a journalist and lives in Berlin.

"I thought I would do something for the Jewish side of my family."

I was drafted into the Wehrmacht when I was 17, and was sent to the Eastern front. I was wounded in the vicinity of Smolensk and was taken to the military hospital in Bobruisk on the Berezina River. I was put in a large room with about 150 to 200 other privates. I kept hearing shooting that I couldn't identify. But one day, I witnessed a scene that told me what it was.

I overheard a few older soldiers discussing the price of a pistol. They couldn't seem to come to an agreement. The one who wanted to sell it said, "This is a really first-rate piece. I tested it out myself. Jews are being shot here. I was out yesterday and shot three or four of them. The gun fits your hand like it was custom-made." Needless to say, this was an extraordinarily shocking experience for me, considering I had a Jewish father. These were not SS men; they were simple privates. Perhaps they weren't even in the Nazi Party or any other such organization. This confession of murder was not politically motivated. It was obvious that these people were not killing out of conviction.

After I got out of the hospital, I went to my commander, stood up to my full height, and said, "Permission to speak, sir." I told him that according to the Nuremberg Laws, I was a half-Jew and thus unacceptable for the Wehrmacht. He looked at me and said, "Are you crazy? I'm not interested in that at all. You're a good soldier; don't cause me trouble." Soon thereafter, I was released from the Wehrmacht with the notation "Unworthy to serve in the armed forces."

Shortly before the end of the war, after I had deserted from a "half-breed detention camp" in Thuringia, I was nabbed on the street in Berlin and sent to a *Volkssturm* unit. As we were marching toward Frankfurt on the Oder, I did the same thing I had done before. I went to my company commander and told him, "Do you know, I'm really in the wrong place here. I actually don't have anything to do with your war. I am a Jewish half-breed." Then I was put into prison where I sat with another man in a cell. He was also a half-Jew. I had a sergeant major who was really a great guy. One evening, he suddenly came and locked us into a truck. He got behind the steering wheel and took off. We drove for a while, and then we stopped. He opened the door and said, "Get out of here!"

I went to Israel in 1947. I thought I would do something for the Jewish side of my family, but I wanted to do it as a German. I didn't want to become an Israeli citizen, and I didn't want to convert—I was a Catholic. When I arrived in Israel, the first thing they did was hold my arm up to see if I had an SS tattoo, the one telling your blood type. Then I was enrolled in the Haganah. Very soon, I was sent to the 7th Brigade of the Israeli army and I quickly advanced to the rank of major and became a battalion commander.

Germany didn't treat me badly; I got to know a great many people who were making an effort after the war to establish something new. I feel a great deal of solidarity with them, and I have never felt out of place here. After all, I didn't grow up in a Jewish household; I grew up in a Social Democratic family. I was not against Hitler because my father was a Jew; I was against him because I was raised to be against him. Both my mother's brothers and my father were Social Democrats. I think of myself as a German, and always have. And I have never had any passport other than a German one.

INGE SCHILZER*

"I am greatly indebted to the British army."

I was expelled from Berlin toward the end of 1940 with one of the last transports. My family was given a piece of paper saying that we weren't allowed to live there any longer. As long as we remained in Berlin, we had to report to a special police station and explain why we were still in the city. We simply didn't know where to go. First of all, it cost money to travel, and second, other countries had already closed their doors to us as well. The more fortunate ones who had a rich uncle in America could afford to go to the United States. But how many of these rich uncles were there, and did they know exactly what we were having to go through? We weren't allowed to go to the theater or to the movies. Signs were even hung on the benches in the park that read: Jews are prohibited to sit here. Later, we had to be off the streets by 8 P.M.

---

* Biography on page 49.

I was sent to Hamburg by the Palestine Office, the Jewish agency responsible for emigration to Palestine from Germany. I was in Hamburg when the first bombs were dropped on the city. I never knew what to think when we were under attack. It was really agonizing. Should I be glad that we are being bombed or should I be afraid? It was a terrible feeling.

I finally wound up on a ship full of Jews hoping to get into Palestine somehow. We sailed around aimlessly for almost three months before finally ending up near the Palestinian coast. Initially the British decided not to allow us to land. The Arabs had given them permission to let in 100,000 Jews, and they were already there. A few Jews who belonged to the underground movement managed to smuggle a couple of dynamite sticks on board. Their intentions were only to cripple the ship so that it couldn't leave, not to destroy it. But the hole they blew in the ship was a little larger than expected, and the ship sank within 12 minutes. Three hundred people died when the ship went down in Haifa harbor.

A war was going on. The British saw us as Germans, as spies. Suddenly I was no longer the Jew. I was the German. We were detained a year in an internment camp. The only thing I possessed was a bathing suit; everything else was lost with the ship.

Later we were considered as shipwreck victims, and had to be treated accordingly. After I was released from the camp, I remained in Palestine illegally.

My first thoughts after my release were: What are you going to do now? How are you going to survive? I knew neither the people nor their language. And I was all by myself. Somehow I managed to get by, living from one day to the next. Working as a maid for a Jewish family living in Palestine was the only work I could find. I worked for them for four years. Israel didn't exist yet. I slept anywhere I could, on park benches, on the floor in the homes of friends, and on top of tables.

I knew I had to do something, so I joined the British army. The reason wasn't exactly unselfish. It was the first time in ages that I had regular meals. It was the first time that I had my own bed and my own clothes. They only gave me a uniform, but at least I was decently dressed. I was, of course, in the women's army. I am greatly indebted to the British army. One day I received a really nice letter informing me that I could now officially live in Palestine. I had already been there for six years.

In 1956, I returned to Berlin for a visit. I went back with very mixed feelings. I walked along the streets, unable to look anyone in the eye. In 1960, I once again visited Berlin. Soon after I arrived, I read an ad in the paper. The British were looking for someone to work in their headquarters. I applied for the job and started work the very next day. I have lived in Berlin ever since. I don't really feel at home anywhere.

Reflecting on Hitler, I don't know what all of the commotion was about. He wasn't even that attractive—I know, I saw him up close once. I can't figure out why all of the women got so excited over him. They were all crazy!

FRITZ NAST-KOLB

Born 1916; employed during the war by the Bosch electric company where, despite being a "half-Jew," he was protected; he and his Jewish mother survived; after the war, stayed with Bosch; lives in Stuttgart.

"My mother looked like a small, emaciated 18-year-old girl."

Because I wasn't allowed to go to a university after receiving my *Abitur* in 1934, I began as a business apprentice with Bosch in Stuttgart. I stayed with the company after I completed the two-year apprenticeship. As an employee of a large armament factory, I had been declared "irreplaceable" and was exempt from the draft. That was in 1940. Even then, it didn't stop the Gestapo from forcing half-Jews to perform hard labor in their *Organization Todt*. By the end of 1943, Bosch said they had to find a way to make certain I was safe. At that time, Bosch maintained so-called Bosch War Service Shops which were situated close behind the front and staffed mainly by Germans. This way, equipment such as generators, fuel injectors, and so forth, could quickly be repaired and returned to the troops. To keep me out of the Gestapo's clutches, Bosch sent me to Minsk, in Russia, at the end of 1943.

In September 1944, I returned to Stuttgart. Bosch set up a special shop for half-Jews and any other people who were out of work or in danger because of political reasons. All in all, there were 30 to 40 of us in this newly established workplace, including 14 or 15 half-Jews. The circumstances were not very comforting. The air-raid siren sounded constantly and you had to keep running back to the bunker. Naturally, we always had a tremendous fear of the Gestapo, there's no question of that. But the air raids and being in the midst of everything that was happening made your own fate seem relatively unimportant, and you suppressed thinking about it. But toward the end of 1944, if you weren't a raving Nazi, you had to come to the realization that it was only a question of time before it would all be over.

As a half-Jew, I was directly touched by the mass murders. My mother, my uncle, my aunt, and my grandmother, in other words, my entire family, was deported to Theresienstadt. We feared that this might mean death, but no one knew anything for sure. We clung to every little shred of information we could get. When we received confirmation that a package we had sent had been delivered, for example, we breathed a heavy sigh of relief. But what exactly happened in Treblinka, in Auschwitz, and in Neuengamme, the systematic elimination of countless people, that I didn't know. You tended always to remain in close contact with those in a similar situation or with others who received information from the front. We did hear something that was filtered through by soldiers at the front to the effect that the Jews who had been transported to Riga back in 1941 had all been shot. That we heard about, I remember very distinctly. There were, of course, rumors, but we didn't know anything for sure. You didn't believe it; you didn't want to believe it. You just didn't think it was possible.

My mother, by the way, survived. I picked her up in Theresienstadt in June 1945. She had always had the tendency to be rather plump, and the first time I saw her, I hardly recognized her. She looked like a small, emaciated 18-year-old girl.

HERMANN ROSENAU

Born in 1926 to a "privileged" German-Jewish mixed marriage; awarded a prize by Nazi leaders unaware of his ancestry; is now active in politics and resides near Koblenz, Palatinate.

"I had been declared the winner of a national competition."

I was the second of three children of a marriage which, according to the Nuremberg Laws, was a "privileged" mixed marriage. My father was, as it was so well put, a "full-blooded Jew" and my mother was officially a "pure Aryan." My father was the director of the last Jewish sanatorium and convalescent home in Germany. This was in Bendorf, in the Rhineland. He wasn't deported along with the others in the sanatorium in 1942 because of his mixed marriage. Such marriages were "privileged" because the children were raised as Christians. As we learned later, this special classification only meant a postponement of deportation. We constantly lived in fear after that day in 1942 when more than 300 people, the sick and the healthy, were loaded on a freight train and deported. Not a single day passed when I didn't ask myself, "Will the others still be there when I go home at night?"

I was seven years old at the beginning of the Third Reich and attended a middle school. There were so-called "maybe-maybe not regulations" regarding us "half-breeds, first class." The schools could, but didn't have to, admit half-Jewish students. And no principal could be forced to take in such a person. Therefore I was unable to go on to the *Gymnasium*. I had always had an interest in technology, but it was only with great difficulty that I was able to obtain an apprenticeship as an electrician.

In the summer of 1943, I was drafted into the Hitler Youth's military training camp. It was run by both the Wehrmacht and the Hitler Youth. The purpose of this three-week camp was to provide 17-year-olds with basic infantry and other military training. When I told them that they had made a mistake in calling me for duty—I was, after all, a half-Jew—they only replied, "This is strictly military business. If you don't go, we'll consider you AWOL. Stop making such a fuss!" So I had no other alternative but to go to the camp.

No one knew me there and I had every opportunity to advance in rank. After one week, I was the senior in barrack-room One. And three days after that, I was the camp senior when it came to organizing different kinds of cultural activities. Besides, I also excelled in all of the tests we were given. As a half-breed, first class, I left the camp with a valid Hitler Youth pass in my hand. This camp pass was even better than the regular Hitler Youth pass because it had your picture in it. Those participants who had really done well were named "war training leaders." Afterwards, I was called a couple of times to serve as such a leader at Hitler Youth fire department exercises.

In retrospect, I must say I enjoyed the time I spent and the duties I had in the Hitler Youth's military training camp. It was the first time I wasn't excluded from taking part. No one treated me like some kind of an exotic crippled insect. I was a normal person like everyone else. Being an outcast, not being able to participate—even during my school days when my good friends, based on their intelligence and other abilities, had become leaders in the Hitler Youth—was naturally depressing. I'm positive I would have actually enjoyed taking part in the field games, going on marches, and everything else they did. And had I been drafted to fight at the front before 1938 and Crystal Night, I would have jumped at the chance.

Later that same year, we were informed in vocational school about the Reich's annual Vocational Contest. I was encouraged to apply as an electrician. My family's idea for survival was, "Don't do anything to bring attention to yourself; if you don't apply, they'll think you're different from the rest," so I filled out the application. When it came to the question, "Are you a member of the Hitler Youth?", I truthfully put "Hitler Youth Fire Department, Bendorf on the Rhine." After all, I had two Hitler Youth honor badges, one of which was the silver achievement badge (actually it was tin). The first contest was held locally. It didn't take long before I found out that I had done fairly well. I was proclaimed winner of our district and invited to participate in the next round.

Not only were we required to take part in athletic events—because "a German boy is physically fit"—we also had to write an extensive essay on our outlook of the world. I remember one topic you could select was, "What do you know about Heinrich Himmler?" And because I had been negatively impressed by Himmler, I knew more than most—his youth, his development, etc. Apparently, I also did well on this test and didn't have to reveal the slightest bit about my true opinions. I wound up winning the provincial competition as well.

For some reason, the officials didn't pay close enough attention and forgot to tell the national judges in Berlin that a half-Jew was still in the running, and I was called to participate in the Reich contest. All of those working in the various metal manufacturing branches were present—from coppersmiths to armature winders, and so on. I, of course, entered the competition as an electrician. And naturally, only one Reich winner would be named from each category. The final competition took place in April 1944. If my memory serves me correctly, the awards ceremony took place on April 28, 1944, in the town hall in Dresden. I was one of the Reich winners.

Among the officials at the ceremony was Dr. Ley. He was the head of the Labor Front, the Nazi trade union. The head of the Hitler Youth, Axmann, was also in attendance. He had lost his right arm, and appeared to be a very calm and rational sort of man. These men exchanged a few words with every third winner they awarded, including me. Afterwards I was interviewd on the Reich's radio network. The Nazis in my hometown in Bendorf heard the same broadcast, and, as you can well imagine, they were beside themselves.

After the ceremony and the interviews, we went downstairs to the Rathskeller where the guests of honor mingled with the contest winners. Then everyone stood and music was played as the big shots, Dr. Ley, Axmann, and a few others, walked in and sat down at our table. For me personally, this was a triumphant situation. There I sat, a "sub-human," with all of the big men, and not one of them knew who I really was. On the contrary, these men had just awarded me a tin medal!

By the time I got home, the place was in an uproar. Finally, I received a letter from the head competition officials in Berlin telling me that I had knowingly deceived them by claiming to be a member of the Hitler Youth. Therefore, they were cancelling my award and expected me to return both the certificate and medal. I didn't comply with their demands. I had my pride. After all, I had been declared the winner of a national competition.

HANNS PETER HERZ*

"This is the most beautiful country in the world, but it had some nasty people for a while."

Our neighbor in Berlin was an SS-*Hauptsturmführer* who worked at Gestapo headquarters. One day he told my father, "Mr. Herz, we've never spoken, but I'd like to tell you that it would be better if you disappeared for a few weeks."

We took my father to my mother's relatives in a small country village. Only 300 people lived there and everybody knew everybody else. My father spent the first week, day and night, shut up in a tiny room in my great aunt's house. Sometimes, when it was pitch dark

---

* Biography on page 47.

outside, he'd go into the courtyard. The head of the Farmers' Association, a party member, lived right across the way; it was a family we had known for decades. He came to my great aunt one day and said, "You can't fool me. Hanns is here. I heard him cough, and I know that cough. He's been here often enough. Okay, so he's here and he has to hide. Why should he hide? He can come out, nothing's going to happen to him here."

My father came out and they talked. First of all, my father got illegal food coupons. After that, the head of the Farmer's Association brought milk, butter, and sausage every day. Then he brought along two other party members and they played cards with my father every other night. And they warned him whenever something was up or whenever a bigwig from the party visited. Three months passed before my father was able to return home again. The village had kept quiet.

Wartime auxiliary duty for students was not just farm work. We also took over regular jobs. Once during the holidays I was assigned to the train station at Friedrichsstrasse. There were four state railroad men in charge of left luggage. They tiptoed around me for two or three days and then asked me how come I wasn't a Hitler Youth. That broke the ice. They brought me fruit from their gardens, and once they even gave me a sandwich. About a week later, the boss took me aside and said, "Listen, none of us here likes the Nazis either. You know, I used to be an engineer, but I was fired because something I said didn't please my boss. Everybody here, in fact, has seen better days. We've gotten used to outwitting those brown gents, and now we're gonna show you how to do it too."

One day an SS man showed up with a huge tin suitcase. One person stood watch while my boss and I took the suitcase to the back. There were large reinforced steel shelves in the back, and my boss said, "Now we'll give this thing some special treatment." He picked up the case and threw it against the shelves, again and again. It wasn't long before something started dripping out of the sides. One side was leaking olive oil and the other perfume mixed with liquor. "Now watch what happens," my boss said. A couple of hours later, the SS officer came back, presented his ticket, and received his case. There was a horrible screech. My boss asked what the problem was. The officer was excited, "Don't you see what's been done to it?" So my boss said, "Why don't you open it up so we can see what happened." He opened it, and there was a heap of broken glass, ladies' underwear, oil, perfume, liquor, and so on. The suitcase had come from France. "I'll report you!" yelled the SS officer. "You're going to pay for this!" "Fine," my boss said, "come with me and we'll go to the station master, but I don't think you're allowed to bring back articles like that." The officer snapped his suitcase shut and disappeared. "See," said my boss, "that's the way we do it." And they did it day after day. It was their kind of resistance, and a kind that left an impression on me.

When I was thrown out of school in 1942, I started an apprenticeship at a scrap-dealer's. There were four other new apprentices and, interestingly enough, we were all children of politically or racially persecuted parents. The manager introduced us to one another and said, "Now you know what to make of one another, and so you'll also get to know me, I want you to come to work 15 minutes early every day." When we'd come in, he'd have a big map on his desk with little flags on it. Then we'd analyze the last London radio broadcast and move the flags to mark the troop movements. By the time the others came to work, we had cleared everything away.

Early in 1942, we were allocated some Russian forced laborers. The Russians had to be picked up by the different firms from a camp in Erkner, near Berlin. My boss called me in and said, "Go pick up the six Russians we're getting. Don't choose strong ones. Take ones that look weak and need help." So I went to the camp, and it was like a slave market. There were huge barracks where they had to bathe and shower. The "buyers" were taken along the windows where they could pick the ones they wanted. I chose six people who looked very weak and who certainly couldn't have pulled their own weight too much longer. I brought them back to the firm where they got pretty good living quarters. The manager appeared and assigned one of our foremen, an old Communist, as supervisor to the Russians. He told me I'd picked the right ones and made the following rule: from then on, we were supposed to bring an extra sandwich to work to give to the Russians. That's how we nourished and took care of them; they never had to do the heavy work. All six of them made it back home when they were freed by Soviet troops.

We'd seen that all our Social Democratic friends and comrades stood by us. After the war father often said, "This is the most beautiful country in the world, but it's had some nasty people for a while." We stayed in Germany because we saw it as an opportunity to help the country and the people. We both grabbed at the chance and we've never regretted it.

In my heart, I feel it was right to stay in Germany—today more than ever—and, above all, to do everything to spare the next generation from the same thing happening to them that happened to us. As long as I can, I'll try time and time again to make it clear that what happened to us isn't a fairy-tale, but a terrible truth no one can ever forget. Sure, you don't have to carry it around with you all day, but everybody's got to know it.

DORA VÖLKEL

Born in 1917 in Poland; a survivor of Auschwitz; lives in Berlin.

"I don't believe there is a God."

I was born in 1917 in the part of Poland that had belonged to Austria before World War I. We spoke German at home. I went to a Polish high school and took German and Latin as my foreign languages. I come from a very respectable family. My father was not an Orthodox Jew. I was the only Jew in my class at school. Anti-Semitism existed in Poland even before the Germans arrived. The last two years it got so bad that classmates of mine stopped talking to me.

We were living out in the country when the war broke out. The sirens started to wail, and we all ran out on the balcony. We thought it was nothing more than a practice alarm over at the Polish air base not far from us. My mother, who had terrific eyesight, said, "No, children, I can see swastikas on the airplanes. They're Germans. The war has started."

The Germans did hardly a thing to the Poles; it was the Polish Jews they took action against. The Germans started by requiring us to pay a "contribution" that was nothing more than a penalty for being Jewish. We had to pay 500 zloty, which was a lot of money considering we didn't have any. And then, of course, we were forced to move to a smaller, unheated apartment. It got really cold that first winter. To earn a little extra money, we knitted. We used to knit in our tiny kitchen on the table next to the gas lantern where it was at least a little warmer. And because it was so cold, we stayed in bed a lot. The Germans soon started to look for men to work.

We didn't wear a yellow Star of David, we wore a blue star. The Jews in Lodz wore the yellow star on their backs. As Jews, we weren't allowed to lock any doors. The front door had to stay open all the time. One day a really drunk Polish policeman stood in our doorway. He was waving his pistol back and forth and threatened to shoot me. He said, "All you pretty Jewish girls do is turn the German soldiers' heads."

We were next moved to a totally Jewish quarter where we were given one room to live in. Things got steadily worse from that moment on. I used to go out with a Christian girlfriend from school. She often said that she thought we looked alike. She always linked arms with me when we walked so that no one could see the Star of David. That kind of thing happened quite often when people saw the star. German pilots used to say to me, "Fräulein, take that thing off and come to the movies with us."

As far as the Gestapo was concerned, we Jews were wild game who could be and were shot on the streets for no reason at all. The Polish population, in general, didn't suffer that much. In fact, many people were actually glad that the Jews were being persecuted and killed. I told my Christian girlfriend, "You know, you can date soldiers if you want. It's war and they can't help it that they have to be soldiers. It's like that all over the world. Not everybody's a Nazi just because he wears a German uniform. Just watch out for the Gestapo man because he's a murderer!"

Our situation turned very serious in 1942. On occasion I worked at the air base where the Germans were whenever they had a special comrades' night or needed someone to clean the tables. One time I was in the kitchen and had to clean out one of those huge pots. And because I was so small, I washed my feet and climbed into the kettle to clean it from the inside. When I bent over to scrub the bottom, my sweater must have slid up my back because when Herr Neumerker, an administrative official at the air base and a very good-looking man, came in, he said, "Say, Fräulein, do you always take your clothes off first thing?" I turned beet-red.

In August, all Jews had to gather with no more than 40 pounds of luggage out in the huge stockyard. Christian friends hid both my mother and sister in their pig sty. Herr Neumerker came to the stockyard to pick out people to work. These people were given a special certificate that stated they were allowed to remain alive. Herr Neumerker saw me and said, "Her I have to have." He looked at me and asked, "Do you have any other relatives here?" I told him that my cousin and my sister were here too. "Anyone else?" Then I pointed to where my father was standing. My father took a little step forward. The Ukrainian militia were horrible anti-Semites and murderers. They nearly beat my father to death right in front of my eyes. Then the people who weren't selected to work, especially the older people and the children, were all loaded up onto a truck and taken into the woods where they were beaten and murdered. That's where my father and all of my Jewish friends were killed.

My mother and my sister were in hiding. My youngest sister was with me. We were marched off to the air base to work. We were still allowed to live in the Jewish quarter. I worked on the base as a cleaning woman. My mother and my sister didn't have work permits, but I was able to smuggle them onto the base. I hid them in the basement next to the room where we kept our brooms and other supplies. I was so nervous. Neumerker must have sensed something because he said, "What's the matter? You know I did everything I could." I told him I had hidden my mother and my sister. He said, "That's terrific! Where did you hide them?" I told him they were here on the base. He was surprised: "What? How did you manage that?" So I told him the whole story. He told me to bring them out during the evening roll call and that he would take care of getting them the necessary work papers from the Gestapo. Later, before he left to go to the Eastern front, he whispered for me to follow him to the laundry room. Then he told me that his cousin was married to a Jewish doctor and that they both had emigrated to Palestine. He was really a wonderful person. I don't know if I would have had as much courage myself to help people as much as he did.

I worked at the air base in Krosno from August 1943 to January 1944. When the Russians started to come closer, we were moved to Plazow near Cracow. It was a labor camp. I remember the day we arrived was a beautiful winter day. There was snow on the ground and the sun was shining. We walked through the main gate and saw a fire. I didn't know what it was, so I said to my mother, "Look how beautiful that is." She said, "Quiet, child! They are burning people over there. First they shoot them, then they throw them in a ditch, and then they burn them." We had to work in this camp. One day in May 1944, we were all called out to the parade ground. They started picking out people to be gassed in Auschwitz that day. They came and took my mother. I had been allowed to wash and delouse her the day before. She was 42 years old and looked like she was 80. She was a wonderful woman, just wonderful, an angel. And because the best people were taken from us is why I don't believe there is a God. I volunteered to go along with my mother, but the SS told me, "Your turn will come soon! You are still young. You can work!"

The Russians kept coming closer and it didn't take long before we were all sent to Auschwitz. We went by train. I still had hope that I would see my mother again. I even fasted during the most important Jewish holidays because I thought if I could see my mother for just a second, there must be a God after all. But my mother had already turned to ashes. She had been cremated immediately.

The trip to Auschwitz was really something. It's my guess that 20,000 people were loaded into cattle cars. We were allowed to get out once at night to relieve ourselves. When we got to Auschwitz, the first thing we noticed was the big sign *"Arbeit macht frei"* (Freedom Through Work).

Then the first selection came, where people were picked out to go straight to the gas chamber. We all had to undress and march naked past a group of SS officers. Another high SS officer was standing all alone with a dog at the side of the group. It was Dr. Mengele. My older sister was absolutely terrified of dying. I said to her, "Don't be afraid. You go in first; I'll be right behind you. If you are gassed, I'll be with you. I won't leave you alone. But don't forget to push your chest out when we walk by!" My sisters and I all had rather full bosoms, and we looked healthier if we pulled our shoulders back and pressed our breasts forward. We marched past the SS men and Dr. Mengele came over to me and touched my breasts. I found out later that he wanted to see if I was pregnant, because pregnant women were gassed first thing. Then all the hair on our bodies was shaved off by prisoners. One of them grabbed my breasts and I slapped him across the face. Next, we were sent to a very large room with nozzles on the walls. We still didn't know if we were going to be gassed or what. When water came out, we knew we were going to stay alive.

With her head shaved clean, my younger sister looked just like a boy we used to know years ago. She started to laugh. In spite of our awful situation, I had to laugh too. It was more a hysterical laugh than anything. I remember I called, "Mathilde, where are you?" She answered, "What's with you? I'm standing right next to you!" I started to laugh again and told her she looked just like Wolf What's His Name from back home. We were given rags to put on and sent to Birkenau.

We were beaten a lot and hardly given anything to eat. You could watch human beings turn into animals. Many people lost all sense of human dignity. We were three sisters and we always saved a portion of bread in case we didn't get anything to eat for a while. My mother had told me, "If I'm no longer around, I want you to watch out for the other girls. You have the most energy and I know you can get them through." I never forgot this and I was convinced that if I wasn't gassed, beaten to death, or shot, I could get the three of us through this alive. I just had to keep alert and not get sick!

I remember there was a really young French girl, maybe 15 or 16 years old. She didn't understand a word of German. The SS women always gave their commands in German. This girl naturally didn't understand and was beaten terribly. The girl yowled like a beaten dog. I can still hear her today.

We were forced to carry heavy rocks from one place to another. We had to carry a rock about a half a mile, set it down, pick up another rock, and carry that back to where we had originally come from. And, of course, there was the fire, the bright fire rising from the chimney. You couldn't help but notice it. It burned night and day. People came from Hungary, and we said, "Today the Hungarians are burning." When was it going to be our turn?

Of course, there were times when we laughed in spite of everything. I saw the fire and I knew people were being cremated, but I also knew I was going to survive. I was incredibly angry. I kept telling myself, "You're going to make it!" And if they did come to get me, I wasn't going to be apathetic like the others.

Then we were moved to another block. The senior occupant, a kind of a Kapo, was a Polish-Jewish woman. She asked us to help her out. She said, "Children, when the SS women come through here, I'm going to have to scream and use the whip, but I'll be careful not to hurt you too badly. If the SS do it, it's a lot worse."

The Russians started bombing the area around Birkenau. They didn't bomb the camps; their targets were the permanent buildings the SS families lived in. The Russians kept coming closer. We were sent to Bergen-Belsen in cattle cars. That was in November 1944.

The rain wasn't heavy, but it was constant. We were first unloaded next to one of the many forests in northern Germany. We had been given blankets that became heavier and heavier the wetter they got; we weren't allowed to set them down. We weren't given anything to eat or drink for three whole days. This was a totally different way of dying—starvation. We finally reached Bergen-Belsen where we thought we were going to be gassed, but nothing like that happened. Starving people to death was the method used there. Then one day, because the Germans were so paranoid about getting some sickness, we were even allowed to wash ourselves. There was a narrow pole only a few steps away from where we washed. That was the latrine. You had to hold onto the pole so you wouldn't fall in. All you needed was a little push and in you fell. We were like chickens perched on a fence.

One day, three civilian men came into the tent looking for people to work. I said to my sisters, "Look, they're civilians. They look like decent people, not animals, not like the SS. They're real people. Stay right where you are." We had to show them our hands, which were heavily calloused from the hard work we had done in the various camps. The men pulled us out of there. On January 3, 1945, we were sent to work in a plant where Junker airplanes were built. Things were relatively good there; at least we were allowed to wash ourselves. My job was to rivet the holes on the wing with a compressed air hammer. Each hole required a different rivet. I caught on rather quickly, more out of sheer fright than anything else. Because I didn't really have the strength to do the job, I tackled it using my entire body. A German foreman worked on the other side. He gave me an apple once and told me to tell the Americans he had been good to me when they came. Both French and Belgian prisoners worked in this factory. I got really lucky once again. One of the French prisoners gave me something to eat. He sold or traded his cigarettes for food. He always brought me buttered rabbit sandwiches. I took out the rabbit meat and gave it to a Ukrainian girl who was free to move about. I told her to trade me onions, carrots, and potatoes. That's how we got by.

We were supposed to be sent to Buchenwald to be gassed, but in March, because the Americans were getting closer, we were sent to Theresienstadt instead. We had to endure a lot during that trip. I was in Theresienstadt from March until May 8. We were supposed to be gassed there, but the gas chamber was never completed. As far as I was concerned, Theresienstadt was a ghetto. It was a ghetto that was on display. Although we didn't get much to eat, the living conditions there were somewhat of an improvement. I met my first husband in Theresienstadt. He was a German Jew who had lost his brother, sister-in-law, and their child in Auschwitz. We were freed by the Russians on May 8, 1945.

When I close my eyes and think back, I can still see the SS guards in front of me. I still can't comprehend how people can act that way. Essentially, they were very primitive people. They were animals. The SS men were most likely all good husbands and fathers. But when it came to us, they beat us, they hunted us down, and they murdered us. They didn't hesitate at all before using their pistols. I just don't understand how a person can be like that.

The women were much worse. They were sadists. When we had to stand naked in Auschwitz, they used to talk to the men and laugh at us. At the time, I remember thinking, "My God, is this really happening?" I felt so ashamed having to stand there naked in front of all those men. I couldn't understand why the ground below us didn't just open and swallow us up. You can't imagine how degrading it is.

ARTURO LEYSER

Born in 1919 to Jewish parents in Berlin; emigrated to Rome, only to find himself in an Italian concentration camp; fled to Argentina and lived in Buenos Aires; returned to Berlin, where he resides today as an employee of the Federal Press and Information Office.

Concentration camp—Italian style.

In early 1939 I left Germany for Italy. I had friends in Rome. Anti-Semitism was non-existent in Italy. In fact, the Italian people spoke of Jews in a positive sense, maintaining that they were good business-men, etc. The anti-Jewish legislation Mussolini later put into effect—against his will—was definitely not very popular among the Italian people.

I returned home one day to find the wife of the couple I had been staying with in tears. "They will be here any minute to pick you up," she told me. She had barely finished the sentence when Italian officials appeared at the door. They were very polite. "We have to ask you to come with us," they said. I was immediately taken to prison in Rome. We were divided up, three to a cell. When two were sleeping, the third either had to stand or sit on one of those lying down. And, there was no toilet—an impossible situation!

Then came the day which I regard as one of the worst in my life, being taken out of prison. First we were shaved by a murderer who had received a life sentence. He shaved us with a very long, sharp knife. We tried to be humorous, and said things like, "You're next! Which way do you think your head is going to roll?" This man had killed his entire family—his kids, his brothers and sisters, and God knows who else. Next, we were taken to the train station.

Apparently the word had gotten around that we were being sent away. There were at least 200 Italian families at the station who greeted and kissed us. We knew some of the people, others were total strangers. One man fed us cherries he had already opened and pitted because our hands had been chained together. Others fed us chocolate—it was smeared all over our faces—and stroked our heads. A young girl I had never seen before covered my face with kisses.

A good friend of mine had also been imprisoned. Although he had been detained in another cell, we had been able to meet every day during the hour we were permitted to walk around in that awful courtyard. One day he said to me, "Arturo, if the time should ever come, I have two pills, one for you and one for myself. Don't worry, you won't suffer. I have them in my pocket." When we were rounded up for transport, we were able to persuade the Italian guards to chain us together. My last name began with an L and his with an M, so it worked out well.

We were all afraid we were going to be sent to Germany. Instead we boarded a train heading for southern Italy, Calabria. I knew then that was our salvation. This was toward the end of June 1940. When we finally reached our destination in Calabria, we walked for a couple of miles until we reached our "camp"—an empty field. The commander came riding over on a horse. He apologized and said, "You will have to build barracks yourself. Otherwise, you won't have a roof over your heads."

Two weeks later, another group of 40 Jewish prisoners arrived. The next transport of prisoners consisted of Poles. More and more prisoners arrived in our camp; for example, prostitutes from Budapest—very attractive women and girls.

All sorts of activities and events were organized. We had, for example, a set designer in our group who set up a stage in one of the barracks using black army blankets and silver paper for the curtains. Our camp had absolutely nothing in common with the concentration camps in Germany.

My parents had succeeded in leaving Germany for Argentina in September 1942. I also eventually obtained legal permission from Argentina to enter that country. The Vatican sent a telegram to the camp stating that my mother had arranged for me to leave Italy. I was sent to Rome, accompanied by two guards. It was impossible to take a boat from Italy to Spain, so my only other option was to fly. My friends in Rome found out that the city's opera house was sending its production of *La Traviata* to perform in Madrid and Barcelona. The ensemble would be flying! My friend arranged for me to be included in the group as the guy who cleans the stage after the final curtain or something. That's how I got to Spain.

I lived in a boarding house in Madrid until I could sail. The day of the big event, I was informed that the Spanish government was refusing to give me an exit visa. Apparently Germany was putting pressure on Spain about people leaving the country. I had no other choice but to go to the German Embassy. The official there accused me of possessing a falsified Italian passport. Of course I did my best to deny his accusations. He decided to send me, along with two guards, to the Italian Embassy, where the authenticity of my documents could be verified. Because the Germans couldn't speak very good Spanish, I presumed that their Italian was just as poor. I did some fast talking in Italian once we got to the Embassy. I told the Italian official that I was in a life and death situation and pleaded with him to help me. I gambled and won! The Germans had to let me go.

INES LYSS*

"You open your mouth about any of this, we'll kill you and your family."

We knew about the "protective custody" camps, as we called them. I was a young girl and a member of the BdM. As far as we knew, no one ever referred to them as concentration camps. We were told that Jews were detained together in these camps for their own safety, so that they wouldn't be killed by people who hated Jews. At the end of the war, they were supposed to be able to leave the country.

Once I talked to an SS soldier home on leave who used to work at the same import-export company I was apprenticing with. I asked him about the camps. He was a cadet at the officer candidate school in Braunschweig. He said, "No problem. I visited the camp in Bergen-Belsen, not far from here. All I can say is that they are receiving the best treatment and are eating well." When you're young, you believe it, you want to believe it. Not even those who had been interrogated in Gestapo basements ever said a word to their families about what had happened to them. They weren't allowed to say anything. They were probably told, "You open your mouth about any of this, we'll kill you and your family." So how were we to find out anything if those who knew didn't even talk?

We knew Jews. My mother had worked for Jews during the First World War. Our doctor was Jewish. We weren't allowed to go to him anymore because my father was a civil servant and the post office wouldn't pay the bill. This Jewish doctor in Hamburg told my father in 1936, "Herr Lüders, I know you can't come to me anymore, but if you need me, I'll come to you. And you won't have to pay me." Then we heard that he had been charged with *Rassenschande* and sent to jail. And after making a few inquiries, we found out that the entire

---

* Biography on page 209.

family had disappeared. Naturally we asked ourselves where they could be, but where could we have gone to find out?

Of course, we willingly believed that these were protective custody camps and nothing else. It was just impossible to believe that people could be so evil and cruel. No one really believed it. I say with my whole heart that we wouldn't have believed it in any case because we just didn't think such things were possible. You tend anyway to pretty much go along with the crowd. You believe certain things because you want to believe them, you want to be able to sleep at night. And I have to admit honestly that I'm glad that I didn't know anything.

DOROTHEA SCHLÖSSER*

Soldiers told me about the horrible things happening to the Jews while I was in Poland singing with a road show to entertain the troops. Everyone seemed to be talking about the truckloads of Jews who were being brought in and killed. The soldiers cried like children when they talked about it.

I will never forget one experience I had while in Warsaw. I was standing off stage waiting for my appearance when I noticed some young soldiers in the audience. There were dancers on stage and one of the soldiers began to laugh hysterically and said, "I already saw some people dancing tonight—the Jews we took away!" Then he suddenly began to sob, "Why don't they defend themselves?"

---

* Biography on page 45.

JEAN CUELLE

Born 1923; French citizen living in Alsace-Lorraine when the Germans annexed it; active in the resistance, arrested in 1941 and deported by the Gestapo to Concentration Camp Sachsenhausen; a businessman, he is president of the French Veterans Association and lives in Metz.

"Parents encouraged their children to spit on us."

I was arrested near Metz shortly after the German invasion because I was denounced as a resistance member. I was denounced by Frenchmen, something which, unfortunately, not only occurred once in a while, but quite frequently. I was the first to be arrested. The whole thing happened at 7:30 A.M. I was interrogated continuously for eight days; there were the famous interrogations which began in a relatively friendly manner on the first day, but became less and less friendly later on because I refused to talk. I continued to be interrogated at intervals of 10 to 14 days.

On December 27, 1942, we were taken by train to the collection camp at Compiègne from which all non-Jewish prisoners were to be deported to Germany. Most French Jews were deported to the known extermination camps: Auschwitz, Birkenau, etc. On the evening of January 22, they assembled us in a large hall, gave us a hunk of bread and a piece of sausage, and informed us that we would board a train for Germany the next morning. Our transport carried approximately 1,700 to 1,800 persons. We marched in rows of five to the train station with an armed Wehrmacht soldier guarding each side. We marched through all of Compiègne to reach the train station, and the entire time we sang the *Marseillaise*.

After we were loaded onto the trains, while we were still on French soil, we threw little notes out of the boxcars for our families. We scribbled something like, "Am being taken in the direction of Germany, destination unknown." I learned later that one of these notes actually reached my mother.

After several days, we arrived in the camp of Sachsenhausen, near Berlin. We were no longer attended to by the army, but had been handed over to the SS. It all took place in an atmosphere of gray morning mist. It was mid-winter, extremely cold, a frightening gray on gray—a scene from a nightmare.

It is often said that the German people didn't know anything about what happened. But I believe that in our case, even if they were unaware of the details of life in a concentration camp, it must have been apparent to them that the prisoners in these camps led a very, very hard life. On our march through town to the camp, we encountered parents who encouraged their children to spit on us. To them, we were French scum, terrorists or Communists. The first sight of the camp told us immediately what kind of a place it was. The first human beings we saw were in such miserable physical condition that we realized this was a camp in which we would slave and suffer terribly.

We all have retained the first roll call as one of our worst memories. We were so thinly dressed, and had had nothing to eat for a long time. It was around ten degrees below zero, and an icy wind blew in from the direction of Berlin. This was the first roll call at camp Sachsenhausen on January 25, 1943.

There were about 6,000 inmates in this camp. We had to get up at 4 o'clock in the morning. We washed ourselves a bit; it was very rudimentary hygiene. We slept in triple bunk beds, and lived in blocks in which every nationality from German occupied or annexed countries was represented. There were Germans there too, Germans of different categories. On my arrival I received the number 58,238. In the end, there were approximately 118,000 to 120,000 prisoners registered in Sachsenhausen.

There were also many political prisoners. Most of them were German trade unionists, Social Democrats, or Communists, who had been quickly arrested as enemies of the system.

The SS used dogs to uphold the iron discipline of the camps. The dogs were mercilessly set loose on the prisoners. An old man, a German, was brought to our barracks one day with his entire body— legs, feet, and arms—covered with bite wounds.

Around 6:45 A.M., we got a half-hour break from work during which we could go back to our barracks and spoon up some turnip or cabbage soup—whatever was available. Our rations became increasingly worse as time passed. We didn't peel the two or three small potatoes we sometimes got, so that we would have a bit more in our stomachs.

We could indirectly determine how large the losses in the German population must have been, because more and more civilians employed at the camp were drafted. At first, the young ones were sent to the front, and then even our SS guards had to go. In the end, they took everyone and sent war veterans to guard us, veterans with only one arm or leg. We watched them limping, and deduced that they were lacking men at the front.

Toward the end of the war, in 1945, I was brought to western Germany and returned to Alsace-Lorraine.

GERTRUDE STAEWEN

---

*Born 1894; a member of the dissenting Prot-
estant "Confessing Church"; because she
risked her life to rescue Jews, she lives today
as the only Gentile in a Berlin retirement home
for Jewish victims of the Nazi terror.*

"We stole groceries and put other people up to stealing for us."

What were the working conditions of a group that wanted to help
Jews and participate in active resistance? Such a group had to work
illegally, with every technique of a secret conspiracy. Nothing written
was permitted to exist. No telephone conversation about a meeting
could take place in clear language. We could never permit ourselves
to speak to someone on the street who wore a Jewish star—not so
much because of informers but rather because every Jew seen in
conversation with an Aryan was immediately and irrevocably lost.
The Gestapo watched very carefully during every service of the
Confessing Church to see if any Jews spoke to us.

Our aid work had to be very carefully planned. In the course of
mobilization everyone was registered with the employment office, so
you couldn't just leave your job and allocate your time as you saw fit.
You had to think up a system with your boss. You had to be in on it
together; the employer had to be prepared to lie for you if necessary;
and, of course, this was only possible if the employer was also an
anti-fascist. It was essential to free yourself from full-time work
because, for years, you were busy night and day, secretly making
your way to the Jews. Needless to say, we helped others besides the
baptized Jews and Christians of Jewish descent who sat beside us on
the church pews. The weakest and most needy among the brothers of

Christ was any person of Jewish descent, whether Christian or Jewish by religion.

Soon our address became known in Jewish circles and, time and time again, a new stranger would ring our doorbell at daybreak—strangers full of fear who had had to avoid every doorman and block leader to come to us and tell us of their plight. And we were always under terrible, nightmarish pressure, knowing that we would only be able to help a paltry few.

When we first began our activities, I remember walking along the Kurfürstendamm in Berlin because quite a few Jews lived in that area. I carried my shopping bag and saw an old and tired Jewish lady shuffling along the street. I walked past her very slowly and carefully so that no one would notice. I whispered, "A friend is speaking to you. Just go home as usual and I will follow shortly thereafter." It worked; she went home and was not afraid. This was the way we operated, and of course, the Jews could always give us many more addresses of people who needed help. It was easy to find people who needed assistance. Much, much more difficult was finding a hiding place for them. My apartment only offered room enough for myself and my children.

One of the most difficult things was feeding the Jews we had hidden. They, of course, didn't have ration coupons when they came to us. We stole groceries and put other people up to stealing for us; we stole in every shop we could. This way, we managed to feed some, even if it was rather meager. On occasion, we were even able to get them a little meat. There was a butcher woman who saw us trying to steal. She came over to us and said, "Here, let me just give it to you." She knew what it was for. There were people like that too.

One time we had a young man, 15 at most, a Jew. He was a highly talented forger and could fake anything. It was so necessary to forge papers. For example, my dear spinster cousin was blessed with eight children—on paper, that is. Helena Jakobs had the largest apartment among the three of us, and she still had a little extra room up in her attic. Although she already had others hiding in the attic, we moved the boy up there too. He did fantastic forgeries for us: passports, birth certificates, and ration cards. He was extremely talented. But one day, we heard that they were on to him and he had to leave. I was terribly unhappy about that. We dressed him up as an old man, the kind who goes to a lot of funerals, and told him to go as far south as he could. He set off with one of his forged passports and actually made it to Switzerland.

Late one night, my helpers and I were walking near a subway station in Berlin-Dahlem. We talked together in the dark behind some bushes because we thought it would be safe there. Suddenly, the bushes parted and there stood an SS man in full war paint. He said, "Don't think we haven't known about you." We thought we were done for. And then he said, "I want something from you. I want money, a lot of money. You come up with it and nothing will happen to you. And, for all I care, you can go on helping all the Jews you want." What a swine! There we stood, three young women, and tried to think of how we could get the money he demanded.

We canvassed all over the place. I didn't tell people what I needed the money for; I only told them that I was in desperate need of it. And because times were so crazy, people gave. We met the SS brute at the prearranged time and handed over a large sum of money. And, in fact, he didn't report us and the Jews we were hiding were safe. This was the kind of thing that was going on.

HANS GÜNTHER SERAPHIN*

"If it is a single person more than none, you're in for it."

Since I was an historian and spoke Russian, I became an assistant to the defense at the Nuremberg Trials from 1946 to the end of 1948. It may be interesting to make some comments on this after forty years.

When I first went to Nuremberg, I had absolutely no idea what to

* Biography on page 118.

expect. In an information sheet for commanding officers which was distributed in Italy in 1944, we were given an exact description of what the Germans did to the Jews in the East. It was presented quite openly and was interpreted, on our part, as a clear case of enemy propaganda. This reminded us of the anti-German propaganda stories we had heard during World War I about the chopped-off children's hands in Belgium. When I went to Nuremberg and read all the official certificates and documents, and heard from the witnesses about what had happened. I was sick. It was all so incredibly hard to believe.

The Waffen-SS, for example. I was an expert witness at 150 trials in German courts, including the trial of the Waffen-SS Cavalry Brigade which had fought in Poland. I found documents afterwards that made my hair stand on end. It is generally argued by members of the Waffen-SS that they have a clean slate. I am extremely skeptical of that.

Most of those accused of murder were not conscious of the gravity of their crimes. For instance, there was a man who didn't feel burdened in the least because, after all, he had only killed 5,000. He said, "Why am I being punished? It was only 5,000; Ohlendorf killed 20,000—that's something completely different." I answered him with, "If it is a single person more than none, you're in for it."

There is a group among us—one that is probably dying out—which still maintains that six million Jews were not killed. But it actually makes no difference. Personally, I believe six million to be slightly exaggerated, and I've had a great deal to do with these things. But whether it was closer to five or six million simply doesn't matter. Some people even claim that the things that are said to have happened in Auschwitz are lies. This is complete nonsense. I know the documents. There are SS reports revealing how many Jews had been killed up to a certain point in time, and that was already a figure of three million. I'm talking about official SS statistics. It is all in there. All of the reports on these operations are preserved in black and white. Everything was precisely recorded.

HANS RADZIEWSKI*

**"If I survived Auschwitz, then it was only
because time and again I met someone who
helped me."**

At the end of June 1943, we were deported from Berlin. After approximately two days and a night in a freight car, we reached Auschwitz. The stench in these cars, the hysterical screaming and so on, were terrible.

Having arrived at Auschwitz-Birkenau, we were driven out of the cars by shouting guards. Our luggage was left behind, and we never saw it again. Next we had to file past a checkpoint, where the SS officers asked our age and occupation. I made myself two years older than I was and told them I was a mechanic. I'd estimate that of us 300 men—there were also 50 to 60 women—maybe 100 were admitted to the camp. The rest were given "special treatment." In other words, they were gassed. When married couples with children arrived, the man would not even be asked; he automatically went along to be gassed with his family. In practical terms, humans were a commodity, and there was so much of this commodity that they didn't know what to do with it all. That was the horror of it. Those SS men who worked at Auschwitz were more or less forced to keep enlarging its capacity for annihilation because the transports were arriving from everywhere.

At Auschwitz-Birkenau, numbers were tattooed onto our arms. Mine is 127071. There were no more names. You were called by your number, issued bread by your number. It was your passport. Those sorted out for "special treatment" were already dead by then. There were no grave markers for them. They were eliminated. The only people left were those who could be rented out to IG-Farben as a numbered means of production.

---

* Biography on page 61.

A typical day in a concentration camp: getting up amid the noises and shouting, washing—everything on the run. Then the beds had to be made, the straw sacks shaken out, and so on. Then out to the main square for roll call. If someone was missing because he had dropped dead, he was dragged out to even up the count. If someone had hidden and had to be looked for, we had to stand until the number was right. And if the men calling roll came up with the wrong number because they couldn't count, they beat us. Roll call would take an hour if everything went smoothly. As it was getting light, we marched off to work accompanied by the music of a prisoners' band. The band was dressed in white and played the most wonderful marches; they were excellent Jewish musicians. And if someone was hanged, the band played afterwards by order of the SS.

The IG-Farben plant at Monowitz was a huge complex of about 3 square miles. We were divided according to skills. The overseers were also inmates, but for the most part they were criminals. If you were popular with the overseers you could avoid work. Otherwise you worked like a dog until you collapsed. I myself had to be dragged to work by my comrades often enough because I literally couldn't stand up anymore. If I survived the one and a half years in Auschwitz, it was only because time and again I met someone who helped me. For example, I used to steal bread from the German foremen until they caught me at it one day. They discussed whether they should report me. I told them that if they did, I would be shot. Well, apparently they didn't want that on their consciences, and from then on they sometimes brought me leftovers, cod-liver oil pills, things like that. All this only because I was also from Berlin and there was some sense of sympathy for me.

There's one thing you can't forget. When the German foremen—there were about 2,000 to 3,000 Germans there who were not prisoners but free men—found out that the undernourished inmates, hunched over and shuffling around, weren't criminals, but Jews who'd been rounded up, and that the strong, athletic, well-fed ones were habitual criminals, there was a tremendous change of attitude.

I don't want to create the impression that Buna was a sanatorium. It wasn't. But I'm a person who tries not to dwell on misery, one who tries to remember how lucky I was again and again—even if I was often starving and in despair. That's how I survived.

In the face of the Russian advance, we were evacuated "home-ward" in 1945. Whoever was incapable of travelling was shot. There was snow on the ground. It was icy cold, about zero degrees. It was a death march. We tried to walk as slowly as possible, hoping the Russians would overtake us, but that didn't happen. Two days later we were loaded onto open freight cars, 80 to 90 people in each. When people died along the way, they were thrown out so that we would have more room. We were supposed to go to Dachau, but they didn't have any room for us there, so we were sent on to Flossenbürg. Flossenbürg was a really bad camp. They had to beat us out of the cars because we couldn't move; we were literally frozen stiff.

I got so sick at Flossenbürg that I didn't even know what was happening to me anymore. Later some of my comrades told me that they found me in a wrecked airplane acting like a little boy, going "zoom, zoom," wanting to fly away.

Then the Americans got me out of there—a black American, tall as a tree, big and strong. I didn't really even understand that I was free. I was 20 years old, weighed 75 pounds, had water in both lungs, frostbite on both feet and legs, and a variety of other maladies. It took a few years for me to begin to come around and get back to normal.

And why have I stayed in Germany after all I had been through? I can answer that question quite easily and with a certain amount of contempt. Who would have wanted me in my condition? I have been classified as totally disabled since 1947. You cannot emigrate with that label attached to your name. No country would admit you.

LOTHAIRE LEVY*

"Why didn't the Pope speak out?"

I already knew about the existence of the concentration camps when I was still a kid, back in 1938, living in Metz, in France. People talked about the German Communists being sent to Buchenwald and Dachau. Quite a few relatives of mine were sent to concentration camps. They were arrested, taken away, and never came back. And I knew of Germans whose family members had been sent to a concentration camp, because when they asked what had become of them, only a small box of remaining personal belongings was sent to them as the answer to their question.

Personally, I can't believe that no one in Germany knew what was going on. Such devastating things as the murders in the KZs (concentration camps)—how can you suppress something like that? What's unbelievable is that the rest of the world silently put up with the crimes for so long! Why didn't the Pope speak out? He was scared. If in 1938-41, the Pope had only told all people who considered themselves to be Christians to defy this, it would have been catastrophic for Hitler. If only all churches had simultaneously stepped forward and said "No!" Hitler's hands would have been tied.

England didn't do anything. They could have broadcast it to the entire world, from morning to night: ". . . this is going on and that is going on. . . ." Someone somewhere would have heard and would have passed it on to a friend, and so forth.

I once met a man in Metz who had come back in 1945. He was a Jew and had been in Auschwitz. His duty there was to pull the dead bodies out of the gas chambers and take them to be burned. He had been arrested with his wife and grandchild, and together they had been transported by train to Auschwitz. One day the gas chamber

---

* Biography on page 51.

was opened and he pulled out a body. It was his wife. She was still holding the grandchild in her arms. The child must have been terrified because it was still clutching tightly onto its grandmother's shoulders. It's too horrifying even to think about.

RUDOLF WÜRSTER*

"We were going to have a lot to answer for if we lost this war."

I was stationed in Poland during the severe winter of 1941. I was still with the Luftwaffe at the time; and one day I was ordered to deliver a package. I found it very strange that dead bodies were scattered all along both sides of the narrow road I was driving on. When I got to the small town of Milec, I immediately noticed that all of the windows in the houses had been smashed. I stopped my car, got out, and asked the next soldier who passed by what had happened. He told me that 3,800 Jews had been taken out the night before. I got back in my car and continued on to my original destination.

On the return trip I heard gunshots coming from a group of buildings that had been used by a Polish gliding club. I grabbed my pistol, got out of the car, and ran to find out what was going on. When I entered the courtyard, I saw young Jews digging graves—large, deep graves. The older Jews were being shot in the back of the neck, I think by Polish militia. I was too horrified to pay much attention. An old woman turned around when her executioner's gun clicked empty. With clasped hands she begged in Polish, "Please help me!" The Pole kicked her in the back, loaded his gun, and shot her.

When a person is shot at close range in the head from behind, everything is blown away, and part of the face falls to the ground.

---

* Biography on page 260.

Even now, the masks worn during carnival season remind me of those shootings.

The sight of all the blood, along with the smell, made me sick and I collapsed. The next thing I knew, some lieutenant or captain, not a soldier, probably a guy from the Nazi security police, was pulling me up by the collar growling, "What are you doing here? You'd better have a damn good reason!" I replied, "I'm terribly sorry, but I was passing by and heard the gunshots. I only came over to see if I could help." That answer saved me from being shot on the spot. I joined our advance unit and confided only to my closest friends my feelings that we were going to have a lot to answer for if we lost this war.

KLAUS SCHEURENBERG*

"It was beneath Eichmann to act like the low-ranking SS brutes."

On May 1, 1943, I saw two men from the secret police enter our house. They were wearing long coats and large floppy hats. They looked so "secret" you could tell who they were a mile away. The building we lived in was almost empty, since most of the tenants had already been deported. The men had come to get us. I was only 17 years old and I had to make a decision. Should I run away and leave Berlin, or should I go along with my parents and try to help them somehow? This was the most difficult decision I have had to make in my entire life. I decided to stay with my parents. I thought I could maybe still run away later on. But that never happened. Later I did have a chance once, but they would have shot my parents right then and there.

On May 8, we were taken to a transit camp in Berlin. A remarkable

* Biography on page 53.

coincidence happened there. My father was walking down one of the hallways, and ran into Herr Sasse, who used to work at the police station in our neighborhood. And because my father had been the administrator of the Jewish House, they had dealt with one another on a number of occasions. They had even become sort of friends. Herr Sasse had been drafted into the Gestapo and was assigned to work in the camp. He took one look at my father and said, "Scheurenberg, what on earth are you doing here?" My father told him, "We're supposed to be sent to Auschwitz. We already have our numbers." Sasse said, "That's absolutely out of the question! Come with me." He went with my father to the camp director, an SS *Obersturmführer.* We turned in our numbers for Auschwitz and received new ones for Theresienstadt. We knew very well that no one was gassed there yet. It was the so-called waiting room for Auschwitz, but at least we knew we had a little more time.

We went to Theresienstadt where we stayed until 1944. Then I was sent to Eichmann's headquarters, a place called Wulkow which was near the concentration camp Sachsenhausen. Because of the frequent air raids, the Gestapo in Berlin had a secret headquarters built in a thick forest. Jewish prisoners, whom they planned to liquidate later on, had to build the new headquarters. Many of my friends were killed, but the Nazis forgot about me once again. Our commandant there was a little pervert from Vienna. He did everything he could to us, but he was never able to break us. He sent some of us to Sachsenhausen to be gassed; he shot some; and he beat some to death with a chain. At some point in the beatings, he always reached a climax and his pants got wet.

During this period of six months, I saw Herr Eichmann all the time. Naturally he never said a word to me, but I saw him a lot. It was beneath Eichmann to act like one of the low-ranking SS brutes. No, he did things his own way. I was in his office one time. It was really spooky. That huge, famous picture of Hitler posing as a commander-in-chief with a coat draped over his shoulders was hanging on a wall. Another wall was full of oil paintings of rabbis and Torah scrolls that had been confiscated from the Jews.

Shortly before the end of the war, on February 11, 1945, I ended up back in Theresienstadt. They couldn't send us to Auschwitz because the Russians had already taken over that camp. And they had to get rid of us somehow because we knew too much. Actually, on one intermediate stop, they wanted to shoot us all. I was already standing in front of a firing squad waiting to be shot when at that exact moment, the German front broke and a flood of German soldiers retreated right across our field. We were all rounded up and loaded into a cattle car—a total of 94 men. Many of them died. We travelled for eight days and eight nights until we finally arrived in Theresienstadt.

In Theresienstadt we had a Jewish administration. It was mostly run by people who hadn't been in the camp very long and were married to Aryans. They were people who basically had little idea what Judaism was and had even less idea of what the rest of us had been through. But at the ripe age of 18, I was a really experienced, expert prisoner who knew all the tricks of the trade. A woman in the administrative office registered me. She asked me what my occupation was. Actually I was a carpenter, but I told her I was a baker, and was sent to work in the SS bakery. I didn't have the slightest idea of what to do. It was difficult, but I finally learned how to bake, and ended up working the ovens and so forth. Working in the bakery is what kept me alive. We were freed on the very last day of the war, May 8, 1945.

PETER PECHEL*

"Even a criminal German government cannot order mass murder."

In May 1943, I had just turned 23 and was sent to Bucharest as a courier for the Supreme Command. It was a sort of reward for my having done a good job in my staff assignment over the past year. I sat

---

* Biography on page 131.

in an express train from Berlin to Bucharest, all alone in the courier compartment, surrounded by sacks of mail I was to deliver in Bucharest. I also carried a briefcase full of top secret documents handcuffed to my wrist, just like a prisoner.

So far, so good. It was already dark when we stopped at Breslau. Suddenly the door of my compartment opened and a colonel from the Engineer Corps stood in the doorway. He was somewhat older, 40 to 45 years old, with several decorations on his uniform. He sat down beside me, and we began to talk. In those times, during the Third Reich, it was possible to find out a person's attitudes and political beliefs within an hour. And after this first hour, it was obvious that the colonel was a front soldier like me, and that he was in no way a Nazi. You could detect it in a lot of what he had to say, the way he chose his words, and in a certain tone of voice when he spoke.

As the train rattled on through the night, we became increasingly frank with one another. We got so confidential that I told him that my father had been arrested by the Gestapo and was in the concentration camp in Sachsenhausen.

A long silence followed. Then the colonel pulled a flask of cognac out of his backpack and said, "Perhaps we should drink to your father's health." I accepted, and then came the decisive point. He said, "You know, you've been very frank with me. You're at Supreme HQ, and you are going back to the front, and I'd like to be open with you too. I have to tell you something you probably won't believe, but I must tell it anyway. We were deployed in Poland to dig trenches for a fallback position." He took another drink and continued. "One of the trenches we constructed was near a train tunnel. One day a locomotive drove toward it pulling open freight cars. People were crammed into these cars. Apparently—we were not far away—they were all Jews. The locomotive pushed these cars into the tunnel, and then uncoupled. Next some heavy diesel trucks drove up with SS men in them. The trucks were positioned at both ends of the tunnel. They let their motors run, with the exhaust directed into the tunnel. Everything else was sealed off so that the gas could take full effect. They let their engines run until everyone in the tunnel was dead. It took over 24 hours. And the people in there, the Jews, must have died a horribly agonizing death. I actually saw this happen, and so did my men."

The colonel had tears in his eyes. He had choked out the last sentences. And then he said, "I would appreciate it very much if you would pass on this information to a person who might be in a position to change something."

I had listened to his account breathlessly, and needed some time to get hold of myself. Then I said, "Colonel, this is so monstrous that I can't believe it. I know that Hitler, Göring, Goebbels, and the rest of them are criminals. But even a criminal German government cannot order mass murder. That is just not possible. It can't be reconciled with our history and culture."

A long pause followed, neither of us saying a word. The train sped through the wide plains of Hungary. The colonel squared his shoulders, leaned toward me, and said, "I can understand that you don't believe me. Will you be seeing your father before you return to the front?" I said "Yes, I'll see him, I have permission to visit him again in the concentration camp." Then he said, "That's good, because there is a much better communication service in the concentration camps than in the General Staff. Ask your father whether what I've told you is true." I said, "Yes, sir, I certainly will. But as much as I've learned to like you during our relatively short conversation, I cannot bring myself to believe what you've told me. Germans don't do things like that." He leaned back, and his voice was ice-cold, as if he was issuing an order, "You ask your father!" I reassured him that I would. He got out in Budapest, and I continued on to Bucharest for the next few hours with heavy thoughts in my mind.

When I got back to Berlin, I requested the usual visitor's permission to see my father, ten days before I left for the front. There was a young SS man from the *Totenkopf* Division present during our meeting. He was a wounded ethnic German, and probably didn't understand much of our conversation anyway. I sent him out to get me some cigarettes. Then I immediately told my father what the engineer colonel had told me in the train, and said, "Father, this cannot be true! Germans would never do that!" Then he said, "My boy, you're mistaken. We know that there are death camps for Jews, and we know that they are no longer being shot, but gassed in the way you have described it to me." My father added almost beseechingly, "Son, believe me, what the colonel told you is true. It's horrible, and it's difficult to comprehend, but these criminals are capable of anything." Then the SS man came back in and we talked of inconsequential matters. I never forgot my conversation with that colonel.

GASTON RUSKIN*

"If I'm going to die,
I hope it goes fast."

On February 27, 1943, I was arrested along with my father and uncle, and taken to Auschwitz.

What can I say about Auschwitz? It was terrible, especially in the beginning. There were 2,000 prisoners in our camp when we arrived. On February 18, 1945, when we left, there were only 32 still alive. It's important to note that Auschwitz didn't consist of just one camp, but I believe there were at least 35 camps there.

I was in labor camp Buna III, in Monowitz, near Auschwitz. The grounds belonged to IG Farben, the chemical concern. IG Farben had an agreement with the SS, and we were "loaned" to them as workers. Skilled workers received 1.80 marks per day while the unskilled laborers were payed 1.20 marks per day—a token wage for 12, 14, or even more hours of work.

We arrived during the night. The train stopped in the main camp. People started yelling, "Get out, you Jews! Get out!" And then they brought out the dogs. We were all really scared. When we got out, a man standing near us started commanding, "Left, right, left, right." I saw him stop an old man and ask what profession he had. When the old guy told him he was a doctor, he hit him in the head and said, "Now you're going to learn how to *really work*!" Later on, I did see the old man at work, but whether he survived or not, I don't know.

---

* Biography on page 42.

My aunt ran over to my uncle one more time to say good-bye. She didn't survive either.

We were pushed onto trucks. We stood like sardines in a can, one right next to the other. Armed SS soldiers sat in the front and back of the truck. My uncle and I were split up. He was sent to another labor camp. We saw people wearing striped uniforms, and we knew we were being taken to a concentration camp. It was freezing cold, about 7 degrees above zero. We were pushed from the trucks. A few suffered their first broken bones—arms and legs—when they fell to the ground.

After a while we were sent to a room and told to undress. We were going to take a shower. I still had a picture of my father with me, a picture of his face which I had torn off from a larger photograph. I held it in my hand. "What do you have there in your hand?" A man came, took my father's picture from me, and ripped it up. Then they shoved us all into the shower room. It really was a shower. I had no idea that gas chambers even existed.

Next, we were given clothes. Even though it was winter, we were given summer clothes: pants, a collarless shirt, a short, light-weight coat, and a cap to put on our heads, where we used to have hair.

Two days later we started to work. I mean hard work. I ran into one of my father's cousins, a butcher, who was used to hard work. He used to carry around a half a cow on his shoulders. Now he had to unload cement. The man broke down after only three weeks and was sent off to the gas chambers.

One evening my father returned and told me they had had to unload parts of a building from a freight car. A wall slipped, and not being able to dodge it, he was hit in the stomach. That night he started shivering. I took my blanket over to him and held him tight. There was no way he could work anymore. They took him back to sick call eight days later. Before going to work, I visited my father and was able to talk to him. While I was there, Dr. Fischer, the camp physician, came in, looked at my father, and said, "Get out!" Some people in the camp told me he had been taken away to be X-rayed. When I returned that evening, a medical attendant, a prisoner like me, handed me a piece of bread and sausage and said, "Your father has passed away." I had seen him that morning, and by nightfall he was dead.

We refused to believe the stories about the gas chambers even though there was a strange smell in the air when the wind blew from Birkenau. Our block foreman, a political prisoner, took me aside and said, "Listen, you have to survive. Within two months this nightmare will be over with." I believed him. I was 19 years old. Those two months turned out to be more than two years.

As part of my work I also hauled cement. I had to carry two 110 pound sacks of cement, and was beaten while walking. A couple of times I fell down and they said, "What, you tore the sacks?" And they beat me some more. I was finished. I couldn't do it anymore.

One day I heard they were looking for a skilled welder. I told them that I was a welder and had experience in the trade. They believed me. Eventually I even got my own welding torch and was able to move around to work wherever they needed me. Once an SS man came over and said, "Hey, you don't know how to weld!" I said: "Of course I can; just watch." He came closer and wore no eye protection. I took the torch and continued with my work. I could see what I was doing, I had my mask on. There was no way he could see. He just said: "All right, all right," and turned around and left. I'm positive it did some kind of damage to his eyes. Anyway, he never came back.

In January 1945, we learned that the Russians had begun their offensive. Late in the afternoon on January 18, we heard that we were going to be moved. We then began our incredible march of 40 miles in 26 hours, stopping only two hours to rest. We reached another camp, in Silesia. That was the first time I had seen Jewish girls since I had been imprisoned. The barracks we were sent to were already full of other people. A total of 350,000 were on the move from various camps.

I ran into a guy I used to work with. We both lay down outside in the snow. Because it was so cold, I knew we shouldn't lie still for too long, so I got up. I nudged my former colleague and told him to get up too. We saw people lying all over the place, frozen to death. That's supposed to be the best way to go. You don't feel anything, you just go to sleep.

We walked over to one of the barracks. I started yelling, "This is *Oberscharführer* Whatever, and if you don't open up, I'm going to shoot the door down!" The door flew open and we ran in. That was our salvation.

One or two days later, we were loaded into freight cars. They asked who wanted to go to Buchenwald, and I volunteered. If you've got to go, you might as well go all the way!

We passed through Prague. The SS soldiers shot into the air when any of the inhabitants of the city tried to throw us some bread. I wasn't hungry, but I was really thirsty. Once when we stopped, I got off the train and went to the locomotive. I asked the engineer if he had any water. He pointed to a faucet and told me to turn it on. Scalding hot water with a film of oil on it came out of the locomotive. I tried unsuccessfully to fish away the oil and drank it anyway. We also scraped the icy snow off the sides of the freight cars, and ate that. We were literally dying of thirst.

I arrived in Buchenwald around the end of January 1945. We walked through the main gate and were immediately sent to delouse. First we had to get undressed, and then we were shoved into a dark tunnel. I remember thinking, "If I'm going to die, I hope it goes fast." We saw light, and then the showers. They were really showers; not gas chambers! We were taken to our barracks. There was no electricity, and most of the boards were missing from the wooden bunks we were supposed to sleep on. I was given a pair of shoes, but they were stolen only two days later. During roll call, I had to stand barefoot in cold slush. I noticed that one of the other prisoners, a Russian, was in bad shape and probably wouldn't live. I stayed near him until he died, and took his shoes. The fact that I took the shoes from a dead man still bothers me today.

HANS-ULRICH GREFFRATH*

It wasn't until January 1947, after I voluntarily saw a documentary film on Auschwitz, that I was forced to believe that the horrible crimes that I had heard were committed by the Nazi regime were really true. Ever since then, down to the present day, my life has been one of terrible shame. Still, I don't believe in collective guilt because,

---

* Biography on page 277.

as troops at the front, we had no way of suspecting that Jews or other groups were being liquidated far behind the front. And I swear that I personally never once witnessed German Wehrmacht soldiers liquidating Jews, prisoners, or civilians. The troops at the front knew that the penalty for rape, pillage, or plunder was death.

WILLI WEISSKIRCH*

It is absolutely out of the question that the military leaders of the day didn't know about the existence of concentration camps and the atrocities which were going on at the time. Even we common soldiers who witnessed the "transports" and heard that the people were being beaten knew that something wasn't right. It is impossible that staff people, who otherwise had their nose in just about everything, didn't know that the Jews were being annihilated.

* Biography on page 22.

CHAPTER 11

Resistance

Resistance to Nazism began as a limited counterpoint to the mass intoxication of the 1930s. Its last prewar chances were lost in 1938 with the Western powers' collapse at Munich. At the outbreak of war, however, an increasing number of Germans began distancing themselves from the goals and the attitudes of National Socialism. The popular enthusiasm of the 1930s reflected hope for the future and relief that the worst did not seem to be happening. By 1942, millions of Germans able to read the casualty lists and hear the air raid sirens were ready to renegotiate the social contract of 1933. To these critics were added disillusioned idealists. Some had believed in Hitler. Others had believed in Germany. As the war progressed, faith turned to hope and hope, increasingly, to despair.

This process was particularly apparent in the Wehrmacht. Historically the relations between enlisted men and officers, and within the ranks of the officer corps, had depended as much on mutual confidence as on formal discipline. From the Reich's beginnings, the generals had offered their enthusiastic public cooperation, however contemptuously they might talk of Hitler and his henchmen in private. This double standard became even more questionable when commanding generals accepted orders that challenged every existing concept of soldierly honor. The commissar order to execute Soviet political officers and the activities of the *Einsatzgruppen,* the SS terror squads, were among the most notorious cases of generals ignoring the Wehrmacht's own regulations.

If few officers were directly exposed to the Reich's atrocities, none could avoid the signs of command failure in conducting the war itself: the careless planning that left an army in the midst of a Russian winter with no warm clothing, or the heedless insouciance with which Germany's high command accepted war with the United States. Since the days of Frederick the Great and Moltke the Elder, avoiding multi-front wars had been a basic principle of German strategy. Where were the men of the General Staff in December 1941? And where were the generals at Stalingrad when an army died at the Führer's whim?

As cadets, the majors and colonels of the Wehrmacht had never been allowed to forget the importance of honor. Now they saw men in the highest posts lacking the moral courage to act on what was happening all around them. The younger generation of Wehrmacht officers was not naive, but neither was it experienced enough to be cynical. At least for some, disillusionment gave way to an active commitment to overthrow the Nazi regime.

The rapid destruction of Communist resistance between 1933 and 1935 indicated that a revolution from below, based on popular support, had no chance of success. Groups like the White Rose, calling for direct public action, were mere way stations to martyrdom. Resistance, therefore, meant conspiracy. But conspiracy by whom, to do what, by which means?

The men and women of the non-Communist civilian resistance represented a mixture of Germany's old and new elites: intellectuals and civil servants, aristocrats and labor leaders. Their specific political aims differed, not least because their central commitment was moral. The resistance spoke of freedom and justice. Its ultimate goals were decency, civility, and the reconstruction of a government that ruled by law. Germany must again be restored to the family of respectable states.

Though critical of the military's role in bringing Hitler to power, the civilian resistance accepted the armed forces as the key to any change of government. The soldiers, for their part, recognized the importance of developing a broader base of support than the Wehrmacht could provide.

Prospective resisters increasingly debated the difference between disloyalty to a particular political system (high treason or *Hochverrat*) and betrayal of the country itself (*Landesverrat*). Some opponents of the regime were willing to cross that line. In the Wehrmacht intelligence service, Admiral Wilhelm Canaris and Colonel Hans Oster passed information to the French and British. Most resistance members, however, regarded direct collaboration with Germany's foes as unacceptable.

This position was sharpened after 1943 by the existence in Russia of the National Committee for a Free Germany and the League of German Officers. The Wehrmacht in particular regarded the members of both organizations as misguided opportunists at best, simple traitors at worst. Any group striking at Hitler now ran the risk of being tarred with the same brush.

Ultimately, the resisters argued, Germany must solve her own political problem. Only then could she seek, under a new government, to modify the Allies' demand for unconditional surrender and negotiate peace.

This in turn led to the problem of what to do about Hitler. It was increasingly clear that the key to success in any conspiracy lay in removing Hitler from power. This generated questions of conscience and procedure. Could a new, moral Germany be built on Hitler's corpse? Civilian intellectuals of the Kreisau Circle, particularly their leader Count Helmuth James von Moltke, rejected in principle the idea of violence, even against Hitler. Pragmatic factors were also involved. Rommel, among others, stressed the danger of making Hitler a martyr. And if the risks of assassination were accepted, the dictator was no easy target. Hitler was personally brave without being foolhardy. His security system was efficient and comprehensive. His uncanny sense of danger had helped him avoid several previous attempts on his life. And he seemed to have the devil's run of luck. By 1944, some resisters wondered if, like a werewolf, he could only be brought down by a silver bullet.

MARTIN KOLLER*

"The colonel dropped my report
into the wastebasket."

After three weeks' leave, I took a train back to the front. Something happened to me en route that I still think about to this day: my encounter with injustice. At one point, a strange officer came into our compartment. He was amiable and polite, and introduced himself in broken German with a Baltic accent as a lieutenant from Latvia. We talked about all kinds of things, everyday subjects, war and private life. And then he said he'd taken part in shooting Jews somewhere in the Baltic. There had been more than 3,000 of them. They had had to dig their own mass grave "as big as a soccer field." He told me all this with a certain pride.

I was completely at a loss and asked stupid questions like "Is that really true? How was it done? Who led this operation?" And I got a precise answer to each. It was true; anybody could check it; they did it with 12 men armed with machine pistols and one machine gun. The ammunition had been officially provided by the Wehrmacht, and a German SS lieutenant, whose name he didn't remember, had been in command. I became confused and started to sweat. This just didn't fit into the whole picture—of me, of my country, of the world, of the war. It was so monstrous that I couldn't grasp it.

"Can I see your identification?" I asked, and "Do you mind if I note it down?" He didn't mind, and was just as proud of what he had done as I was of the planes I'd shot down. And while I scribbled his strange name down on a cigarette package, my thoughts somersaulted: either what he's told me is true, in which case *I* can't wear a

---

German uniform any longer, or he's lying, in which case *he* can't wear a German uniform any longer. What can, what should I do? My military instinct told me, "Report it!"

I returned to the squadron and was right back in action. I flew and fought as best I could. I didn't think about the Latvian's story. Then the orderly came to collect my laundry. That's when I found the shirt I'd worn on the train. I emptied the pockets, and there was that piece of paper with the address. I finally had to do something. The same night, I wrote a report to the squadron leader.

The commander remained seated behind his desk when I came, still in my flight suit, to report. He pointed to my paper: "What do you want me to do with this?" I shrugged and ventured, "Forward it, of course, Captain."

I had done my duty; now I could forget it. Then I received a message that told me I was to report to Colonel Bauer at Simferopol in the Crimea two days later.

The colonel had my report in hand. With all the stamps and entries on it, it had become an official document.

"I wanted to speak with you," said the colonel, "before I act on this report. Do you understand that?" "No, Colonel," I said stupidly.

He leaned back, took a deep breath, and said, "My dear young friend. . . ." My dear young friend? No superior had ever said that to me before. I felt good.

"What do you think I should do with this?" I sat stiffly on the sofa and didn't know what to do with the question. What does a colonel do with reports? I swallowed and said, "I don't know, Colonel. Maybe forward it?"

The colonel slid closer and put his arm around my shoulder. I smelled his good after-shave and was frozen. "Son," said the colonel with a frown. Son? He was talking like my father, but I liked it. Then he offered me cigarettes. We smoked. The colonel said, "If I pass on this report, son, you'll be jumping out of the frying pan and into the fire."

Then he nudged me and said, "You know what, son?" I shook my head and looked at him, "If we get out of this alive, we'll go home and clean up that mess. Thousands, believe me, thousands will be with us!"

And the colonel picked up my report, held it over the wastebasket and asked, "So, do you want to jump into the fire, or do you want to be there with the rest of us, for the big clean-up? Can I quash your report?" "Yes, sir, *Herr Oberst*," I said, convinced.

"Thank you, Lieutenant," the colonel said, and dropped my report about the Latvian lieutenant and the execution of the Jews into the wastebasket.

KLAUS VON BISMARCK*

"What depressed me the most was the almost pathetic helplessness of our own army's commanders."

At this point, I would like to talk about the generals. General von Bock and General von Manstein had both been my predecessors as commander of the battalion in Kolberg. I visited them on a couple of occasions during the war. They asked me, "How are things going? What do the soldiers think?" I told them, "We are all very concerned! While we are out at the front fighting enemy forces much stronger than our own, total megalomania has broken out among the staff in the rear areas!" I told them that the men had lost all confidence in the senior army commanders. It was high time for one of our generals or field marshals to finally have the guts to stand up to Hitler and speak his mind.

I would like to give yet another example of the field marshals' conduct during this time. I was flown out of the Demyansk Pocket in a Fieseler Storch, and landed at some other airfield. It was winter. Off to one side of the road, every 300 to 400 feet or so, I noticed small heaps or bundles which were covered with fresh snow. I recall

---

* Biography on page xxxv.

thinking "What is that? Are they sacks?" I then told my driver, who had been sent from the Army Group H.Q. to pick me up, to stop the car. I walked over and looked at two or three of the little heaps. They were Russian prisoners! They had been shot! The number of them I saw along the road seemed endless. I presume we drove 10 to 15 miles, and I kept seeing Russians lying next to the road, unarmed Russian prisoners.

I tried to reconstruct in my mind how it was possible for this to have happened: "What went on here? Were there too few guards? Had the guards then panicked and shot the prisoners who couldn't keep up with the rest of the group? Had the guards shot them because they didn't know what else to do? The prisoners couldn't have been transported out. Is that why they chose to simply execute them?" These were the thoughts that crossed my mind.

I went straight to Field Marshal Busch, commanding Army Group North, "Whatever is going on here is disgusting! I'm going to file an official report!" Busch was a fatherly type of man. His reaction: "This is really incredible! The head of the SS is responsible for this! Things happening here in the rear area of the army are bad enough. I receive daily reports about what's going on, also reports concerning the partisans, but this, this is terrible!"

I was shocked! How was it possible for a German army to treat its prisoners in this manner? It was just totally unbelievable! And Busch said, "You are right! You are completely right! I am going to see what I can do to find out who is responsible for this. I am definitely going to look into this!" I wrote up my official report and left it behind. I never heard that Busch did anything. What depressed me the most was the almost pathetic helplessness on the part of our own army's commanders in this aspect of the war, by letting something like this happen.

JOHANNES STEINHOFF*

"We will no longer stand for Göring denouncing us as cowards. . . . Göring has to go!"

This was about the time when a small group of Luftwaffe wing commanders began to meet to devise a plan to get rid of Göring. Our meeting place was known only to the handful of people we had decided to take into our confidence. Our agenda: "We will no longer stand for Göring denouncing us as cowards. It is essential that Hitler revise his decision withholding the new jet aircraft from the fighter pilots. We can no longer just sit back and watch our cities being leveled almost at will. With the help of the jets, we could stop the bombing offensive, if only temporarily. Göring has got to go!"

The Chief of the Luftwaffe General Staff wrote to Göring: "It is my impression that a very serious crisis of confidence is developing which, if nothing is done to stop it, may lead to very serious tension and ultimately to catastrophe." He suggested that Göring meet with the mutineers immediately for a frank discussion in order to clear the air.

This happened around the end of January 1945. Göring then summoned all of the conspirators to meet in Berlin at the Air Ministry. When I walked into the conference room, a few of my friends were already there, including Colonel Günther Lützow, who we had decided would be our spokesman. In an obvious attempt to neutralize the "mutiny," Göring had invited other wing commanders to attend the gathering as well. The air was tense. We briefly greeted one another, and that was it. Any further conversation was superfluous considering we were all more than aware of what was at stake.

The door opened, and Göring walked in, followed by his usual

---

* Biography on page 7.

entourage: his adjutant, his personal general staff officer, the chief of the general staff, and a few others. Apart from a strained "Good morning, gentlemen," no "Heil Hitler!," no handshaking, no "How are you?" He took no notice of us and went directly to his seat at the round table and sat down with a groan. Very soon it became clear to me that he wasn't going to play the role of the arrogant, insulting big man. Was it even conceivable that he was going to have us arrested or liquidated?

The Chief of the General Staff thanked Göring for his readiness to meet with the fighter pilots, and he asked him to accept Colonel Lützow as the speaker for our group. Göring nodded. Lützow stood up. What he then said to Göring was really something. Because he knew that Göring never listened to anyone for any length of time, except the Führer, without interrupting, Lützow began with, *"Herr Reichsmarschall,* I must ask you to hear me out to the end. If you interrupt me, sir, I believe there will be little point to this discussion."

Göring went pale. With his fat, hanging cheeks and bags under his eyes, he looked like an old lady sitting at that table.

Lützow talked about our dilemma. He complained about the poorly equipped wings. He talked about the fact that the Luftwaffe, especially the fighter arm, had been bled to death after more than five years of war. He also went on to say that the fighter arm was no longer prepared to accept the charge of cowardice.

Göring couldn't stand it any more. The exchange between Göring and Lützow became louder and louder. Finally, it was only Göring who was doing the talking; no one else present dared to say a word. And when Lützow drew a deep breath and opened his mouth to protest, Göring flew into a rage and jumped, or rather with great effort rose out of his chair and yelled, "That's enough! I don't want to hear any more! What you are demanding is downright mutiny! What kind of an officer are you, Lützow? I'll have you shot!" And with that he stormed out of the room, followed by his dazed entourage.

What was he going to do? Could he possibly get away with ordering his bravest pilots shot? It was humiliating enough for him to have to explain all of this to Hitler. Lützow and I were dismissed from our jobs and transferred for "disciplinary reasons." I found myself, as it were, back out on the streets. I spent the next couple of weeks travelling around. The fact that we hadn't been successful in effecting any change didn't give me any peace of mind.

I decided to try and see Lützow, who had been sent into banishment as the Fighter Commander, Upper Italy. It was banishment because there were no longer any fighter pilots left in Italy to take charge of. I set out for Verona, but didn't get very far. My papers were checked at the Brenner Pass, and when I got off of the train in Verona, I was met by two MPs and taken to the guard commander, who then asked me to sit down and wait. They finally got a telephone connection through to the chief of staff of the air forces in Italy. "Steinhoff, what brings you to Italy?" he asked me. "I came to visit my friend Lützow," I told him. Without beating around the bush, he snapped back, "Steinhoff, I order you to go back immediately!" "Where to? I don't have a job or an assignment at the moment." "I told you to return to Germany on the next train. Do you understand me?" "Yes, sir, *Herr General!*" And so I waited an entire night until the next train heading for Germany stopped in Verona.

At Munich, we had to go into an air raid shelter, but, thank God, the train station was not attacked. The next time the train stopped was in the middle of nowhere, in an open field between Munich and Ingolstadt. MPs ran along the track shouting, "No one's to leave the train!" I had already seen the contrails in the sky and sensed a big attack was in the making. I rolled down the window, jumped outside, and ran across the field. The privates took this as a signal and followed me. It didn't take long before half of the soldiers on the train were making off over the open area heading for the shelter of the trees. The fighters dived down over us . . . Mustangs! They zeroed in first on the locomotive, then on one passenger car after the other. Windows shattered. I was sitting maybe 200 meters away, crouched behind a bush on a slope, and witnessed the entire catastrophe. An hour must have passed before we felt it was safe to go back to the train. Only then were we able to see the actual extent of the damage. There were *Blitzmädchen* in the next compartment where the officers had been seated. The train commander had ordered them not to leave the train and, as a result, two of them were severely injured and one was dead. I briefly lost my control and yelled at the train commander, who looked more like an over-aged high school teacher than anything, "You idiot, how could you let this happen to these girls?" He stuttered something about having received strict orders. "What's the use?" I thought. Several hours passed before they brought in another engine, and we finally continued on to Berlin.

In February 1945, I received a phone call from General Galland: "Macky, how would you like to fly again? Hitler wants me to set up a squadron—a small unit of fighter jets—to finally prove the Me-262's fighter capabilities!" What a fantastic challenge! I grabbed at the opportunity without hesitating a second.

It was a rather unusual unit of young men. All but a few of the 12 pilots were highly decorated, experienced aces. The Reich had shriveled down to a tiny enclave north of the Alps. We had plenty of Me-262s, the fantastic new jet. As soon as they were completed, they were parked out on the autobahns. What the Third Reich had accomplished here was a masterpiece in improvisation. It succeeded in mass-producing highly modern jet airplanes built in open fields and, in part, by concentration camp inmates. Not only did we even have enough fuel to get into the air; we also had a perfect radar organization. Technically, we were an entire generation ahead of our enemies.

By now it was the end of March. The Soviets had already penetrated into German territory. The Allied forces had crossed the Rhine. And we, what remained of the Luftwaffe, experienced one last major air battle. We were shot down by the bombers we attacked; our bases were bombed; and we suffered major losses. Even though we were in a state of deep depression, all of this activity and commotion didn't give us much opportunity to hang our heads in defeat. For us, our efforts in this grand finale seemed to be in part a kind of retribution, and possibly we were able to prevent even more German cities from being bombed.

The evenings we spent in our quarters were agonizing. Even though everyone was well aware that the Reich's days were numbered, no one dared to think about what the end would bring or what would happen afterwards. We continued to fly, though at times we flew with a certain degree of apathy and indifference. But the ecstacy of flying twice the speed of the Flying Fortresses, the ecstacy of flying such a superior aircraft, motivated us to fly those last few missions over what was left of the German Reich.

Private accommodation had been arranged for pilots in the Munich area. I lived with a simple family in their house. These people, the civilian population in general, looked upon us pilots as a group of lunatics who really didn't have much to do with them anymore. I don't recall ever discussing our situation, or the catastrophe, with them. Nevertheless, the same questions continued to surface: What will tomorrow bring? How will this war end for us? What will happen afterwards? The thoughts and proposals dissolved in uncertainty, even though it was clear to everyone that the Reich was lost long ago.

I crashed on takeoff in my jet, which was overloaded with munitions, on April 18, 1945, and was badly burned.

In retrospect, I must admit that I was not aware of the horrible crimes committed during the war in the name of the German people. On one occasion during a stopover in Poland prior to the Warsaw ghetto uprising, I did hear that the SS had devised a "clever" method of eliminating Jews. I couldn't assess that information. I had spent five and a half years serving as a fighter pilot, concerned primarily with daily operations. The fighter pilots' revolt came too late. We lacked the overall information known only to those in high staff positions or otherwise close to the center of power.

I endured the final days of the war under the pain-killing influence of opium. I found myself in a state of almost hopeless depression. My good friend Lützow never returned from his last combat mission. The Americans gave the SS one last battle near the military hospital I was in near Tegernsee, south of Munich. I had no idea where my wife and two children were; I hadn't seen or heard from them in six weeks. Then it was all over. We had lost everything.

INGE AICHER-SCHOLL*

**"The executioner said he had never seen
anyone die like that."**

My brother and sister and their friends are known to history as the
"White Rose" resistance group. But at first their own family didn't
know what Hans and Sophie were doing. Hans came home from the
University of Munich for a few days of vacation in the fall of 1941.
That was when we found leaflets reproducing the sermons of Bishop
Galen in our mailbox. We read them with great enthusiasm, of
course, and were amazed that something like this could still circulate.
And I can still see Hans standing there with the leaflet in front of him,
saying, "If only I had a mimeograph machine."

In November 1942, Hans came home again for the weekend. We
took an evening walk along the Danube, which was quite close to our
home. It was a beautiful evening, and Hans said, "Many Social
Democrats and Communists have been sentenced and executed, and I
tell you, we have to act. It's time the Christians finally did something
about it." And I, in my fear—already having been arrested by the
Gestapo once, I was always afraid—said, "Hans, we're already
political suspects. God knows we've already stuck our necks out.
Keep out of it." Hans hesitated, then replied, "Yes, you're right. For
the resistance movement you need people who have no record. Each
person must know only as much as is absolutely necessary."

Silence was the two-fold scourge of the Third Reich. The people
who worked and fought against it had to keep quiet to avoid incriminating anyone else. The others kept quiet because they were afraid.

While in Berlin, during the semester holiday of 1942, Hans met a
member of the resistance, Falk Harnaek. This is also when Hans
developed a plan to establish illegal student groups in every univer-

* Biography on page 26.

sity to carry out sudden, concerted "leaflet operations" scattering pamphlets in university buildings.

Several weeks later, Hans received a warning that the Gestapo was on his trail, and that he could count on being arrested within the next few days. Hans chose to ignore this. Apparently he thought they were people who only meant well and were trying to scare him into abandoning his dangerous activities.

Should he have given up this difficult life in Germany, with its constant threats, for a free life in Switzerland? For an athletic person like Hans, it would have been no problem to cross the border illegally, over the Alps. But what would happen to his friends and family? His escape would have made them immediate suspects. He would have had to watch them being dragged off to concentration camps from his safe perch in Switzerland. He wouldn't have been able to bear that.

On a sunny Thursday, February 18, 1943, Hans and Sophie filled a suitcase with leaflets before they went to the university. They were both pleased and in good humor when they set off. But Sophie had had a dream that she couldn't quite shake off: the Gestapo had arrested them both.

They reached the university, and since the lecture rooms were due to open any minute, they hurriedly emptied the contents of the suitcase in the corridors and from the second floor into the entrance hall. But the janitor saw them. All doors of the university were locked immediately, sealing their fate. The Gestapo was notified at once, and arrested them.

The interrogations began, day and night, hour after hour. They were cut off from the world, not knowing if their families or friends even knew where they were. The circle of friends that had formed around Hans and Sophie in Munich went with them along the dangerous path of active resistance with indescribable fidelity. Alexander Schnorell, Christopher Probst, Willi Graf, Professor Kurt Huber—all of them were to die for their cause.

I should add that my parents and I didn't know a thing. We only knew that the leaflets existed. Sophie brought one home once and told my father, very coolly and cheerfully, that this kind of thing was being distributed at the university. My father said, "Sophie, that's wonderful, but you two won't get involved, will you?" And she said,

"Where did you get that idea? We wouldn't do anything like that; don't worry." When we learned what had happened, we feared the worst. But we hoped that the trial would last a long time, that perhaps the war would even be over before the verdict came.

Everyone who came into contact with Hans and Sophie, the other prisoners, the pastors at the prison, the guards, and even the Gestapo officers, were deeply moved by their courage and their noble bearing. Their calm and composure made for a strange contrast to the hectic tension of that place. Their activities worried party and government officials right up to the top levels.

Two days after their arrest, it became clear to them that they could expect the death sentence. There was only one thing to do: remain prudent and rational, involve as few people as possible, and embody, in all clarity, the freedom of the human spirit.

When the last morning came, Hans asked his cellmate to bid good-bye to our parents. Then he gave him his hand, kindly, almost ceremoniously, and said, "We want to say goodbye while we're still alone." With that, he turned around without a word and wrote something on the white prison wall. There was silence. He had barely put the pencil down when the guard came to handcuff him and lead him into court. The words on the wall were Goethe's words, words which his father had often murmured when pacing back and forth, the pathos of which had sometimes made Hans smile: *"Allen Gewalten zum Trutz sich erhalten"* (To stand defiant before overwhelming power).

They were not allowed to choose their own lawyer. They were appointed an official counsel for the defense, but that man, of course, was nothing more than a powerless marionette.

During these last nights, Sophie slept like a child—when she wasn't being interrogated. After her indictment she lay down on her bed and talked about her death in a soft voice, "Such a beautiful, sunny day, and I am supposed to go. But how many must die today on the battlefields? How many young, hopeful lives? What does my death matter if our activities have awakened thousands of people?"

A short time later, her cell was also empty. A piece of paper remained behind—an indictment, in one word, "Freedom."

My parents learned of their arrest the day after it occurred, first from a woman student we knew, and then through an anonymous phone call from another student. But what could they do? It was a weekend, and no visitors were allowed in the prison. On Monday, they took a train to Munich with my brother Werner, who had been unexpectedly on leave from the Russian front.

They hurried to the courthouse and pushed their way through the courtroom crowded with invited Nazi guests. The judges sat in red robes, Freisler raging with fury in the middle. Calm, erect, and very solemn, the defendants sat across from them. They answered freely and confidently. Sophie said once—she said so little otherwise—"So many people think like we do, only they don't dare speak out." My parents arrived just in time to hear the death sentence pronounced. My mother collapsed and had to be carried out. My father shouted, "There is a higher justice!" My mother collected herself immediately and concentrated all of her strength on asking pardon for her children. She was wonderfully composed. My brother Werner elbowed his way forward and took Hans and Sophie by the hand. When tears came to his eyes, Hans gently laid his hand on Werner's shoulder and said, "Remain strong—no compromises."

My parents succeeded in visiting their children one more time before they were executed. They hurried to the prison between four and five o'clock. They did not yet know that these were to be their children's last hours. Hans was brought to them first. He wore prison clothing, but his walk was light and erect—as if nothing external could harm him. His face looked drained and exhausted, as after a struggle. He leaned over the barrier separating them and held their hands. "I have no hate; I have left everything behind me." My father embraced him and said, "You will go down in history. There is a higher justice."

Afterwards, Sophie was led in. She wore her own clothes, and walked very slowly, calmly, and erect, with a smile on her face. She gladly took the sweets my parents had brought, which Hans had refused, saying, "Good, I haven't had lunch yet." She had also become a bit thinner, but her skin glowed, and mother noticed once again how red her lips were. "Now you will never walk through our door again," said mother. "Oh, it's just a few years," replied Sophie. And then she said something similar to Hans, "We've taken the blame for everything that might cause problems." Her biggest worry during these days was whether mother would be able to stand losing two children at once. But when mother stood beside her, so courageous and composed, Sophie was relieved.

After that, they were taken away, the girl first. She went without flinching. The executioner said that he had never seen anyone die like that before. And Hans, before he lay his head down on the block yelled loudly enough for his voice to resound throughout the prison, "Long Live Freedom!"

Where did my brother and sister get this strength from? I would say the first source was their relationship to Christ and God. The second source, almost inseparable from the first, was the knowledge that what they had done was right, and that someone eventually had to stand up for these convictions.

Note: Part of this text is adapted, with Frau Aicher-Scholl's consent, from her *Die weisse Rose* (Frankfurt am Main, 1982), pp. 69 *passim*. An English version was published in 1983 by Wesleyan University Press, Middletown, CT.

WOLF-JOBST SIEDLER

Born 1926; court-martialed for defeatism at 17; became a publisher after the war; lives in Berlin.

"When Hitler is hanged, I will personally walk barefoot from Berlin to Potsdam to help pull on the rope."

My best friend was the son of Ernst Jünger, the legendary "Pour le Mérite" officer of World War I. After World War I, Jünger became a nationalistic author who, around 1933, did an about-face against nationalism and refused to be nominated president of the Reich Authors' Association and the Poets' Academy. His son had a deep dislike of vulgar mob rule. The two of us founded a group to oppose the Hitler Youth at our boarding school. We also discussed what would happen if the war was lost. There were 17 of us, and the 17th was a Gestapo agent. At the end of 1943, we were arrested.

My friend Jünger had, for example, written: "This war will never be ended unless an assassination attempt on Hitler succeeds. As long as Hitler is alive, there will never be an armistice." And at the end, as a 17-year-old will do, he wrote, "When Hitler is hanged, I will personally walk barefoot from Berlin to Potsdam to help pull on the rope." Naturally, that was recorded.

We were put on trial in January 1944. We had already been serving for several months as helpers in a naval anti-aircraft battery. So the question was, were we naval auxiliaries and therefore under the jurisdiction of a military court, or were we students or Hitler Youths and therefore under the jurisdiction of the Peoples' Court? The latter would have been tantamount to a death sentence. Ernst Jünger was at that time an officer in the German military command in Paris. He set the wheels in motion to have us tried by a military court. Needless to say, it worked. As 17-year-old naval auxiliaries, we were sentenced to nine months.

We were imprisoned in Wilhelmshaven along with political prisoners. There were constant executions. Many cases were far more harmless than ours. A little sailor got drunk one night and said, "If things go wrong here, the bigwigs will surely have planes ready to fly them off to their villas in Switzerland; nothing will happen to them." He was executed.

PHILIPP FREIHERR VON BOESELAGER

Born 1917; served as a general staff officer in the Russian campaign of 1942; president of the German forest estate owners; today he lives in Kreuzberg, Palatinate.

"Kluge could not decide whether to accept the consequences of acting on what he knew."

During Operation Barbarossa I was a lieutenant in a reconnaissance battalion. I was badly wounded and sent back to Germany. When I recovered, I was ordered to report to Army Group Center as an aide to the commander, Field Marshal Günther von Kluge. That was in early 1942. By the time I settled in, it was clear that Kluge's staff believed it impossible to win the war in the East. Instead, some sort of political solution had to be found.

An opportunity presented itself when some patriotic Ukrainians offered to enter the war against Stalin openly, if the Ukraine would be guaranteed partial autonomy during the war and independence afterward. Already a million Russians were serving as auxiliaries in German uniforms. Three and a half million more were in German POW camps. The proclamation of a Ukrainian state was sure to bring many of them over to our side. It was a calculated risk, a chance to come out of the war a victor.

The Army Group staff recommended the plan. After a while we heard Hitler not only refused to consider the proposal; he intended to destroy the Ukrainian people for fear they would become a new Russian elite. We already knew Hitler couldn't care less about the ordinary soldier. We'd also learned that Hitler became lost in details. He issued orders that had no relationship to the kind of general directives a High Command is supposed to give. He'd determine the position of individual machine guns, and decide specific targets for guns or tanks.

I accompanied Kluge to Hitler's headquarters several times. Hitler never seemed sympathetic or attractive in any form. He was very intelligent, but he projected nothing at all. I never understood how, for example, officers who were flown to Hitler to be decorated were so charmed by him. They always said how they were going to take the chance to tell Hitler what really was going on at the front. But most of them came back converted.

To give you an idea of how Hitler worked, let me describe his relationship with Kluge. Hitler was commander-in-chief of the army, so before making any important decisions Kluge had to get his consent. This meant making arrangements for a telephone call well in advance. When *Wolfschanze* reported, the duty officer would call me and say, "I'm connecting you with the Führer. Please remain on the line." I said, "I'll connect you with Field Marshal von Kluge." When I made my call, I could hear Hitler breathing. He always took his time beginning the conversation—it made Kluge nervous. Then he'd say, *"Heil, Herr Feldmarschall!"* Kluge would answer: *"Heil, mein Führer!"* And then they'd get down to the subjects at hand.

We orderly officers were responsible for monitoring the conversations on another line, keeping a record of what was said. The clever way Hitler set the tone was most impressive. When he didn't want to make a decision, or when his decision was different from Kluge's wishes, and things got tense—these conversations were only held on really important subjects—then Hitler always steered away from an open confrontation at the last minute. He'd say something like, *"Herr Feldmarschall,* I took the liberty of sending your wife her favorite flowers for her birthday, and by the way, we'll have to think a bit more about the questions we've been discussing. I'll call you again." Of course he never called, nor was he available for Kluge. So the decision was made the way Hitler originally intended.

Once, though, more than flowers were involved. It was Kluge's 60th birthday, and Hitler called to congratulate him. Somehow he had learned Kluge wanted to build a new barn on his wife's country estate. At the end of the conversation Hitler said, "*Herr Feldmarschall,* I understand you want to build a new barn. I am pleased to inform you that for your services to the German people I am making 250,000 Reichsmarks' worth of building material available to you. You will receive a check for the appropriate amount in the very near future."

After they hung up, Kluge called me into his office. I saw how uncomfortable he was that I had listened in. He said, "Boeselager, you heard what the Führer gave me for my birthday. What do you have to say?" I promptly answered, "*Herr Feldmarschall,* I cannot remember that the Kings of Prussia ever made such grants to their generals during a war. As far as I know, such things only happened after the final victory. I would give the check to the Red Cross." Kluge answered, "I'll have to think about it some more," and told me I was dismissed.

I never heard anything more from Kluge about Hitler's gift. I'm afraid he accepted it. I couldn't understand. I knew that in Prussia a victorious field marshal was always rewarded by his sovereign. But not during the war, and not because he was 60 years old! That was simple bribery!

To understand Kluge and the other senior Wehrmacht generals, you have to understand their backgrounds. After World War I many officers stayed in the army because they couldn't afford to leave it. They had no estates to retire to after the Kaiser fled to Holland. They had married young, had one or two children, and joined the Reichswehr before the Kaiser absolved them of the oath they swore to him. And that was important, because many of them were then expelled from the officers' associations of their old regiments as oathbreakers.

These men entered the Reichswehr with backs already bent, grumbling about their one-time friends who were rich enough to stand aside and criticize. Then Hitler came. All of a sudden, this generation of officers saw their careers flourish. Officers who had *left* the army were now coming back as reserve officers or as emergency commissions in their old ranks as first lieutenants. The majors and colonels they now served weren't the old breed of Prussian officer, they were men who had learned how to bend. They were men who had been educated in isolation, in the old imperial cadet corps. They lived on their pay, which was very low. That meant they lived in the officers' mess, because they couldn't afford to socialize outside it. The Reichswehr officers' horizons were narrow. They had very little contact with civilians, because they couldn't pay the bills for, say, dinner at a hotel. On the other hand, the officers' club had all the amenities, plus a congenial circle of friends.

This narrowness was professional as well. In 1941, the military leadership was arrogant. "In six weeks," they said, "the war will be over." But the real breakdown in confidence came with Stalingrad. Kluge said that attacking in two directions at once, toward the Caucasus *and* towards Stalingrad, would never work. After Stalingrad it was clear to him that the war was lost and that Hitler had somehow to be removed if Germany's defeat was not to be calamitous.

Kluge despised the Nazis. He hated Himmler and Bormann. He knew how dangerous and unpredictable Hitler was. Kluge had been an army commander during Operation Barbarossa, and never passed on the commissar order to his subordinates. He was a Christian—not a strict Protestant, Lutheran, or anything like that, but he was a Christian. Murder was murder. You could give him facts about the shooting of Jews, or the murder of mental patients in the homeland, and he would listen.

I would say Kluge first learned about the concentration camps in February of 1943. Who would have told him? No one dared at first. But in the regular briefings, the more we learned about the geostrategic situation, the more we learned about what was happening in America, it was frightening to listen to the cold statistics of what they were producing. And we junior officers finally said, "It's time to tell Kluge. Also that not only Jews are in these camps. There are millions of Germans 'unworthy to live,' and even soldiers, being killed."

But Kluge could not decide whether to accept the consequences of acting on what he knew. He couldn't commit himself to the resistance, not because he was afraid, but because he feared to go down in history as a traitor. In March 1943, Hitler visited Army Group Center's headquarters. Several officers proposed simply to shoot him. Kluge knew about the plan, but in the end forbade it. Himmler would not be accompanying Hitler, and Kluge feared a civil war

Youth leaders were war enthusiasts who acted like commanding generals. Schirach, for one, had never even been in the army, but told bloodthirsty World War I stories. My father found this irritating.

Until I was 16, I must admit that had anyone asked me if I was a National Socialist, I would have answered this question loud and clear with "Yes." Of course, had anyone asked me why I was such a convinced supporter of the party, I would have had trouble answering. We had been told wonderful things about the Teutons, Germany, the fatherland, and so on. The young generation of that time was very cleverly manipulated psychologically by the National Socialist regime. To put it simply, young people were talked into believing they were a few years older than they actually were. The sense of inferiority, which usually surfaces during puberty, was alleviated by promotions, oath taking, and the distribution of guns and ceremonial daggers. We were told, for example, that it was exceptionally fun to march past a church on a Sunday morning and disturb services by playing fanfares on our trumpets. Of course, the fact that respectable citizens were less than enthused delighted us that much more.

I thought all of this was marvelous. And sometimes when my father was at home during the war—which was rare—I told him about some of the things we did. But he didn't want to hear anything about it. He said, "You know what? You can talk about it wherever you want, but not when I'm sitting here at the table. I don't want to hear it!"

A few of my father's younger orderly officers agreed with me; they were delighted by my frank and straightforward opinions. But looking at people that age, 21 to 22 years old, from today's perspective, I would say they were more adolescents than they were adults.

I was drafted into the anti-aircraft at the beginning of 1944. I had just turned 15 and was incredibly proud to be given a uniform and treated like an adult. Naturally, there were times when we did act like kids and do some childish things. I recall one incident at a train station. We saw a navy officer, a lieutenant-commander, and decided we would ask him when the next train left. He was supposed to think we mistook him for a railroad official. He got terribly angry and asked us if we had ever seen a stationmaster wearing an Iron Cross First Class before. And in chorus we replied, "*Jawohl, Herr Kapitänleutnant,*" and laughed. We were so proud of ourselves!

My attitude changed after the death of my father. I began to realize that not everyone had the positive outlook I had. The question has been raised, how could you let yourself be enslaved by Hitler like that? But that some form of "slave psychology" was practiced is just not true. German potential was simply overestimated. As a young person, you were always 100 percent, even in the face of defeat. When you have been swept along in the wave of enthusiasm and are actually taking part in what is going on, you don't feel as though you have been robbed of any liberty at all. Just the opposite is true. No one challenged you on any of the basic questions. In a democracy there is always someone who speaks out in disagreement, and that person is allowed to express his views.

My father and I had always been very close. Whenever he came home, he always gladly shared his free time with me. We became even closer after he was wounded in France. He was hit by bullets fired from low-flying British planes on July 17, 1944, and only regained consciousness several days later. I still have a letter he sent to my mother; it was typewritten on July 23. He couldn't even sign his name; his signature was an illegible scribble. He had himself transported back home. He also requested that I be transferred to him from my flak unit so that I could read for him. He had extreme difficulty reading anymore. He had suffered a quadruple skull fracture which left him shortsighted and almost blind in one eye, and far-sighted in the other. And because of the head injuries, he couldn't tolerate wearing glasses. He suffered from excruciating headaches. And so I always had to read to him.

The officer who was responsible for my father's war diary had kept very literal and precise notes. My father had me read the diary to him. He wanted anything that was incriminating stricken from the record. He redictated everything he didn't like. He had a secretary, a sergeant, who destroyed the original pages.

This was quite a dangerous undertaking after July 20. But it brought us that much closer together. Due to his skull injuries, my father had difficulty sleeping at night, and he would sit downstairs in the dark for hours and talk. It was during these nightly conversations that he expressed his sincere doubts concerning ultimate victory. He was totally convinced that the war was as good as lost. He knew it was all over after Montgomery's breakthrough at El Alamein in

North Africa. In 1943, he told Hitler that Germany was not going to win the war and that we should concentrate on getting out as best we could. Then Hitler said to my father, "Remember something. Nobody, but nobody, will make peace with me."

The July 20 assassination attempt was another thing my father mulled over. He had always warned against such an undertaking, because he believed a dead Hitler would prove to be more dangerous than a Hitler who was still alive. My father told me he had wanted to surrender in France. He had even talked to the Waffen-SS, to Sepp Dietrich, about it. Dietrich admitted to my father that he didn't believe the Western front should be held until the Russians reached Berlin. Then my father asked Dietrich, "If we decide to surrender, whose side are you going to be on?" Dietrich replied, "You are the supreme commander here, we'll go along with you." These are the kinds of things my father talked about.

My father did not believe that Hitler was murdering Jews in masses. German troops in Africa had been isolated from the rest of the world. He didn't believe the British radio broadcasts either because they said so many false things about him. His idea was, if we were going to lose the war, we had to end it with as much dignity as possible.

What troubled my father the most was that Hitler was apparently going to fight to the bitter end regardless of the consequences of defeat. He once told me that had they capitulated in France, and had the Western front collapsed, then the Germans should have let the Americans and British go as far east as possible; they should have opened the way for them. He also told me that he probably wouldn't have been able to send my mother and me to safety prior to surrendering. Hitler would have most likely sought revenge on the two of us.

During the weeks my father spent at home, he expected that at some point he was going to have to answer for his point of view. During that time, the Gestapo never left our front yard. He requested that a guard from the army post in Ulm come to our house because he said, "I'm not just going to sit here and let them come in and shoot me in the dark of the night."

He displayed an incredible calm when dealing with problems such as this. Even the day Generals Burgdorf and Maysel came to pick him up, he remained very cool and calm. Just after we were informed we were having visitors, my father and I took a walk in our yard. He said, "Either I'll be dead by this evening, or they are coming to give me another assignment at the front." That was the one thing left he really wanted—a decent and demanding assignment.

When Burgdorf and Maysel arrived, they said they wanted to talk to my father alone. It was a beautiful fall day. Afterwards, he went to my mother and told her that he was going to take the cyanide the generals had given him. My mother couldn't believe what was happening was true. She didn't want to believe it. Then my father called for me and told me he had ten minutes to say good-bye. He told me the poison they had given him needed only three seconds to take effect. After that they were going to take him to a military hospital in Ulm. Approximately 20 to 30 minutes later, we would receive a phone call informing us he had had a cerebral hemorrhage and was dead. That is exactly what he said. Then Alldinger, his adjutant, said, "But aren't you going to put up a fight?" My father said, "No. I've thought about it and it wouldn't do any good. It would be absolutely senseless. They told me if I complied, nothing would happen to my family. The Führer has even promised to give me a state funeral in recognition of my accomplishments in North Africa." He also told us how essential it was for us not to utter a word to the outside or talk about it to anyone.

Then Alldinger said, "But you still have your guard." My father responded, "Alldinger, I am no longer allowed to give even a single soldier an order. That's all in the past. There's no use even talking about it. And taking everything into consideration, it's best we leave it as it is."

They got into the car—the two generals and my father—and drove away. Then we received the phone call, "Your father has just died of a massive cerebral hemorrhage."

After that, everything proceeded routinely and according to plan. It was almost unreal, even up to the telegram we received from Hitler expressing his condolences.

I accompanied my mother to the funeral, and was preoccupied with taking care of her. Field Marshal von Rundstedt, who in the meantime, had been reactivated into the military service, represented

Hitler. At one time he had been my father's immediate superior. It was strange, but he hardly exchanged a word with my mother or me. In fact, he hardly said anything at all. He held a speech which he read, and he had great difficulty even accomplishing that feat. The fact that he stuttered and stammered his way through his speech made his apparent insecurities all the more obvious. He disappeared immediately after the funeral.

Later, von Rundstedt is supposed to have said that he didn't know the causes of my father's death, something I find very strange. My father had talked about Rundstedt as a man with highly respectable convictions, who at one time had described Hitler as a "corporal from Bohemia." When Hitler relieved him from his position as Supreme Commander West, he was supposed to have said that he was happy that everything was over with, and that Hitler could kiss his ass! But apparently the field marshals and generals were so morally paralyzed by then that they just numbly continued to do what was asked of them.

JOB VON WITZLEBEN

Born 1916; member of a distinguished military family; deserted to the Russians in the aftermath of the plot to kill Hitler; retired colonel of the East German National People's Army; citizen of the GDR; lives in Potsdam.

"Hitler and his gang had to be eliminated, quickly and by force."

I first learned of the plans to get rid of Hitler and his accomplices in late autumn of 1943. I had just returned from the Eastern front as a captain and battalion commander to be trained as a General Staff officer.

During my few days of leave, I visited a distant uncle who was a favorite of mine, Field Marshal Erwin von Witzleben. At the time, he was already discharged from service, and later he was bestially executed at Hitler's orders—hanged from a meathook with piano wire. I visited him because I wanted to exchange ideas with a sober expert about the military situation and the future of the war. During our conversation, he asked me what I knew about the "Seydlitz Committee" and what I thought of it. I knew, from my experience on the Eastern front that the Russians had distributed a great deal of material from the National Committee for a Free Germany and the League of German Officers. I found their standpoint not only informative, but—despite some unwarranted assumptions—quite reasonable, and this is what I told my uncle. His reply to this was that he knew General von Seydlitz very well. He had a spotless reputation for civil courage and honor.

In principle, my uncle wanted the same things as Seydlitz. Hitler and his gang had to be eliminated, quickly and by force. He had wanted to try this as early as 1938, when he commanded Military District III in Berlin. But now, in 1943, everything depended upon the attitude of the German Wehrmacht and, above all, its generals. If the National Committee caused the officer corps and the troops to see his own views all the more quickly, my uncle could only welcome it. We could only hope that the "Seydlitz Committee" would continue its activities while my uncle used the limited influence he had left to fight the whole Nazi mess. My opinion was that the officers of the "Free Germany" movement were honorable and patriotic men who were on the right track, though their powers of negotiation were naturally limited in Soviet captivity. I felt that if I were ever to find myself a POW, I would join them.

I had nothing to do with the July 20 conspiracy. But my uncle was involved, and a few days after July 20, Himmler held a disgusting speech about this gang of officers and generals, these traitors whose ashes were now strewn in the gutter, and that now we must all unite in the fight for Germany's destiny. The reaction of most of my colleagues to this speech was one of complete rejection. They said, "It's easy for Himmler to talk, the stupid idiot! What nonsense."

PETER PECHEL*

"Don't you want to accumulate some plus points for the Fourth Reich?"

"Not permitted to leave the camp alive" is how the card read, the card that accompanied my father from the Gestapo prison on Prinz Albrecht Street in Berlin to the concentration camp in Sachsenhausen near Oranienburg. In other words, it was the death penalty.

It all started in April 1942. My father, the publisher of a well-known monthly magazine, the *Deutsche Rundschau,* was arrested by the Gestapo for having written articles critical of the regime. After spending some time in detention, he was sent to the concentration camp in Sachsenhausen, north of Berlin. At the same time, I was in a military hospital in Berlin recovering from a wound I had received in the fighting near Moscow during the winter of 1941. As long as I was in the hospital, I was able to visit my father once a month. I was allowed to write him once a month, send a small package once a month, and receive a letter from him once a month. But whenever I brought up the subject of release, it was as if I were talking to a wall; the officials either changed the subject or remained close-mouthed.

Time passed and I returned to the front, first back to Russia, then to France, where soon afterwards the invasion began. In the meantime, my mother had been condemned to 8 years hard labor after the July 20 assassination attempt. She was liberated by the Russians at the end of the war.

One day in December 1944, shortly before the Ardennes offensive, I was notified to report to the Supreme Command of the Home Army in Berlin immediately. Once there, I found myself in the office of the general for whom I had once served in 1942–43 as adjutant. He had me assigned to his staff so I could, as he put it, do everything possible to get my father released from the camp, because there

---

* Biography on page 131.

wasn't much time left. It is this man I have to thank that my father did, in fact, survive the war.

I assumed my new responsibilities in Berlin. In the few hours between duty hours and air raid warnings, I continued to pursue my father's and my mother's release. I went about it in several different ways, all without any success. Time was of the essence. It was already the beginning of April 1945, the Russians had reached the Oder, and I hadn't accomplished anything. I certainly did notice, however, that the Gestapo people I had been dealing with were becoming more polite and talkative. They were already contemplating their fate at the war's end, and weren't particularly overjoyed at their prospects. And it was this insecurity that put an entirely different light on the situation and gave me an entirely new idea of how to carry on. I had to play on the anxieties of the Gestapo, their fear of what tomorrow might bring, and I had to make my way to the top.

It was a desperate idea, but then so was the situation and that's why I decided to go through with it. In the beginning of April—I think it was the 8th—I called Reich Security Headquarters and asked to talk to *Obergruppenführer* Müller's adjutant. *Obergruppenführer* Müller was the feared and despised chief of the Gestapo, the state's secret police. He was called "Bloody Müller" because his hands were stained with the blood of countless innocent people. When the adjutant answered the phone, I told him my name and added that I was calling from Home Army Headquarters. I told him I had an urgent message for the *Obergruppenführer,* and asked if it was possible to meet him the following day. After checking, the SS officer gave me an 11 o'clock appointment for the next morning.

I spent that night memorizing exactly what I was going to say. I reported to the adjutant's office at exactly 11 A.M. My heart was beating like crazy. I inconspicuously felt for the gun in my belt. After a short wait, the adjutant said, "The *Obergruppenführer* is ready to see you now." I walked a few steps. The door shut behind me. I was standing in a large, brightly sunlit room. Sitting behind a desk was a squarely-built man with a remarkably yellow-tinted face and impenetrable, almost black eyes. I was standing directly across from "Bloody Müller."

Müller asked me politely what I wanted. I replied just as politely that I wished the release of my father, who had been detained in the

Sachsenhausen concentration camp since 1942. "So that's your real reason for coming here to see me," he said. His eyes narrowed, "I am very familiar with your father's case. He hates the Third Reich and he hasn't changed one bit since he's been imprisoned. Do you really believe that we would release an enemy of National Socialism?"

I had been expecting something like this. Now I had to act. The sun continued to shine through the large windows. For a brief moment I thought how wonderful it would be to be far away right now, far away from everything, not be at war, not have a father in a concentration camp. But the reality of the situation quickly brought me back to my senses.

I turned and looked directly at Müller. "Let's stop pretending, *Obergruppenführer,*" I heard myself say in an icy, indifferent tone. "Let's stop lying to ourselves. You know exactly what the military situation is at this point. You know it and I know it. The Russians will be here in Berlin in three weeks at the latest. The war is finished; so is the Third Reich. Don't you want to accumulate some plus points for the Fourth Reich? Considering everything that is connected with your name, you could stand a few plus points. Wouldn't it be wise to release my father—immediately?"

A long silence followed. Maybe one minute passed, maybe two—I don't know. I had gambled, I had just played my highest trump card and I didn't know if it was enough to take the trick. The little man sitting opposite me still had the power to eliminate my father, my mother, and me. All he had to do was to call for his adjutant. But nothing even close to that happened. Suddenly, Müller looked up. He rose. He said, "I want to think about it. Call me tomorrow morning."

I was dismissed. How I made my way out of the building and back to my office, I do not know. The tension of the conversation gradually let up, but I immediately found myself engrossed in new, feverish speculation. Had I really won? Would my father be released after all? Or, had he just said that he wanted to think about it? Could he have, in the meantime, given the order to have me followed and arrested when I got home that night? Anything and everything was possible during those days in April 1945. I decided that, in any event, I would spend the night at a friend's house, a place they would hardly suspect me to be. If, in fact, the Gestapo was really after me, I wasn't, by any means, going to make it easy for them.

I didn't get any sleep that night, the tension was too great. The next morning I lifted the telephone receiver at least a dozen times only to let it fall back into its place. That phone call was going to be final. What would happen if the answer was no? I didn't even want to think about it. Finally, at 12 o'clock noon, I made the call. Once again, the adjutant answered the phone. He spoke only one sentence: "You can pick up your father at the camp tomorrow at 1300 hours." Mechanically, I said thank you and hung up. Tomorrow at 1300 hours. I had won. Nevertheless, I was still skeptical: "Are they perhaps luring me into the camp only to arrest me? Once you're inside the camp, they can do whatever they want with you." These thoughts were not very comforting and I tried to suppress them. I didn't succeed very well, and decided to spend the night again someplace else.

I took the commuter train to Oranienburg the next morning. It was a beautiful spring day, one on which it was difficult to imagine that there was a war still going on. I took my time and walked slowly from the train station to the camp. How often had I walked this same route, loaded with packages, to visit my father. Was today really going to be the last time, the day for which I had been working and waiting for the last three years?

It was pointless to continue to think about it anymore. What had been started must be carried through to the end. I reported to the camp commandant's office and was seen through without delay. He was a pale man with restless eyes. The minute I saw him, I knew I was safe. These guys were really terrified. They surmised what they were in for. "Your *Herr Vater* will be here shortly," the commandant told me. *"Herr Vater"* and not "Prisoner Pechel." Through the open window, I could hear people singing outside. A group of prisoners was returning from work. They wouldn't be in this camp much longer either. Suddenly the door opened. My father walked into the room, dressed in an old suit, no longer wearing the zebra-striped clothing with the red triangle that signified the political prisoner, the clothes he had worn for the past three years. We embraced. The commandant said something else, my father was free to go.

A few minutes later, we were walking through the camp's main gate in the direction of the train station. My father had left the camp alive after all.

CHAPTER 12

July 20: Rebellion of Conscience

The decisive turning point in the German resistance came with the transfer in September 1943 of Colonel Claus von Stauffenberg to a staff post in Berlin. Stauffenberg, a scion of the old Swabian nobility, had long since lost any illusions about the Nazi regime. Severely wounded while serving with the Africa Corps, he took advantage of his new post as Chief of Staff, Home Army, to galvanize a movement that was in danger of focusing on problems instead of on opportunities. In particular, Stauffenberg was a catalyst for the idea of assassination. Planning for Operation Valkyrie, as the action was code-named, began in the summer of 1943.

The conspirators were handicapped by dissension in their own ranks, by Gestapo counterintelligence, and by simple bad luck. A successful coup depended on combining the assassination of Hitler with a prompt takeover of the state machinery. Stauffenberg used his staff position to alter emergency security orders in such a way that army troops could occupy key administration and communication centers in Berlin on the news of Hitler's death. Sympathizers throughout Germany and occupied Europe were ready to take similar action on Stauffenberg's word.

But who was to kill Hitler? Those officers with regular access to the Führer were unwilling to make an attempt on his life. Their reluctance is generally explained in terms of misplaced loyalty to their oaths, or to some form of moral cowardice. It can also be reasonably suggested that squeamishness played a certain role. The ability to shoot down an unarmed man in cold blood is not particularly widespread, even among professional soldiers.

Ultimately, Stauffenberg decided to perform the mission himself. This created two crucial problems. It was impossible for him to use a pistol. His right hand was gone; his left had only three fingers. Stauffenberg, moreover, had made himself indispensable to the conspiracy in Berlin. Now he had to travel to East Prussia, assassinate Hitler, and return as quickly as possible. He could neither make certain of success nor set the plot into immediate motion.

The results are familiar: a conference held in a flimsy wooden building instead of a concrete bunker that would contain the shock waves of an explosion; a briefcase casually moved under a table; an afternoon lost as the conspirators waited for Stauffenberg's plane to land. By the time Valkyrie was well under way, news of Hitler's survival was reaching Berlin through too many channels to control. Officers already corrupted with medals, country estates, and cash grants were quick to jump to what seemed the winning side. Stauffenberg was shot by a firing squad in the courtyard of the War Ministry. Former Chief of Staff Ludwig Beck shot himself. They were among the lucky ones.

In the following days an orgy of arrests followed—men, women, and children. Some were hanged on meathooks, dying by slow strangulation. Others were beheaded. Still others were shipped to prisons and concentration camps to await the Führer's pleasure. The army, concerned to the last with the appearances of honor, expelled uniformed victims from the officer corps before turning them over to the Peoples' Court.

July 20 had little prospect of success. Yet for all its shortcomings, Operation Valkyrie marked the end of the German concept of the state as a metaphysical abstraction, above human intervention. In that sense it helped to lay the moral groundwork, at least, of the Federal Republic. But July 20 symbolized something else as well: a recognition of the need to challenge a system that perverted every value it touched. For the participants in the uprising, success was less important than honor.

HERBERT BÜCHS

Born 1913; Luftwaffe staff officer; spent much time in Hitler's headquarters; present at the July 20 assassination attempt; after the war was a lieutenant general in the Bundeswehr; he currently lives in Meckenheim, Rhineland.

"There was an explosion, a bright yellow flash that forced everyone down. It was total chaos!"

In the West, after the invasion and prior to the July 20 assassination attempt, the Allied beachhead in Normandy was contained. It wasn't until July 25 that the Americans were able to break through near Avranches. But in the East the situation was extremely critical. During their summer offensive, the Russians had succeeded in destroying 28 divisions of Army Group Center and had advanced far into Poland. The entire situation was exceptionally grave. Also the weather was very hot and the humidity high; conditions that Hitler didn't like. The overall mood in the *Wolfschanze,* Hitler's headquarters, was tense and nervous.

On July 20, the daily noon briefing was held as it had been over the last several days, in the briefing room, and not the main bunker. This briefing room was located in a specially designed barracks built to withstand incendiary bombs, although it was totally ineffective against explosions.

I arrived at the briefing just after it had begun, so I neither saw Stauffenberg nor can I make any statement concerning the briefcase that was brought in. I only remember that General Heusinger was in the middle of his presentation.

I went over and stood at Hitler's left on the far left side of the huge briefing table. Hitler had the door to his back. I remember it was 12:37 P.M. The briefing had begun punctually at 12:30, so I had only missed the first few minutes. Stauffenberg must have already left the room by then. There was an explosion, a bright yellow flash that forced everyone down. It was total chaos. I saw Lieutenant Colonel John von Freyend, who was standing near the window, jump out. Since no one knew what was going on, I jumped out of the window too.

My first reaction was to run around the building. I saw other briefing participants come out of the barracks, but I really didn't pay much attention to whether Hitler was among them or not. All I knew was that there had been an explosion and that I had to inform Göring. I ran down to the communications barracks which was located about 150 feet from the briefing room. Once I got through to Göring, I said, "*Herr Reichsmarschall,* there's been an explosion here." Then I ran back to the barracks to find Jodl.

Shortly after the assassination attempt, we found out that we were all suspects, even those who had been in the room when the bomb went off. We were all screened and Himmler had Fegelein inform us that we had all been cleared. It was a time of total uncertainty for everyone.

The noon briefings continued without interruption. They were held in another barracks; in a somewhat smaller room, with fewer people in attendance. Hitler became sick with a kind of hepatitis and spent much time in bed. I personally took part in the briefings concerning the Ardennes offensive when Hitler was present in bed. Hitler was a broken man who still had the capability of getting himself back on his feet by clutching at any straw. For him, the straw became the planning of the Ardennes offensive. This was another attempt to take the initiative into his own hands, to turn the tide of the war.

FRIEDRICH GEORGI

*Born 1917; Luftwaffe staff officer involved in
the military conspiracy against Hitler; publisher after the war; makes his home in Berlin.*

"Are you for or against the Führer?"

Since the summer of 1942, I had been a general staff officer at the
Supreme Luftwaffe Command in Bernau near Berlin. I worked for
the General of the Anti-Aircraft Artillery and was directly responsible for the organization and operations of air defense. I had no idea
that Count Stauffenberg was going to make an assassination attempt
on July 20. The first piece of information that intimated an assassination attempt could possibly have taken place was a teletyped order
that a certain Heinkel 111 approaching Berlin from East Prussia was
to be shot down under all circumstances. I delayed passing the order
on because I suspected that it had to do with Stauffenberg's airplane
and I wanted to give him ample time to land in Berlin.

The first Valkyrie Order reached our office that afternoon. The
entire post was shut down, and, unless you had a specific order, you
weren't allowed to leave. In the early evening, I received a telephone
call from my father-in-law, General Olbricht. He asked me to come to
the Home Army Headquarters on Bendler Street as soon as possible
to see him. The duty officer, who was also a friend of mine, gave me
his pistol to take "just in case."

I went directly to Bendler Street. My father-in-law told me everything that had happened that day. He also said he was certain that
Hitler was still alive, which, in other words, meant that the attempt to
overthrow the government had failed. Furthermore, he said it could
only be a matter of hours or days before he and his confidants were
overwhelmed by SS units. He wanted to die like a soldier. Then he

said, verbatim, "So many decent soldiers at the front and men and women at home have already died so senselessly, it's high time people give their life for a good cause and sacrifice themselves for the fatherland." He handed over his briefcase to me with the instructions that I was "under all circumstances to make sure that the contents never got into the hands of the Gestapo." Moreover, I was to try to get out of the building, which in the meantime, was most likely already surrounded.

Before I could leave, the door to the secretary's office was thrown open and a group of five officers armed with submachine guns forced their way into my father-in-law's office. They demanded he explain what was going on. Furthermore, they demanded to talk to Colonel Stauffenberg immediately. During this violent dispute, I ever so slowly made my way to the door, so that I could flee if and when the opportunity arose to do so. The door flew open once again and a very excited Colonel Stauffenberg walked in. When he saw what was going on in General Olbricht's office, he immediately turned around and tried to escape. By blocking the door, I was able to give him a few seconds' head start. Stauffenberg fled down the hall. A few of the officers in my father-in-law's office ran after him while the remaining men blocked the office door.

What followed was a brief exchange of gunfire, and utter chaos. In the confusion, you could hear officers asking other officers, "Are you for or against the Führer?" I made my way to the secretary's office. The door leading to the hallway was standing wide open. There was another officer, someone I didn't know, standing in the door across the way. He had a gun in his hand. He asked me the same question, to which I only replied, "How do I get out of here? I don't know my way around." He told me to "go straight down the hall and take a left at the stairs, but get out of here fast because we need a clear field of fire!" I said good-bye to my father-in-law with a long, hard handshake.

With a firm grip on the briefcase, and without drawing my gun, I didn't run, but walked quickly down the corridor and down the stairs until I reached the courtyard. The main gate was barricaded by a line of armed army soldiers. The civilian gateman saw me—he knew who I was—and helped me to escape. He showed me another way of getting out, a way of avoiding the barricade. My car was parked across the street. It used charcoal for fuel and took a good 15 minutes to get started. Those 15 minutes seemed an incredibly long time.

I returned to the command post and looked over the contents of the briefcase. I removed all of the incriminating documents, especially the list of names of those involved, and burned them, piece by piece, in a bucket. Then I got rid of the ashes and hid the bucket.

Four days later, on July 24, two army officers showed up in my office; allegedly they came to escort me to a hearing. They took me directly to Gestapo Headquarters in the Prince Albrecht Street, and handed me over to a Gestapo official who was waiting for me. Everything was taken away from me; my medals were removed with the instructions to "take those things off!" I ended up in solitary confinement in a cell in the prison basement.

My imprisonment in Prince Albrecht Street lasted only a few days. There were no interrogations, at least initially. During the air raid alarms at night, two prisoners were always handcuffed together and taken to the bunker. Even though we were very closely supervised, these air raid alarms provided us with the welcomed opportunity to exchange this or that word, and bits and pieces of information. After approximately ten days, the majority of us prisoners were moved— to make room for new prisoners—to a special Gestapo prison in Berlin-Moabit, where an entire wing had been vacated to make room for "20th of July" people. There is where I remained until my release at the end of October 1944.

We were all in solitary confinement. We were only allowed to leave our cells when called for interrogation. We were not allowed to walk in the courtyard; we had no visitors, no contact to the outside world; we weren't allowed to write or receive letters; and, in the beginning, we weren't even allowed to read. At night, we had to lie on a bed directly underneath a bright headlight. We always had to lie with our hands on top of the blanket and, sometimes, though not always, we were even handcuffed. And through the peephole in the door, we were constantly under observation, day and night.

I was interrogated many times by a variety of people, but I was never tortured. During such sessions, it was crucially important for your interrogators to be under the impression that you honestly wanted to contribute to the investigation. It was also imperative that they believed you had a totally clear conscience. It was wisest to tell the Gestapo everything they already knew or would most likely find out. You could implicate only those individuals you knew with absolute certainty were already dead.

My strategy for survival was based on instilling my interrogators with the feeling that even though I had a certain degree of intelligence, they were intellectually my superiors. You had to ardently deny anything and everything that was self-incriminating. However, as General Olbricht's son-in-law, I had to admit everything I should have known. Moreover, not one of my interrogators ever demanded that I make derogatory remarks about General Olbricht. In spite of everything, it was apparent that the Gestapo had a special respect for the man. They naturally condemned his actions, but they never once expressed doubt concerning the integrity of his motives—at least during the interrogations they didn't.

In the meantime, my commanding general had done everything he possibly could to persuade the Gestapo to release me. He was the one responsible for giving the Gestapo the impression that my absence placed the launching of the V-1 in serious jeopardy. He also made certain that I wouldn't be forced to give up my uniform. Even though the Gestapo constantly ordered me not to do so, I was able to wear a general staff officer's uniform the entire time I was there. That in itself offered a certain amount of protection against mistreatment. And because the Gestapo couldn't prove there was a connection between the army conspirators and the Luftwaffe, even though they surmised that one somehow had to exist, he was able to convince them that their only hope of establishing a connection was by releasing me and keeping me under constant surveillance. That way they would most certainly come to learn with whom I made contact and who made contact with me. Moreover, I was a Luftwaffe officer and, considering the fact that the attempted revolt was organized and initiated by the army, I was nothing more than an unimportant accessory.

LUDWIG FREIHERR VON HAMMERSTEIN-EQUORD

Born 1919; son of the Reichwehr's former supreme commander; an officer, he participated in the July 20 conspiracy against Hitler and lived in hiding until the war ended; after the war he became director general of RIAS, the American-German radio station in Berlin.

"As a medical student, you'd better pay close attention to the corpse you dissect—it just might be someone you know!"

I was sent to Home Army Headquarters on July 20, 1944, with three fellow soldiers. Our first assignment was to arrest and disarm a certain *SS-Oberführer* who had come to Bendler Street with an escort to arrest von Stauffenberg. We did just that. The *SS-Oberführer* allowed himself to be disarmed while jeering at our superior numbers. Next I went to General Olbricht's office to await further instructions. General Olbricht had me come into his office to guard the Deputy Commanding General of Berlin, who apparently wanted no part of what we were in the process of doing. We couldn't let him leave the building at this point. The general made his position quite clear. He told me that he was a soldier, not a putschist. His remarks reflected the attitude of many of the other generals and senior officers. The idea of mutiny was just too much for them.

After a brief conversation with General Beck later that evening, I realized that we had failed in our attempt to get rid of Hitler. Between 9 P.M. and 12 P.M., I noticed officers walking around armed with submachine guns and hand grenades. While on the way back to my guard duty, several armed officers pushed past me and went into a room. I didn't follow, and remained in the hall. A shot rang out. All soldiers instinctively grab for their weapon when they hear gunshots. I did the same. A short general staff officer was standing behind me and said, "Leave your gun where it is. It wouldn't help anyway." So I left my pistol in the holster. Who was this officer? Was he one of us or was he on the other side? Only a few moments later, the door opposite to where I was standing opened, and out walked General Olbricht's adjutant, a lieutenant colonel. He had his coat on and was about to leave his office. The general staff officer standing next to me gave a signal to another officer standing in the hall who suddenly grabbed for his gun and pointed it at the adjutant. It was then clear where these other officers stood. They were definitely not on our side.

Then Stauffenberg was shot at and wounded. There was return fire, probably from Stauffenberg's orderly. By now there were six or seven of us officers standing out in the hallway. A lieutenant colonel with a gun in his hand came to us and said "Someone is trying to stage a coup against the Führer, and we have to counter it! Gentlemen, you are under my command." We were ordered to block off all hallway exits immediately. I didn't utter a word, while ever so carefully removing myself from the rest of the group.

It was clear to me that Hitler was still alive. These general staff officers, apparently not in on our plan, had organized a counterattack, thereby making the putsch a lost cause. The only way our plot could succeed was if Hitler was killed. The situation being as it was, I had no other choice but to try to escape. Only because I had once lived on Bendler Street, and was more than familiar with the area, was I able to get away with my life.

I managed to call my sister, and told her that I had to disappear immediately. Then I went home and woke up my mother. I told her the attempt to overthrow the regime had failed, and that I had left my briefcase with a pistol and my papers in General Olbricht's office. I had to leave at once; they would most certainly look for me at home first. But where could I go? I remembered a young lady I had met only a few days earlier at a friend's dinner party. She was a medical student, and definitely not a Nazi. We had joked with her that evening by saying, "As a medical student, you'd better pay close attention to the corpse you dissect—it just might be someone you know!" She didn't exactly appear to appreciate our morbid sense of humor, but I decided to go to her house anyway. Afraid of waking up her younger sister by ringing the doorbell, I threw stones at her window. I told her the Gestapo was on my tail, and asked her if I could possibly stay at her place for a couple of days. She immediately said yes.

Within the next couple of days, my older brother found me another place to stay. I never stayed in one place too long. Friends, friends of friends, even officers, were constantly helping me find a new and safe place to hide. During this time, I always had enough to eat. I was even supplied with false identification papers. Many people risked their necks to help me. Because of my involvement in the assassination attempt on July 20, my older brother was forced into hiding. My younger brother was arrested and imprisoned until the end of the war. My mother and youngest sister were arrested in November, and were detained in the women's prison in Berlin. I lived in hiding till the end of the war.

WOLF-DIETER ZIMMERMANN

Born 1911; an active member of the dissenting Protestant "Confessing Church"; is a pastor and lives in Berlin.

"Our problem is how to keep things from becoming even worse."

One day in the summer of 1941, I sat together with Pastor Dietrich Bonhoeffer and Werner von Haeften, Stauffenberg's aide. We spoke of a potential assassination of Hitler. Von Haeften asked, "Should I shoot him? Do you think I should shoot him? Since I'm Stauffenberg's aide, I know how to get a gun into the main headquarters. Should I shoot him?" Bonhoeffer was completely quiet for a moment, and then said, "The problem is, what comes afterwards? Shooting him is pointless when the next two Hitlers are waiting in the wings. Our problem is not shooting the man. Our problem is how to keep things from becoming even worse."

REINHARD GOERDELER

Born 1922; son of resistance leader Karl Goerdeler; army officer arrested by the Gestapo after the July 20 assassination attempt on Hitler; today is top manager of a law firm in Frankfurt.

"My father wanted a democracy of the Ten Commandments."

My father, Karl Goerdeler, would have become Chancellor of Germany if July 20 had succeeded. He was Lord Mayor of Leipzig until he resigned in 1936.

If one can describe his attitude in the years between 1933 and 1936 as a period of critical distance from the regime, then 1937 and 1938 can be seen as the turning point, the years in which he was driven to thoughts, and then actions, of resistance. The transition from thought to deed went very quickly.

My father's warnings to British officials during his visits to London began, at the latest, in 1938. He suggested that the British government no longer compromise, but assume a clear and definite stance toward Hitler. I believe that thanks to his connections and contacts in Germany, he knew that Hitler would take one step after the other to expand the Reich as long as he encountered no resistance from London and Paris. And ever since Hitler had occupied the Rhineland in 1936, it was clear that the West had little desire or inclination to oppose him.

But it was not possible to dissuade the British under Chamberlain from carrying out policies of appeasement, with the result that the Treaty of Munich was signed. My father, very disappointed by the lame attitude of the British government, became active in fighting the Hitler regime. This, of course, meant that we certainly didn't make any open statements over the telephone, or anywhere else. My father had many contacts in the Reichswehr, and later the Wehrmacht. Whenever a name was dropped, we could assume my father knew that person. Generally speaking though, my father was extremely cautious in mentioning names, and was quite reserved in speaking to us children.

You have to realize that for a child growing up under the conditions of a dictatorship at that time, there was a total lack of information even from your own parents, let alone the other limitations put on the freedom of information, of speech, and of the press. This has remained very strong in my memory, and it is the basis on which I judge my environment today.

My father exercised a certain amount of caution, even at home. But we knew that after he resigned as mayor of Leipzig in 1936, he was not only critical of the regime, but that he did everything he could to prevent war from breaking out. My father behaved as carefully as he could under the prevailing conditions. For example, he memorized as many telephone numbers as possible to avoid writing them down anywhere.

I received my father's last letter when I was at the front in Italy. In this letter he wrote: "After the death of your brother Christian, I have doubled my efforts." I destroyed this letter before I was arrested and taken to Berlin because it could have been used as evidence against me. Nonetheless, it remains unforgettable to me.

I heard the name Stauffenberg mentioned once when I was at home, and therefore when the name came up after July 20, I suspected what might be in store for my father and for all of us.

The military men who were sympathetic to the resistance wanted plans and strategy papers. This is how my father's political papers and letters ended up in the hands of the Gestapo. A portion of these letters had been written with the intent of convincing the generals that it was time to act. When I saw my father for the last time in February 1944, before going to the front, I recall that the situation was full of frustration. As a civilian one could not act alone; one was always dependent on the military.

That my father was a central figure in all this almost surprised me, even though I knew he had an endless number of contacts, not only in the military, but in universities and churches as well.

It would be an exaggeration to claim that my father was a deeply religious man, but he was concerned with justice and truth. He wanted honesty, truth, and respectability, a democracy of the Ten Commandments.

In retrospect, one can say that Karl Goerdeler didn't do everything right. But one thing remains in my mind about my father, and that is, the longer this regime went on, the more complete became his horror of the injustice, the despotism, and the oppression of freedom. And I would like to tell the young historians, the German as well as the foreign ones, that they must try—which is admittedly difficult—to imagine life under a dictatorship. Sometimes even the small things in everyday life brought great dangers with them.

Let me add a few words about the approach of the conspirators toward the Allied powers. Based on the conversations that went on in our household, I remember that the call for "unconditional" surrender made all efforts of the resistance extremely difficult. It was especially the German generals who argued that the demand for unconditional surrender was, in fact, nothing but a challenge to continue with the war, cost what it may! In all probability, the military tried to persuade the leaders of the resistance—whenever they met during the war in such neutral countries as Switzerland and Sweden—to try and clarify if the terms of "unconditional surrender" could be mitigated. Or perhaps they could even determine how the enemy powers (the U.S., England, and the Soviet Union) would react to the idea of an internal revolt against Hitler.

Naturally the entire situation became that much more critical after the catastrophe in Stalingrad in January of 1943. The conspirators were running out of time. By July 20, 1944, the Red Army had almost reached the German border, the Western powers had a strong beachhead in Normandy, and there were heavy air raids over the Reich. The prospects of overthrowing the regime were diminishing. Undoubtedly, it was the hopeless military situation in both the East and the West that ultimately led to the decision to go through with the assassination, no matter what. On the one hand, it would provide a basis for negotiation, while on the other hand, as Henning von Tresckow put it, it would be, at least in part, an attempt to restore the honor of the country.

I believe the call for unconditional surrender placed an incredible burden on all those involved, men who were all serious, responsible, thinking individuals. Then, of course, you can't dismiss the fact that the United States and England weren't always in total accord with the Soviet Union. Even if the putsch had succeeded, who knows whether or not they would have occupied the rest of Germany after all. However, in spite of everything, the conspirators must have had a flicker of hope somewhere.

Even though it wasn't openly discussed, the conspirators were all very much aware of the danger that their activities could result in a stab-in-the-back legend. But I am convinced that their personal moral and ethical commitment to restoring or at least saving some of the country's honor won out over the risks involved in such an undertaking.

After the war some members of the German opposition were criticized for taking a stand against Hitler only after it became obvious that the war was not to be won on the battlefield. The claim that the entire German opposition—military men and civilians, the so-called conservatives and the liberals, the Social Democrats and Communists alike—was nothing more than "a bunch of rats jumping from a sinking ship" is absolutely ridiculous and absurd. This has not only been openly refuted by the family members of the dead resistance fighters, but has been discredited by well-known historians as well.

COUNT FRANZ LUDWIG VON STAUFFENBERG

Born 1938; son of Count Claus von Stauffen-
berg, the leading figure in the July 20 assas-
sination attempt; was arrested by the Gestapo
after July 20 and put in a concentration camp;
after the war became a member of the Bun-
destag; now serves as a member of the Parlia-
ment of the European Community and resides
in Bavaria.

"We were to remember that our parents were outstanding, wonderful people."

I was one of four children. At the end of the war, I was seven years old; during the war, I had no idea of my father's involvement in the resistance. Although my mother was aware that he was a member of the resistance group, she did not know that he was the key figure in the plan to overthrow the regime. She was only generally informed, and she found out about the role he had played from the radio.

Our family life with father was sporadic during the war. I remember Christmas 1943, when he came home after having been wounded in Africa during an air attack. He had lost an eye and two fingers from his left hand. He was forced to take on a new assignment until he had completely recovered.

After the assassination attempt and after my father had been executed, mother told us children that he was dead. I can't remember her having given any long explanations, but then I wasn't old enough for much logical reasoning.

Two days later, the Gestapo found out where we were and assigned two men to guard our house. The next day we were told that my mother and my great uncle—an uncle on my father's side who had been visiting us—had been taken away. A few days thereafter, the news came that my grandmother and her sister had suffered a similar fate. Two cousins were executed. We were taken to a home in Lower Saxony that had been established for the purpose of housing the children of resistance members. I remember a village pastor telling us that we would be taken away—no one knew where—but whatever happened, we were to remember that our parents had been outstanding, wonderful people. This preacher risked his neck in saying this; someone could have reported him.

Twice we were told we would rejoin our relatives at a place known as "Buchenwald," which was nothing more than a name to us. This never happened. Once we were actually driven in the direction of the concentration camp, but we were returned before arriving there. During the wintery trip, I watched bombs fall and noted the delay between the sounds and the visual explosions.

Later there were rumors of plans to donate this "worthwhile genetic potential"—we children and others in a similar position—to childless SS couples, but our almost being sent to Buchenwald contradicts these reports. And we were lucky, as the matron of the home, who had a relationship with the county supervisor, kept us protected.

Of course only a few generals were involved in the July 20 plot. I do not like to pass judgment on the high-ranking generals of that time. Some of the generals certainly were subjected to too many demands and were incapable of coping with the situation they found themselves in. But my father was disappointed because he experienced great difficulty in enlisting help for his plan.

Anyone in a public position from 1933 on no longer served the common welfare. He served an evil state, and he experienced this change suddenly.

The combination of Versailles and democracy was a heavy burden for Germany, one that brought us the economic woes that Hitler exploited. But I still don't know all the reasons why a highly civilized people could have been so completely carried away by what happened during the Nazi era.

In the 1950s, when I listened to recordings of speeches by Goebbels and Hitler, I wondered how this use of the voice, of language, and of argument could have exerted such an immense influence on people. In the 1950s, I felt the speeches were repellent, foreign, and unreal. Today, however, it no longer seems so far-fetched to me that rhetoric aimed at eliciting hysterical reactions should be effective. I feel this holds true for any country in the world.

The July 20 plot wasn't a conspiracy of one minority against another. It was a collective effort of widely differing groups against a political regime. The conspirators, including my father, realized that regardless of whether the attempt succeeded, something significant would happen. This is important for the leaders of the Federal Republic to remember. I am not sure whether they understand it.

MICHAEL MAAS

Born 1926; an officer candidate when his father was executed for his part in the July 20 conspiracy; became a public relations manager and writer after the war; lived in Berlin; deceased 1988.

"What about father?" "He was executed."

My father was a member of the SPD, and because he felt that his duties were in Germany, he refused an offer to emigrate to the United States. Very early on, I asked him what a concentration camp was. He explained the meaning of the word to me very precisely, which he was able to do since friends had told him about what sorts of terrible things had happened in them. Most of these people were from the Berlin area. Most were in the infamous "protective custody," as it was officially known, of Sachsenhausen.

In 1938 came a turning point that had a very strange effect on my father's career. He and others began organizing illegal labor unions, to the extent that this was possible. They had no great effect; the National Socialists and the Nazi workers' association had practically smashed the labor unions. During this time, Colonel Graf Stauffenberg came to our house on two occasions, dressed in uniform, and left late in the evening.

One evening in June 1944, my father practically let me in on the secret with the words, "I have to put a burden on your shoulders, since now you are a soldier." He then told me in great detail about his activities in the civilian resistance movement. He was an absolute supporter of the concept of surrendering to the allies after a successful assassination. That way at least all of the troops, especially those in the East, could be brought back to the old Reich territory. Inwardly he was a skeptic, an opponent of the assassination. But he saw that in all likelihood we would have no other chance to make clear that there were not only Nazis in Germany.

I was stationed near Frankfurt on the Oder, 60 kilometers east of Berlin. After the unsuccessful assassination attempt, I received a postcard. It was meant to inform me only that nothing had happened. In August, I got a pass to go home. My mother was there, and I asked, "What about father? What is going on? I haven't heard anything from the two of you for ten days now." For those ten days he had been under arrest. My mother knew where he was—in the notorious Gestapo interrogation building on Prince Albrecht Street. He was then sent to a special concentration camp in northern Germany.

When the trials commenced, my mother was able to send me permission to visit my father in the concentration camp. I had to report to my commanding officer. I was arrested a few hours later. It was completely clear to me that what my father had feared had happened, and that I had to think seriously about what I knew, and what I didn't know. I was interrogated, and apparently they believed what I told them. They released me, and I went back to my unit.

On October 29, in the afternoon, I was told to report to the orderly room. I thought, "Something is up with my family." I received travel orders for Berlin, along with the message that my visit to my father in the concentration camp had been approved. First, however, I was to go home.

It was late at night when I arrived at the Zoo Station. There was an air raid, and I had to go into the bunker at the zoo. Afterwards, I walked home, and I was very astonished that my mother opened the door for me; normally she never opened the door. She fixed me breakfast, and then we were alone. My first question was, "What about father?" And then she said, with unbelievable, almost rigid composure, "He has been dead for two days now. He was executed."

My mother had tried everything to rescue my father. Later, I worried that a human being who had tried with every bone in her body to perform such a rescue would not be able to survive afterwards.

I returned to my unit. I returned on exactly the day the examination of the cadet officers was to take place. I passed the exam. We were sitting around talking when the commander came to me and said, "Please report to my office in half an hour." I wondered what was up. This man, a captain who looked younger than he was and who wore a golden Hitler Youth badge, said that he knew what had happened. Then he said, "I have to tell you—I'll say it in one sentence. Do not forget your father. He was a very honorable, a very decent man." This captain risked his neck to tell me that. After a brief pause, when I was just about to click my heels, he said, "One thing is clear—don't do anything stupid."

My mother and I telephoned every evening, and each time I asked about her health. One evening I received the news I'd been fearing, something was wrong. Rushing home, I found my mother lying in bed with a nervous collapse. I stayed by her side until she was taken to the hospital. She got pneumonia, then double pneumonia. A few hours after she had been taken to the hospital, she was dead. This was only six weeks after my father's execution. I was an orphan at 18.

In December, before Christmas, I was suddenly ordered to go to the army personnel office in order to have a direct confrontation with the chief, General Burgdorf. I didn't learn the reason until after I arrived. In a waiting room, I met four other cadet officers like myself, and we soon understood each other by simply exchanging glances. They were all sons of executed men and were there, as I was, because they were supposed to change their names. In a brutal conversation, General Burgdorf told me what a swine my father had been: a traitor to his fatherland and his country, a man guilty of high treason. And his wife was basically no better.

Then he stopped, and I fought to keep myself under control. He said, "We demand that you change your name. After all, you are an officer cadet in the reserves." I said, "Fine. I am willing to change my name." The general's face brightened up. My grandmother's maiden name was von Zolligkofer. He asked, "What do you want your name to be?" I said, "Michael Maas-von Zolligkofer." The general went into such a rage that I thought, "Now I'm in for it." Then I said, "Do you really believe, General, I would change my ways and thoughts by changing my name?" The general shouted, "Get out!" I thought I would be arrested, but nothing happened.

KURT MEYER-GRELL*

"I sat down on a bench across from that bust of Hitler, and I began to weep bitterly."

National Socialist ideology was impressed on us children systematically—indoctrination so thorough that ten years after the war's end I still thought like a National Socialist, even though I'd learned about the atrocities.

I was in the officers' mess of an air base near Berlin on July 20, when the loudspeaker announced an address by Reichsmarshal Göring. Göring said that an assassination attempt had been made on Adolf Hitler. He also appealed to the Luftwaffe to remain loyal to the Führer. The Reichsmarshal hadn't finished speaking when I jumped up, fastened my gun belt, and was on my way to my unit to alert them about what had happened. I intended to issue them live ammunition.

---

* Biography on page 139.

I should add that we'd had some drinks at the mess, so I was slightly foggy.

To get outside, I had to go through the lounge, past a bust of Hitler—a bronze bust across from a marble bench. And I freely admit that I couldn't pass this bust, because I simply couldn't imagine anyone, let alone a soldier or an officer, a general, lifting a hand against the supreme commander. I sat down on the bench across from that bust of Hitler, and I, a 24-year-old man, began to weep bitterly. At some point, I pulled myself together, telling myself this wouldn't get me anywhere. I ran to my unit, alerted them, and issued live ammunition.

A short while later, an officer came to relieve me in the name of the commander, right in front of my entire unit. The commander had heard that Lieutenant Meyer-Grell was lying drunk under the Hitler bust! This was immediately retracted once I set him right that, after all, I was the only one on the air base who'd immediately acted in line with the Reichsmarshal's orders.

CLARITA VON TROTT ZU SOLZ

Born 1917; wife of Adam von Trott zu Solz, one of the key figures of the resistance, who was murdered by the Nazis; became a psychiatrist after the war; resides in Berlin.

"I believe I can die honorably, perhaps, but I can't hide"

When Adam and I became friends, everything changed for me. He gave me a whole new perspective, and through it, I gained the courage to trust his judgment. He had an unyielding goal: to bring about the downfall of that criminal government. And he wasn't alone.

Several friends, all young men who had strong and attractive personalities, formed a group. They accepted the priority of mutual goals over personal interest. We wives often played the part of observers at these meetings. Never again could I trust the character, judgment, and energy of a group so completely.

How can I best describe the atmosphere we lived in during that time? Even during our discussions at home we covered the telephone with a cushion; we thought this would protect us from being bugged. Often we talked in English because, although our housemaid was reliable, her National Socialist fiancé certainly wasn't. It was very difficult when Adam had to work on dangerous papers at home. We didn't have a good hiding place in the apartment. I took them to bed with me at night, along with matches, and hoped that in an emergency, I'd be able to burn them and flush them down the toilet.

When women and children were evacuated from Berlin, communication became very difficult. I suggested that Adam disguise important messages as reports on someone ill. We gave our friends codenames like "Heart," "Head," "Stomach," and so on. This little code played an important part in the negotiations of the circle. You had to be extremely cautious. It was painful, but you couldn't even talk to sympathetic family members, name any names, or share any thoughts or plans that had any illegal content. These people could have caused damage by unknowingly giving something away.

Adam was arrested on July 26. I cannot describe the paralyzing emotion of the following weeks. I was still a free person, but I couldn't use this freedom to rescue Adam. And I simply could not imagine the monstrosity of our little daughters being directly endangered.

I met with a close friend in Berlin on the day of Adam's trial, August 15, 1944. He did something then for which I remain grateful to this day: He had the courage to tell me that my children had been taken away. That is something that you can't overcome easily, and it hasn't been until recently that I have been even able to talk about this experience. At the time, I just went numb and walked into the old courthouse inwardly half-dead.

I tried to find the room where my husband was being tried. The trial was being held in a large hall, the doors of which were guarded by SS men. I tried to find a place to wait, in the hope that I could see my husband when he and all the other prisoners were led out. I hoped I could give him one last glance that would say everything, a sign of all our love and one last reassurance about us. But from where I was standing in the hallway, in front of the enormous doors of the courtroom, I could hear Freisler yelling. It was only by a miracle that I managed to avoid being arrested right then and there.

At this point I could have gone underground. Through a series of incredible coincidences, I was able to speak to Pastor Poelchau, the pastor for prisoners in Moabit. I managed to give him a farewell letter I had written to Adam. He pleaded with me to go underground, and, although I considered it for awhile, I felt that this was just something I didn't have in me. I told him, "I believe I can die honorably, perhaps, but I can't hide."

COUNTESS MARION YORCK VON WARTENBURG

Born 1904; widow of Count Peter Yorck von Wartenburg, a leading participant in the July 20 plot, who was consequently murdered by the Nazis; after the war, became the first German woman appellate judge; resides in Berlin.

"The time I spent in prison was almost a salvation."

The Kreisau Circle was a very tight, close-knit group. Everyone was down to earth, never really interested in wracking their brains over intellectual issues. Life was so real, so immediate. Of course, one feels much more aware when confronted with danger.

The group met just about every evening at our apartment. There was always a pre-set theme which was thoroughly discussed. Nothing, absolutely nothing, was ever talked about on the telephone or written down. There were no informers among us, not a single one. Everything was based on mutual trust. New members were brought into the group only with great care. Initial conversations were conducted with utmost caution and a great deal of sensitivity. That's one thing I believe men have over women: their intense feeling of comradeship and mutual trust. At that time, this was very special.

I was so intimately involved in what had happened that the time I spent in prison after July 20 was almost a salvation. The seclusion, just being able to be alone with my own thoughts, was a blessing in disguise. I spent the first two weeks in solitary confinement. I didn't talk to anyone. I didn't leave my cell. I had nothing to do and nothing to read.

Once in a while, a Gestapo man would look in on me to see if I had suffered a nervous breakdown. That was, after all, the purpose of solitary confinement. On one such visit, he took notice of my ripped stockings. They had been torn when I fell down the stairs. "Ah ha," he said, "now you've had a nervous breakdown!" I replied, "No, why? Should I have?"

I felt an extreme closeness to my husband during this time. Even when awake, I never really knew if I was dreaming or if this was reality. Ever since that time, I understand how a person who has recently lost someone they love feels an incredible closeness to that individual. You continue to live and suffer with your lost one. In a dream, my husband told me how he died and what he felt.

I knew my husband had written me a letter immediately preceding the execution, but it was in Gestapo hands. After my release from prison, I made three trips to Berlin in an attempt to find the letter. On the fourth occasion, I was summoned to Berlin by the SS. They offered me a widow's pension. I refused adamantly: "My husband did not give his life so that I could receive a widow's pension." The man I was dealing with sat back and after a while said, "Do you want his letter?" I finally got it. With this precious treasure in hand, I returned to Silesia. I sewed the letter in the lining of a small linen bag and took it with me wherever I went. It was written on war paper and has become very fragile over the years; the print is barely legible.

Those who maintain that the entire German nation consisted of criminals are wrong. I met quite a few decent human beings in high positions during the Third Reich, people who were at least willing to listen and help. I found this so even in prison. The two SS men responsible for taking the pictures for the "Criminal Photo Album" were almost pleasant to me. The one asked me my name. "Yorck," I replied. He looked at me—his eyes nearly doubled in size—and immediately said, "Won't you please have a seat, Countess?" Through small gestures such as that, people could show their respect for a man who had just been executed. This type of thing happened many, many times.

Upon my release from prison, I had to report to Gestapo Headquarters for interrogation. It was an eerie place, to say the least. After reaching each floor, a heavy iron gate would slam behind you. Even on the top floor, where the main interrogation office was located, there was a woman on guard. Once I reached the top of the stairs, she quickly pulled me into her cubicle and said, "I saw your husband every time he was brought in for questioning. He always said hello; he had such wonderful eyes." You can't imagine what her words meant to me, especially in a place like Gestapo Headquarters.

I came to realize that if people spoke openly about what was really on their minds, they would never betray you.

I regret that so little has been done to honor the fallen soldiers. It is unfortunate, especially for our citizens. They have no symbols. They have nothing in which they can take moral pride.

CHAPTER 13

Collapse

In the aftermath of the Battle of the Bulge, the Allies pushed steadily forward into Germany. On February 8, 1945, British and Canadian troops launched a major offensive through the Reichswald. Further south, U.S. and French forces closed on the Rhine river, the last great geographic barrier in the west. Plans for a pontoon crossing were discarded when on March 7, 1945, troops of the 1st Army's 9th Armored Division managed to seize the undestroyed Ludendorff Bridge at Remagen.

The crossing of the Rhine marked the beginning of the war's last act. Two U.S. armies encircled the Ruhr, as the rest of the Allied forces fanned out into Germany against collapsing resistance. Supreme Commander Dwight Eisenhower continued to focus on defeating the Wehrmacht and crushing all possible sources of future resistance. His intelligence reported plans for a "national redoubt" in southern Bavaria and Austria, combined with plans for nationwide guerrilla warfare by the so-called "werewolves." Preventing this meant overrunning the entire country, including outlying rural areas, as rapidly as possible. British troops drove for Bremen and Hamburg. American spearheads reached the Elbe river, fought through Munich, and crossed the pre-war frontier into Czechoslovakia. Thousands, then hundreds of thousands of German soldiers surrendered rather than risk Russian captivity. Others threw away guns and uniforms, seeking to blend into the columns of refugees fleeing the advancing Red Army and make their private ways back home.

Germany had a foretaste of what to expect from the Russians in October 1944, when Red Army spearheads overran the East Prussian border village of Nemmersdorf. Counterattacking Wehrmacht troops found a scene of desolation and massacre whose details lost nothing in repetition—particularly to veterans of the East who remembered the devastation caused by the German army in Russia. Officers whose loyalty to the Nazi regime was wavering now saw no choice except a fight to the death with the Soviets, to the last man and the last round.

For three months Hitler ignored appeals to withdraw German troops still in the Baltic States, and to evacuate the urban populations of Upper Silesia and East Prussia. Instead the Führer ordered house-to-house defense. He declared such cities as Königsberg and Breslau "fortresses" to be held to the last man. On January 12, 1945, the Red Army broke out of its Vistula bridgeheads and marched toward the Oder River and the Baltic Sea. Refugees took to the roads as T-34s drove through and over the columns of farm wagons. Heinrich Himmler assumed command of an "Army Group Vistula" that existed mostly on paper, while the German navy called on its last resources to evacuate refugees through the ports that remained open. Within two weeks Silesia, the Reich's last industrial center, was in Russian hands. The Soviet offensive exhausted its supplies only 40 miles from Berlin.

As the Red Army completed overrunning Hungary and the Balkans, the eyes of Stalin and his generals turned to the greatest prize in the history of the Soviet Union. On April 16, 1945, the final offensive began. Two-and-a-half million men, 42,000 artillery pieces, and more than 6,000 tanks encircled the Reich capital and began to squeeze it. Opposing them were the fragments of an army: old men and boys hastily thrust into uniform; SS troopers from half of Europe; survivors of once proud divisions and corps. Underneath a dying city Adolf Hitler moved phantom relief forces on a map disintegrating from his perspiration. On April 30, the Führer committed suicide. On May 2, Berlin capitulated. Five days later Hitler's successor, Admiral Karl Dönitz, surrendered what remained of the Thousand-Year Reich.

THEO HUPFAUER*

"We had to leave them scorched earth!"

As the Allied armies got closer to Reich territory in the second half of 1944, there were advisers in the Führer's headquarters who believed that when the enemy came, he must find nothing intact. We had to leave them scorched earth! Since 1943 I had been working under Albert Speer. I was what amounted to his deputy in the Ministry of Armaments. A scorched earth policy meant that all the factories, food, and medical supplies, all the dikes and dams, all bridges, all transportation facilities, were to be blown up. In other words, all infrastructure would be eliminated, so that it would be virtually impossible to operate in these areas.

Hitler wanted this even though it would have meant the end of Germany and the German people. As early as September 1944, guidelines were prepared for the destruction of plants and factories under a direct threat of enemy occupation. These guidelines, however, were opposed by a great majority of party, state, and economic leaders. Albert Speer was the leading spokesman against this self-destruction. His so-called "implementation instructions" said, "We must remain ready for battle to the end. Factories can be made non-operable, but they must not be destroyed. Evacuations must only take place in highly sensitive cases."

Later, in December 1944, it became clear that we couldn't win the war. Two very stubborn supporters of the scorched earth policy were Bormann and Keitel, I know this from Speer. And these were naturally the two men who pulled the most weight with Hitler; they were with him constantly.

I never met Bormann personally, never exchanged a word with him, but he was the man who pulled all the strings. I got the

---

* Biography on page xxv.

impression that his big role model was Stalin. Stalin wasn't a top man at first either; he was Lenin's secretary. But Stalin was constantly by Lenin's side and never left him alone, just as Bormann never left Hitler alone. Hitler had all kinds of odd working hours, but he only managed by using medication. His so-called "doctor," that gangster Morell, taught him to use amphetamines to wake up and barbituates to sleep. Bormann managed all this without drugs. In the end, everything rested on Bormann's shoulders. There weren't any cabinet ministers anymore, except Speer, who had direct access to Hitler.

Although Speer was a favorite of Hitler's, and in this case he certainly tried to use that advantage, Speer could only talk to Hitler on a now-and-then basis, so he was at a tactical disadvantage from the start. What Speer did next, in my opinion, went beyond "civil courage." Speer actually beat Hitler at his own game and turned Hitler's own weapons against him. Speer argued, "The scorched earth policy must not be implemented. You yourself, *mein Führer,* say time and again that the territory we lose today will be recovered very shortly. I'm sure you are still of the same opinion. Retaking scorched earth will not help us at all. We must retain the possibility of putting the factories and civilian life back in order as quickly as possible. So we must merely dismantle the important machinery and hide the parts. Then, after we've taken back these areas, we need only re-assemble things. Our duty," Speer told Hitler repeatedly, "is to preserve the basis of life of our people." Personally, I'm convinced that Speer risked his life by doing this.

Speer had a plan to get the Führer a new circle of advisers, with Bormann and Keitel out of the way. He didn't plan to have them murdered, only arrested and somehow handed over to the enemy. The Allies could do what they liked with them. But this would only have been possible if Speer knew who would replace Bormann. Keitel wouldn't have been a problem, but Bormann was. His replacement had to be someone whom Hitler admired and who was well known not only in the party, but in military and economic circles as well. Speer considered the Gauleiter of Hamburg a good candidate.

To rally support against the scorched earth policy, Speer made many trips in October and November 1944. He went to Hamburg, the Western front, to Austria, all the way to Silesia, and I was his constant companion. Speer spoke with every important military leader. He talked to the Gauleiters and the commanding generals in Germany to convince them that a scorched earth order should not be carried out under any circumstances. Of course, he used Hitler's own arguments to make his point.

When we arrived back in Berlin, we received a call from Kaltenbrunner, head of the Police Ministry and next in line to Himmler. I knew Kaltenbrunner. We were both fraternity men, and that was really our only contact. Kaltenbrunner asked if he could speak with me. I said, "Herr Kaltenbrunner, I'm the younger one, I'll come to you." And he said, "No, no, I'm the one who wants something from you. I'll come to you."

I went to my office and thought, "Oh God, now we're going to be arrested. One of the Gauleiters has reported us." I phoned my wife and said, "Krista, listen. I'm about to have a visit from Kaltenbrunner, and I'm not sure how it will turn out. If you don't hear from me by seven this evening, call this number." I gave her the number of Luftwaffe Field Marshal Milch, whom I knew very well.

Kaltenbrunner came to my office and said in a friendly way, "Look, we know each other well. But I'm obliged to tell you something. You and Speer have travelled all over, demanding and encouraging things which oppose the orders of the Führer." "Speer and I oppose the scorched earth policy," I replied, "you're right about that. But the Führer says we will retake these areas, and he doesn't want a devastated countryside." "All right, all right," he answered, "I just wanted to let you know that if it comes down to me being required to take action against you, I won't allow old acquaintance to stand in the way." I said, "Fair enough; it was very good of you to come. I appreciate it." And with that, he left.

Given Speer's campaign against the scorched earth policy, you might well wonder whether he personally believed in final victory. He didn't. He hadn't for some time.

ROLF PAULS

*Born 1915; as an officer in the tank corps he
lost an arm in Russia but continued to serve;
was ambassador to the United States and
became the Federal Republic's first ambassador to both Israel and the People's Republic
of China; resides in Bonn.*

"The *Volkssturm* can hardly wait to get out of here!"

I had lost my left arm in Russia, but continued to serve as a staff
officer. During the final stages of the war, we were ordered to bring
tanks and artillery to the right bank of the Rhine, near Cologne. The
next morning, we were ordered to go down to the vicinity of
Remagen and meet the Americans for a last stand—it all ended in the
vicinity of Düsseldorf. Herr Grohé, the *Gauleiter* of Cologne, enthusiastically told the division commander that he would send three or
four battalions from the *Volkssturm* consisting of approximately
3,500 men. He maintained that the *Volkssturm* could hardly wait for
the opportunity to defend their own hometown.

Hearing that, my boss blew up, slamming his fist down on the table
so hard that the hats flew up into the air. He yelled back, "I'll tell you
what the *Volkssturm* can hardly wait to do—they can hardly wait to
get out of here! The last 24 hours have proven that—they are taking
off in all directions. And to tell you the truth, I can't blame them."
Herr Grohé was rather shocked by this outburst and left. He crossed
the Hohenzollern Bridge, had it blown up, and reported us to Army
Headquarters, but nothing happened.

During this last phase, Field Marshal Model once asked me if the
troops were receiving enough newspapers. I said that we hadn't had

any for some time. The Field Marshal fetched a great quantity of the newspapers from his car and gave them to me. The headline read, "Bitter Resistance Instead of White Flags." As I read this, my glance fell upon the houses in the village street where I was standing. The first white flags were already hanging from the houses.

Later, when the Field Marshal asked me what the people were saying, I told him that they were saying that after they had been so mistreated, they at least wanted to bring the whole affair to an end with dignity. The next day we were overrun by the American 13th Armored Division.

HEINZ SCHWARZ

Born 1928; anti-aircraft auxiliary in 1945; participated in the defense of the bridge at Remagen; a career politician after the war; long-time member of the Bundestag; lives in the Rhineland-Palatinate.

"We're blowing the bridge!"

As a young *Flakhelfer,* I was at our command post during March 1945. It was located in the bridge tower on the Rhine, just opposite Remagen. It was my job to make the telephone connections. One day I transmitted an important call, a call which signified the beginning of the end of Hitler's Third Reich.

Captain Prattke, the combat commander in Remagen, wanted to speak to our bridge commander, Captain Friesenhahn. Naturally, we weren't supposed to listen in on such conversations, but we did anyway. There were rumors that the Americans were on their way to the Rhine. That's why I distinctly remember this particular conversation so well. It went as follows: "Friesenhahn, this is Prattke. The Americans have passed through Rheinbach, 25 kilometers away. They are on their way to Bonn and Remagen. Prepare to blow up the bridge. Heil Hitler, Friesenhahn!" "Heil Hitler, Prattke!"

That telephone conversation made more of an impact on me than anything I had experienced as a flak auxiliary until that time—and that included the bombing raids. Now I knew the war was just around the corner. It was going to hit home any time now! My parents only lived about five miles from the bridge. It was March 7, 1945. The Americans reached the bridge the following day.

The bridge had been the target of several air raids the week before. It had been damaged by the bombs, and was being held together by railway ties so that motor vehicles could still cross the river. That first week in March, entire German units returned, with cannons being pulled by horses, by motor vehicles, and yes, even by soldiers. In other words, the German army was retreating from the left bank of the Rhine 24 hours a day. That's when it really became clear to me that this war could never be won.

The retreat was really something to see. The older soldiers in our unit stayed down below, but the rest of us were curious and went up to the bridge tower to get a better look. We were all still kids, around 16 years old. There was no continuous fighting. In fact, long periods of time elapsed during which absolutely nothing happened. It was a shock to see the condition of the returning German soldiers—totally exhausted and worn out.

The Americans advanced along the left bank of the Rhine on March 8. One of my comrades, another young flak helper who lived in a village on the left side of the Rhine, received the order from his unit commander to "blow up the ammunition and beat it back home as fast as you can!" His superior was merely taking consideration of the fact that the "soldier" was just a kid. He was really concerned that the boy made it home safely.

Just like a kid, I told my friend, "Wait a minute before you blow the stuff up. I want to run up to the bridge tower first to see the fireworks go off!" After it was over with, and before I left the tower, I grabbed an ax and cut through the telephone lines, making sure they couldn't be used again. I was under fire when I ran back out onto the bridge. I dodged into the tunnel entrance where I knew I was safe from the war, for the time being at least. The bridge tunnel was bomb-proof. Then the order rang out: "Everybody down! We're blowing the bridge!" We heard a dull bang. We thought the bridge had been destroyed, and we were saved. Then the word spread quickly that the bridge was still intact and the Americans were crossing it.

At the time, I had no idea why the detonation had failed. The only thing that mattered to me was the fact that the Americans were across the Rhine. I knew I had to somehow get myself out through the rear entrance of the railroad tunnel and run home to my mother as fast as I could. Fortunately, I had grown up in the area and knew of a few side roads which led to my house. I don't know how many times I asked "where are the Americans now?"

It was really something when, 15 years later in 1960, I met Sergeant First Class De Lisio, the first American soldier to set foot on the right bank of the Rhine. That made me acutely aware of just how much the world had changed from 1945 to 1960.

SIEGFRIED KÜGLER

Born 1926; volunteered for the Luftwaffe because he wanted to fly, but wound up as a paratrooper; after the war, became a top manager at the Siemens Company; lives south of Munich.

"Didn't that guy Hitler learn any geography, or what?"

I volunteered for service in 1943 at 17. I had the feeling I had to do something. Politics had absolutely nothing to do with it; we didn't even know what that was. Sure, we all knew who Hitler was and yelled the obligatory "Sieg Heil" when necessary. And, of course, I was in the Hitler Youth too—after all it was mandatory. But it was more of a sports-and-games club to us; whenever it got military we got around it somehow. There were political lessons too, but we just goofed off during them. They didn't interest anybody. You have to differentiate between National Socialism and—I don't want to say "reasonable nationalism"—but just the feeling that you're doing something for your country. That's something totally normal, and not necessarily typically German.

I volunteered for transfer to the Luftwaffe paratroops. That was the only place you could go in the Luftwaffe other than the "Division Meier."[1] I didn't want to run around with the Hermann Göring arm band.

It took a lot to get through training, but afterwards I knew I'd done the right thing. I really learned how to operate in the field, to camouflage and protect myself. We didn't do any jumps; there wasn't any fuel left for transport planes. Apart from that, training was typical: small-scale warfare, no large groups—we called it "red

Indian war"—don't be seen, camouflage, practice hand-to-hand fighting.

I became a corporal; we always said it was the most dangerous rank of all. The Allies were saying they'd shoot all the corporals, so there would never be another unknown corporal like Hitler.

We first saw action in January 1945 in Holland, and in February we crossed the lower Rhine. We lit some fireworks behind the American lines at night. I'll never forget this, because at night you could see something I didn't know: if you crack open a tank with a bazooka, it melts the metal. This was the first time I had seen anything like that. That glowing metal sprayed high as a church steeple. You could only see that at night; it was an unforgettable sight. We also shot up a couple of trucks, but we didn't do any hand-to-hand fighting.

The Americans were marching toward the Rhine. When we saw everything that was going past, all the artillery, tanks, and trucks, well I've got to say I just flipped. I thought: how can you declare war on such a country? We asked ourselves, "Didn't that guy Hitler learn any geography, or what?" No matter how good or bad the Americans were as soldiers, their equipment alone was enough to win the war.

Ultimately, we had no choice but to surrender. We had to wear those so-called "bone bags,"[2] and there were at least two guards per prisoner. They didn't let us out of their sight. They were scared to death of those "bone bags." We were the paratroops.

---

[1] Refers to the Hermann Göring Division. Göring boasted at the start of the war that if any bombs fell on Germany, "you can call me Meier." By 1944, logically, the division's nickname became "Division Meier."

[2] Idiom for the camouflage garb of the paratroopers.

WOLF-JOBST SIEDLER*

"I would not have deserted."

Along with my friend, Jünger, I had been jailed for criticizing Hitler. We were 17 years old. Jünger got out of prison before I did, but we managed to be assigned to the same unit, the 6th Panzer Grenadier Division. We were sent with them to Italy. On our release papers it said, "Not permitted to become a civil servant, and never to be promoted in the Army." The war could have lasted 30 years and I would have always remained a private. That was in September 1944.

On our way to action on the Southern front, our train was bombed near the Italian border. We jumped out, leaped into the bushes, and watched the train disintegrate.

I was sent to the east of the Po Valley, to Forlì, and saw action the first night. At that time we still had relatively new bazookas, and we were sent to knock out an English defense position. I had to throw myself down, crawl forward, stand up, and fire this huge tube five yards long. There was a violent blast, which I thought was normal considering the size of that thing. And then it hissed and everything was smoky. It was the propellent charge going off in my hand. In fact, I still cannot move my hand very much today. In the field hospital the doctor told me, "Well, son, you won't become a pianist or a secretary, but as for the important things in life, holding a glass and caressing a girl, you'll be able to do both."

So I was sewn up and had a wonderful time in the hospitals in Padua and Venice. Venice was an open city; only wounded soldiers were allowed to go there. Since it was already infested with partisans, after dark we had to go through the streets in threes. One of us always carried a submachine gun. Frequently a soldier would disappear in the canal with a knife in his back.

---

* Biography on page 357.

I was sent to the front one more time, for the Allies' last great breakthrough battle south of the Po. Only the remnants of armies were left; there were no organized units. People had only carbines and pistols, no heavy weapons; there just weren't any left. I came into this mess, and luckily contracted malaria. At the decisive moment I had a fever of 104 degrees. My company commander was a charming man who had been a carpenter, had fought from the first day of the war to the last, and had been promoted to officer because of the exceptional bravery and competence he had shown in the field. He said, "Kid, we'll get you out of here. This will only last a few more days. You'll get marching orders—and get yourself into the nearest hospital with that fever." I still wanted to stay. You felt so lost without your outfit; and virtually the whole countryside was in the hands of the partisans. But he gave me my orders, and I set off alone through upper Italy, searching for a hospital and hoping to reach Germany.

Jünger was put into the front lines near Carrara and was killed in action on the first night "on the marble cliffs," the title of one of the books his father wrote. Even today, the father still has not been able to accept his son's death and the fact that his son fell at that particular spot. The book had been written five years earlier.

I ended up in captivity after all. My fever rose to 106 degrees, and I collapsed in a hospital town near Padua. During the night the hospital was stormed, and we were taken prisoner by partisans loyal to the Italian king. They behaved very correctly: went to each bed, lifted the mattresses to look for weapons or ammunition, asked about SS men—I don't know what they did with them—passed around cane wine bottles, and said, "La guerra é finita, comrades! Celebrate!"

A few days later we were handed over to the British. We were taken to Taranto in southern Italy, where there were already thousands of POWs. So there were no rations or accommodations, only barbed wire. At first we didn't even have tents. It was June, and burning hot.

Next I was brought to North Africa, to a huge tented camp near Benghazi. My papers proved to be very helpful there. Suddenly I was called to a British major, who was actually a German who had emigrated to Palestine and joined the British army there. He had examined my papers and the point "Aiding and Abetting Illegal Jews" made me especially likeable to him, even more than my other resistance activity. I was signed up as an instructor in the British Intelligence Department for the Re-Education of German Prisoners of War. I was supposed to give lectures on German history and the democratic traditions in German literature.

I told this ex-German, "Major, I can't do it. I have been in prisons since I was 17. I am completely incapable of lecturing thousands of prisoners—judges, senior doctors, officers, probably even university professors." He replied, "The library is at your disposal. We have 35,000 books here; you can read up on what you need." I was given a house in Benghazi, a jeep, and a special pass permitting me to move about freely.

So I held my lectures, and inspected the POW camps together with British officers who were bored stiff after years of war stuck in the desert. They said that we shared the same background—same education, school system, etc. They had the old yachts of the British colonial army, and so for months of the summer of 1946, I did little more than sail up and down the entire North African coast with young British officers.

I stayed until the end of 1946, and even then I was not sent home to Germany. The British sent me to Wilton Park, a POW college near London. I only returned to Germany at the end of 1947.

I never thought of deserting during my time as a soldier, despite my antipathy for the regime. I was never really confronted with the question, because I was severely wounded my very first night at the front, and had to spend months in the hospital. When I finally made it back to the front, everything was already collapsing. But in retrospect, I suspect that I would not have deserted even if I could have. There were archaic principles of honor involved here: one simply didn't do that kind of thing. I suppose I would not have shot a deserting comrade, as so many did. It would have been an unthinkable thing to do.

As to whether we knew what was going on, and whether this burdens us as soldiers and Germans, I should tell a story from my time in prison. During air raids we had to go to the bunker. This was our only opportunity to talk, because we were kept in solitary confinement. We particularly tried to edge up to the political prisoners. One time an army captain, who was sentenced to death and executed two weeks later, told us that massive liquidation of Poles, Russians, and Jews was taking place in the East. All the political convicts agreed that there were murders, shootings, beheadings, hangings, and torture, but insisted that the talk of gassing was all war propaganda. We recalled the tales of chopped-off children's hands in Belgium during World War I. Even in January 1944, prisoners on death row still thought all this to be BBC atrocity propaganda, and said such things were not possible.

HORST WEGNER

Born 1929; he and his family fled their home in eastern Germany before the Russian invasion; lost both his parents in an air raid; is a postman in Bad Godesberg, near Bonn.

"I'll tell you, I've had my fill of war up to here."

At the age of 14, I had to live in a dorm where the Navy Hitler Youth also lived. I was in my first year of apprenticeship at a shipyard in East Prussia. I was learning to become a technical draftsman. Every morning we had to fall in for the flag raising ceremony—that was tradition. One morning in February 1945, we lined up, raised the flag, and waited for the "Fall Out!" order so we could go to the canteen and eat breakfast. No one moved. Nothing happened. There was no one around to give the command—no superiors, nothing! And there we stood, 500 to 600 of us. All our superiors had run off. You could already hear the artillery fire.

The Russians were coming. It was every man for himself—head west! I saw the first Russian tanks roll into the city; Russian infantrymen were sitting on top. I was able to jump on a train at the very last minute. I was home about eight days before the Russians came, and we had to move on.

Since my mother couldn't walk too well, I had to sit her in the basket on the front of my bike and push her. My father, who had been wounded in World War I, walked alongside us. We walked to Kolberg on the Baltic Sea, about 30 miles away. The Russian tanks caught up with us just before we reached Kolberg. The infantry sitting on top of the tanks started to shoot wildly all over the place. My father got shot right through his thigh. We were near a farmer's house, and sneaked into the barn to catch our breath and rest a little. I was dog-tired from pushing my mother on the bike. The Russians found us and pulled us out of the barn. They were Mongolians. They had huge scars and pockmarks on their faces. And they were draped in jewelry—they wore watches up to the elbows. They came in and pulled out everyone wearing anything military—a military coat, for example. They were taken behind the barn, shoved against a wall, and shot. They weren't even all Germans; some of them were foreigners. They even shot the private who had bandaged my father's leg.

It was really cold out. It was February and there was lots of snow. We kept on moving west, on and on. The Russians started firing at us again—artillery fire. We decided to stay put until they had to stop to reload, and then we ran like hell. I was still pushing my mother on the bike and my tongue was dragging on the ground. We finally got to Swinemünde. We thought: "We finally made it! We're in the West now!" We found room for my parents in a school. They were assigned a place in the hallway. Getting into a room was out of the question; they were already crammed full of people. After all we had been through, all I could think of was going to sleep. We spent the night there. The next day, March 12, my mother said, "Let's go down and get something to eat." They were passing out some hot soup from a kind of field kitchen. We went down and stood in a long line. But before we had gotten to the front of the line, the first bombs began to fall. It was chaos. Everyone panicked. There had been no warning at all. The first time we heard them was when they hit. There was no alarm, no nothing.

I was standing next to an ash-pit and jumped in. It was a 10 to 12 feet long container made out of brick. I was standing up to my neck in ashes. I had to hold on to the cover really tight because it flew open every time a bomb exploded. The noise from the bombs exploding was really, I mean really loud. I knew I was at least safe from all the metal and stuff flying through the air.

The attack lasted about an hour. I kept praying for it to stop, but they just kept coming back, wave after wave. You can't imagine how scared, how deathly afraid you are. You're all alone. You don't know if your parents made it to the basement or not. You're just sitting there, waiting. An hour can really be a long time.

Things gradually quieted down. I could hear people yelling and shouting. One was crying out for his mother; another was calling for somebody else. I lifted up the lid of the pit. I saw a lady walking around holding her head together with both hands. She'd been hit by a bomb fragment. Children and old people who'd never even had a chance of getting into the basement, were lying all around the schoolyard. I got out of the pit and went to look for my parents. But it was going to take at least four to five hours before anyone could begin to do anything. The school building was gone—the ground where it used to stand was level. The basement ceiling had also caved in. What kind of bombs had they dropped on us? It was like they had used a scythe to cut the whole area clean. There was nothing left— nothing.

Hours later, they pulled my mother out of the basement ruins through a hole they had managed to dig. You could still hear people screaming from below. But my mother, she was blue. I had the feeling she had suffocated. I never saw my father again. He was probably buried underneath the basement ceiling when it collapsed. They took my mother over to the grass area in front of the school where the hundreds of other bodies were lying. There were men, women, children, babies, old people—dead people of all ages. And my mother too. I still hoped I would somehow find my father. I hoped for two days. I even helped carry away the ruins myself. We listened to see if we could hear anyone knocking, or any other signs of life from below. But I never found my father. I'll tell you, I've had my fill of war up to here. I was 14, and from that moment, I was on my own. I started to walk west along the Baltic coast.

ANDREAS MEYER-LANDRUTH*

"Only the moment counted."

In 1944, the front came closer. In July, the Warsaw uprising took place, and after that we heard artillery fire day and night. We heard about the fighting in Warsaw from the wounded whom my mother nursed. Cossacks serving with the Wehrmacht came through our area, some of them in traditional garb, and some in SS uniforms. They came with families, with horse-drawn carriages, and with camels. Suddenly the atmosphere became very tense.

The front around Warsaw broke around the beginning of January 1945. It caught up with us on the 15th. I fled with my mother and sister. My father remained, and my brother was on the front.

On the next day, we heard that Posen would have to be evacuated. In the evening, we went to the train station, which was completely full. It was eerie. There were large groups of young Poles singing the German hit song about how "everything would pass." We waited on the platform for hours wedged in among masses of people. Finally the train came. It stank, and it was full and kept getting fuller. The trip to Breslau took two days and nights.

There were scenes during this train trip that reflected the entire tragedy of human actions and existence. Families were pulled apart. Some people yanked others out of the train, and then threw in their own belongings and jumped in. Along the way, we saw German soldiers who had been hanged. They had signs around their necks saying, "I was a coward and tried to run away." We saw slaughtered cattle scattered on the road, where some people had failed in the attempt to take their cattle with them. There was a woman in our compartment who was over 80 years old. She went crazy during the course of the journey. Only the moment counted, only the moment

---

* Biography on page 101.

had to be endured. We gave no thought to what might happen afterwards. We really had no fear.

Toward the end of January, we travelled on to Lübeck. When we arrived there, we found that in spite of the war, public life in Lübeck functioned wonderfully. We were freed by British troops in March 1945.

RUDOLF WÜRSTER*

"Our 27 Royal Tigers destroyed more than 300 heavy Russian tanks."

We eventually received new tanks, Royal Tigers, and were transferred east, to the Oder River sector. There we dug in. At 4 A.M. on April 16, 1945, we were attacked by Russian fighters, artillery, and just about everything else. But nobody broke through our position. According to the Wehrmacht bulletin, our Waffen-SS battalion consisted of 27 Royal Tigers, and we destroyed more than 300 heavy Russian tanks. One of our men, a guy by the name of Bismarck, knocked out 25 "Josef Stalins" in a very short time.

I still remember those last fights. South of Berlin, we were defending an anti-tank obstacle. As the Russians approached, I returned fire. At first, I didn't even notice the three Russian T-34s crossing a field and heading in my direction, but I knocked them out, too.

Another time I was ordered to keep the road leading out of a village under observation; Russians were supposed to be inside. Relying only on eye judgment, I estimated the range at around 1,750 meters. We set our sights accordingly, loaded armor-piercing shells, and waited. Suddenly four Russian T-34s came out of the village from behind a hedge. We flamed one before it could even get into

---

* Biography on page 260.

firing position. We hit the second one too. We hit the turret of the third tank, and the rear of the fourth. Then, while shifting into reverse, our tank threw a tread. We weren't able to fix it. At four o'clock in the morning, when the Russians began firing signal flares in our direction, we bailed out. I put explosives in our tank's gun barrel and we jumped onto another tank nearby. Our deserted Tiger was burned out.

The Russians kept closing in to the south of Berlin. One night somebody suddenly cried out, "Russians!" I went to ground head-first, and one of our quad-twenty AA guns was just mowing them down when one of my buddies came running up shouting, "Stop! They're all Germans!" Another time, we moved through a burned-out gunnery range. Bodies were lying all over the place. At dawn I noticed a group of people lying in the woods nearby. One was a lieutenant wearing a pair of binoculars around his neck. I said to my buddy, "Gee, we could really use those." Just as I was about to slide the binoculars over his head, the lieutenant opened his eyes, looked at me, and said, "Get lost! Can't you see I'm sleeping here!" He had been there the entire night, and didn't even realize that he had been sleeping amid the dead.

We continued marching in the direction of the Elbe. My sixth sense warned me to get rid of my newly awarded Iron Cross, my Tanker's Badge, and my Silver Wound Badge. I knew if the Russians caught me wearing them, I would be killed on the spot.

ERWIN LOESCH

Born 1924; fought for three years on the Russian front, winding up at the siege of Danzig; became a teacher after the war; lives near Wuerzburg, Bavaria.

"This was the mass grave of an army."

It was August 1944 in Estonia. The sun blazed, and the sweat trickled down our bodies. We found two foxholes directly behind a small house.

Everything was surprisingly quiet for the next few hours; no sign of the enemy. We went into the house and rummaged through drawers and cupboards, where we found German books that interested us. All the doors and windows were open so that we could be seen from the enemy side—this was careless of us. Suddenly, there was a loud bang—it didn't hit us, but went over the house. We ran out through the back door and dived into our foxholes. A second shell hit the house, which caught fire immediately. Then came shell after shell, and machine gun fire. We couldn't see a thing through the smoke. To our right, a German machine gun crew was falling back. "Tanks!" they shouted. We immediately picked up the radios by the straps and darted back 100 yards, taking cover where we could.

We ran behind some shocks of wheat, set up our transmitter, and made radio contact at once. We saw that the Soviet tanks and guns had reached the foxholes we'd just left. We transmitted the message, "Fire immediately on own position. The enemy has broken through!" With that, German shells streamed over our heads and we hit the dirt. The enemy tank was hit, damaging one of its tracks. Then a platoon of about 30 German *Landser* and a sergeant reached us. They were supposed to counterattack. "Everyone scream 'Hurrah!

hurrah!' as loud as you can," the sergeant told us. "The Ivans won't know that we're such a small bunch." And, in fact, the charge succeeded in turning back the advancing Russians.

This kind of rear-guard action was typical in our retreat from Russia. By March 1945, I was fighting in front of Danzig. Enemy planes flew over us toward Danzig non-stop, and the city was lit by fire. Artillery rumbled on all sides. The enemy had loudspeakers blaring music. Then an announcement, made loud and clear: "German soldiers! Comrades! Give up resistance! Throw down your weapons! Your fighting is senseless! In a few days we'll chase you into the sea! Your death is certain! Surrender and you will see home again!" Then music played again, the artillery thundered, and machine guns hammered. Afterwards, the whole thing was repeated again and again: music, the call to surrender, music, and more shells. This loud, shrilling music in the face of death!

It was an eerie night on the hills around Danzig. It was as if the devils were dancing. Only a few steps away from the fighting line, we were confronted with a bloodcurdling picture: German soldiers were hanging from the trees along the street with ropes around their throats. Some were barefoot, and almost all had signs pinned to their chest that said something about cowardice. Several of them even had military decorations on their jackets. We were stunned! At this moment it was crystal clear to us that this was the end.

All of a sudden there was an explosion in a house on the right side of the street. One of my comrades called to me from a deep underpass. I swung myself down to him; many frightened civilians were already crouching there. My comrade shone a flashlight on me. I badly bruised my chin, and shrapnel had entered my knee. With two men supporting me, we moved on. We wanted to catch up with the others in our unit, and there was no time to lose.

After we reached the hospital, someone announced that the lightly wounded could try to make it back to the Vistula River, where there was a possibility of being transported out by a ship. The soldier next to me gave me a nudge and said, "It's our last chance." After weighing the pros and cons, we decided to go for it.

The road was full of shelled and burning military vehicles and refugee wagons, dead soldiers and civilians strewn among them.

Time and again new attacks of fighter-bombers increased the destruction. This was the mass grave of an army; not only an army, the mass grave of women and children as well. There were collisions of vehicles in threes and fours, burned out and still smoking; the ragged and charred corpses of people and horses; and a horrible smell. I had already seen quite a bit in the course of this war, but this outdid everything by far. Death still hadn't had enough. He kept hammering without letting up.

Shortly before 6 A.M., we got our first view of the Vistula River. A huge mass of people, mostly refugees, were crowding the dock. Finally, shortly before midnight we were called to board a navy ferry. There must have been 5,000 to 6,000 people on the ship when it left port on the evening of March 28, 1945. Russian planes attacked the ship. But all the bombs missed us and dropped into the water amid heavy defensive fire from the ship's anti-aircraft.

At 9 A.M. on March 31, 1945—the Saturday before Easter—our ship entered Copenhagen harbor. We were saved!

BERNARD SCHMITT*

"That boy heaved himself up, spat in my face, and shouted, 'Long live the Führer!' "

Being Alsatian, I made up my mind to fight with the French instead of waiting to be drafted into the Wehrmacht. I was able to reach the Free French Army, but I was in pretty bad shape. I only weighed 82 pounds, and for a man of almost five feet six inches that isn't much. They fed me, and two months later I weighed 125 pounds and felt decidedly better.

I was wounded for the first time during the liberation of

---

* Biography on page 113.

Strasbourg. I got a bullet through my leg. The days before I received my second wound, we didn't encounter any German soldiers. It was early April 1945. We were in Germany, and there appeared to be no more soldiers left, only Hitler Youths, all 13, 14, and 15 years old. They were part of the so-called *Volkssturm.* Wehrmacht regulars were nowhere to be found.

Anyway, that day a young boy was brought into my hospital tent with multiple shrapnel wounds. I can still picture his face. He was about 14, and looked like he was in a trance. I leaned over him and said in German, "You dummy! Look at what this has gotten you!" Well, that boy suddenly heaved himself up, spat in my face, and shouted, "Long live the Führer!"

I was wounded the next day by another Hitler Youth. He fired a bazooka at my jeep. My driver was killed, and I caught 14 splinters in my right lung. The wounds healed very quickly, and I was back in action only two weeks later. The real effects only became apparent later on. In 1947, I began to spit blood, and in 1948, they had to do a pneumothorax because I had four holes in my lung. Now my lung is shrunken to the size of a fist, and is no longer usable.

I would like to relate another situation I got myself in. It was in the Ulm area toward the end of the war. I went into an inn one morning and ordered myself a drink. I noticed a man who had lost his left arm sitting in the corner. I was certain it was the result of a war injury, so I stood up and said in German, "Allow me to propose a toast to the health of not only a former enemy, but also a fellow soldier." The man stood up, clicked his heels, and said, "Excuse me, sir, but I don't drink with my enemies." I said, "But I'm not your enemy. The war is over—or practically over." He said, "The war isn't over yet. It might be over for me, but it's definitely not over for the German people." He clicked his heels again, and said, "Excuse me, I can't stay here any longer." And he left.

In a small Swabian village, 15- and 16-year-old girls came running towards us yelling "Chocolate, chocolate!" They thought we were Americans, and in our Free French uniforms we looked just like them, too. So we gave them our chocolate. Suddenly an older woman rushed out, yanked one girl aside, and screamed, "Aren't you ashamed of yourself? You whore! Your father's still fighting at the front and you're flirting around with Frenchmen!" That was at the end of March 1945.

As far as the Germans are concerned, I don't believe in collective guilt. As Napoleon once said of the Alsatians, "They speak German, they think German, they even pray in German, but they die as Frenchmen." So I don't believe in collective guilt. The first words I spoke were German.

GOTTFRIED FÄHRMANN*

"We cried watching our 20 Me-262s explode."

We were sent back from Russia to defend the home front. Going against four-engine bombers was always a hard job. In contrast to our German aircraft, the American "Liberator" as well as the "Fortress" had immense fire power from the rear. Flying through one of their formations without taking hits was totally out of the question! You could be guaranteed at least one hit every time you were in combat with them.

At the end of the war we were assigned the task of setting up a wing of the new jets, the Me-262.

Flying this jet gave us young pilots the feeling that we were finally sitting in a superior aircraft. We were naturally eager to try the plane out in combat, and we saw no other way out but to continue to fight for our country.

Toward the end of the war, we experienced severe logistical and supply problems. Jet turbine engines were extremely difficult to obtain. Our maintenance people worked diligently day and night until the end. Our small unit suffered in that both General Galland

---

* Biography on page xxxiii.

and Colonel Steinhoff had been wounded. Colonel Lützow had been killed in action. When the Americans began to close in on our base, which was located near Salzburg, we blew up all of our airplanes. We cried watching our 20 Me-262s explode. Then we retreated to the mountains where the "Alpine Redoubt" was supposedly still being held by the SS. Of course, we found no trace of them.

When we first heard that Hitler had committed suicide, we believed it to be a false report. We hadn't forgotten the reports we had heard on the radio or read in the newspapers at the beginning of the war. How were we to know if the information we had been given was accurate or not? How were we to know if, as Hitler maintained, we just shot back on September 1, 1939? Did the Poles initially attack us or not? We were unable to determine whether Hitler had been killed in action or whether he had actually committed suicide. The aura created around Hitler and Goebbels appeared to fit nicely into our scenic surroundings. After a most beautiful spring, the Bavarian and the Austrian countryside disappeared under a layer of snow. It was May first. It was a sign—a sign telling us "It's over!"

We never really knew what was going on. We were limited to what we heard on the radio. We knew about the bombing raids. We knew our cities had been totally destroyed. But we were never informed about the other horrors of the day.

HERBERT BÜCHS*

The last time I personally saw Hitler was on April 20, 1945, his 56th birthday. It was in the *Führerbunker* in Berlin. As usual, everyone gathered to offer him congratulations. The briefing participants stood in a row and without saying much, shook Hitler's hand as he passed by. Hitler himself appeared abstracted, lost in thought. He didn't look at me. He looked right through me.

* Biography on page 376.

JÜRGEN GRAF

Born 1927; anti-aircraft auxiliary who deserted to Berlin when the Red Army marched through Germany; after the war became a radio and television reporter in Berlin, where he still resides.

"Their main problem was liquor."

The first Russian troops arrived in Berlin on April 24 or 25, 1945. I was 17 and a half years old. I was wearing a pair of Lederhosen and a T-shirt, so the scars on my right leg from a car accident were quite visible. When the Russians saw these scars, they thought I was a member of the SS. But after I explained about the accident, everything was fine. They were very friendly and sometimes brought us things to eat. Since our house was rather large, they decided to set up quarters there.

There were no bedrooms on the ground floor, but there was a beautiful mahogany-paneled library with a few good paintings, a large living room, a dining room, and smaller sitting rooms. This was all perfect for their officers' mess. They stored peas, jars of fat, and meat in the basement. There were thousands of cans of sardines in our wine cellar. Once in a while we swiped a few, but the Russians didn't care. We started trading things for food with these first Russians, and commerce flourished. They liked jewelry and cameras, and since we had two or three cameras, we traded them for butter.

This went well for exactly 48 hours. Then the next wave of Russian troops arrived, and they settled in to stay. These Russians were really bad. Their main problem was liquor, and they were the ones who started the period of rape and destruction in Berlin. My father had stored most of his good paintings outside the city, but he kept a few just because he couldn't live without art around him. The second troops used these paintings as dartboards, and slashed them with knives. My father also had a 500-piece set of porcelain that had originally been given to Hindenburg for his 80th birthday. This was very valuable so we stored it in the garage. The Russians found it, and when they'd gotten drunk enough they had a good time smashing these precious dishes against the garage wall, watching them break into a million pieces.

Then they decided to destroy the rest of my father's antiques that were still left in the house. Statue after statue was smashed. They butchered our carved wooden madonnas with their knives. After that, they decided to see whether carved wood like this would burn, so they built a big fire out on the lawn. The Russians got a real kick out of watching the madonnas burn.

That's what living with the Soviets was like. The first troops were friendly and gave us food. They had officers with them who spoke German very well and told us to be calm, that everything would be all right. These officers explained that first they would take Berlin, and then a form of self-administration could be set up to replace Nazi rule. All of this was very encouraging. Just 48 hours later, houses were burned, women were raped, and people who had gone underground, who had worked against the fascists for years, were taken away and shot.

BRUNHILDE POMSEL*

"Fritzsche personally dictated to me the declaration of surrender."

I was stupid during those last days. Instead of staying at home with my parents in a Berlin suburb, no, I had to go into the city. After all, I had to go to work, the office couldn't do without me! I took one of the

---

* Biography on page 282.

last trains into the city. When I reached the Ministry of Propaganda, where I worked, the building was on fire. We all moved into the air raid shelter, where I wrote proclamations to a German army that was supposedly positioned outside of Berlin ready to kick the Russians. I personally didn't believe that would happen, but then I didn't believe that everything was lost yet, either. The idea was simply inconceivable.

There were bombs exploding all around us, but we felt secure down in the shelter. Little did we know that the place wasn't safe at all. The noise from the "Stalin organ" rocket launchers was constant. There was a continuous flow of wounded being brought in from the streets. We were able to stay in touch with the Reich Chancellery via messengers from the Ministry of Propaganda. They reported that Russian snipers were already on top of the buildings.

Then Hans Fritzsche of the Propaganda Ministry came down and personally dictated to me the declaration of surrender of the city of Berlin. This declaration was to be handed over to the Russian commander, General Zhukov. Next, we spent hours sewing white flags out of flour sacks. A White Russian woman who was with us translated the declaration of surrender into Russian. Then Fritzsche and a couple of others left the shelter carrying the declaration and a huge white flag.

We sat in our shelter and waited for the intermediaries to return and tell us that the war was over. A gang of about 20 Mongolian-looking Russians arrived instead. It was horrible. We didn't understand them and they didn't understand us. Using their guns, they just rounded us all up and forced us out on to the street. We didn't know what was going on. Once we got on the street, we saw our intermediaries walking back with the white flag. The Russians pushed us back down into the shelter where we stayed for the next couple of hours. Finally, they made us walk from our shelter all the way to Tempelhof, about three and a half miles away.

The war had just come to an end. The walk through Berlin was horrible—dead horses and dead people everywhere. Russian military police women were already out directing traffic. Once we got to Tempelhof, we were locked into an apartment. Our little group consisted of about 20 people, all from the Ministry of Propaganda. That day was the beginning of my imprisonment.

We were interrogated separately during the first two to three days in that Tempelhof apartment. I told them that I was a shorthand typist in the Ministry of Propaganda. I didn't say anything that would make my position sound important. I never feared being harmed or shot, because I knew that most of the reports concerning the horrible things the Russians did were exaggerated. Of course, some of the reports were true, but the majority of them had been magnified out of proportion. The Russians didn't touch a hair on our heads. I wasn't raped, either. We were lucky to have been captured by these particular soldiers, who were part of Zhukov's troops. They were very disciplined and treated us correctly.

I was separated from the rest of the group, though I never found out why. Another woman, a very refined and elegant elderly lady, was also picked out from the group. She was a White Russian married to another White Russian who had worked as a translator for the *DNB*, the German News Agency. He had also been arrested, but he wasn't with her.

Young Soviet soldiers constantly kept coming in to see us. We presumed they were our guards. I was still young, and at first naturally thought they were interested in me. But they came because they wanted to talk to Frau Junius, the White Russian. They always came with vodka and onions. They set everything down on the table and got out the water glasses. I had to pour the vodka and drink along with them. They sat and talked with Frau Junius for hours. When they left, I always asked Frau Junius what they talked about. She said, "They are all such nice boys. They wanted to know what living in Russia under the Czar was like."

LOTHAR RÜHL

Born 1927; served in the Luftwaffe ground
forces as a teenager and helped defend Berlin;
at war's end became a journalist and later an
undersecretary in the West German Ministry of
Defense; now a journalist again; resides in
Bonn.

"The SS are shooting themselves."

The Soviet offensive against Berlin began in early April 1945. Our
company, which had started with 140 men, was left with only 12 to
15 survivors after a Russian attack. Our commander ordered us to
return to Berlin in small groups. The assembly point would be the Air
Ministry.

We did indeed all meet there. We were organized into a battle
group and defended an old drugstore with bazookas and machine
guns. Our real battle was against the Russian tanks; we saw very little
of the infantry. We put several tanks out of action and we took a few
Russian prisoners.

I was picked up by the SS on April 29 or 30. An SS patrol stopped
me and asked me what I was doing. Was I a deserter? They told me to
go along with them and said that all cowards and traitors would be
shot. On the way, I saw an officer, stripped of his insignia, hanging
from a streetcar underpass. A large sign hung around his neck read,
"I am hanging here because I was too much of a coward to face the
enemy." The SS man said, "Do you see that? There's a deserter
hanging already." I told him that I was no deserter; I was a messenger.
He said, "That's what they all say." I wound up at an SS assembly
point. One of our platoon leaders sat there. He saw me and yelled,

"Hey, what are you doing with one of our men?" The answer was, "We picked him up." The platoon leader asked, "What do you mean 'picked him up'? This man is our messenger and I know him very well. Let him go so he can get back to his duties." They finally let me go.

On May 2, 1945, we were told that the garrison in Berlin had surrendered. We knew that Hitler was dead; we had heard that the day before. Then all of those who were able to walk were ordered into the Schultheiss Brewery. Now and again, we heard shots. The Russians were still far away, so I asked who was doing the shooting. I was told, "Come around to the back, the SS are shooting themselves." I said, "I don't want to see it." But I was told, "You have to watch." People were actually standing around shooting themselves. Mostly, they were not German SS men; they were foreigners, some West Europeans and some East Europeans. The group included a number of French and Walloons.

When the Russians rounded us up, we were divided into different march columns at a large old drill ground outside Berlin. The Russians didn't select anyone in particular; they just said, "You go here, you go there, and these men go sit in the square." We also had to sleep in the square. No one was allowed to stand up. If anyone tried, the Russians immediately fired live ammunition at head level.

Once during a noon rest, we were permitted to take a short walk. The Russians were being so generous because they were receiving warm food again for the first time, and couldn't take their eyes off the big pot of goulash. A comrade and I hid ourselves in the cellar of a ruined house. There were piles of beets down there, and we burrowed into them. We ended up spending the entire day in that cellar. The others had marched on and we were left behind. Then the two of us swam over the Elbe and wound up in American captivity.

A few days later, while we were herding cows in a village, the Russians came and recaptured me. They had lost too many prisoners, and since they had reported many more to Moscow than they were now able to deliver, they had to somehow make up for the deficit. Thus I came to be a prisoner of the Russians for a second time.

The next day during interrogation, a bored Russian officer said in broken German, "Take off your shirt." I had a good idea what they were after, so I held up my arms. I didn't have the SS tattoo giving my blood group. He asked me if I was a soldier. I told him, "I no soldier. I tuberculosis. I come from Ruhr area." He wanted to see my hands. They were all marked up from working on a farm. Finally he took a piece of paper out and wrote on it. I asked him what it was and he said, "Propusk." I said, "Propusk? What's that?" And he said to me in German, "For freedom."

LEO WELT

Born 1934 in Berlin; lived through the Russian conquest of Berlin to be "adopted" by Americans; today is a company manager and lives in Washington, D.C.

"At the age of 11, I was already a man. I had seen German soldiers hanged, children shot, women raped."

When the war started, we lived quite well. But then, as the bombing offensives began we decided to leave Berlin. All of our friends had left and the schools were closed. My mother decided that we would go to Silesia. My father was already dead. He got killed in 1942 in Italy. So now we were on our way to a farm and a flour mill that belonged to my mother's cousin in Silesia.

Then when the tide of war started to turn and the Russians from the East came closer, we went back to Berlin. At that point the air raids had increased. We lived in our house during the raids, but at night we slept in the basement. We had a well-constructed shelter down there, with special wooden supports and a steel door. Bunk beds were installed in the basement for my whole family, and sometimes my grandmother also came to stay with us. There were usually six of us.

The air raids kept getting worse. Sometimes the whole city was on fire. At times, you could not differentiate between night and day. When you went outside you had to have a wet cloth over your face, because there was so much dust and dirt in the air that it was impossible to breathe. Our house had been hit a few times, but not seriously. Once an incendiary bomb fell into the house, but luckily one of my uncles was with us and he had had a lot of experience in handling incendiary and phosphorous bombs. As a matter of fact, all of us had been trained in how to handle these bombs. It took quite a time for them to explode. If you knew how to handle it, you could just pick it up and throw it out of the window. This was not the case with phosphorous bombs; they were more dangerous. But incendiary bombs fell by the thousands every day. Sometimes we could even stand in front of our house and see the sky just glistening in the distance with incendiary bombs.

You could also see shells bursting, especially at night. Although the noise was very frightening, we gradually got so used to it that we actually slept right through the air raids except when big bombs exploded so nearby that the house shook and rattled and the wall plaster began to fall.

When the big bombs fell, it wasn't just that the house shuddered, the ground shuddered too. We were very lucky. Most of the houses in my area were totally destroyed. This was the section with many government buildings and it had special camouflage with dummy trees hanging from ropes over the streets. I remember very well the night when the zoo was hit. The next morning alligators and snakes were crawling across the streets. Chimpanzees were hanging from the trees. After an air raid, we children used to wander around looking for bomb splinters and other things. We even looked for souvenirs in crashed planes.

We knew that the war was turning when we started to hear artillery fire. Hearing artillery is horrible. When you have an air raid, it comes and then it stops, but artillery goes on all the time. The front was still far from Berlin, but you could hear the rumbling day and night. That meant that the Russians were somewhere, but you weren't sure where, or if they could be held off. There were trenches dug everywhere. Streets had to be cleaned and roads repaired because of debris. The fighting got so bad that we could not leave our basement. When there was a lull, we went up and saw soldiers marching, carrying their weapons, and lines of horse-drawn wagons. There were endless lines of people walking or pushing carts with their belongings. You could hardly walk in the streets anymore because of dead horses, dead pigs, or dead people. There were burned-out trucks and passenger cars.

One morning we heard a terrible pounding on our steel door. My grandmother opened it, and there were two Russian soldiers with guns. We clung to our mother. The Russians searched our house looking, maybe, for soldiers. They took my mother's jewelry and her watch, then they left. During the day, more troops came. Women started to run away because of—I didn't know what sex was like until I saw it in the streets—rape. There was a lot of rape and looting going on, and people were being shot.

The SS shot a lot of German soldiers because they were not interested in fighting anymore. They killed not only young boys who were crying they wanted to go home, but many soldiers because they had lost their will to fight. They were even hanged from the lampposts as traitors. And I remember quite clearly when my brother and his friends went into the basement of a house that had been bombed: there were five German soldiers sitting there, all shot. Then the Russians did the same things, only much worse because the women had to run for their lives. My mother had to run into the house and let herself out of the window on sheets to get to her hiding place in the garden. She escaped, but many of our neighbors weren't as fortunate.

For example, a woman friend of ours was shot in the back when she tried to run away after having been raped many times. A doctor came to treat her, and asked me to get some water. I had two pails, and on my way back from the pumps a Russian soldier stopped me. He wanted to take my water, but I just kept on running. When I got to the house, there was not much water left in the pails, but it was enough to sterilize the instruments to take the bullets out of her back. The lady did recover physically. Mentally she never recovered.

Then German prisoners of war held by the Russians started to clean up the city. Bodies had to be taken down from the trees where they were hanging. And everybody was afraid of typhoid or cholera. We were instructed to drink only boiled water.

Germany surrendered shortly after the fall of Berlin. One of the luckiest things that happened was that in the fall of 1945, the part of the city I lived in became the American sector. One morning we woke up and saw an American tank and American soldiers on the next corner. That was a wonderful sight. We still wandered around, scrounging and stealing things. The Americans gave us chocolate and so forth. As a matter of fact, the Russians also gave us food and candy.

Life started to stabilize, although we didn't have any stores or shops. We still had to improvise when it came to getting food. The region was known for its vegetable and potato fields, so we used to bicycle to the country and wait until dark. When it got dark, we went into the fields and dug potatoes. When the Russians played searchlights across the fields, we ducked into the furrows.

For us, this period was an adventure. We even started to play with hand grenades and bazookas. There was military hardware lying everywhere. Naturally, as young boys, we exploded many of these things. We used the bazookas to go fishing in the Spree River. We shot a bazooka into the water, all the fish came up, and we went home with buckets full of fish. We used to take shells apart and make trails with the powder and explode bombs, things that were terribly dangerous. We used to roll hand grenades down hills to see how far they would go before they exploded.

Besides playing with military hardware and stealing food, we traded things we found in the empty houses at the black market near the Brandenburg Gate, where the Americans and the British were selling things to the Russian soldiers. The soldiers traded cigarettes and margarine, and when the MPs came, everybody ran. The MPs gave us coffee, chocolate, and cigarettes, and we sold them afterwards.

Actually, when I think about this period, it seems very unreal. Money was lying in the streets, for instance, and nobody wanted it because they said it was worthless. There were thousands of marks lying around, and we didn't pick them up.

I left Berlin in 1951 under the auspices of the Catholic charities. I had a foster family in America who made it possible for me to finish high school and go to Princeton University, where I graduated in 1958. Since 1958, I have worked in international trade. Today I am a specialist in offset and counter-trade. And I always tell people that I am more qualified to do this because I got my training on the black market in 1945 at the Brandenburg Gate, trading the family belongings for food.

At the age of 11, I was already a man. I knew how to handle pistols and machine guns. I knew how to shoot a bazooka and how to throw a grenade. I had seen German soldiers hanged, children shot, women raped. I had seen everything. I was a man.

CHAPTER 14

German Women in Total War

World War II played a major and unexpected role in emancipating Germany's women. In principle, National Socialism insisted that women's role was limited to "children, home, and kitchen." But the rhetoric of domesticity foundered on the increasing need for labor. Not until after Stalingrad did Hitler authorize the direct mobilization of women for war work. But since 1939 women had stepped forward to replace men called into the Wehrmacht. "Woman's place" became anywhere work needed to be done. As train crews and streetcar conductors, behind the desks of the Reich's bureaucracies, on the farms and in the factories, women kept Germany going throughout the war.

Women dealt with shortages and air raids. They stood hours in lines, rode miles by bicycle and streetcars to buy food or to fill out forms. They nurtured a generation of children whose fathers were at the front, maintaining at least the illusion of normality as the Reich crumbled. And women sustained private lives, family lives, as an alternative to the Nazi rhetoric of community. Whatever it took in time and energy, German women literally kept home fires burning in expectation of the day the war would, somehow, come to an end.

When the Eastern front collapsed, the refugee columns consisted of women, children, and the few men too old or too frail for the *Volkssturm*. Time and again it was the women who brought the columns through, pulling wagons out of snowdrifts, nursing exhausted horses, and being raped by Russian soldiers in an orgy of victory. It was the women, the *Trümmerfrauen,* who began the task of clearing the Reich's bombed-out cities—one brick at a time. If the men came back from the prison camps morally and physically broken, it was the women who said, "We've made it this far; we'll get the rest of the way." Germany's reconstruction owed much to the courage and will power of a "second sex" that by 1945 was second to none.

RENATE HOFFMANN

Born 1916; wife of an officer; she and her children were caught in the Soviet breakthrough in eastern Germany in 1945; lives in the Rhineland.

"The only thing you could do was to pretend you were a rock or dead."

When the war broke out, I was living at Greifswald Air Base, not far from Peenemünde. My husband was commanding a night fighter squadron in the Rhineland, near Cologne. I was lonely and decided to visit my mother for a while. She had been widowed at the end of World War I, and I grew up surrounded only by women. I missed my father very much. My grandfather and his only son also died during that war.

We listened to radio broadcasts constantly. Naturally we listened only to the German stations. My aunt once said to me, "If you want to know what is really going on out there, you have to tune in to the British stations." We were all very much aware that anyone caught listening to them could be sent to a concentration camp. My aunt chose to listen anyway. I personally felt I would be betraying my husband if I listened to the British network.

I returned to Greifswald Air Base and continued to live there for the next three and a half years. Both of my children were born during that time. Our apartment building housed four families. Living there gradually became more and more difficult. The war was beginning to take its toll. Of the four young couples, three husbands were killed and I was the only one who still had her husband. The women were all so young. They had just had their first babies. In one case, the child was born a few months after the father had been killed. It was a very painful time.

I moved away from Greifswald during the last year of the war, because we feared that the air base would be bombed. I moved to a farm nearby. It belonged to a relative who took in refugees on the run from the East. I was able to have two rooms to live in. We remained on this farm throughout the last year of the war.

The overall situation worsened during the winter of 1944–45, when the number of refugees coming from East Prussia and the German eastern regions increased drastically. Their paths took them right by the farm. They came with horses and wagons in tow. I'll never forget one wagon. It had a cart attached to it with an old dying man lying in the straw. They continued their journey to the West the next morning over the bumpy dirt road. It became clear that the situation was getting more and more serious. But we continued to believe that the Eastern front would hold somewhere.

Suddenly one day in March 1945, my husband showed up at the farm, riding on a small motorcycle. He had flown to Greifswald from his base near Berlin, and he came to tell us to flee. The Eastern front had totally collapsed and the war was as good as lost. We had a difficult time comprehending what he was saying. We had never expected it to be so bad.

He flew back to his squadron, and there we sat, my cousin, her husband, and I. We tried to figure out what to do next. The area between the Oder and the Elbe was packed with millions of people on the move. It didn't make any sense for us to pack a wagon and join the dense flow of people. We decided it would be best to stay on the farm and wait things out.

Not much later, we heard on the radio that the Russians had crossed the Oder, and that we could expect Soviet troops in our immediate area as early as the following day. They were on their way to Greifswald and the farm was located two miles from the road. We knew the Russians couldn't miss us. We also knew that they had shot all of the owners of the neighboring farms. They turned the houses upside down and behaved like madmen. We were told not to have the least bit of alcohol in the house. We also heard that the Russians attacked and raped women.

The German front had ceased to exist. During the night of April 29, my cousin and I convinced her husband to leave. Naturally, his wife and children were terribly upset, but had he stayed he would have been shot by the Russians as a kulak.

My cousin had three children and I had two. The wheelwright's wife lived in a small house next to ours on the farm. She also had two children, so there were a total of seven children between us. That night two German soldiers dressed in civilian clothes—they apparently had thrown away their uniforms—spent the night in our barn. That was what was left of the German front.

We had to think carefully about what we had to get rid of so as not to endanger ourselves. We decided to throw all of the farm's hunting rifles into the small pond in front of the house, along with any liquor we had. We emptied my cousin's entire wine cellar into the pond. After we were finished, we dressed, and, lying on our beds, we waited for morning to come.

Around 10 o'clock the next morning, we saw a Russian ride through the main gate on a horse. He must have been drunk because he fell off. A second Russian came, then a third. They staggered and reeled their way to the door and entered the house. It was worse than we had ever imagined. One of them went straight to the telephone, ripped it off the wall, and threw it on the floor. With that, we were cut off from the rest of the world. Another Russian went to the radio and threw that on the floor, making sure we no longer heard any more news broadcasts. More men came in. They raged through the house, going from room to room. They stormed into the kitchen and demanded the cook make them something to eat. There must have been about forty soldiers.

I took the children outside and hid them behind some bushes. Inside, we ran from one corner to the other, not knowing what to do.

A man from the nearby village passed by and reported that the Russians were acting like animals everywhere. He was, of course, referring to their mistreatment of women in the area. After hours of this, a Russian officer showed up with an interpreter at about five o'clock in the afternoon. He was wearing a perfectly tailored uniform, an impressive looking man, and also wearing white gloves! This officer told us, through his translator, that he was confiscating the house and was giving us five minutes to leave the estate.

We threw a few essentials into a covered wagon. Someone hitched a horse to it and we climbed in. The 80-year-old gardener was our driver. Our group included three mothers and their seven children, the cook and her niece, a refugee from Berlin, a young nurse.

As we rode through the main gate, we decided to head for the city of Greifswald to the west. At the main crossroads, a Russian military policewoman was directing all German refugees to the east. We were met head on by the entire Russian advance. The seemingly endless flow of Russian forces rolling toward us was unbelievable. The first day, all we saw were tanks and trucks bumper to bumper. After that came the supplies, transported by small horse-drawn carts.

German fighter aircraft attacked and strafed these Russian advance columns. I sat up in front next to our driver, while the others were in the back. They couldn't see the sparks as the bullets hit the concrete road.

I told the old man to stop. We took the children, dropped them into a ditch, and jumped in after them. The planes disappeared and we got back on our wagon. After that, everything came to a standstill because a Russian horse had been injured and was blocking the road. The Russian soldier leading the horse walked up to us, looked at us, and ever so casually unhitched our horse. But he was nice enough to harness his injured horse to our wagon. So we had to continue our journey being pulled by this bleeding Russian horse.

Thick woods stretched along either side of the road. I decided that we would take the first path that led off the main track. We made our way into the woods between the trees and over the grassy ground looking for a good place to hide. In the process, we got so stuck in between three trees that we could move neither forward nor backward.

Although we heard Russian troops in the distance, our immediate area was suddenly quiet. Darkness set in and we all crawled underneath the awning of the wagon. We all wore our warm winter coats and sat on our suitcases. We ended up staying there for seven days and seven nights. The Russian advance never let up during this entire time; tank after tank, one horse cart after the other. Why hadn't our leaders warned us that we were in imminent danger of being overrun by a massive Soviet army?

Our food supply ran out on the third day. We didn't have anything to drink either. On the fourth day, I decided to see if I could find a house somewhere. The nurse went with me. Quite a distance from our wagon, we did find a house secluded among some trees. We sneaked up to the house. Suddenly three Russian soldiers came around the corner. They pointed their guns at us and forced us into the house. We realized right away that we had walked into a trap. And we knew what they had in store for us.

We were separated. They put their guns to our heads. Any attempt to defend ourselves meant certain death. The only thing you could do was to pretend you were a rock or dead. I don't want to talk about what happened next. . . .

When the three men left the house, I opened the door of the room I was in. Another door opened down the hall and the nurse came out. We just looked at one another. All we said was "water!" We were nauseated and felt miserable. Thank God there was still running water in the house. After reviving ourselves somewhat, we were more determined than ever to find the things we were looking for. There was a large bucket of lard still on the table. We took it. And we got water, potatoes, and an ax. We took everything back to the wagon.

I was filled with a tremendous anger. I took the ax and chopped down a tree, which freed our wagon. But we didn't leave immediately. There was still too much Soviet activity on the main road.

Every morning we all spread out to pick grass for our injured horse. He ate and appeared to get better. Then one day we heard a commotion and shouts of joy coming from the road. We couldn't understand the Russian words, but we assured each other, "That can only mean that the war is over and they have won!" We all had the same thought: "My God, the war is over and we're still alive!" The sun was shining, it was a beautiful day. We were about to resurface after the flood.

We got back out on the road and headed for Greifswald, where we went directly to a friend's house. He was a professor at the university there. He didn't recognize us. After all, we hadn't washed in a week, and we had wrapped our heads in awful scarves to look as bad as possible. It took a while, but our friend finally said, "It's you! Of course you all can stay here. We have three rooms upstairs we don't use." We asked if he was sure that the Russians couldn't climb up the wall and into the windows at night. Our friend laughed at us and said, "But here in the city everything is over with! You have nothing to be afraid of!" But we were all still so frightened that we—the old man, the women, and the seven children—camped out together in one room that first night. We had discovered that human beings are like animals, and feel much more secure in a pack.

The next morning, the professor asked the obvious question, "Did anything happen to you women?" We immediately knew what he was referring to and said "yes." Then he told us we had to go to the clinic with him right away: "In the university clinic we only have enough medication left for a few days. Right now we are treating about 500 women." We had had no idea that so many Russian soldiers had venereal diseases and had infected an entire population. We went to the clinic with him and found out we had been infected as well. Most likely, the nurse and I were two of the last to receive any medication at all. We received enough to be healed. Thousands and thousands of women must have been infected with this sickening disease. Then I thought we might be pregnant, but fortunately, this wasn't the case. The old man returned to the village, while the rest of us stayed at the professor's house.

About four weeks later, I heard that the pond in front of the farm house had almost dried up—the weather had been very warm—and the guns we had thrown in were showing. I received an official summons from the Russians living on the farm to give them an explanation.

I walked back to the farm. Two Russian officers were sitting in front of the house in large leather chairs. A phonograph was playing music to which two Russian girls were dancing on the porch. It was a bucolic scene. The sun was shining on the farm house and its dark green shutters. It was as though total peace prevailed!

I was taken into the house to make a statement as to how the guns got into the pond. The Russian—he spoke German—began to ask me questions. What was my ulterior reason for trying to get rid of the guns? He tried to accuse me of throwing the guns into the pond only to return for them later on to initiate a revolt or something crazy against the Russians! I repeated time and again that I was only thinking of our own safety. I was finally able to convince him that my intention was to destroy the guns and nothing else. He finally let me go.

The door from the living room led directly into the main hallway. I remembered I had hidden a small package of jewelry in the large grandfather clock in this hall. The first Russians to enter the house had snatched my purse containing all our passports, documents, and money, but they didn't get their hands on the jewelry. Now as I stood all alone in the hallway, I thought: "Do it! Take a quick look to see if the package is still there!" I reached inside and was amazed to find it. I felt like a king! As I left the house I began to think of all the things I could do with this jewelry. I could trade it for groceries or anything else.

Five weeks passed before the first train left Greifswald for Rostock. This was the first sign of postwar Germany waking up. I had to find out if my mother was still alive, if her house was still standing. Although I hadn't had any news from my husband, I still had great hopes that he was still alive. When I last saw him in March 1945, he was still flying to try and stop the massive Allied bomber offensives.

I left my children with my cousin and got on the train to Rostock, a large harbor city on the Baltic Sea. That's as far as the train went. My home town was about ten miles from Rostock. The train station was packed with refugees who were camping out on the stone floor. It was awful to see people having to live this way, crowded, sitting on the floor waiting to be transported out. I saw several people die during the one hour I was there. People sat there for weeks and waited.

There was no train to my home town. So I set out on foot, alone. A few Russians drove by in cars, but no one bothered me. I had covered about half of the distance when I first noticed the familiar red-shingled rooftops and the single, narrow, pointed church steeple along the horizon. I was elated because I thought if I could still see the red shingles, the town can't be in that bad of shape after all! The closer I came, the better everything looked. As I reached the outskirts of the town, a woman crossed my path. She looked me straight in the face and said, "Oh God! It's you!" I asked, "My mother, is she still alive?" "Yes," she replied, "she's alive. So is your aunt." "How is the house?" I asked. "Fine, everything's all right," she said. I turned the street corner and saw the house. I recognized the two benches to the right and left of the front door. My mother and her sister were sitting in front of the house, and they saw me coming. They had almost given up all hope of ever seeing me and the children alive again. "Where are the children?" they wanted to know. I told them that the children were safe in Greifswald.

Naturally, their house had also been ransacked by the Russians. My aunt and my mother were both over 50 years old, and both had been raped by young Russian soldiers. To my knowledge four out of every ten women were raped.

I returned to Greifswald to pack our things. Now I had to figure out a way to find my husband. I didn't know where to begin to look. A message, just a piece of paper, was delivered to our house several days later. It read, "Your husband is wounded. He's been burned and is in a hospital in Bavaria near Tegernsee, south of Munich."

I immediately packed my rucksack and set out to find him. Some people helped me get across the border. We had to wade through the Saale River on a weir. We heard border guards fire shots off into the distance, but we all made it across the border to the American side unharmed. I was able to get on a train and went to Tegernsee. It took me seven days to make the trip. The trains were overcrowded and I spent most of the time riding out on the steps.

I had friends in Tegernsee and went directly to their house. "Come in," they said when they saw me. "Of course he's alive. He's visited us a couple of times, but he's not here anymore. Right now he's in the eye clinic in Munich. You don't have to worry. Our children are not afraid of him." I didn't know what to say to that.

I went to Munich and saw my husband the next day. The entire situation was handled awkwardly. At the hospital, my husband's friend walked me to a door and said, "He's in there, but you go in alone. And plan to come back to our house tonight." There was no doctor in sight, and no one told me anything about my husband's burns and what to expect. So, looking straight ahead, I walked through the door and saw a bed in front of me in which someone was sitting. It had to be my husband. Unfortunately, he noticed my hesitation, as brief as it was. A doctor should have made me aware of the severity of the burns so that my husband wouldn't notice that I didn't recognize him.

We fell into one another's arms. We talked and I immediately realized it was the same voice, nothing had changed. My husband got out of bed and put on his robe—the same motions, the same movements, the same figure. But it had still been a shock, because the face was no longer there—it was gone.

We quickly agreed that I should go back to the Soviet zone to get the children and return to Munich as soon as possible. That is exactly what I did, and in the autumn of 1945 we were reunited as a family once again.

COUNTESS TERESA SOLMS

Born 1932; grew up on a farm during the war; is the wife of Count Solms.

"My father looked in on the Poles every morning."

On the farm there were POWs of many different nationalities. In our area they were mostly Poles. Each farm was given specific guidelines regarding the POWs. For example, close contact between the farmers and the POWs was not permitted. They were only to receive a certain amount to eat, and there was a curfew.

We dealt with these rules very leniently. After the bombings at night, for example, my father would make the rounds with the Poles on our farm to check whether any incendiaries had been dropped. Incendiaries were quite tricky. They stuck somewhere and would not explode until there was wind. My father looked in on the Poles every morning to see what they had to eat, and you can be sure that it was no different from what we had ourselves.

After March 8, 1945, when the Americans marched in, the Poles were interned in camps. Our Poles refused to leave the farm because they felt people still needed food. Of course, and I know this for a fact, there were other cases in which the farmer was lynched by the Poles working on the farm because he had mistreated them.

One day after the war, one of the Poles from our farm came to visit. He wanted to see how things were with us. He called on my mother at her apartment—my father had died in the meantime—kneeled before her, and called her "Chefin" (Boss).

Everything concerning food supplies functioned very well in spite of the war. There was never a situation in which the population could not have been fed. It was all a question of organization. As to meat, I can say that none of us on the farms ever suffered from hunger. Every farmer was told how much livestock was to be slaughtered per month. The farmers' district leader, in our case my father, supervised this, and it was strictly forbidden to slaughter animals secretly. I remember that sometimes up to ten of us sat in the cherry trees picking fruit when the dive-bombers came in low and shot at us. We let ourselves down the ladders and lay down in holes. This was part of everyday life, and nobody grumbled much about it.

We had endless streams of refugees from both sides: first the refugees from Aachen on the Dutch/Belgian border, and later those fleeing from the East. On our farm, for example, there were 12 to 14 of us; after the collapse, there were 26 people there. We didn't have a living room anymore, people slept there—teachers, officers, and so on—who had come back. But the organization and integration was marvelous. Entire school classes often picked fruit and planted potatoes. They got their breakfast and coffee for that, or a sandwich and coffee in the afternoons. What am I saying—coffee? There wasn't any real coffee; it was the famous coffee substitute.

During the last days of the war, shortly before the Americans arrived, we received orders to drive the livestock away. The livestock and the farm machinery were to be sent across the Rhine, away from the Americans. This was "scorched earth." My father strongly opposed this order and actually went to the surrounding farms at night with my sister to talk to the farm women. He pleaded with them not to carry out this order. He asked them to think about what was to come, and said that at least they should herd the livestock into the arms of the Americans instead of away from their farms. At that point one could get away with going against the orders and requests of the party, but it still took a great deal of courage and character to do so.

My father's land was between Bonn and Bad Godesberg, near where the U.S. Embassy was later erected. At the time of the American advance, around March 8, there was a German flak battery situated there. As the Americans came closer, the people of Friesdorf received the order to leave their homes and assemble in our bunker, an old mining shaft where mushrooms had been grown.

An American came to my father with a translator and asked him if he had any influence on the flak battery, and whether he would negotiate with its officers so that the battery would surrender. My father, along with an American officer—who had, incidentally, removed his weapons beforehand—drove up to the flak battery to speak with an officer my father knew. They talked. They had half an hour. The time was almost up. There were many young boys in this battery, 15 and 16 years old. The German officer told my father that he was sorry, but he had just gotten a new battery commander two days earlier, and this man was determined to fight to the last drop of blood. My father asked for more time. He took this officer aside and suggested he have the guns blown up in five minutes time. And five minutes later there was a detonation, and the guns were indeed blown up. The battery surrendered.

HILDA RUBIN

Born 1908; an office worker in a small north German city during the war; today a retired nurse living in Memmingen, Bavaria.

"No one knew what the right thing to do was anymore."

As you can imagine, we were all excited to see my brother, Günther, suddenly standing at the front door one day in 1945. But it didn't take long for us to realize that he had come home illegally. He had had travel orders to Berlin and had decided to make a side trip home to see us. He was 16 and a half years old and had been drafted a year and a half before. We hadn't seen him during that entire time and he was homesick.

My mother was absolutely terrified. We were all scared that he was going to be arrested. Only a short time before, a young man from our neighborhood had returned home and hidden in his parents' house. We found out about it later when he was arrested and shot as a deserter. Of course, we feared that the same might happen to my brother. It was impossible for him to leave from the train station in our town. He would have most certainly run into the hands of the many MPs there who were looking for deserters.

We decided my brother should leave from a small station about five miles away. That night, my sister and I got out our bikes—my brother sat on the back of mine—and rode over the bumpy paths. We were really relieved when we reached the little village and dropped him off. The tiny waiting room in the train station was a sad sight. The place was filled with boys, all around 16 or 17, who had also made a quick visit home and wanted to avoid the MPs.

My mother was almost happy that my brother was gone again.

"Now at least nothing can happen to him. He can't be arrested and won't be shot," she said. After that, we didn't hear anything from him. It was as though he had evaporated into thin air. We received no mail. My mother had a terrible time dealing with the fact that she had forced her only son to return to the war. Time and time again she said, "We should have hidden him, we should have just kept him here!" At that time, no one knew what the right thing to do was anymore.

JULIANE HARTMANN

Born 1925; the sheltered daughter of an upper-middle-class family, she was in a Berlin suburb when the Russians came; after the war she was posted to the United States with the German Foreign Service; now resides in Bonn.

"He pointed his gun at me and said, '*Frau komm!*' "

It was the autumn of 1944. My father was at war, and, in the meantime, my stepmother had moved with my younger brothers and sisters to a farm in Bavaria. I was 19 and decided to stay in Berlin. Berlin was, after all, my home. Not much later I was drafted into the labor service and had to work 64 hours a week in an ammunition factory. Thank God I didn't end up in the main hall, but instead was sent to work with two wounded soldiers in a small room. It was said that we were doing solder work on some secret weapon, but all I recall soldering were pots and pans. I got up at five o'clock every morning and rode my bike to the factory to begin work at six. I worked 10 hours a day, 64 hours a week for "our Führer."

About that time, we began to really feel the food shortage at home.

There was nothing left to hoard, and we had used up what we had in reserve. We relied totally on the official rations. Our noon meal consisted of cabbage and potatoes, while in the evening we generally ate potatoes and carrots. Besides my aunt and me, there were up to 35 refugees living in our house. I remember having to divide a tiny piece of butter up into "Monday to Friday"; the daily portions were never even enough to spread on one piece of bread.

I remember distinctly, it was April 14, 1945, when there was a major attack on Potsdam. From that day on, we had neither running water nor electricity. The telephones weren't working either. The first wave of Russians arrived shortly after that. The first thing we did was to hang a white sheet out the window. What followed was worse than anything we had ever imagined. Today, I am able to say that "I was the first victim on the street." The never-ending stealing and looting became a daily occurrence over the following weeks and months.

The man who lived next door had been bombed out of his house in Berlin. One night he was visited by an entire horde of Mongolians who pointed their guns at him and asked, "Where woman?" Since he lived alone, the only thing he could say was that there were none in his house. And so they went to the next house, which was ours. They forced their way through the front door. I can't tell you now exactly how many of them there were. They went through the entire house—which was very large—with flashlights, from the basement to the attic. Some of the people living in the house were able to hide. As for myself, I fell into the hands of one of the Mongolians.

That was actually the second time. The first time occurred when I mentioned I was the first victim on our street. It was the middle of the day. One Russian went into the garage and the other headed for the house. Not having the slightest idea of what would happen, I followed the man into the house. First, he locked all of the doors behind him and put the keys in his pocket. I began to feel a bit funny when we got to one of the bedrooms. I wanted to go out on the balcony, but he pointed his gun at me and said, *"Frau komm!"* We had already heard about a few of the horrible things going on, so I knew one thing for certain and that was "Don't try to defend yourself." An upper-middle-class child, I had never been told about the facts of life.

I had heard that the ransacking of homes and looting were supposed to be prohibited, and was naive enough to believe that we would receive some kind of support. While Russians were once again going through our house, I grabbed the one bicycle we still had around and rode to see the area commander. I did get to see the man and tried to make myself understood. Two Russians on motorcycles followed me home. When they saw our beautiful house and realized that Russian officers were among the soldiers looting, they joined right in too.

I was 19, not that young by today's standards. We were just so happy that the war was over, that we were still alive, and that no more bombs would fall. Of course, we contemplated what the future would have in store for us, but primarily we thought we were lucky to be alive at all. I was examined, and fortunately I hadn't been infected with venereal disease. At least I knew I was all right, though I admit that I did have nightmares for quite a while after that. But looking back at what happened to me, it's as though *I* wasn't really being violated. Instead I was standing next to myself, alongside my body, a detached observer. That feeling has kept the experience from dominating the rest of my life.

ANNA HUMMEL

Born 1921; secretary for the Gestapo in Norway; a housewife married to Oskar Hummel; make their home near Aachen (Aix-la-Chapelle).

"I always accepted whatever came from above without criticism."

I was a secretary to the commander of the security police in Oslo. In Germany it was called the Gestapo. I was in Department 5, which was criminal investigation. For the first time in my life I had contact with political people, prisoners who were members of the Norwegian resistance. Once I went on the troop transport *Monte Rosa* along with 5,000 soldiers through the Skagerrak and down to Hamburg. There were three of us girls on board who guarded the prisoners being taken to Germany. It was the first time I'd ever had anything to do with prisoners—there were also hostages among them—and it was the first time I began to wonder "Why?" "What for?" But you know, I'd just gotten married and suppressed these thoughts.

Nonetheless, in the criminal investigation office in Oslo, I sometimes had doubts. My work involved the Norwegian resistance. Of course I knew they were against us. But it never even dawned on me that something might be wrong with what we were doing, that we had absolutely no business there. That absolutely went past me. I mean, I could maybe have done something at one time or another, but I didn't. But what can you demand of people who are 20 or 21 years old who have never seen or heard of anything else? I always accepted whatever came from above without criticism.

My real doubts only began after Stalingrad. After a half-year of training, a cousin of mine was sent to the Russian front, where he was killed immediately in 1943. You know, he wasn't even there long enough to write us one letter. One of his buddies came by and explained that they had to leave him lying wounded, that they couldn't go back to him. He was only 19 years old. That outraged me so; it was a real eye-opener. I thought, my God, does this have to be? What are those boys doing that far into Russia anyhow? But doubt didn't succeed in breaking through altogether. I wouldn't have done anything, and I wouldn't have dreamed of joining the resistance. And I never had anyone to talk with about it. Except for my husband at the front, I didn't have family of my own, and you didn't trust anyone outside of your family.

HEDWIG SASS

Born 1903; was in Berlin when the Russians conquered the city; became a Trümmerfrau; *lives in Berlin.*

Most of us tried to make ourselves look a lot older than we really were. We wore old rags on purpose. But then the Russians always said, "You not old. You young." They laughed at us because of the old clothes and eye-glasses we were wearing. They knew what we were up to!

ANNA MITTELSTÄDT

Born 1900; worked in a Berlin factory during the war and was later drafted as a Trümmerfrau; *lives in Berlin.*

"Your feet are on fire!"

I worked in a factory that manufactured land mines for the German army. It was my job to put in the firing pins. I had been drafted. My sons were away at war.

After the Russians arrived, women were employed by civilian firms to remove the ruins and to clean up the streets. We worked like dogs. There were no men around. They were either dead or prisoners in some camp.

We had to walk long distances to reach our work area. A few fortunate ones were able to use the *S-Bahn*, which amazingly, in spite of all of the bombing, was still intact and operating. I organized and led the *"Trümmerfrau-Brigade"* in Berlin.

I remember during one attack, we ran to a basement for protection. The corner house across the street was totally destroyed. Panic-stricken, we left the basement and ran out onto the street. The streets were covered with phosphorus. The people behind me were screaming at me, "Frau Mittelstädt, your feet are on fire!" Everywhere I stepped, I stepped in phosphorus, in flames. But I didn't care. I just kept running.

HANNA GERLITZ

Born 1907; wife of a banker; experienced Russian occupation of Berlin; lives in Munich.

"Stay very calm; otherwise they'll shoot us all."

The Russians occupied our section of Berlin on April 22, 1945. We were sitting in the basement when the Russians entered the house. They came downstairs and naturally found the liquor. They proceeded to get drunk. They sang songs and my husband courageously sang along with them, only he sang, "Hide, hide yourself in the corner. . . ." The Russians realized what was going on, and to prove that their pistols were loaded, they shot at the jars of preserves on the shelves. The place was a mess. My husband said, "What pigs!" At that, a Russian said, "What you say? Pig, you say?" He put his gun up to my husband's forehead. My husband looked him straight in the eye and said, "Yes, you pig!" Then the others came back and grabbed me. My husband was beside himself. I said, "Stay very calm; otherwise they'll shoot us all." Thank God it didn't happen in the same room. There were two of them. It was horrible for my husband as well.

I remember thinking, "If you don't go with them, they're going to shoot us all. Maybe I can save us. And if you sacrifice yourself now, you'll get over it later. You will have done your duty and we'll come out of this alive!"

They were young, and they were drunk. They weren't Mongolians; they were, in fact, rather good-looking officers who had doused themselves with perfume and cologne so as not to smell so repulsive. At least they made that part a little more bearable for me. Although I didn't find the experience that repellent, I wasn't exactly elated either. I can only thank God I wasn't infected as so many other women were.

The funny thing about it was that I was wearing a ski suit, and had my jewelry in my pants' pocket the entire time. They didn't find it; they didn't even look for it. I guess the other thing was more important. When they were done, they fired their guns into the air. The others thought the Russians had shot me until I yelled out, "It's over with!" Afterwards, I had to console my husband and help restore his courage. He cried like a baby.

BARONESS IRMELA VON FÖLKERSAMB

Born 1921; served in the compulsory Women's
Labor Service and as a nurse's aide; makes her
home in Bonn-Bad Godesberg.

"I don't have a heart anymore."

During the war I was drafted into the Labor Service and sent to East
Friesland. We were there to help the farmers plant turnips and so on.
The nicest girls were delinquents from the harbor areas of Bremen
and Hamburg, who could neither read nor write. They were very
sweet. We always read them the letters from their boyfriends at the
front, and we also wrote letters for them. We had the great "privi-
lege" of going out at night when the air raid alarms went off and
sitting in slit trenches alongside convicts that had come from various
prisons to work on the moors. These were not people from concentration camps, but ordinary criminals.

Then I received word to report to an orphanage. These children
were between the ages of six and fourteen, the poorest of the poor.
Few were actually orphans; most came from bombed out cities like
Hamburg, or cities in the Ruhr. These boys and girls, who were
really badly off, could recuperate for six weeks. The boys were nicer
and less complicated than the girls, who constantly suffered from one
thing or another. Some of these children arrived sick, filthy, and
infested with lice. You were really confronted with the misery of the
poor: destitute, starving, and undernourished children who had not
had a good night's sleep in ages because they were always lying in
some cellar.

When I returned to the Rhine, toward the end of 1943, I immediately received another assignment. I could either work in a munitions factory or in a hospital, and I chose the hospital. It was very trying. The hospital was in Ahrweiler, so we received the wounded soldiers from the Western front. Later, of course, we also treated many civilians who were wounded in the air raids. There were always between 200 and 300 patients, all of them surgical cases.

It was one big butcher shop. The days the hospital trains arrived were especially bad. We often spent 10 hours at a time among moaning, wounded soldiers. There were amputations, and of course many shrapnel injuries, all of them patched up with horrible, filthy casts.

When I went home I said, "I don't have a heart anymore. I can feel no pity." And my father said, "Be happy you no longer feel anything, otherwise you could not stand it."

At first I did feel pity for these poor young men, who arrived badly wounded and screaming for their parents, and who were dead inside two hours or so. Your heart was breaking constantly. You cannot weep along with the soldiers for a year and a half, at a hospital. You must become hardened. This actually happened to me quite quickly—there was just too much suffering. All of these men were very young. The ones that really got to me were the ones who mutilated themselves. Soldiers had wounds that just would not heal. And then we realized they were poking around at their wounds with something they had concealed under their bed sheets. They did this out of sheer terror of being sent back to the front. In my opinion, these men were always the worst off.

Once there was an air raid while we were frantically unloading patients from the hospital train. Suddenly the officer in charge shouted, "Hit the dirt! Fighters!" He threw himself on top of me and was mortally wounded. He saved my life, got a splinter in his lung, and was dead just a few days later. That was one of the worst experiences I have ever had: slowly realizing that the man who had saved my life had suffered a fatal wound.

KÄTHE SCHLECHTER-
BONNESEN

*Born 1909; lost her husband and children in
the war; lived in Cologne after the war;
deceased in 1987.*

"My two children were pulled out dead."

We had hardly been in Cologne two weeks. In fact, our suitcases
weren't even unpacked yet, because we were planning on leaving
again, when the daylight attacks began. On September 27, 1944, I
wanted to take my two small children, who were three and six years
old, to the insurance company in the city to apply for the orphan's
pension, since my husband had been killed at the front. We passed a
kindergarten in the suburb of Mauenheim on our way. The kindergarten teacher, who knew me and the children, saw us and said,
"Don't take the children into the city. There could be another air raid;
they're safer here." My six-year-old son pleaded, "Oh please, let us
stay here. We'll play with the doll's kitchen." I gave in and travelled to
the city alone.

The air raid warning sounded while I was sitting in a streetcar. I
had to get off and go into a bunker. All I could think about was my
children. As soon as the "all clear" signal sounded, I ran frantically
back to Mauenheim to look for them. At first I looked in the bunker
where the children normally went during an alarm, but I didn't find
them. I saw other children, but I couldn't find my own two. My
mother was in the bunker, but she hadn't seen them either and didn't
know where they were. Later that afternoon, I heard that a whole
group of people had been buried in a house on Nibelungen Street,
including children from the kindergarten. It was true—late in the
day, more and more people were pulled out of the cellar of that house.

The bombs had fallen immediately after the alarm. Because there was an open area between the house and the bunker, many people had run into the house. Then a heavy bomb had fallen in at an angle and hit the cellar. Not all of the people in the cellar had died right away. Some were still alive; but as soon as they came out into the fresh air, they keeled over and were dead. My two children were pulled out dead. You could hardly see any injuries on them. They only had a small drop of blood on their noses and large bloody scrapes on the backs of their heads.

I was in a state of total shock. I wanted to scream, right then and there. I wanted to scream "You Nazis, you murderers!" A neighbor, who had only been released from a concentration camp a few days before, grabbed my arm and pulled me aside. He said, "Do you want to get yourself arrested too?"

HILDEGARD ANDRES

Born 1915; witnessed the bombardment of Dresden in 1945; wife of Erich Andres; lives in Hamburg.

"Dresden won't be bombed—Churchill's aunt is supposed to live there."

It was February 13, 1945. I was working in the center of Dresden at one of the city administrative offices. Because of the influx of refugees from the east, we were very busy. My apartment was located near the large park in Dresden. I had barely gotten home that evening when the sirens began to wail. On the previous occasions when they had sounded, nothing had happened. Dresden was totally intact. We always said, "Dresden won't be bombed—Churchill's aunt is supposed to live there." We were so certain nothing would happen to us, we didn't even have any bunkers.

Almost as soon as the sirens went off, you could hear the first bombs begin to explode. I immediately ran down to the basement. The bombing was really heavy. The first attack lasted about 30 minutes—from 9:45 to 10:15. The neighbor's house was hit right away and was burning. After the air raid, we stood in a line out on the street, passing buckets of water in an attempt to put out the fire.

While we were doing this—it was around midnight—the sirens sounded again. We were bombed a second time. Once again, we all ran to our basements. I was four months pregnant with our first child at the time. I remember lying on the floor thinking, "I hope the roof doesn't cave in on me!" Our house was hit, not by incendiaries but by demolition bombs, and by the winds started by the fire storm. All of the windows and doors had been literally blown out. There was no way we could live in the house after that second attack.

I was able to salvage two suitcases. My husband's suit and his Leica camera were in one, and baby clothes were in the other. I knew I had to save at least these few things. Then I started walking. Everyone was heading for the outskirts of the city. With my gas mask on, I'd walk a bit, stop and put down the suitcases, and pick them up and walk again. I kept this up until I finally reached a friend's house.

The next day was Ash Wednesday. The streets of Dresden were filled with debris and bricks. You had to walk on top of it to get anywhere. Dead people were lined on either side of the street— women, children, and soldiers. I remember seeing children with backpacks lying there with their faces to the ground. While walking down that street I heard a man cry out, "Mother!"—I can still hear him today. He was standing on top of a huge pile of bricks, under- neath which his mother was buried.

I continued walking toward the office. I saw more dead, mum- mified and scorched because of the heat. I really didn't take it all in. I was pregnant, and kept thinking, "Just don't think about it; just get through—somehow." But my office building was gone. The entire inner city was in ruins. There were so many dead that they had to be cremated at the old city market place. We still have pictures. There was no other way to bury so many people. I heard that in the end, a lot of cellars were walled up with cement because it was impossible to dig out all the dead.

Although we didn't have much to eat, we didn't starve. Actually it was worse after 1945. I remember, because my daughter was born in July 1945. I couldn't nurse her, and I received a few potatoes and 4 pounds of bread, for a baby!

It wasn't until November that my husband found out he was a father. He saw his daughter for the first time when she was 10 months old.

JUTTA RÜDIGER*

"I rejected any use of girls as soldiers."

I still hear today that the Third Reich encouraged out-of-wedlock pregnancies. In fact, the slogan "Give the Führer a child" was the work of a few fanatics during the war. I got letters from the front asking me where I got the idea of encouraging girls to get pregnant. The whole thing was new to me. I made some inquiries in party circles, and was told my correspondents had been listening to enemy propaganda!

It is true that Himmler once spoke to the leaders of the League of German Girls and said that when so many soldiers were dying in the war, if a man got a girl pregnant and then went back to the front, we should be generous and assume that they plan to get married, especially if the man was killed. An unmarried mother should not be driven to suicide, as was earlier so often the case.

We agreed, and said, "Good. If a woman is expecting a baby, the League of German Girls will help her." But even Himmler never went so far as to say "you must give the Führer a child," or "every woman

---

* Biography on page xxvii.

should get pregnant." He didn't dare. All of us were glaring at him, and he probably noticed it. At the end of his speech he even said that any SS man who seduced a minor would be severely punished. The SS *Lebensborn* homes, the "Wells of Life" were not breeding farms, but places where unmarried mothers could go to have their children in peace, away from the reproaches of their relatives.

We in the League felt even more strongly about using women in combat. Early in 1945 Arthur Axmann, Schirach's successor as Reich Youth Leader, told me that Martin Bormann wanted me to make BdM girls available for military service. Bormann planned to create a women's battalion. I said spontaneously, "That is definitely out of the question! There's no way I will allow it! First, if we're so desperate only the women can save us, then it makes no sense anyway. Second, I am of the opinion that for purely biological reasons, women can't be used as fighting soldiers. It contradicts their nature. Women bring life into the world; they don't destroy it. I am ready to see my girls even in the front lines, as medical orderlies or supply personnel for our comrades in the Hitler Youth. But a women's battalion is out of the question." Axmann shrugged and said, "It's your responsibility." I replied that indeed it was.

I never heard anything more on the subject from Bormann or anyone else. I rejected any use of girls as soldiers. At the very end, I issued an instruction in Berlin that the leaders of the League of German Girls learn to use pistols for self-defense in emergencies. We'd heard what the Bolsheviks were doing to German women. But if girls fought in Berlin, they did so on their own initiative.

INGEBORG WORLITZ

Born 1920; survived the air raids on Hamburg; continues to reside in Hamburg.

"I had a baby carriage. I was rich!"

I didn't want to leave Hamburg, no matter how bad things got. But—well, then I met my husband, he worked for the railroad, and I got pregnant, and we had to get married. He wanted me to leave Hamburg because of the baby. They were still bombing us—no more big attacks, but they'd drop these air mines, and when they exploded the pressure burst your lungs. People would be standing on the street, the mine would drop, and they'd just fall over because their lungs were gone.

Finally I gave in. I went to Neustadt, a small town outside Hamburg. In January 1945, I had my baby. But I had nothing else—no diapers, no baby clothes, no baby buggy. There was nothing anywhere for a child. But some people who hadn't been bombed-out tore up their sheets for diapers. Someone gave me a little jacket; someone else a pair of tights—you can't imagine how people helped. And in March, when my daughter was eight weeks old, I saw a woman pushing a baby carriage. She was using it to haul coal! And I said, "I have a baby girl. Could you sell me the baby carriage?" "I'll give it to you instead," she told me. And it was a really fancy one, with big wheels. I had a baby carriage. I was rich! I could take my daughter out for a little fresh air!

CHAPTER 15

The Children's Crusade

"Whoever controls the young," the Nazis asserted, "controls the future." They made every effort to bring Germany's young men and women under the New Order's influence. The Hitler Youth and its female equivalent, the League of German Girls, consumed an increasing amount of time and energy. Before 1933, membership in the Hitler Youth was a way of challenging the establishment: parents, teachers, preachers. Now the Hitler Youth was part of the establishment.

But one element of the experience remained vital. Most German adolescents of the Nazi era were white-hot patriots. Their elders' doubts about the war were seldom passed on, in good part because of fear of the results if charged with "defeatism." Nazi wartime propaganda focused on glorifying young heroes. Newsreels, magazines, even postcards featured men in their early twenties who performed feats of individual valor, yet survived to receive their medals from the Führer himself. These specific factors worked in a general climate of limited sophistication. "Adolescence" would become a familiar concept in Germany only in the postwar years, and only then as an import from the West. In the traditional German family structure, until one was an adult one was a child, with nothing to say, and no reason to be told anything in particular. Especially among the middle classes, enthusiasm untempered by rational calculation was regarded as a positive quality, indicating a lofty spirit that would soon enough be tempered by experience.

The environment of Germany's youth, in short, did not encourage taking critical distance from a Reich that demanded ever more from them as the war progressed. The only question was, "When do we get our chance?" Urban teenagers were mobilized as messengers, first-aid assistants, and rubble cleaners. The SS formed a division from Hitler Youth members. High school students manned anti-aircraft guns. Then in October 1944, Hitler created the *Volkssturm*. All physically fit males between 16 and 60 became eligible for military service. Boys who had dreamed of the Knight's Cross suddenly found themselves in foxholes or on street corners, aiming bazookas at Allied tanks. Their sisters hid from prowling Russians, or weighed virginity against a carton of cigarettes from a GI. It was a rude awakening.

LOTHAR LOEWE

Born 1929; attacked tanks in Berlin with a bazooka at the age of 16; after the war was a television correspondent and director general of the SFB, Berlin's radio and television station, lives in Berlin.

"The image of Soviet subhumans I had carried with me finally collapsed."

Why didn't we do anything to get out of Berlin? Why didn't we turn and run? We wouldn't have known where to go. I was at home in Berlin; at least I had an aunt there. We didn't have an apartment, but we didn't know where else we could go either. I didn't have any relatives in the west, and I wouldn't have been able to get there anyway. Apart from that, there was an atmosphere of doom, of the end of the world, because of the reports from the east, of the Russian advances into Germany.

We began to believe what Goebbels had said so often: If the Russians invaded, they would kill everyone, and whoever wasn't killed would be sent to the mines in Siberia, and whoever was sent there never came back. We would simply join ranks with the army of forced laborers there we'd heard so much about. Every civilized, organized form of life would come to an end.

It was the courage of desperation which motivated the soldiers. Berlin was defended so bitterly only because so many of the soldiers, so many of the civilians were afraid of Soviet imprisonment. They wanted to save themselves, to keep the Russians out of Berlin for as long as they could. Everything possible was done to stop them, to gain a little more time. If we were lucky, the Americans or the British would get to Berlin first. This is what any intelligent person hoped for.

To me, Bolshevism meant the end of life. And in my opinion, that's the reason for the terribly bitter fight in Berlin, which wasn't only street to street, but house to house, room to room, and floor to floor. The Russians and the Germans suffered such horrible casualties here because every single brick was bitterly fought over for days on end.

In mid-April, my Hitler Youth unit was mobilized. The fighting was in an area of Berlin I knew like the back of my hand. At 16, I carried messages under fire. My CO was a lieutenant with a wooden leg and a medal. He spent nights with his girlfriend. Every evening he stopped the war and said, "Come back at 8:00 tomorrow morning." The next day, we'd go back to the front on some street or other.

We had bazookas. I had a Belgian pistol and an Italian tommy gun with no safety catch. Once it almost went off and killed a sergeant. My CO always wanted me to wear a helmet, but I didn't like them. The things were so big they slipped down on my nose, and besides, I couldn't hear when I wore one.

It was a bad war. The nights, when the women in the occupied side streets were raped by Russian soldiers, were awful; the screams were horrible. There were terrible scenes. But these, on the other hand, only encouraged us all the more. We were genuinely afraid the

Russians would slaughter us. They didn't take prisoners. That's when I knocked out a tank with a bazooka.

Three tanks had broken through, and I shot at them along with another older soldier who had several stripes on his sleeve for knocking out tanks. I fired from a cellar door. It had quite an effect because there was a wall behind me, and the bazooka's backblast was really something. The tank flew into the air—an impressive sight to a teenager.

The Russians retreated, and then I had a horrible experience. This had all happened on one of the side streets of the Kürfürstendamm. People who lived there had put out white flags of surrender. There was this one apartment house with white bed sheets waving from the windows. And the SS came—I'll never forget this—went into the house, and dragged all of the men out. I don't know whether these were soldiers dressed in civilian clothing, old men, or what. Anyway, they took them into the middle of the street and shot them.

I was infuriated. Of course we didn't dare do anything about it. But anywhere you went, you saw military police. Even when the Russians were already in sight, you could see police a hundred yards farther on, still trying to check people. Whoever didn't have the right papers or the correct pass was strung up as a deserter, and hung with a sign saying, "I am a traitor," or "I am a coward."

I was wounded on May 1. After I was hit, I was always afraid of being wounded again whenever the shooting started. I had never been afraid before, but now I was really scared. I'll never forget sitting in a bunker and hearing of Hitler's end. It was like a whole world collapsing. The report was that he'd been killed at the head of his troops in the heroic Battle of Berlin. Adolf Hitler's death left me with a feeling of emptiness. Nonetheless, I remember thinking that my oath was no longer valid, because it had been made to Hitler. We had sworn an oath to the Führer, but not to Dönitz, his successor. So the oath was null and void.

Now the trick was to get out of Berlin and avoid falling into the hands of the Russians. Close to dawn everything started moving. I went out into the streets. Berlin burned: oceans of flames, horrible clouds of smoke. An entire pilgrimage of people began marching out of Berlin. I spotted an SS Tiger tank unit with room in one of the tanks, so they took me along. I assumed this would be a sure thing because the tank was a heavy one. The SS men made a very determined impression; they didn't want to fall into the hands of the Russians, and neither did I. It looked as though we had a good chance of reaching German troops who were supposed to be still fighting a few miles away.

Somewhere along the way I peeked out of the hatch and saw the rest of my unit, which I had lost. I told the tank driver to stop, and I jumped out and went back to them.

Hospital trains were supposedly ready and waiting outside Berlin. The picture of white beds on a train which might roll all the way to Hamburg was very appealing to me. I hadn't washed in ten days and was bloody, wounded, dirty—a real mess. We pushed our way right across a troop training field. And there I saw a firefight between Labor Service people and Luftwaffe soldiers. The Luftwaffe thought the Labor Service men were Russians because of their brown uniforms. And the Labor Service people thought, because they were being shot at, that the Luftwaffe men were Germans fighting on the Russian side. They could yell as much German as they wanted; they didn't believe each other, and continued to shoot at one another. This went on for about half an hour, and a few were killed. I just laid low and thought to myself that I was about to be killed in German crossfire. Finally, some experienced officer suddenly stood up and commanded everyone to hold their fire, stand up, fall in, and march. And they obeyed and said, "Sorry about that, buddy," to one another, and moved on as if nothing had happened! An eerie scenario.

Everything ended on May 5, in a village south of Nauen. Thousands of soldiers had gathered there: a few generals, our unit, and many wounded. The Russians had surrounded us, and we were being shelled. At one point there was a pause in the firefight, and the Russians sent a couple of parliamentarians over to encourage us to give up. The generals were emphatic about the wounded being sent to a hospital by truck before the rest would lay down their weapons.

My commander didn't like this. He had a great deal of experience on the Eastern front. There were only about 20 of us left when he said, "I dismiss you all from the Wehrmacht; I dismiss you from duty. Hand over your military passes. I personally do not intend to surrender, and neither does my aide. We plan to take a half-track with a full tank of gas and break out of this dump when it gets dark. Our last chance is to take this vehicle full speed ahead cross-country at night." His theory was not to parade out of there, but to keep it subtle. "I won't force anyone, but whoever wants to come along may join us."

There were 10 or 12 people on the half-track with bazookas, tommy guns, hand grenades, and light machine guns. Some wore helmets, others didn't. It was a mixed crowd; a few women air force helpers were also with us. And we actually succeeded in breaking out. The Russians didn't shoot. I believe they weren't interested in chasing anything anymore.

We drove cross-country for a while, then turned onto a highway. Suddenly, we encountered a Russian column turning in from a side road. My commander's driver spoke Russian; he was a Volga German. He told them we were Russians, and we joined the tail end of the column as the last vehicle. The column was rolling west, that was the important thing, so we went along, happy as pie. By this time many Russians were driving German vehicles, so no one thought anything about us.

Then the column turned, and we drove on alone straight ahead. The Russians wanted to stop us, they yelled "Stoj!" and swung red flashlights. My commander told us to keep going, and only to shoot if we were shot at. They fired into the half-track. Several of us were killed or badly wounded. We continued for about three miles, but the radiator had been hit, so we stopped and got out.

We continued on foot until we ran into a Russian company. They formed a skirmish line and came right toward us. The question was whether we should fight a last battle or not. The commander told us there was no point, and we raised our hands. There were about six of us left. The squad that took us prisoner lined us up against the wall of a shed where there were two dead civilians lying on the ground. I was sure we were going to be shot. There was a big discussion with one of the officers, and then suddenly they just came up to us and took our rings and watches. But I also found myself with two packs of cigarettes I hadn't had before—the Russians pressed two packs of German cigarettes into my hands.

They led us to some trucks and took us to the next town, where they handed us over to a Ukrainian artillery unit. And the image of Soviet subhumans I had carried with me finally collapsed. This unit had a woman doctor with them, and the first thing they did was to see to the wounded. After that, we got something to eat from these Bolshevist "subhumans." The average Russian sympathized with young boys like us, and there were quite a few of us in this campaign. I had neither a mess kit nor a spoon. I had nothing; I'd even thrown my pistol away. And it was this Bolshevik, this person I'd always believed to be a monster, that lent me, the Nordic German, his mess kit and spoon to eat with.

I had seen many Soviet POWs during the war. And I had also seen how they were treated. All POWs were treated better than the Russian prisoners we had. The Soviets were always beaten, really, and they never got anything to eat. They were made to look like the subhumans we imagined them to be. The idea that a German soldier would give a Russian prisoner his mess kit and spoon to eat from was simply unimaginable to me. And the fact that this Soviet gave me his, voluntarily, happily, because he felt sorry for me, shook the foundations of my image of them.

That's when I told myself that maybe the Soviets were much different from what they had told us to believe. This was my first encounter with Soviet people, and I'll never forget it for the rest of my life. And it has continued to influence my feelings toward the Soviet Union.

KARL DAMM

Born 1927; Hitler Youth member who was drafted into the anti-aircraft auxiliary and sent to the front to defend Berlin; after the war was a member of the Bundestag; high school teacher; lives in Hamburg.

"I was a victim of Goebbels' propaganda."

On February 15, 1943, five days before my 16th birthday, I reported, like almost all of my classmates, to the 2nd battery of the 267th Heavy Anti-Aircraft Battalion for service in the flak auxiliary.

Service in the flak auxiliary had many fascinating aspects. In the first place, we were impressed by the fact that we were now soldiers. Then there were our guns, the heavy 8.8cm and the light 2cm guns. Finally, we were intrigued by the technology of target acquisition and target tracking.

Once, I believe it was in the summer of 1943, a damaged B-17 Flying Fortress flew only a few hundred meters over our position. We kids, red-faced and yelling with excitement, pointed out the big fat target. We were disappointed and indignant when our battery commander expressly forbade firing at this aircraft. Naturally he was right, but in that moment it seemed to us that he had just thrown away the victory. The B-17 crew, by the way—this was made known after the war—is said to have been killed by enraged citizens. I can remember that their burned corpses were found after the end of the war and that the guilty received their due punishment.

Needless to say, we got our school instruction at our gun positions. Almost all of us had been wearing uniforms since we had been 10 years old, every time we had to participate in some sort of service. It began with the *Jungvolk,* and then, when we were 14, we went into the regular Hitler Youth.

As youngsters, it gave us a sense of power when our squad would go singing through the streets, accompanied by the deep march beat of the drums and the sharp tones of the trumpets. And the mood at many of the social evenings, when we would sing the songs of the youth movement to the accompaniment of a guitar, was terrific.

As a child, I had wanted to fly. When I was 14, I reported to the Hitler Youth pilot training program. I passed all of the sailplane tests and got my pilot's license in June 1944 in the Pre-Military Instruction Center. After my time in the center I joined the Luftwaffe as an officer cadet. None of us recruits could grasp the idea that Germany was in the sixth year of the war and that the Wehrmacht was retreating on all fronts.

In the middle of April 1945, our training battalion was ordered to move out as quickly as possible. Each of us received a rifle—French rifles from the First World War—and ammunition. Each company received several bazookas to form a "tank-destroying squad." We were not even shown how to use them! I think it was April 14 when our battalion left for the front—30 miles east of Berlin.

We dug trenches for two days. At first nothing happened. On the second day, the scene changed. Around noon, individually or in small, disorganized groups, retreating soldiers appeared at our positions. These dirty, terrified figures belonged to the *Gross-Deutschland* Division, and they told us that the Russians had succeeded in breaking through because Russian soldiers in German uniforms had attacked at dawn. They had called out, "Comrades, don't shoot, we're Germans!"

That night, along with a comrade, I had sentry duty from midnight until 2 A.M. About 4 A.M., weak rifle fire could already be heard. As the first signs of daylight appeared over the eastern horizon, we saw about 50 Soviet tanks moving along the road past our position.

I don't know how long we waited. It must have been about noon when our sergeant called to us, "We're getting out of here." We grabbed our rifles and followed the sergeant toward the communications trench that would give us cover. But we stopped after only a few meters. The trench was occupied by our dead comrades—it was filled almost to the halfway mark with their bodies. Those were the first dead people I had ever seen in my life! But naked terror followed the horror. We stumbled over the comrades who had been mowed down, comrades we had gone through the past six months with. We were afraid to walk on the corpses, but we were even more afraid of joining them.

As we were fleeing, an officer with a pistol in his hand ordered us loudly and clearly to stop. There was a short exchange of words; we tried to make it clear to him that we were no deserters. He cut us short and commanded, "You stay here! We are mounting a counterattack!"

A fleet of German tanks, Tigers, Panthers, and one monster I think was a Royal Tiger, came up and opened fire. The tank battle lasted for perhaps half an hour, after which the Soviet tanks were burning, immobile monsters. Our first two days at the front made us realize we were nothing more than cannon fodder. Nonetheless, we never considered deserting. We wanted to find our unit, or, if it no longer existed, at least get to another Luftwaffe unit that could give us some kind of protection, and a chance to carry out a sensible military mission. We retreated into Berlin and joined the defense of the city.

The end of the grisly game was clear. We had only restricted movement and defense possibilities. We were like pin pricks—able to delay the Russian penetration here and there, only to increase the city's suffering. It was clear to every participant that there would be no escape.

The older soldiers, which meant the twenty-two and twenty-three-year-olds, may have recognized the uselessness and the irresponsibility of this street battle. But we youngsters, who had had our baptism of fire only a week before, were still naive.

In part our sense of obedience, which seemed to be taken for granted, made us continue. Nonetheless, I hesitate to speak of "blind" obedience. What role did the ideological training to which we had been exposed for twelve years play? You may not believe me if, in looking back, I say "none." In the real battle situation, the main motive was simply to survive. Thoughts about the "Führer, our people, and the fatherland" did not move me. Our people and our fatherland, yes—we were Germans, and opposite us were Russians, "Bolsheviks." Perhaps the tenacity of our defense would have been less if we had been fighting against the Americans or the British. I don't know. I didn't expect anything good from the Soviets. To that extent, I was a victim of Goebbels' propaganda. But who was there who had not either approved or spoken Goebbels' sentences: "Führer command us; we will follow you!" and "Führer command us; we will bear the consequences!"

RUDOLF VILTER

Born 1929; at 16 was forced to fight in the Volkssturm *against the Russians, and was severely wounded; worked as a journalist after the war and lives in Berlin.*

"We were afraid of our own MPs."

I turned 16 in January 1945, and I was drafted a few days after the beginning of the Russian offensive. At first, we were members of the *Volkssturm,* and felt like second-class soldiers. Later we became real soldiers, all right. Perhaps it was pride that motivated us. We did not run to the army with banners waving, the way they did in 1914. Neither was there any enthusiasm or patriotism. Nor did we have the feeling that the final victory could be won only with us and by us. I think we were filled with skepticism and fear.

We received miserable training. One reason was surely that we lacked weapons and didn't have enough ammunition. We had to be very sparing in our use of the bazooka. We shot at tanks that had been taken out of service, which is very different from firing at the real thing. In addition, our trainers were mediocre—I don't think they were really interested, or saw any sense in what they were doing.

The Russians crossed the Oder River on April 16, and the attack on Berlin began. About April 20, we were sent into action north of Berlin. Fear, and only fear, controlled us during our first encounter with the Red Army. I will never forget the first T-34 tank I saw. I thought it was coming directly at me, and I wanted to hide ten meters underground. Our platoon leader, an old sergeant, stood out in the open and shot at the tank with his bazooka. He showed us that such things could be hit. They were just as vulnerable as we were.

Our great hopes were the Elbe River, the British, and the Americans. We had a panic fear of the Red Army and of captivity in Russia. We received orders to break out to the west on April 24. A stream poured out of Berlin as the city was evacuated: women, children, wounded, POWs, foreign workers—it was a picture of horror.

A major, along with two officers and a few MPs, stood by the side of the road. These were also people we were very afraid of—an important reason why we didn't desert. We saw what happened to deserters who were caught; they were hanged from trees with signs reading, "I'm hanging here because I was too cowardly to defend my fatherland."

To clear the way we had to attack a village occupied by the Russians. I witnessed a really terrible incident during the attack. A non-commissioned officer (*Unterscharführer*) in the Waffen-SS rolled one of the wounded Russian soldiers onto his stomach and shot him with his sub-machine gun.

We heard rattling and whizzing, but we didn't see anything of the enemy. Suddenly I received a heavy blow, as if someone had struck me on the shoulder and the leg at the same time. Mortar fragments had struck my collar bone and lodged in my ribs and my lungs. I must have been unconscious for some time; I remember only that there was a flash when I came to again, and I was terribly groggy. I was bleeding from the shoulder and couldn't move my right arm. I crawled to the nearest house, found it locked, and went on to the next one, which was open. Other wounded men were there, too, and a classmate of mine who had been wounded only slightly attended to me and bound up my wound.

We thought that the Russians would come and shoot us, and they did indeed come very soon, but they didn't harm us. On the other hand, they didn't help us, either. Those who had light wounds tried to find towels and things for bandages in the surrounding houses. They also searched for water; a terrible moaning was going on in this cellar.

Just by chance, I had been wounded in the vicinity of our home town. My classmate went there and told my family about my predicament. My father immediately obtained a hand-drawn cart from the landlord and got him to come along, even though the landlord had five children of his own to look after. They came and got me and wheeled me home on the cart. I remember nothing of the trip.

There were three major reasons why we never considered deserting. The first I've already mentioned; we were afraid of our own MPs. If a deserter was caught, he was dragged before a drumhead court-martial, sentenced, and hanged or shot. Another reason we didn't desert was our fear of Soviet captivity, which was described to us as being the worst experience imaginable. A third reason was our hope of meeting up with the Americans, whose POW camps we almost longed for.

WOLFGANG KASAK

Born 1927; fought as a flak auxiliary in the defense of Berlin; POW in Russia; presently director of the Slavic Institute, University of Cologne.

"I gave him my styptic pencil and marched off into captivity."

In 1945, I was drafted as an auxiliary into the anti-aircraft. I can still remember being in my father's study when he told me I had been drafted. I remember my mother's despair. I remember the clear realization that this event had ended my childhood, and that now complete subjugation to the regime would begin, which might even include deadly danger. I had just turned sixteen.

I joined a medical corps training unit. We had outstanding instructors. It was similar to studying medicine, but there was also some military nonsense. One day the order came, I think it was on April 24, 1945, that we were to go to Berlin. I arrived there and wanted to call my mother. But Potsdam had been burned to ashes on the night of April 14, and I couldn't reach my parents. I waited the entire day in the barracks to see if my mother would visit me to say goodbye. On the way from the barracks to the front, I met her by pure coincidence. I'll never forget this twist of fate. Potsdam had been destroyed, but we were able to see each other again. This meeting with my mother remained a source of strength for me throughout the entire period of my captivity.

A few days later we were at the front. We didn't know exactly in which direction the enemy, the Poles, could be found. They were either in front of us or behind us, we didn't know. As a medic, I had the duty of attending to the wounded. When the command came for us to retreat, I was left alone in my foxhole. When I came out I was shot. The shot didn't exactly hit its mark, however; I was only grazed and felt some pain in my head. I asked the soldier who had shot at me to help me. I gave him my styptic pencil and marched off into captivity.

I was led away by a very nice Polish soldier. Without saying a word, he made it clear that I would be interrogated and that everything would be taken from me, so why didn't I give him my watch.

KLAUS BÖLLING

---

*Born 1928; Hitler Youth; became anti-aircraft
auxiliary at the end of the war; his Jewish
mother was sent to Auschwitz; journalist after
the war; chief government spokesman under
Chancellor Helmut Schmidt; resides in Berlin.*

"How dare a civilian degrade me like this."

At the university my father belonged to a student duelling fraternity.
Though most of the other members were of the nobility, he gained
their respect through his academic excellence. As a lawyer, he was
one of those young intellectuals who was in opposition to the Weimar
Republic; and who, as the strength of National Socialism increased,
supported it at first.

I grew up like many sons of civil servants. I always considered my
father a civil servant, though he had been forced to retire after 1933
because my mother was of Jewish descent. It was his desire that I
attend the *Gymnasium*. He was a humanist and had been an excellent
student; he still corresponded with his teachers in Latin. I was more
than challenged when it came to school—particularly in Greek—but
I had to fulfill my father's wishes. From 1939 on, I was a passionate
member of the *Jungvolk*. It was a world I was happy to be in, I
belonged.

When we were called to the ack-ack, we considered it to be the
first test of our manhood. We felt redeemed from our inactivity—all
the older students were already in the Wehrmacht. For most of us,
there was a strong urge to get involved. We wanted to line up with the
men in field-gray, or whatever the popular rhetoric was at the time.
That was in May 1944.

My mother was arrested that summer. Only then did I find out she was Jewish. I first found out through my father, who visited me when I was a flak helper. He said, "We always hid it from you, but now your mother's been arrested. She made a careless comment, someone informed on her, and there's nothing I can do for her. Personally, I believe mother is an illegitimate child and not Jewish at all.[1] "I'm trying to save her on this account, but proving it will be very difficult. I've already tried; but the chances are slim. You can visit her this week in Berlin at the transit camp—I've arranged that. You can go there, but from there your mother will be taken to a concentration camp."

It didn't really dawn on me what this meant; my idea of a camp had nothing even vaguely to do with the reality of what was later called the Holocaust. I regarded it all as a mistake that would be corrected in due time. The term "Jewry" had absolutely no relevance to me. I didn't know any Jews, and the few Jewish acquaintances my parents had were no longer in Berlin. It just wasn't a topic of concern for me; until I was 16 or 17, my life had been just like anyone else's.

My mother was of a Jewish background, but had no relationship whatsoever to the community or the religion. People who aren't familiar with the history of the Third Reich are unaware that there were many Germans Jews like her in this situation. My parents had no political disagreements, and I know that emigration was never a point of discussion. As a young woman in the 1920s, my mother went to conservative nationalist rallies with enthusiasm. She had volunteered for service in World War I, and had worked as a nurse in hospitals on the Western front.

I had absolutely no idea what would happen to my mother. I knew she had been arrested, but I imagined her to be in something like protective custody. My father knew, of course. He'd discussed it with others and knew that the Nazis had decided on the Final Solution to the Jewish question. This information was available in literature, and had been read by the intellectuals. Only a few were so naive as to

---

[1] Allegations of illegitimacy were a frequent means of evading the restrictions and penalties imposed on Jews in Nazi Germany, especially among the educated classes and those with contacts in the bureaucracy that facilitated preparing—and fabricating—the necessary documents. Bölling senior was laying the ground for such an attempt in this conversation.

doubt the seriousness of the threat, even if they didn't know anything about the extent of the Holocaust.

I went to the transit camp in north Berlin. A man came up to me, a Gestapo officer in civilian dress. He just couldn't believe that suddenly someone in uniform—with a swastika armband—was coming to visit a camp which was nothing more than a compound for penned-up Jews who, like my mother, wore the star. That just didn't fit into his picture. After he identified me, he ripped the armband off my uniform. That really got to me. After all, I felt like a soldier. How dare a civilian degrade me like this? This was even worse for me, because I didn't take the threat to my mother seriously. I couldn't be afraid for her because I had no idea of what she'd have to endure. As banal as it sounds, this scene is unforgettable. It was a turning point for me and helps explain why—with great emotion—I joined the Communist Party after the war. It was a logical step for me; this was the party that was going to grind the Nazis to pulp. My mother survived, but only because she had training as a nurse. She worked in the Auschwitz medical division.

Visiting my mother shortly before she was transported to Auschwitz changed my whole attitude toward the regime. I had the feeling that National Socialism was my personal adversary—the epitome of injustice. I felt that I'd done my duty as a flak helper, and the fact that I came out of it alive was pure coincidence. There were some attacks when bombs fell left and right and many kids my age—15 and 16— were killed. Having my armband ripped off made me realize that, not only did they disregard what I'd done to serve our country, but quite obviously I was a nothing to them. That's the way they treated me.

Everything began to happen at once. There was only a few months difference between the day I received notification that I was supposed to be a half-Jew and the fall of the Third Reich. I witnessed the latter in Berlin with the occupation of the city by the Red Army. The Russian occupation was gruesome, especially the rapes. I saw that there were suicides in our neighborhood, and so on. But I also experienced a great deal of spontaneous kindness at Russian hands.

The occupation by the Americans was completely different. I remember exactly how their indoctrination led to a totally different approach. My mother had just returned from Auschwitz. She spoke very good English; she'd been engaged to a British officer at one time. She worked as a translator for the Americans and presented her papers showing that she'd been at Auschwitz. The Americans had a good laugh at the papers, said, "All Germans were Nazis," and confiscated our belongings. This implanted, indoctrinated hate for the Germans has also remained in my memory.

WALTER KNAPPE*

"There was no spirit, no sense of pride."

I was part of a group of disabled prisoners of war exchanged from Canada in January 1944. I thought we were returning to the country I remembered. I was devastated to discover the striking changes that had occurred in Germany. My trust in the country was shaken. There was no spirit, no sense of pride.

In January 1945, I was sent to the Luftwaffe officers' school. There we learned how to sail, how to dance, and how to give orders. The graduation dinner consisted of unpeeled potatoes with herring. We had learned how to wield a knife and fork skillfully so that we wouldn't swallow any bones. Then, as a lieutenant, I was sent to a fighter aircraft control station at Küstrin on the Oder. This was at the end of March.

With the Eastern front collapsing, I was sent to Berlin and assigned Hitler Youth as soldiers. We fought tanks with bazookas. There was a great danger that my eager Hitler Youth would run into Russian fire without even being able to fire their bazookas properly. I was so glad when our mission was called off, and I could release them all. Only too well could I understand their crazy enthusiasm; they went to their doom in the belief that they were fighting for Germany.

---

* Biography on page 74.

The willingness of the soldiers to make sacrifices was unlimited. I remember an event that occurred when we were coming back from our last mission. We possessed maps of subterranean Berlin. We were thus able to move from cellar to cellar under the city. We had to fight in subway tunnels, and that is the worst possible sort of combat. You see only flashes of fire coming at you: flame throwers and tracer ammunition. The battle in Berlin was hopeless.

During our retreat, we ran into a trap. As we were marching ("marching" is somewhat exaggerated; we were running), we were shot at from the left with sub-machine guns. Many of us fell, and a great rage and despair overcame me. I saw Russians, threw down my gun, and slipped into a cellar I saw in front of me. In the cellar I saw German civilians with their hands above their heads. They shouted at me that they had already been searched, and that I should leave. Otherwise I would be shot. I went out, climbed the stairs, and practically fell into the arms of the Russian soldiers.

Two Russian officers, breath smelling of a mixture of alcohol and perfume, stood before me. I was put into a POW camp.

HELMUT KOHL

Born 1930; as a youth in the Palatinate near Ludwigshafen, lived through Allied bombardments; after the war became a politician and leader of the Christian Democratic Party; Chancellor of the Federal Republic of Germany since 1982.

"I can still see how they lay there with blue faces."

I have several very strong memories from the war. The first is from September 1, 1939. The night before, my father had been called up for military service. On that day, we—my mother, my brother, who was to die in the war, and I were downtown, standing on the Rhine bridge between Ludwigshafen and Mannheim. We saw the first refugees of World War II go by; they were peasants from the South Palatinate who had been evacuated. They had miserable nags—at that time they didn't have tractors—and a few cows. A calf followed behind. There were bedclothes piled up on a small wagon. The people were all very serious, and many women were crying. I was nine at the time.

Another recollection is the most indelible of my war memories. Beginning in 1943, the air attacks against Ludwigshafen reached such proportions—the Ludwigshafen/Mannheim area was one of the most heavily bombarded targets—that we had student fire brigades. These brigades took turns sleeping at the school, and while they were on duty there they had to work continuously putting out fires.

I can remember helping shovel aside debris of a destroyed house in order to reach the people trapped in the cellar. I was perhaps 12 or 13 at the time. When we got to the people, they were dead—not from the bombing, but from the lack of oxygen. To this day, I can still see how they lay there with blue faces from having suffocated. When I go past this site now—another house stands on it—I can't help but think of this scene. I was an anti-aircraft helper when the Americans came at the beginning of May 1945. We just started for home. We walked on the railroad tracks, because the roads were full of Americans. We had our Hitler Youth winter uniforms on, since we had no civilian clothes. We spent the night on straw in a signal box. The next morning we heard the news that the war was over.

HERBERT MITTELSTÄDT

Born 1927; an anti-aircraft auxiliary; was a "true believer" in spite of a strong Catholic upbringing; became a journalist after the war; resides in Berlin.

"I truly believed we would be the victors."

I was drafted as a Luftwaffe helper on February 15, 1943. I was sixteen years old. This was a para-military form of military service. As incredible as it sounds, our regular school teachers came out to our firing positions and held 22 hours of classroom instruction a week, literally between the guns. You can imagine how excited we were about that. We were more than happy when an air raid warning occurred either before or during such a session because that meant that class would be cancelled.

The first time I was actually aware of a KZ (concentration camp) was when I was a Luftwaffe helper. We were stationed in Falkensee, a suburb of Berlin. The KZ was very close to our anti-aircraft emplacement. This was not an extermination camp. I believed that those detained there were being kept in isolation and apart from the rest of our nation's people because they were criminals and homosexuals. I only found out about Auschwitz and Buchenwald after the war had ended. I presume that had I heard about the extermination camps and other atrocities going on during the war, I probably wouldn't have believed it. If anything, the one thing the National Socialist movement succeeded in was to instill, especially in the young generation, a strong and conscientious feeling of nationalism and belonging.

In 1943, I believed without a doubt that we would ultimately win the war. We considered our defeat in Stalingrad to be only a technical problem. One could read from the military reports that a "planned retreat" had begun on the various fronts. In addition, the Africa Corps had begun to make its move. We boys thought that they were the absolute heroes. We dreamed about fighting under Rommel's leadership in Africa, where it was warm. We found it fantastic when we saw films of soldiers frying eggs on the hot tanks.

I truly believed we would be the victors. This was stimulated by the fact that the parents of many of my classmates had fairly high positions within the Nazi Party hierarchy. Although we did receive some political schooling, we did not take it too seriously. Our battery commander, who was responsible for it, often took all of us to the movies instead. Still, none of us ever doubted Germany's ultimate victory.

I began to have my first doubts about the outcome of the war toward the latter part of 1944, when our forces began to suffer major defeats. After the invasion, we surrendered Paris. Enemy troops were moving in closer and closer to the Reich's borders. The Russians were at our back door. Nevertheless, we remained under the influence of Goebbels' propaganda, and continued to believe that Hitler still had one more super weapon left for us to employ. When the first V-1s were launched against England, we were convinced that this was the beginning of an offensive phase engaging a series of "secret weapons" which would turn the tide of the war for us.

On January 6, 1945, I was drafted into the army and sent to a sector opposite French troops. We were told that the first French attack wave consisted of blacks from Senegal who supposedly carried knives between their teeth, and never took prisoners. They supposedly immediately cut the throat of any German they caught.

We retreated systematically, and by the end of April, ended up in what is now part of Austria, Vorarlberg. On May 1, 1945, our lieutenant approached the 25 of us, and gravely announced, "I no longer believe that there is any way possible for us to win this war. I am going to discharge you, and whoever wants to, can continue to fight with me as a 'Werewolf.'" Only one guy raised his hand. His family was in East Prussia, and the possibility of his ever returning was extremely slim anyway. Since the lieutenant only had a single ally, he said, "The whole thing is not worth it. I'm going to discharge myself as well!"

HUGO STEHKÄMPER*

"An eight-year-old had destroyed a tank."

In February 1945, two months before my 16th birthday, I was drafted into the *Volkssturm*. They stuck us in the old black SS uniforms which you hadn't seen anymore during the war, brown Organization Todt coats, and blue air force auxiliary caps. We thought we looked like scarecrows. And we were ashamed of the French steel helmets they slapped on us. This didn't fit the picture of a German soldier for us. As boys of 15, well, if we were going to be called up, we wanted to be real German soldiers, not imitation French.

I never did any fighting. All the same, in April 1945 I ended up as an Amercan prisoner. I didn't have any weapons, but they found military maps on me which I'd picked up because I thought they were pretty! Because of that I was accused of being a "Werewolf."

I was interrogated by an American officer who spoke very good

* Biography on page 218.

German. A soldier sat behind me, a big, strong man with a thick, black beard. Whether it was part of the interrogation, or he just got excited, I don't know, but this man jumped up, put his pistol to my head, and screamed "You Werewolf!" Up to then he hadn't said a word and as you can imagine, I believed it was all over for me.

Then I was put through a second interrogation that ended with a similar result. Apparently I answered questions too poorly or too clumsily. I can't exactly praise myself for holding up very well. I was 15 years old.

Then I was put in with other POWs. We found ourselves in a stream of prisoners marching to the fields along the Rhine. I only had a sweater to protect me from the pouring rain and the cold. There just wasn't any shelter to be had. You stood there, wet through and through, in fields that couldn't be called fields anymore—they were ruined. You had to make an effort when you walked to even pull your shoes out of the mud.

Today it's incomprehensible to me how we could stand for many, many days without sitting, without lying down, just standing there, totally soaked. During the day we marched around, huddled together to try to warm each other a bit. At night we stood because we couldn't walk and tried to keep awake by singing or humming songs. Again and again someone got so tired his knees got weak and he collapsed. Then the whole group would fall over, and everybody bitched because they'd fallen in the mud.

Later I was sent to a special camp in France for youths under 18. I remember an eight-year-old there who had destroyed a tank with a bazooka. He was a bright little kid, a child who wanted to do something against Germany's enemies. The American camp commander took him in so that he didn't have to live under prison conditions.

We were transported through Belgium, and there we experienced real hatred. When we marched through Namur in a column seven abreast, there was also a Catholic procession going through the street. When the people saw the POWs, the procession dissolved, and they threw rocks and horse shit at us. From Namur, we went by train in open railroad cars. At one point we went under a bridge, and railroad ties were thrown from it into the cars filled with POWs, causing several deaths. Later we went under another overpass, and women lifted their skirts and relieved themselves on us. We found that much less dangerous than the railroad ties.

KLAUS MESSMER

Born 1929; an active "Werewolf" at the war's end; became an industrial engineer; lives at Lake Constance.

"We really did some pretty dumb things."

It was so depressing for us to see the first French military vehicles drive into our town. For us "Werewolves," it was only natural that we resist in any way we could, and we really did some pretty dumb things. We snuck out and made our way to the vehicles. We smashed dashboards to pieces, and poured sand by the handfuls into the gas tanks. After a while we decided to change our tactics and began to blow them up. We would ride our bikes the 12 miles to the Siegfried Line, where we knew our soldiers had planted land mines only a few days earlier. There were gaps and holes all over the place, and we could see exactly where the mines had been planted. This was crazy, but we would carefully pull the mine out and take off the lid. Then, holding the pin steady with two fingers, we would deactivate the bomb. Next, we would remove the detonator to take with us. We took hundreds of them and used them to blow up French military vehicles.

Our church youth group had a small cabin in the mountains. We used it as our main headquarters and as a place to store our weapons, hand grenades, carbines, and all of the explosives we had removed from along the Rhine. And it was there we planned all of our attacks.

We soon realized that our efforts to resist had done absolutely nothing to change anything. A new era had begun and there was nothing we could do about it. It wasn't until much later that we were capable of realizing and assessing what we had done. And I don't regret it. I strongly believe that our reaction was logical, especially when you consider what our country was like before the war and the way we were raised.

THEO LOCH*

"Of my 32 classmates, only 13 returned."

After the war came the big question: Why did I join the Waffen-SS?

The best answer might be for me to read the letter that I wrote to my parents on February 14, 1940. As a minor, I was required to obtain my parents' permission to volunteer for the Waffen-SS. The passage from my letter to my parents reads as follows: "Everybody says that the Labor Service is the worst of all. In addition, we would have to start in the winter, and then we would have to go into the army for two years, perhaps even after the war, since we know that the war is going to be over very soon. . . . For this reason, and for others as well, the school director made the decision that all of us who are still here should join the SS in April. The Waffen-SS will take us as officer candidates. You will surely see that the director of our school was right when he ordered us to join the SS this spring, and that this move, like everything I have done here thus far, will turn out to be very useful." That was how I came to join the Waffen-SS.

In August 1940, I was assigned to the training battalion of the *Leibstandarte* in Berlin. There I received recruit training. In March 1941, I was sent to the field regiment of the LAH, the *Leibstandarte Adolf Hitler*. There I served in the campaign in Greece. To my great

---

* Biography on page 10.

surprise, we received orders to attack the Soviet Union on June 21, 1941. I fought in Russia until I was seriously wounded in hand-to-hand combat in the Ukraine that autumn.

I was sent back to Vienna, to a hospital, where I remained for several months recuperating from my wounds. After a short period in the depot battalion of the *Leibstandarte,* I was transferred to the SS cadet school in Bad Tölz, where I took part in a four-month officers' training course. Then I returned to Berlin and was transferred to the SS junior officers' school in Lauenburg, in Pomerania.

In the summer of 1944, I was assigned to the Western front to what was called the XII SS Corps. In reality it was a mixed bag, SS in name only. I was assigned to command an "assault company." A fifth of my men were Waffen-SS, a fifth were U-boat crewmen, the rest were air force and infantry. But we were all fighting the same war. It ended for me when I was badly wounded one last time.

After Stalingrad, a great deal of questioning went on even within the SS itself. I can honestly say that many heretical, critical conversations took place with greater ease in the Waffen-SS then elsewhere in Germany. We said to ourselves, "They can't do anything to us—we're part of the same unit."

The Waffen-SS was in no way homogeneous. There were idealists who were fresh out of high school. There were those who had been drafted. There were the many foreigners, the ethnic Germans, and then there were the "Legions"—the Dutch, the Walloons, the French, and the Italians—it was indeed an interesting mixture. The overriding thought on everyone's mind was, "When are we going to get to the front; where will the next mission, the next test at the front be?"

I would like to quote a short passage from Kogon's *SS Staat,* a sentence I subscribe to one hundred percent. It says that the Waffen-SS "was an arm that Hitler created for his policies, which, however, consisted of young idealists and the sorts of people who work as mercenaries." In addition, as the Waffen-SS grew, it thought of itself more and more as a fourth branch of the Wehrmacht. Its members had special privileges as far as armament was concerned. They were the first to receive camouflage jackets; they had outstanding equipment; and they knew they had the honor of being used wherever they were desperately needed. "They were born to die."

Basically, two things are important for me today in my position concerning National Socialism. The first is that, of my 32 classmates, only 13 returned. The rest were mercilessly used as cannon fodder. The second, which devastates me even more, is that the Gauleiter and the other party big shots, who were initially in the internment camps with me after the war, were separated out. When they met us 22-year-olds who had returned from the front (and my wounded leg was still aching), they more or less said, "Hitler? Who *was* that anyway? We were never Nazis; we were always against all that. If you had not fought so well, all of this would never have happened." And I stood before them and thought to myself, "These are the men who, as party functionaries, convinced the German people to keep on going, and now that they are behind barbed wire, they maintain they never knew anything about it at all."

That was when I made the big break from what had happened. That was when I truly recognized how grossly betrayed we had actually been. A generation had been raised to die—to pass the big test—and then it was betrayed.

GUSTAV SCHÜTZ

Born 1921; lost an arm, but led teenagers into combat at war's end; became a teacher after the war; lives in Fulda.

" 'Operation Tank Destroyer Brigade' was ridiculous."

After the amputation of my left arm in February 1942, I was assigned to service in the Hitler Youth along with about thirty other wounded soldiers. I was in the Hofgeismar area where several *Landdienst* camps were set up, each for about thirty boys between the ages of fourteen and fifteen.

Everything went fine until 1945, when the U.S. and British armies came closer. I'd gotten married in February. On March 30, we were ordered to evacuate. The boys got everything ready for the march. I found them in a downright war-like mood. Many of them had gotten weapons from farming women, who gladly wanted them out of the house—either because they thought they might cause them difficulties with the Americans or because they didn't want them to fall into the hands of the foreign POW workers. The boys proudly displayed their air rifles and small-caliber weapons.

After two days' march we reached the training complex. They had rations and accommodations for us. Apart from ourselves, there were about sixty boys and fifty girls all between 15 and 16 years old. They'd already been on the road for weeks. In addition, there were high-ranking Hitler Youth and BdM leaders, some of them with their families, a police unit of about 100 men, and a Wehrmacht unit with several assault guns. One officer told us that the American army had broken through with armor, but that they were trying to close the breach.

My wife and I set out on the march to the Harz Mountains with over a hundred of these young men. In a train station restaurant in Hattorf, we heard a radio announcement. It spoke as if the German army was still intact and still had the terrible "wonder weapons" at its disposal. When I heard all this I was deeply ashamed that someone could think us stupid enough to actually believe such reports. I felt betrayed and cheated, my love for the fatherland shamelessly misused. The kids were thrilled with the idea of fighting as 'soldiers' for the final victory. We could hope to bring them back safely, if only the war would end soon.

The boys were now stuck into German army uniforms, most of them too big—pants and jackets that had been mended in every way possible, army and air force uniforms mismatched. The only thing there was no shortage of were steel helmets though not everyone even had a belt. Everyone had a gun, but the guns were an odd collection of different origin. Officers and sergeants got pistols and machine pistols. Each company got two horse drawn carts for baggage transportation.

Dusk had already set in when the local Gauleiter declared that we were the newly formed "Tank Destroyer Brigade Kurhessen" and part of the *Volkssturm*. He was dressed in an army major's uniform and gave a short speech from a podium. He told us that our assignment was to prevent enemy tanks from entering the Harz Mountains at all costs.

Although we thought that "Operation Tank Destroyer Brigade" was ridiculous, and foresaw that going into action with a bunch of totally untrained boys was suicide, we didn't dare refuse. In the afternoon we got bazooka lessons, and following that we got instructions on how to behave during fighter-bomber attacks.

As we marched down the forest paths, the column fell silent. Suddenly a lieutenant stood in front of us, ordered the other noncom to make sure that no one lagged behind, and waited with me until there was some distance between us and the column. Then he said, "Schütz, you're the only one I've known for a while and believe I can trust. There's already been one Children's Crusade, and none of those children came back. I don't want to be responsible for being involved in this one. We've got to prevent a bloodbath when we meet American tanks. What do you think?" I told him that I considered it suicide to take these inexperienced boys into battle against well-trained troops.

We'd reached the town of Heiligthal and had just settled in, when suddenly a sergeant I didn't know and our platoon leader rushed over from the neighboring garden shouting, "The tanks are in town, run!" We couldn't see the tanks, but my wife and I ran after our platoon leader into a cherry orchard. When shots whizzed by us, I pulled my wife to the ground and we pressed ourselves to the earth, totally out of breath, our hearts beating wildly. The two platoon leaders got up again and ran, fountains of dust spraying around them. I dragged my wife up, and we ran again too, until we were shot at. We hit the dirt. We continued to jump up and dive down again until we finally reached a valley that offered shelter. MG bursts brought branches down on us. We looked beyond the village, which was hidden from view, to the landscape opposite us—and we couldn't believe what we saw. On the meadows and fields more than a hundred tanks were neatly aligned in two rows. Trucks drove along the roads supplying the tanks with gasoline.

We hadn't gone far when we were confronted with a hideous sight.

Shredded tents, equipment strewn about, dead men with bloated stomachs, and the repulsive sweet smell of decay were everywhere. They wore brown Labor Service uniforms with yellow armbands: *Deutsche Wehrmacht*. But there were no weapons lying about. This was a Labor Service camp that had been torn to pieces.

On a field we saw traces of tank treads and several knocked-out American tanks. So there'd been fighting here too. We didn't see any dead near the guns and tanks on our side, but on the other side of the road more than a hundred dead Labor Service men were lying in long rows—all with bloated stomachs and bluish faces. We had to throw up. Even though we hadn't eaten for days, we vomited.

We ran away from this gruesome place as fast as we could. A woman in the next village told us what happened. A flak battery manned by Labor Service men had camouflaged itself to allow the tank spearhead to go past in order to attack the rest of the column. But a man from that village had betrayed these plans to the Americans. So the leading tanks started through the village, then turned immediately while the next tanks opened fire from the cover of the forest. Even though the Labor Service men were surrounded, the Americans suffered considerable losses. So after the Labor Service men had been taken prisoner, the Americans shot them as partisans and put their corpses by the roadside as a deterrent.[1]

Wolfhager and the boys decided to head home. Horst Ehrlich, my wife, and I went on. We breakfasted on cough syrup and sugar, and marched for hours and hours with empty, rumbling stomachs. We looked as ragged as hobos. The people planting potatoes in the fields were mistrustful and unfriendly. So were the people in the towns. We no longer dared even to beg for food. Here on the country roads U.S. military vehicles were less common than on the main highways. But finally a half loaf of bread was thrown to us from an enemy truck. We left it lying because we thought we had to show our pride. But after we'd gone about 50 yards I went back and picked it up. "Let's not be silly," I said.

---

[1] The Geneva Convention in effect during World War II required a visible sign of combatant status as a condition of being treated as a prisoner of war. An armband was usually considered enough to fulfill the legal requirement. In practice, whether surrender was accepted under these circumstances often depended heavily on the number of casualties the victors suffered during the fight.

From time to time along the way, U.S. soldiers threw us small packages with crackers and cheese. That's what we lived on. We walked about thirty miles a day. One morning it was so bitterly cold that we awoke quite early in the barn where we'd spent the night. It must've been about 6:00 A.M. I peered through a chink in the barn doors and couldn't believe my eyes. About 50 yards away, an SS unit was marching past single-file, heavily armed with MGs and machine pistols, about 60 men! Staying under cover in the bushes on a low slope, they gradually disappeared.

We went back to the road and started walking. A U.S. soldier threw us a package, and among the crackers, chocolate, and candies were cigarettes and matches. I lit a cigarette and after the first puff I was dizzy, with green and blue spots dancing in front of my eyes.

CHAPTER 16

Gulags West and East

Surrendering is arguably the most dangerous thing any soldier can do. Its experiences in Russia made the Wehrmacht determined to avoid deepening "the filth of war" in other theaters. Particularly in North Africa, a kind of chivalry developed between the combatants—a chivalry that paid dividends in Tunisia, Italy, and northern France, when hundreds of thousands of Germans became Allied prisoners of war.

Until mid-1944, most of these prisoners were sent to the U.S. or Canada, both for security and because it was easier to feed them. Their initial reaction was usually shock. Some prisoners looked around them and asked how Germany could even have thought of challenging such resources. Others turned inward, believing Hitler's genius and the Wehrmacht's skill at arms would still somehow produce final victory. American efforts at re-education and re-indoctrination produced, at best, limited results.

With Allied victory seemingly no more than weeks away in the summer of 1944, prisoners were increasingly held on the continent of Europe for eventual postwar repatriation. As their numbers increased, the level of treatment declined in the early stages of captivity. German prisoners at this stage of the war were also influenced by wishful thinking. Images of the good life in Anglo-American hands were widespread, developed partly as a contrast to the Russian alternative and partly as a reason for continuing to fight. But realities of poor food, no shelter, and orders punctuated with a rifle butt could be disconcerting. Until Stalingrad, falling into Russian hands was perceived as amounting to an automatic death sentence. The Soviet system that had murdered millions of its own people and that was now engaged in an enormous war, had few resources to spare for prisoners. Nor did Stalin care for the lives of Russians in German hands. His own son died in captivity. By 1943, however, the number of German prisoners had reached critical mass. There were enough of them to be useful for propaganda purposes, and as labor to rebuild what the Wehrmacht had destroyed. At the same time the POW community was large enough to be somewhat self-sustaining even in the context of the Soviet Gulag.

This did not make entering or enduring Russian captivity any easier. Prisoners of the Americans might be disturbed when the first meal did not include steak. Men surrendering on the Eastern front were relieved not to be shot out of hand. They were grateful for a slice of bread, for elementary medical care, for gestures of sympathy from new masters who themselves had little or nothing. Few prisoners taken in the East returned home in the weeks after Germany's surrender. Instead, they were shipped to Russia's interior, becoming, along with many deported civilians, part of a system of forced labor that took on renewed life in the postwar years. They were released haphazardly. Not until 1956 did Konrad Adenauer's government negotiate a formal agreement for the return of the surviving POWs. Thousands of others, civilians as well as soldiers, disappeared forever into unmarked graves.

JOSEF HÜHNERBACH*

"We didn't live badly as soldiers. But the Americans! They lived like gods!"

I was captured at Anzio, Italy. We had fortified positions when the Americans came with bombers, hundreds of them. And then the fighters came and shot up our trenches. At dawn our company commander deserted to the Americans. We said to ourselves: If our leader takes off, why should we stay around and get our heads shot off? We weren't crazy. First we get it pounded into our heads to hang in there and fight, and then the commander runs away. He just took off, deserted. The Americans attacked with tanks, and our tanks fought back. It was a heavy tank battle.

I was taken prisoner by the Americans. Then it was off to America. I thought to myself on the way that we didn't live badly as soldiers. But the Americans! They lived like gods!

We arrived in Norfolk, Virginia, and from there I was taken to Pennsylvania, Texas, Arkansas, and finally to Louisiana. It was real hot there. The guys that worked in the woods would bring back snakes and baby raccoons. We could play soccer, tennis, or put on plays in a big hall. It was great.

The only people who bothered us were German paratroopers who came in fresh from France. They came with all their decorations and medals that they wouldn't allow to be taken away. And if you wanted to go to English lessons, they hassled you and called you a traitor. They still believed in victory.

We picked cotton and earned money. With that money we could go to a big camp store and buy everything. I bought rings and crosses—everything 14 carat, I still have them—and tobacco and stuff. We were allowed to take 50 or 55 pounds of stuff from America back to Germany.

---

* Biography on page 134.

They treated us very well. There was an American Catholic priest there too, and I was his altar boy.

ERHARD HECKMANN

Born 1912; taken prisoner by the U.S. army in Italy in 1944; worked as a journalist after the war and lives in Cologne.

"Every document also went to the Soviet Embassy."

We landed at the 52nd Street Pier in New York in the fall of 1944, climbed aboard one of those sight-seeing boats, and were taken across the Hudson River to New Jersey. An all-glass boat—we had never seen anything like it. When we reached shore we were ordered to board a waiting train, where there were waiters dressed in white. A three-day ride took us to Camp Forrest, Tennessee. Given the circumstances, the rations were very good, but more was still to come. At Camp Forrest we were put into a normal American barracks camp. At first, we just waited to see what they would do with us. When we saw the kitchen our eyes almost bulged out of our heads. What we saw in the refrigerator was simply unbelievable to us: crates of frozen chicken, slabs of meat, and so on. We had never seen anything like it in our lives. We got our first meal, and soon we settled into everyday camp life. We had different jobs like cleaning the barracks and weaving camouflage nets.

We were rented out to farmers in Alabama; I think the farmers had to pay eight dollars per POW per day. At one point we underwent a selection process. They wanted to find people with technical experience who spoke English in order to analyze German technological documents. Those of us who passed were sent to a German Document Evaluation Center. The material was all about Peenemünde back then. We summarized and translated these documents.

The head of the Evaluation Center was an American major. There were also civilian army employees, and it was all funded by the industrial firm General Electric. The Americans were amazed at the results. Rocket technology had existed in America since the 1920s, but they had never considered the possibilities of military applications. The translated documents were made available to interested parties via a distributor in Washington. As a result, every document also went to the Soviet Embassy, and the Russians helped themselves.

ROBERT VOGT*

"I saw black American soldiers for the first time."

As a prisoner of war I ended up in Rouen, where I saw black American soldiers for the first time. When we saw them we were scared stiff and thought, "Oh Lord, now we're done for." This feeling came from—and here I must say that we were lied to in the Third Reich—being told these people were subhuman, barbarians, etc. Even at school we were told that. So we were terribly afraid. But my fear disappeared 20 minutes later, after I'd spoken with a black American.

He said that in a little while we were going to unload some ships. The trucks were already arriving and I said, in English, "We are very hungry." In fact, we were half-starved when we were transported out of the last camp. I was down to 98 pounds and had stuffed towels into my clothes to make it look like I could still work. Whenever I moved too quickly everything went black in front of my eyes.

---

* Biography on page 253.

The man looked at me and didn't say anything but "come." He put me in a weapons carrier and drove me to the field kitchen. He loaded it up with all kinds of food and we drove back. We were a group of about 50 men, and when I said, "Food, boys!" they dropped everything, ran up, and used their hands to shovel it into their mouths like animals.

I must say that I came to consider these black soldiers as our protectors, which is when I began to have serious doubts about the Third Reich's propaganda. Here I had proof that we had been lied to. Okay, when they got drunk they did some pretty crazy things, but they weren't brutes. We liked them better than the white Americans. They said to us, "We're black slaves, you're white slaves." They were very kind to us. This major experience with the blacks made me wonder: If what they told us about blacks was a lie, what else had they lied to us about?

HERRMANN BLOCKSDORFF*

"You get your rations today from the best fed army in the world."

On April 24, 1945, I was taken prisoner by the Americans and brought to the Sinzig POW camp. There were 1,000 men to a camp. They were split up into groups of 100, and then into groups of ten. Each group of ten was given the outdoor space of a medium-sized living room. We had to live like this for three months, no roof over our heads. Even the badly wounded only got a bundle of straw. And it rained on the Rhine. For days. And we were always in the open. People died like flies. Then we got our first rations, and I swear to God, I'm telling the truth: we got one slice of bread for ten men. Each

---

* Biography on page 264.

man got a tiny strip of that one slice. In addition to that we got, per ten men, a tablespoon of milk powder, coffee, grapefruit powder, and one tablespoon of sugar. Per man, that was a strip of bread, and a teaspoon of the above mentioned powders. And this went on for three long months. I only weighed 90 pounds.

The dead were carried out every day. Then a voice would come over the loudspeaker: "German soldiers, eat slowly. You haven't had anything to eat in a long time. When you get your rations today from the best fed army in the world, you'll die if you don't eat slowly."

That was the end of April. The bombers continued to fly over us. We looked like scarecrows. We looked like the concentration camp victims in the films they showed us later on. On June 21, we were discharged and brought home by train in cattle cars.

I had my own little house. How happy I was that it was still standing! When I rang the bell, Americans came to the door—my wife's new friends. They asked me what the hell I wanted.

KARL BAUER

Born 1919; battalion commander in the German infantry; was a POW in Russia until 1948; owns an art gallery; lives in Wuerttemberg.

"Banishment, jail, punishment camp, it's been the Russian fate for centuries."

On November 3, 1937, I joined the infantry. I wanted to get my military service over with as quickly as possible so that I could go on to the university. When the war broke out I was a sergeant in the reserves. During the war I was a company headquarters squad leader, platoon leader, company officer, company commander, and battalion commander—roughly in that order. And I was always an infantry officer.

In the spring of 1945, I was active in the defense of Danzig, the Hela Peninsula. On May 8, I became a POW. I was one of the last Germans to leave Hela, and I got an excellent impression of our Soviet escorts. I had a VW amphibious car, and Major Kuno Bajev, an Uzbek, accompanied me. At the end of the column there was a horse cart with a sergeant and two Red Army soldiers. There was no way to watch us, since there were 1,600 of us. Mainly, they served to protect us from reprisals by Soviet troops in the Danzig area. They did so in a truly exemplary manner—very friendly, obliging, and polite all the way to the POW camp. The first immediate impression I had of a Soviet front officer was a positive one. Major Bajev had been chief of a headquarters battery in an artillery regiment during the whole war and—this happened in the Soviet army—he'd never had a single day of leave in four and a half years of war. He'd never been home.

Our regiment was from Danzig, and as we marched down the main street—the same one we marched down for the victory parade after the French campaign—the whole population of Danzig, or what was left of it, stood by the roadside. And we marched in singing—the Soviets practically insisted—with me in my VW reviewing the parade.

It was grotesque. I had a sergeant and many other soldiers who marched along holding hands with their wives and children, because some of their families lived in Danzig. After all, we were the Danzig regiment. And the incredible thing was that the German soldiers actually believed they'd be home by Christmas. This was a rumor that was systematically spread. Even worse was the rumor that British warships had arrived in the Danzig harbor and that the British would make sure that the German POWs could go home right away. So with these kinds of rumors circulating, everybody marched into imprisonment like good boys. Whereas I knew all along—I don't know why—that we'd be there a long time. But it would've been completely futile to try to do anything about it. It became a long march. A march that lasted many years.

I was interrogated by an NKVD state security officer, who accompanied me throughout the questioning during the following months. I was asked about a unit, about officers and men, about places in the central sector of the Eastern front that I'd never heard of. I was never even assigned to the central sector.

At the end of this questioning I was asked about a Private Ayring. I said I didn't know anybody by that name. And then I was led out to be taken back to my barracks, and I saw a German soldier standing in the dark hallway. I looked at him and knew right away—that's PFC Ayring. The one I just said I didn't know. Ayring had been transferred to my unit eight days before the capitulation because I'd had heavy losses in the last firefight and had insisted on replacements.

Well, that's how the story of my trial in the Soviet Union began. What I didn't know back then was that the Soviets were systematically searching for war criminals. It was quite a simple tactic; it's just that we were so naive we never got the message. Going into imprisonment, we'd all simply been asked about our military past: Where were you during the war? With which unit? And the Soviets had then prepared a list of all units which, in their opinion, had committed war crimes—and some, to be honest, had. Each of us had quite truthfully said where he'd been. Ayring had been with a replacement battalion on the Central front and had, in fact, taken part in the executions which were the subject of the trial.

And now I was accused of having ordered these executions! It was a really simple NKVD method. They told Ayring: "You were just a common soldier. Tell us who your commander was, and nothing happens to you. You were just following orders." And maybe Private Ayring just wasn't smart enough to see that it was a trap. He simply named—and given his acute distress I understand that today—an officer he knew. And that was me. He didn't know anybody else.

So suddenly I was the accused Captain Bauer, Commanding Replacement Battalion X, a job I'd never had. The subject of the trial was real. What was wrong was that *I* was the accused. That was my problem.

First of all the NKVD tried to get me to confess by using physical pressure: hunger, beatings, a cold cell (it got down to 14 degrees), letting you sit there for days, hearing nothing, seeing no one. Actually it became clear to me when I thought about it later. This method brings you to the brink of what human existence means to a West European. And when you've been driven to the brink of what human existence means to you, you might just tend to collapse and say, "What's the point?"

After I'd been cooped up with up to 60 Russians in one cell, I began to see the NKVD and later the KGB as a Soviet system that had evolved throughout history. It had variables, ideological variables. But basically nothing had changed. I can well remember being in a cell with a Soviet teacher. He spoke good German and said, "Basically we are seeing the repetition of what our fathers and grandfathers have gone through: banishment, jail, punishment camp, it's been the Russian fate for centuries."

I'm sure I survived because of two things. I understood pretty quickly how the system worked; and understood that no matter what, I'd be dead in the end—the death sentence was still in effect back then. If I'd admitted to what I hadn't done, the death sentence would have been mandatory.

The German was in a completely different situation from the imprisoned Soviet citizen. Soviet families could bring food through the prison office once a week. I got nothing! I was completely dependent on prison food, which consisted of a half-pint of hot water in the morning, a bit of bread each day, and twice a half-pint of watery soup per day. Physically you can stand that for about three months. For seven months I didn't have any underwear, no socks, no shirt, and no change of clothes. Today I can't even imagine living like that.

When I was interned in that infamous concrete bunker at Minsk airport, I got first and second degree frostbite. That was after the first interrogation and before the major one when I got beaten so terribly. It was always around 20 degrees in that bunker; no blanket, no bed, no nothing. Thank God I had a coat left—a private who was interned with me had nothing but his uniform jacket, and that was split at the seams. And lice were an enormous problem. We got the usual running sores and so on.

When it got to the point where it looked like I'd die, the NKVD let up, because that would've ruined their whole objective. So I was taken to the hospital. It was equipped with German field beds, and there were about 300 to 350 very sick people in one huge room. I know this sounds outrageous, but you'll just have to believe me: there were about five to seven people per two beds. You just can't imagine it. Because my left foot and some of my left ribs had been broken in the beatings, I could only lie on my right side. It was really touching how my bed-mates managed that, because it was only possible to turn over if everybody did it at the same time.

It was typical that nobody ever asked—no one sharing that bed, no German doctor treating me, no German medic helping me—nobody asked why I was in such sorry shape. Everybody knew: NKVD. Everybody knew, but no one said a word. That was a taboo. If you got caught in the works of the NKVD, you were written off. You became a non-person. That was the terrible thing about it.

I've seen tragic cases of collapse in people from whom I would never have expected it, dishonorable to the point of shamelessness, just because of hunger. I saw that happen with a military judge, a colonel from Potsdam, I don't want to mention the name. Grotesquely enough, he was head of the prisoners' court—such a thing existed, almost perverse—and in that capacity he always decided on the rationing. Twice I personally caught him trying to allocate himself double rations. And double rations meant that somebody would go without. That's the kind of thing that was going on.

Finally the charges against me were withdrawn. The witness had been proved a liar. I was released in June 1948.

KURT MEYER-GRELL*

"We marched into Russian imprisonment singing."

Early in 1945 I was transferred to ground force training. We couldn't fly anymore; there was no more fuel. Then I was sent to Breslau. First I was given a Luftwaffe field company. Later I directed all the air operations of the so-called "Fortress Breslau." I was involved in blowing up the Kaiserstrasse and the pylons of the Hindenburg bridge to create a runway in the heart of the city. I personally participated on the ground in the cargo glider operations. We received the gliders and saw to it that ammunition and weapons were distributed to the right units. Until the end, ammunition was parachuted in large amounts.

On May 7, I was captured by the Russians. We were all beset by a sense of doom, because we were afraid of being put at the mercy of the Russians. Even in 1945, many of us believed the Russians didn't take prisoners. And I remember very clearly that when we were marched out and loaded into trucks, many of us expected to be taken into the nearest ditch and shot.

I recall how my men and I sang the national anthem from the bottom of our hearts in front of Breslau city hall on the evening of May 6. The next day we surrendered in good order, wearing our decorations and our sidearms. Officers were permitted to retain their weapons, but I'd thrown my service pistol into the river the day before. So we marched into Russian imprisonment singing.

At first we were very decently treated; there's no other way to put it. I saw Russian officers salute us as we marched past them through streets full of rubble. I was badly wounded at the time and walked with a cane. So I got special permission written in Russian which

---

* Biography on page 139.

entitled me to use a cane with a rubber tip. I greeted the Russian officers, my interrogators, with the Hitler salute. I was then asked if I was a fascist. I said I wasn't, that I'd only been in the Hitler Youth. I can only say that admitting this never got me into trouble.

JOSEF LÜCKING*

"The escapees had to be brought back dead or alive."

I was imprisoned by the Russians for four years. At first I was sent to Auschwitz. The camp was totally overcrowded, so people had to sleep on the bare ground. Columns of people were put to work dismantling the IG Farben plant nearby. The Russians took everything that wasn't nailed and bolted down and shipped it east. We even saw them take down roof tiles, load them in wagons, and send them east. After about three weeks in Auschwitz, we were put on a transport bound for Russia. Russian medical officers, women, were stationed at the camp gates and asked each person if he'd ever had typhoid, cholera, syphilis, or any other kind of contagious disease. They were terribly frightened of epidemics. We said, "No, we're healthy, and we'd like to stay together." We had misgivings about saying we had any kind of disease. Whoever did that would've been suspect from the outset: "Get rid of that man, shoot him!"

So we were loaded into train cars, 120 men into each. The toilet was at the head end of the car; it was just a hole sawed in the floor. The *Landser* were crammed right up to it, and whoever needed to go had to climb over at least four of them. They were lucky if they didn't get it on their face or back.

Our rations consisted of three drinking cups of flour soup a day.

* Biography on page 269.

That was it, and it stayed that way for weeks on end. But the situation wasn't much different on the other side either. To be honest, the Russians were suffering horribly from hunger themselves. I mean, I saw for myself in Moscow that the Russians would say they'd picked up so and so many dead off the streets that day, people who'd died of malnutrition in 1945.

We changed from narrow gauge to wide gauge tracks. Of 2,400 prisoners on the train, roughly 70 percent couldn't even make it from the one train to the other on their own two feet. We had to climb up a slope because the wide gauge track was set higher. We were stiff from lying or sitting still for so long. For example, if a person lying down wanted to turn over, the whole row had to turn over with him, it was that crowded. About 10 percent of the people died on our train.

As for life in camp itself, we worked in three shifts. Every ten days we got a free day which we had to spend in camp, within the barbed wired enclosure. There were three fences surrounding the camp. The first one was low barbed wire, the second high, and the third low again. The patch of ground between the fences had to be raked daily so that as soon as someone stepped over you could see the footprints.

Several people tried to escape and some even succeeded. They had themselves tipped out along with the coal, which was half-suicide in itself. They packed themselves into the coal carts. I later learned that two of them made it as far as Kiev and hid out in a town nearby. They were given food by the civilians. In the end, though, they were caught.

The guards on duty got five years of exile in Siberia if someone succeeded in escaping during their watch. The escapees had to be brought back dead or alive. Once the guards actually did the following: They shot two Russians coming back from a work shift, rolled them in a tarp, and left them at the camp gate for 24 hours. In the morning when we marched off to work, the camp commander addressed us: "I know you men want to go home, but before you try what these two did, you should think twice. In case anyone would like to try anyway, I'll leave the gate open tonight. He can go right ahead and try!" All three shifts had to march by those two dead men that day.

JOB VON WITZLEBEN*

**"One general in particular immediately
disguised himself as a supercommunist."**

Since my name is von Witzleben, I was under constant suspicion after July 20. I had to undergo some rather unpleasant experiences: interrogation by the Gestapo, a temporary discharge from the Wehrmacht, and other harassment. But because they couldn't prove a thing, I was transferred to the Eastern front to "prove myself" again.

At the beginning of 1945, I was in the besieged city of Königsberg when my corps' chief of staff told me that I was to be flown to Vienna. There, I was to be court-martialled for my peripheral involvement in the conspiracy. He said he believed it would end with my being executed. I could only save my life by surrendering to the other side.

At the beginning of April, I told Lieutenant Schröder, the officer in charge of the corps signal station, to make contact with the Russian division stationed opposite us. I had him say that I was threatened and intended to continue my fight against Hitler by taking advantage of their repeated offers to surrender. On April 9, 1945, a Russian officer made his way into Königsberg and took me on a pre-arranged route across the German lines to the Soviet side. A captain accompanied me. Lieutenant Schröder bade me farewell, wished me luck, and shot himself.

The Russians questioned me very thoroughly about the July 20 plot because their own information about it was still sketchy. I was taken to Moscow. Then, around early June 1945, I was transferred to Camp 27 at Krasnogorsk. I felt that becoming a member of the League of German Officers was both honorable and an unavoidable consequence of my actions. I joined it from deep conviction and with a good conscience.

---

* Biography on page 368.

My new camp was a center for prisoners with information particularly interesting to the Soviet leadership. It was also a place where people with special information in technical areas were sent: atomic researchers, electronics experts from Siemens, and so on. Many inmates were general staff officers or intelligence specialists. In 1945, approximately 150 generals from the Luftwaffe and the army arrived, in addition to a couple of admirals. After that, scores of technicians and engineers joined us, as well as prominent foreigners, and various international spies.

The Americans handed over the infamous Field Marshal Schörner, a brutal Nazi die-hard who was known for drumhead court-martials and summary executions, to the Soviets. He was sent to our camp. This was a dramatic event. There was a bunch of soldiers from Schörner's army group at camp, and word got around pretty fast that he was coming. He arrived dressed like a Bavarian farmer. There were about 200 POWs waiting for him alongside the main street of the camp with a rope. They wanted to string him up then and there. But the Soviet guards stepped in and drove us back to the barracks. They really gave us a beating for even daring to try this. They told us that Schörner was under Soviet protection, we didn't have the right to sentence him without a trial, and, furthermore, we could do that back in Germany. Surely we'd rather have him alive for that?

Schörner lived in a special barracks for generals. The ranks there went from brigadier-general to full general, and they kept exclusively to themselves. From a political standpoint, with the exception of a reasonable few, they were all completely stuck in the mind-set of the war. When they strolled along the camp road in the evening, entertaining each other with why Stalingrad had been attacked from the right and not the left, and other nonsense, reliving their lost victories and fighting battles, it was like watching a caricature, a cartoon. I didn't have much respect left for the generals at this point, but seeing this forced me to acknowledge that the military leadership had thrown our chances to the wind.

One general in particular immediately disguised himself as a supercommunist. He voluntarily removed his shoulder straps and decorations. He came to me right away and said, "Witzleben, it's time for us to learn new things and make a fresh start." And then he acted like a supercommunist. I didn't find his act very credible. He was only playing along to get back home as soon as possible.

I met many officers who were very rational without being in the National Committee. They did not choose to involve themselves politically, but in their hearts and minds, they were prepared to make a break with fascism. I knew a Captain von Wangenheim who had been the operations officer of a division on the Eastern front. When his division commander sent him orders sentencing Russian partisans to death, Wangenheim told him, "No, I refuse to sign these." That commander was hanged by the Russians. But the papers and documents of their headquarters proved that Wangenheim had done his best to resist these war crimes. What he did took a lot of courage, and the Soviets really admired him for it. He wasn't particularly friendly toward the Soviets, but they said he was an honorable man, a real German officer. He died in camp. There were openly fascist officers as well, who were still celebrating Hitler's birthday in 1946.

When the Russians disbanded the National Committee, we became aware of how the entire structure was changed. It became an anti-fascist POW camp committee, but it wasn't the National Committee anymore. That was over. It had served its purpose for the Soviets, and it was finished.

WOLFGANG SCHÖLER*

"Under the circumstances, we were treated pretty well."

Toward the end of the war, I was taken prisoner, along with the rest of my company, by Czech partisans. We were then handed over to the Russians. I must say that, under the circumstances, we were treated pretty well. The prison commander, a lieutenant colonel, was an old

---

* Biography on page 136.

soldier who still showed us a certain amount of respect. The Austrian troops tried to set themselves apart from us Reich soldiers. One time an Austrian major got a group of officers and privates together and tried to get special treatment from the commander. The prison commander told him, "You fought against us just like the Germans, and if you don't like something here, then I can always handle you like the cook handles raw potatoes!" I remember him saying that because it was so unique.

From Czechoslovakia we were taken on a long train trip to Rumania. From there we were sent in a big convoy of more than 1,000 people to an unknown destination in Russia. I could tell that we were headed in the direction of Rostov. On Christmas Day in 1945, we were even allowed to air out our blankets before being sent off again. We finally wound up in Azerbaijan, right on the border. In the distance we could see Mount Ararat.

Frankly, I don't think anyone needs to tell us about the living conditions in concentration camps, because they weren't much different from ours. For example—just to name some numbers—initially there were approximately 9,000 of us, and within a very short time, at least 1,800 had died very unpleasantly. We were physically exploited through bad treatment and the subtropical climate. I got very sick myself. But there again, I experienced something which confirms the kindness of the people in Russia: I was taken to a Russian hospital and cared for by Russian doctors and nurses. And I never had the impression that they would have treated us any differently had we been their own.

BRUNO WEIK

*Born 1927; became a Russian POW in 1945; is
a farmhand and lives in Gimmersdorf, Rhineland.*

"They liked us Germans!"

I was taken prisoner in Danzig. I was wounded and lying in an aid
station. When the Russians got close; we put out white flags with red
crosses. The Russians didn't mistreat us. They gave us shots and
dressings for our wounds. They showed no hate, and they didn't
threaten us. A young Russian doctor treated us very well, I might
add. Later other Russians told us "Yes, doctor sick, too much work,
tomorrow." They shared drinks with us. Most of the time they didn't
even know what was in the bottles. They had French cognac and let
everyone have a shot. But if an officer—a "politofficer" as they
say—came around, then they went out. When they were thirsty they
came back, saying, "Commissar no good."

They also gave us meat from dead horses killed in the fighting.
They did the best they could. You can't say they are third class
people, or that they are inferior. There were some intelligent people
among them. A lot of the noncoms and officers had even gone to
college. They could speak German. And when I was a prisoner in
Russia we had better chances with the Russian women than the
Russians themselves. The women said, "Russian man is pig. Goes to
a woman, second woman, here children, there children." But they
liked us Germans!

ALBERT SCHOEB*

I wasn't a POW in Russia itself; I was in Stettin, where, from August 1945 to January 17, 1947, I loaded ships. The Russians completely exploited Germany. They dismantled the factories and train lines, and sent locomotives, grain, and sugar to Russia. That was our job as POWs for one and a half years.

When I was in Stettin I once tried to speak to the camp commandant about being released on the basis of my French citizenship. You see, I knew that foreigners were being allowed to go home. He didn't even listen to me. He just said, "Alsace-Lorrainers are just as German as we are." Loud and clear. He was one of those men from the Seydlitz Army, the National Committee for a Free Germany. But I felt French, like all the other Alsatians drafted by the Nazis.

Thousands came home in 1945, others in 1946, and others in 1947. The last French POW that was released came home in 1954, from Siberia. He was from Strasbourg.

----

* Biography on page 116.

WOLFGANG KASAK*

**"I copied the dictionary onto five 'volumes'
of cigarette paper."**

One thing I will never forget about the march into captivity was the shooting of a 15-year-old boy right before my very eyes. He simply couldn't walk anymore, so a Russian soldier took potshots at him. The boy was still alive when some officer came over and fired his gun into the boy's ear.

It took all of our remaining strength to stay in the middle of the extremely slow-moving herds being driven east. We kept hearing the submachine guns whenever a straggler was shot.

We had our first encounter with helpful Russian people, who had had their own years of experience of the terrible aspects of life in the Soviet Union. After all, the Russian concentration camps were considerably older than the German ones. Once, as we were being transported into Russia in cattle cars, we stopped at a station where we were permitted to get out. The guards had orders to keep everything under control. A woman began bringing water to the soldiers who had gotten off the train. When people dying of thirst have a chance for water, a certain commotion occurs. The guards drove the woman away. But she kept on bringing water, bucket after bucket, to the places where no Russians were standing guard. I know now the Russian soldiers closed one eye and took a long time in following their orders to keep the woman from giving us something to drink.

When we got to the Volga River, we had to build our own camp. Anyone who didn't work was put into the "cooler," and 14 days in the cooler meant either certain death or pneumonia.

Then we were to go to yet another camp. I packed the few things I had, including a coat I had taken from a man who had died next to me

---

* Biography on page 480.

the night before. I hesitated to take the coat at first, but since winter was coming and I didn't have a coat of my own, I decided to take it after all. We were put onto a ship and sailed down the Volga River. It was beautiful—even starving prisoners couldn't help but admire the scenery. A third of the prisoners aboard died within two or three days.

After that I spent a year in a hospital that had been set up in a school. We received about a third of what a person needs to eat in order to survive. I figured I could survive by using my brains and learning Russian. I managed to get hold of a small instruction book for Russian soldiers and a small dictionary. I copied the dictionary onto five "volumes" of cigarette paper—50 papers to a volume. After six weeks I was made an interpreter in the kitchen. I knew about enough to tell "spoon" from "cleaver."

I became sick, so sick that my friends came to pay their last respects. I had a huge boil on my knee from which liters of pus were drained. But I survived.

I finally went home on November 16, 1946. The strongest impression I have from the time after I returned home is of how my father stood up to death. Soviet soldiers had dug six graves across from our house in Potsdam. They stood my father, my mother, my aunt, my father's secretary, and two other residents of the house in front of the graves in order to shoot them. The soldier who was to perform the execution lay in the doorway of our house behind a machine gun. But there was no officer present to give the order. My parents said good-bye to each other. Suddenly a Soviet soldier came up to my father and pulled him away from the open grave. Only a very long hour later did my mother finally learn what had happened. It turned out that there was a party going on across the street that needed a piano player! It was a macabre situation. My father improvising cheerful songs at the piano after almost being shot! He always said that from a certain point of view, life was over for him at that moment, even though nobody was shot after all.

BRUNHILDE POMSEL*

"You, you're always kissing!"

After spending a few days locked in a small apartment in Tempelhof, the Russians pulled us out of bed in the middle of the night and loaded us onto horsecarts—something I'll never forget. And there we sat, sliding back and forth, being driven out of the burning city of Berlin. We were first taken to some stables along with Vlassov soldiers, Russians who had fought on the German side. The stables were huge and the floor was covered with straw. We were lying in a row, and across from us, about six feet away, was an entire company of these Vlassov soldiers. One guard was sitting on a foot-stool holding a flashlight and was watching over us and the Vlassov soldiers. Darkness set in and we were supposed to sleep.

I started to doze off and was already half asleep when I felt someone touching my leg. I let out a scream. A Vlassov soldier was already half on top of me. He had tried to take advantage of the situation. Afterwards, I was almost sorry that I had screamed because the guard kicked the Vlassov soldier and then beat him up. It was really horrible. Now comes the cute part. The guard walked down the entire row of Germans carrying his flashlight. And then he picked out a really sweet boy, a 20-year-old German soldier, and told him to lie down next to me. He was nice. He told me he was definitely planning to escape. I told him he shouldn't even consider the idea.

We were then loaded into freight trains and taken to Posen where I stayed for six months, until November 1945. Now that was a real prison camp. People died there like flies. There was hardly anything to eat. It was incredibly filthy and the vermin were awful. I came down with typhoid. No one had even the slightest bit of hope that I would survive. I lost all the hair on my head. But I'm one tough cookie and came through after all.

---

* Biography on page 282.

Next, we were sent to Buchenwald, the camp that had originally been run by the Germans. Everything there was pretty well organized. We women spent a relatively decent time there. There were approximately 150 of us. We were the ones picked to do work like cleaning, sewing, peeling potatoes, and so forth. Nevertheless, I still had absolutely no idea why I was still being held prisoner. I was never told why the entire five years I was there. Once in a while and for form's sake, a Russian officer came by and asked if we had any complaints or wishes. Whenever we told him we'd like to go home or to be able to write a letter, he said, "The day will come when you will all be free to go home."

There was a Russian officer responsible for cultural affairs in the camp who was absolutely superb. He was a wonderful, understanding person who made a lot of things possible for us. He was very sympathetic toward young people, for example, Hitler Youth and 17 to 18 year olds who were locked up. Who knows why they were sent there? Anyway, the Russian officer set up a cultural group providing the young people with the opportunity to folk dance. The Russians themselves appeared to really enjoy such clowning around and theatrical kinds of things.

There were also some really talented people among the prisoners; for example, there were members of the Berlin Philharmonic Orchestra. Somehow they were able to get some instruments. Then there was also a prisoner who had been director of a Berlin orchestra. The story of how he ended up in Buchenwald is interesting. He was living in Berlin at the end of the war. Russians appeared at his house and told him they had arrested a certain individual who used him as a reference. The man arrested wanted him to testify on his behalf. So the director went along with them. The whole story was a trick and the director was imprisoned. He later died in the camp.

We started up a regular little theater group. They came to me and said, "You used to work for the radio, so you must be able to act." "Sure I can!" I took on the leading part in a comedy and became well-known throughout the entire camp. I was even popular among the Russians. The Russian sergeant whose job it was to keep an eye on us was really nice. In one of our plays, an art professor had to give me a big kiss on stage. Right in the middle of the performance, one of the Russians called out, "You, you're always kissing!"

The food we got to eat was probably the healthiest you can imagine. Morning, noon, and night we ate barley-broth. It was awful, but a doctor once told me, "You should be grateful. You couldn't have eaten anything healthier. In the event your diet is very one-sided, barley-broth is the best. Everything you need is in it."

All in all, I can say today that I have good memories of the time I spent in Buchenwald because I survived without having to suffer a lot. Of the five years I was held prisoner, the years I spent there were the best. In November 1947, a messenger suddenly appeared and said, "Brunhilde Pomsel to the main gate." That meant you had five minutes to pack everything you owned—I didn't have much—and get yourself to the gate where you disappeared from the surroundings you had grown accustomed to over the last two years.

I then spent half a year in a factory in East Berlin run by the Russians. I built radios and sewed women's and men's suits. Just as unexpectedly as I arrived there one morning, I was sent away again. I was taken to Sachsenhausen which, as it turned out, was my final destination. That was the worst part of the whole ordeal. In the meantime, the camps were thoroughly organized. The Russians had not only taken over the camps from the Germans, but they had also learned to run them with German perfection. The old haphazard ways of the Russians had become non-existent. Everything functioned so much better, but it had become automatic and harsh. It was a terrible time, especially considering three whole years had passed since the end of the war.

The most difficult part was having to cope with not knowing why you were still being detained. I experienced some pretty horrible things. At one point, I really considered suicide. But how do you do something like that? I knew I didn't have the courage, but even if I had, I didn't know how to go about it or what to use. You didn't have anything. I couldn't even hang myself. As far as I am concerned, there is absolutely no situation you can't get yourself out of. But was I really going to end in a prison camp? And suddenly you reach the point, which I basically reached the first day of the almost five years I spent in prison, where you say, "Shit! Tomorrow I'm going home!" You keep living with the thought, "We're going home tomorrow, or next week for sure."

I was released one day all of a sudden. I was given 13 marks and a bill which read, "Five years of 'hospitality,' wages minus room and board, etc., leaves 13 marks." I bought myself a train ticket for Berlin-Charlottenburg at the Oranienburg station. When I got home I said, "Look, mom, this is what I earned in the last five years!" She said, "But that money is worthless; that's only East German money. That's only worth 3 marks here." Today's U.S. equivalent would be about $1.75.

EPILOGUE

This book is the tip of an iceberg, the product of two years' interviewing and two years' reflection. It is comprehensive. Concentration camp victims and SS men, resistance activists and teenage Nazis, emigrés and true believers stand side by side in its pages. But above all, this is a story of ordinary people—the men, women, and children of the Third Reich's front generation. They have spoken for themselves, without interjection or comment by the authors. They have in common only an identity in place and time: They were Germans between 1933 and 1945. And in 1945 they saw the end of their world.

"Enjoy the war," ran a joke familiar in the Reich's last days, "because peace will be terrible." Twelve years of Nazi rule had left Germany's cities destroyed, its people scattered, its government abolished. Foreign soldiers walked its streets as masters while millions of refugees sought safety from an Eastern Europe staging its own solution of the German question by systematic, brutal expulsions.

What was going to happen next? Would Germans be deported as forced labor? Would they face a permanent future as Europe's new "subhumans"? And should the worst be averted, how were they to live? What would they be allowed to do to feed themselves?

Morally too, 1945 was a year of uncertainty. The Reich's former leaders were distancing themselves from the system they had served so well. Like many young men who had believed in Hitler, Peter Petersen noticed the vanishing Nazis:

We were most bitter about the party officials who, now that the war was over, were busy telling each other and the denazification commissions that they had always been against Hitler. They said they had only joined the party in order to keep worse things from happening. All of the Nazis disappeared overnight; suddenly everyone had been in the resistance!

Nor was this denial of National Socialism confined to those with something obvious to hide. Anna Hummel, who was also a true believer, remembers that

> there was relief that it was finally over. There won't be any more dying, any more raids. It's over. But then the fear set in of what would happen afterwards. We were spiritually and emotionally drained. Hitler's doctrines were discredited. And then the desperation set in of realizing that it had all been for nothing, and that was a terrible feeling. Surviving, finding something to eat and drink, was less difficult for me than the psychological emptiness. It was incomprehensible that all this was supposed to be over, and that it had all been for nothing.

What had become of the cheering crowds of 1933? Of 1938? Were the wartime Germans a generation of opportunists, rejecting the Nazi order only when the bill came due? This question is particularly significant because of the nature of the National Socialist regime. It was not a state like all the rest, a state which made its bid for world power, fought a war, and lost. It was a criminal system that committed its atrocities "in the name of the German people."

But questions of right and wrong are seldom as obvious at the time as they seem in retrospect, even under Adolf Hitler. It might be more accurate to say *especially* under Adolf Hitler. The Third Reich changed the history of the world, yet it endured for only a brief moment in time—twelve years. The pace of events alone was rapid enough to sweep along millions of people with a current that seemed to flow ever faster. Modern states and modern ideologies have the means to blur processes of choice and action. Particularly for young people, there was no time to catch one's breath, no time to reflect, no refuge from the endless pressure to participate.

This pace grew worse after September 1, 1939. War is the province of disruption. National Socialism's norm was war, and Germany reaped the whirlwind. Seven and a half million of its people died, one-third of them civilians. Everyone over five or six years old was somehow involved. World War II had no parallel in history. It was waged without rules or mercy. It assumed a life of its own, as though it would go on forever. Yet at the same time it was waged with malevolent intelligence. No one in Europe escaped it. World War II mobilized children for the front. It made women the prizes of victory. It demanded the annihilation of entire peoples. It generated realities worse than any nightmare. Auschwitz, Stalingrad, and Berlin have in common that the abnormal became the stuff of everyday life. Chaos seemed natural. It was the way things had always been, the way things always would be.

Stalingrad and the Allied bomber offensive added desperation to chaos. The millions of men by now conscripted into the Wehrmacht saw themselves as fighting not for the Third Reich, but for their families and their homeland. Isolated in hostile occupied countries, confronted by increasingly superior enemy forces, the *Landser,* the ordinary soldiers and their junior officers, had no solid moral basis for judging the crimes of the regime they served. In Germany, the massive air raids produced similar results. The Allied attempt to break a people's morale by destroying its cities was a major strategic and political error. Instead, the raids distracted the German people's attention from anything beyond immediate problems. Clear thought was further discouraged by ignorance based on lack of information. Books, newspapers, radio, all were rigidly controlled. Even private conversations involved significant risk. Totalitarian societies offer few opportunities for facile moralizing. Soldiers, whether at the front or in home garrisons, were in an even more restricted environment than civilians. Thousands of men in Wehrmacht uniforms were executed or imprisoned for "damaging the national war effort" by "crimes" as insignificant as listening to foreign radio broadcasts.

If guessing was risky, knowing too much posed more than simple physical danger. Those who by chance glanced into the Nazi abyss promptly looked away. They denied it existed. They talked of "exceptions" or "excesses." They forced themselves to forget. Anything was preferable to the truth, because the truth was too horrible to acknowledge.

This placed a corresponding burden on those Germans who understood, or came to understand, the realities of National Socialism. Here the Wehrmacht high command bears a major responsibility. Adolf Hitler could not be removed from office by impeachment. The Nazi regime ultimately responded only to force, and in a modern state the locus of effective force is the military establishment. A soldier, moreover, is a man whose profession commits him to taking risks essentially different from the ones incurred by intellectuals, civil servants, or attorneys. Too many senior officers in the Third Reich refused to accept the responsibility of their position and their heritage. The generals boasted of "traditional Prussian honor." To Americans, Prussia is generally identified with unthinking, unconditional obedience. For Germans, Prussian qualities were more comprehensive and more positive. They involved self-discipline and self-mastery: willingness to accept the consequences before God and man of one's actions, whatever might be the cost. By 1945, all that remained of honor was its form. The substance had been eroded by twelve years of compromise. Too many of Germany's generals abandoned their men in a form of desertion far more disgraceful than any mere physical flight from the battlefield.

The moral failure of these warriors left resistance to the Nazi system in the hands of two small groups: the heroes and the martyrs. Often in the Third Reich, they were one and the same, like the doomed youngsters of the White Rose. Yet the link was not inevitable.

Heroism in Nazi Germany took three forms. One was conventional courage, the courage needed to knock out a tank or climb into a fighter cockpit. Often taken for granted, it is nevertheless a quality not to be despised. Without its presence, other forms of heroism too readily fade before the torturer's grim arts. The second form of heroism highlighted in Nazi Germany is best called the heroism of routine. Whether on the battle fronts of a total war or in a concentration camp, extraordinary responses became a standard, earning only fresh demands. These demands in turn evoked the third form of heroism: the heroism of resistance. Even in a totalitarian dictatorship, resistance does not demand sainthood. Human qualities suffice—if they are properly used. Resistance under the Third Reich involved more than planting bombs in restaurants, and far more than taking advantage of a constitutional society's freedoms. It required above all the courage to follow conscience in isolation, even in the face of death, while at the same time maintaining a sense of the relationship between ends and means. For all their shortcomings, the men and women of the July 20, 1944, assassination attempt on Hitler saved the honor of their nation. And without honor, no people can survive.

The men and women who share their lives in these pages challenge three familiar myths about Germans under National Socialism. The first is the myth of collective opposition, the myth that the German people from the beginning rejected Hitler's siren call. The myth makes everyone at heart a Christian, a Marxist, a simple soldier, or something else having as little as possible to do with National Socialism. Its devotees probe the Nazi years for signs of "everyday resistance," no matter how trivial, no matter how limited the risk: "In my heart, I was part of the resistance. I came to work late whenever I could. I never said 'Heil Hitler!' And one night I even whispered to my grandma that things would turn out badly!" Susanne Ritters, 17 at war's end, offers a bitter critique:

> We believed in Hitler. We believed in the whole system, the entire leadership. There we were, already half-dead, still believing in victory. We could not do anything else. That was our generation and he was our idol. We didn't just adopt something. It was a given. It came from inside of us. And we sucked it in like mother's milk.

Yet these pages also deny an opposing myth, the myth of collective guilt that makes every German living through this period an active, committed Nazi, endorsing when not supporting every aspect of the regime. Richard Löwenthal, forced into exile as a Jew and a Social Democrat, says he was very much aware that anti-Semitism had always existed in Germany, but before Hitler's time it was confined to a very small minority. If I were to compare Germany with other countries before Hitler, I could say that there was considerably less anti-Semitism in Germany than in France, to say nothing of Poland or Austria.

What many people fail to realize is that Hitler did not come to power because of his anti-Semitism, or because there was a massive wave of anti-Semitism in the country at the time. Hitler's coming to power was based on a wave of nationalism and the miserable economic situation in Germany.

What attracted millions of Germans were National Socialism's positive appeals. Family, community, homeland—these values are not contemptible in themselves, nor were they invented by the Nazis. Hitler spoke to a desire to have things better. He promised something for nothing—or at worst, something at the expense of vague, almost invisible "others." He even delivered on his promise, at least for a while—long enough to add the German people to his list of victims.

Our interview partners finally challenge a third myth—the myth of oblivion, sometimes described as "Waldheimer's Disease": live long enough and you forget you were ever a Nazi. German history neither began nor ended in 1945. The Federal Republic sometimes speaks of a "Zero Hour" from which all somehow began anew. East Germany boasts of a postwar revolution which swept away the old order. But the generation that bore the burden of Hitler's Reich and Hitler's war remembers, far too well for its own comfort, the part it played. For the survivors, their war was not a collective experience. It was a composite of personal events and decisions, random happenings, and blind chance against a background of confusion. They have struggled—not least by participating in this project—to come to terms with their country's history on a personal level. If recollection sometimes finds positive elements—courage, comradeship, empathy—that should occasion neither alarm nor surprise. Such memories are not harbingers of a Fourth Reich. They are rather part of the process of mastering a painful past.

A favorite question regarding the Nazi experience is its specificity.

Was National Socialism a kind of tragic historical accident? Was it a function of particular German experiences—some tragic flaw in the social structure, or the national psychology? Or was National Socialism the monstrous product of an industrialized, secularized Western civilization? This book suggests that National Socialism owed its genesis to German needs and German problems. Its success, however, reflected a quality that cannot be restricted to one people or one time. The experiences of our interview partners demonstrate that Germany between 1939 and 1945 was not a nation of criminals. Still less was it a nation of saints and martyrs. Individually and collectively, the Germans adapted.

Since 1945, Western thought has been permeated by a utopianism leaving no room for misjudgment, no room for immaturity, no room for conversion. What is important is being right, morally right, the first time and from the first hour. In both Germanies younger generations say, "It would never have happened to us." They declare themselves too clever, too sophisticated, to have become part of Hitler's Reich. Our interview partners' experiences suggest another important lesson: the potential to learn from error, to learn from history, which remains a record of mistakes made for good reasons. They have been taught humility, and have paid high prices for the instruction.

"Greater Germany" died with Adolf Hitler. But "Germany" remains a living concept on both sides of the current border. The emphasis may differ, but the roots are the same: two states, but one ethnic and cultural entity, one nation. The war generation built this new Germany as it had fought for the old one. After the war, this generation had to ask itself: What is more important, yesterday or tomorrow? Its answer can be seen by any visitor to Germany. Civilization owes these men and women, if not gratitude, then at least recognition.

Glossary

Terms

Abitur—Examination for admission to a university or equivalent program; usually taken at the conclusion of one's Gymnasium (q.v.) studies.

Ahnenpass—Nazi document officially confirming Aryan ancestry.

Aryan Nachweis—Papers officially establishing one's "non-Jewish" heritage.

Blitzmädchen—Nickname for Wehrmacht women auxiliaries in the telecommunications services.

Commissar Order (Kommissarbefehl)—Order to execute all Soviet political officers captured during Operation Barbarossa, as opposed to recognizing them as prisoners of war.

Crystal Night (Kristallnacht)—Government-inspired anti-Jewish violence on November 9, 1938, so-called from the acres of broken glass that littered the streets next day. The most visible public demonstration of Nazi anti-Semitism, a traumatic turning point for many Germans, Jewish and gentile.

First of May Rally—Traditional labor day, celebrated with major demonstrations by Marxist parties. Later a Nazi holiday as well.

"Fortress Breslau"—In the winter of 1944–45, major cities of eastern Germany such as Breslau and Königsberg were declared "Fortresses" by Hitler, to be held at all costs by whatever forces were available.

Gauleiter—Chiefs of the party districts into which Nazi Germany was divided. Existing alongside the official administrative structure, they increasingly became responsible for political and economic mobilization during the war, and ultimately for the defense of their Gau.

Golden Party Badge—Sign of a long-time member or one who had performed unusual services for the party.

Golden pheasants (Goldfasanen)—Contemptuous Wehrmacht nickname for party officials, derived from the brown color of their uniforms and the elaborate trimmings with which they were adorned.

"Green triangles"—Concentration camp prisoners' uniforms were marked with triangular badges whose colors indicated their offense. Green was for criminals, red for political prisoners, pink for homosexuals, blue for deportees. Jews added to this a yellow triangle, the two forming the Star of David.

Gymnasium—German secondary school whose program was roughly equivalent to a U.S. high school plus the first two years of college. Admission was based on a combination of merit and ability to pay the fees; most students were drawn from the middle and upper classes.

Hague Convention—International agreement regulating the conduct of military operations in order to avoid unnecessary violation of human rights.

Horst Wessel Song—Nazi Party anthem celebrating a young man allegedly murdered by Communists for his Nazi political beliefs.

Kapo—Supervisors in concentration camps, in most cases criminals.

Kapp Putsch—Attempted right-wing coup against the Weimar Republic, staged in March 1920, and defeated by a combination of a general strike and the army's refusal to participate.

Knight's Cross (Ritterkreuz)—Highest grade of the Iron Cross, instituted by Hitler. It could be awarded in several grades; with oak leaves, swords, and diamonds in various combinations.

Krautjunker—East Elbian aristocrats who lived on their sometimes heavily indebted estates.

Landser—Term for ordinary German soldier, equivalent to "GI" or "grunt."

"Night and Fog Actions"—On December 7, 1941, Hitler authorized the seizure of all persons deemed "dangerous to state security." Victims of this decree were not to be publicly executed, but to vanish "into the night and fog." The term came to be applied retrospectively, to any sudden disappearance during the Third Reich.

Nuremberg Laws—Comprehensive Nazi legislation, legally defining Jews and setting them apart from the "Aryan" German community.

Pour le Mérite—Nicknamed "Blue Max," this was the highest decoration Imperial Germany could bestow. During World War I it was awarded only to officers, for outstanding bravery and leadership.

Rassenschande ("Racial Shame")—Offenses against the Nuremberg Laws, specifically those paragraphs prohibiting sexual relations between Jews and "Aryans."

Reichsheini—Nickname for Heinrich Himmler, derived from his official title of "Reich Leader of the SS."

Reichsparteitag—Annual National Socialist Party congress held at Nuremberg from 1927. After the seizure of power, these became massive spectacles, designed to impress Germans and foreigners alike with the strength of the new regime.

Röhm Putsch—Alternate name for Hitler's "Blood Purge" of the SA and other political rivals in 1934. Derived from Hitler's charge that SA leader Ernst Röhm was planning a coup against the Third Reich.

Rollbahn—Originally, a Wehrmacht term for the main axis of advance of a Panzer division. Later, commonly applied to major Russian highways. These were often so badly paved that traffic "rolled" parallel to the road, but yards away from it.

S-Bahn—Elevated train in Berlin.

Scorched Earth Order—Stalin's instructions given in the wake of Operation Barbarossa, to destroy and burn everything in the path of the invading Germans. Hitler later used the same concept.

Sippengesetze, Sippenhaftung—Nazi laws making families responsible for all their members. Used to hold women and children as hostages for their men at the front, to prevent surrender, desertion, or disobedience to Hitler's orders. After July 20, applied automatically to families of the people involved.

SS Tattoo—Waffen-SS men were tattooed under the left armpit not, as so often stated, with SS runes, but with their blood group.

Stab-in-the-Back Legend (Dolchstoss-Legende)—Belief held after 1918 by many Germans that their country did not lose World War I in the field, but was "stabbed in the back" by traitors at home.

"Strength Through Joy" (Kraft durch Freude)—Nazi program of state-subsidized leaves, vacations, and other entertainment; intended primarily to win over the working classes.

Trümmerfrauen—Women mobilized to clear away rubble after the war.

U-Bahn—Subway in Berlin.

Volksgemeinschaft—Best translated as "folk community," the word had strong emotional overtones. It conveyed a sense of belonging, of affirming one's own identity through membership in the German ethnic group.

Wehrkreis (Military District)—Germany was divided into these for recruiting, mobilization, and other matters of military administration.

Wolfschanze ("Wolf's Lair")—Code name for Hitler's headquarters in East Prussia.

Organizations

Bendler Street in Berlin—In peacetime, headquarters of the armed forces. H.Q. of the Home Army during the war.

Brandenburgers—Wehrmacht special operations formation, performing missions analogous on one hand to Ranger and Commando forces, on the other to the OSS.

Charlemagne Division—Waffen-SS formation of French volunteers.

Confessing Church—Organized in protest at Nazi efforts to integrate the Protestant state church into the Third Reich. Its name came from its leaders' insistence on the importance of prayer.

DNB (Deutsches Nachrichten-Büro)—Nazi-controlled national news agency.

Döberitz—Major army training camp west of Berlin.

Einsatzgruppen—Mobile terror squads under the direction of the SS. They were assigned to suppress opposition behind the front lines in Russia by killing everyone they considered dangerous. Well over a million people were murdered by these units. Most of the victims were Jewish.

Freikorps—Volunteer military units formed after the November Revolution in 1918 for border defense and internal security. They also served in the Baltic States, where they cooperated with the British against the Bolsheviks. Originally organized or sponsored by the Weimar Republic's Defense Ministry, they took on an increasingly right-wing, anti-democratic attitude with the passage of time. Märker's *Landesjägerkorps* came closest to the ideal expressed in several interviews: a force for underwriting bourgeois/conservative ideas of order.

Gau—Party administrative unit in Nazi Germany; not officially part of the civil administration.

German Peoples' Party (Deutsche Volkspartei/DVP)—Right-of-center, upper-middle-class party of the Weimar era; closely identified with its chief figure, Gustav Stresemann.

Gestapo (Geheine Staatspolizei)—Secret state police, most common terror instrument of the Third Reich.

Grossdeutschland Division—Elite division of the army, originally recruited heavily from volunteers.

Home Army (Ersatzheer)—Responsible for administration of troops in Germany, and for providing supplies and training replacements for the operational forces.

I.G. Farben—German chemical cartel, which after 1942 operated plants near several concentration camps using slave labor.

Jungvolk—Junior division of the Hitler Youth, including boys 10 to 14. Generally considered to be less "political" than the older age groups.

Kreisau Circle—Group of officers and civilians formed in 1940 to oppose National Socialism. Among its leaders were Helmuth James von Moltke and Peter Yorck von Wartenburg.

LAH—Leibstandarte Adolf Hitler—Elite formation of the Waffen-SS expanded from a regiment to an armored division in the course of the war.

Labor Service (Reichsarbeitsdienst)—Eventually compulsory for all able-bodied men and women. Males were usually drafted for six months prior to conscription into the Wehrmacht. The Labor Service thus also functioned as a form of pre-military training.

Landdienst—Service on farms by boys and girls too young for military conscription during the war.

League of German Girls (Bund deutscher Mädel, BdM)—Girls' counterpart to the Hitler Youth.

League of German Officers (Bund Deutscher Offiziere)—Founded in Russia after Stalingrad by German POWs in an effort to win support from those officers disgruntled with Hitler and his conduct of the war, yet unwilling to collaborate fully with the USSR. Also called Seydlitz Army, for its chairman General Walther von Seydlitz (q. v.).

Moabit—Maximum-security prison in Berlin where political prisoners were interrogated and detained prior to execution.

Napola: Nationalpolitische Erziehungsanstalten (National Political Training Institutes)—Nazi Party schools designed to train selected candidates for high leadership posts in the Third Reich.

National Committee for a Free Germany (Nationalkomitee Freies Deutschland)—Organization of German POWs and Communists established in the Soviet Union after Stalingrad to work for Nazi Germany's defeat. Linked to League of German Officers (q. v.).

Neuengamme—Concentration camp near Hamburg.

NSFO—Nationalsozialistische Führungsoffiziere—Introduced in the armed services in December 1943, as analogs to Soviet Russia's commissars; responsible for political indoctrination of the common soldier and political supervision of the officers. They lacked, however, the independent authority of the commissars, and possessed little standing in the *Wehrmacht.*

OKW (Oberkommando der Wehrmacht)—Armed forces supreme command.

Organization Todt—Semi-military force established in 1938 for heavy construction work. Its members were civilians, but functioned under military law and discipline.

Prince Albrecht Street—Berlin headquarters of the Gestapo.

Ravensbrück—Concentration camp for women, located about 80 miles north of Berlin.

Reichsbanner—Paramilitary organization formed for the defense of the Weimar Republic. Originally intended as non-partisan, it became in practice quickly identified with the Social Democrats.

Reich Central Security Office (Reichssicherheitshauptamt)—Main headquarters of the secret police of the Nazi system.

Reichswehr—Name for the German armed forces under the Weimar Republic.

Rotfrontkämpferbund—Paramilitary organization of the German Communist Party prior to 1933.

SA—National Socialist (Nazi) paramilitary organization of storm troopers.

Seydlitz Committee, Seydlitz Army—Wartime names for the League of German Officers and the National Committee for a Free Germany.

SS—Initially small paramilitary organization maintaining security at Nazi Party rallies and protecting Hitler; eventually became large autonomous military and police organization.

Stahlhelm (Steel Helmet)—Organization of conservative veterans of World War I.

Der Stürmer—Notorious anti-Semitic newspaper edited by Julius Streicher.

Totenkopf Division—Waffen-SS formation, originally formed from concentration camp guards. Throughout the war there was a significant exchange of personnel between the division and the camps.

Unter den Linden—Principal avenue of Berlin prior to the partition; route of the Reich's major military parades.

Vlassov Army—Russian POWs who served against the Soviet regime in separate units under their own officers; commanded by General Andrei Vlassov, who surrendered to the Wehrmacht in 1942. The name was also applied to the Russians, almost a million of them, who served the Wehrmacht after 1941 in any capacity.

Werewolves (Werwölfe)—Organization of guerrillas, mostly Hitler Youth, set up at the end of World War II. Intended as a resistance movement. It never became an effective fighting force.

Personal Names

Axmann, Arthur—Successor to Baldur von Schirach as chief of the Hitler Youth.

Bonhoeffer, Dietrich—Protestant theologian and leading figure in the Confessing Church (q.v.) murdered by the SS in 1945.

Brüning, Heinrich—Leader of the Catholic Center Party; Chancellor of Germany, 1930–1932.

Burgdorf, General Wilhelm—Became head of the Army Personnel Office after July 20, best known for his persecution of resistance members in the officer's corps.

Dietrich, Josef (Sepp)—SS officer; commander of the *Leibstandarte,* later SS corps and army commander.

Fegelein, Hermann—Representative of the Waffen-SS at Hitler's headquarters. He was married to the sister of Eva Braun, but Hitler nevertheless ordered him shot when he attempted to flee Berlin in 1945.

Flex, Walther—Idealistic lyric poet venerated by the German youth movement; killed in action during World War I.

Freisler, Roland—Presiding Judge of the "People's Court" (Volksgerichtshof) that tried the White Rose and the principal July 20 defendants. Notorious for his vulgar and abusive behavior, he was killed in an air raid on February 3, 1945.

Fritzsche, Hans—Senior official in the Propaganda Ministry; chief commentator and "anchor man" for the *Grossdeutscher Rundfunk,* the national radio network.

Galen, Clemens August—Cardinal Archbishop of Münster, an outspoken opponent of the Nazi regime.

Goerdeler, Karl—Resigned as mayor of Leipzig; became leader of the resistance movement; had the conspiracy of July 20, 1944, been successful, he would have become Reich Chancellor.

Heusinger, General Adolf—Chief of the Operations Section of the Army General Staff; passively sympathetic to the resistance; later Inspector General of the Bundeswehr.

Jodl, General Alfred—Chief of Operations, Wehrmacht High Command. Executed as a war criminal, 1946.

John von Freyend, Lieutenant Colonel—Adjutant to Field Marshal Wilhelm Keitel, who was present at the July 20 conference in the "Wolf's Lair."

Ley, Robert—Labor Minister and head of the Reich Labor Front, the Nazi organization that replaced the independent trade unions. Sentenced to death at Nuremberg, he committed suicide before his execution.

Model, Walther—Wehrmacht field marshal, prominent in the war's later years as a loyal Nazi general; committed suicide after the surrender of the Ruhr Pocket.

Moltke, Helmuth James—One of the founders of the Kreisau Circle (q.v.); arrested in January 1944, and executed.

Ohlendorff, Otto—SS commander of Einsatzgruppe D in Operation Barbarossa; responsible for the mass murder of over 90,000 Jews. Later a key member of Himmler's SS bureaucracy. Hanged as a war criminal in 1951.

Papen, Franz von—Chancellor of Germany in 1932; largely responsible for Hitler's entry into the government in 1933. Served briefly as Hitler's Vice-Chancellor; later Ambassador to Turkey.

Pieck, Wilhelm—Chairman of the German Communist Party; postwar leader of the Socialist Unity Party in East Germany and first president of the German Democratic Republic.

Polish Corridor—To provide the new state of Poland with an outlet to the sea, the Versailles Treaty established a "corridor" cutting the province of East Prussia off from the rest of Germany. This was a major grievance in Weimar Germany.

Ribbentrop, Joachim von—Nazi Foreign Minister, 1938–1945; his appointment marked the eclipse of professional diplomacy in the Foreign Office. Sentenced to death at Nuremberg; hanged 1946.

Rokossovsky, Konstantin K.—Polish-born; field marshal in the Soviet Army; one of the Red Army's leading strategists and field commanders; responsible for the final destruction of the Stalingrad pocket.

Schirach, Baldur von—Head of the Hitler Youth, later Nazi Gauleiter of Vienna.

Schumacher, Kurt—Crippled by wounds in World War I; imprisoned as a Social Democrat and brutally tortured by the Nazis, he played a major role in reorganizing the SPD, and was its first postwar chairman.

Seydlitz, Walther von—One of the senior German generals captured in Stalingrad; chairman of the League of German Officers (q.v.).

Seyss-Inquart, Arthur—Gauleiter of Vienna, later Nazi governor of the Netherlands. Sentenced to death at Nuremberg; hanged 1946.

Skorzeny, Otto—German SS officer who organized and led several daring operations behind allied lines; a committed Nazi who escaped to Spain after the Reich's collapse.

Sorge, Richard—German journalist and long-time Communist who worked in Japan as a Soviet agent. Among other things, he informed Stalin of German intentions to attack Russia in 1941, and that Japan would remain neutral.

Speer, Albert—Favorite of Hitler; architect; Reich Minister for armaments and war production.

Streicher, Julius—Chief Nazi anti-Semite; Gauleiter of Franconia and editor of *Der Stürmer* (q.v.). Hanged in Nuremberg.

Student, Kurt—Creator of the German paratroops; highly respected by the men who served under him.

Treskow, Henning von—Leading member of the military resistance; committed suicide in the aftermath of July 20.

Udet, Ernst—World War I fighter ace; later world-famous stunt flyer and playboy. Appointed head of aircraft development and procurement by Göring despite his lack of technical expertise. Committed suicide November 17, 1941, in the wake of repeated failures of new aircraft designs.

Ulbricht, Walther—German Communist leader who went into exile after Hitler's seizure of power and spent World War II organizing opposition to the Nazis among German prisoners-of-war. Later head of the Socialist Unity Party and Chief of State of East Germany.

Weapons

Fieseler Storch—Light plane similar to U.S. Piper Cub, but better able to land and take off in rough terrain.

"Giant"—Me-323, a glider with auxiliary French-made engines; possessed an extraordinary carrying capacity for its era.

"Josef Stalin"—Heavy Russian tank; counterpart to the German Tiger and Royal Tiger tanks.

Lightning P-38—U.S. escort fighter and fighter-bomber.

"Mandolin"—Nickname for the Russian submachine gun, derived from its drum-shaped magazine.

Mosquito—RAF light bomber and reconnaissance aircraft.

Mustang P-51—U.S. escort fighter and fighter-bomber.

"Rommel Asparagus"—Obstacles laid to block allied landings in northern France.

"Sewing Machines"—Russian PO-2 biplanes, used as trainers before the war, then employed for night harrassing raids on German rear areas. So called from the sound of their engines.

Stalin Organs—Multiple free-flight rocket launchers, known in the Red Army and the West as Katyusha.

T-34—Principal Soviet tank of World War II, first saw action shortly after the beginning of the German invasion.

Thunderbolt P-47—U.S. escort fighter and fighter-bomber.

Typhoon—British fighter-bomber.

West Wall—Known as the Siegfried Line to the Allies, built before the war, ostensibly as a counterpart to France's Maginot Line.

Equivalent Ranks

SS	Army/Luftwaffe	U.S. Army
Oberstgruppenführer	Generaloberst	General
Obergruppenführer	General	Lieutenant General
Gruppenführer	Generalleutnant	Major General
Brigadeführer	Generalmajor	Brigadier General
Oberführer	—	—
Standartenführer	Oberst	Colonel
Obersturmbannführer	Oberstleutnant	Lieutenant Colonel
Sturmbannführer	Major	Major
Hauptsturmführer	Hauptmann	Captain
Obersturmführer	Oberleutnant	First Lieutenant
Untersturmführer	Leutnant	Second Lieutenant

Chronology

November 11, 1918	Armistice ends World War I.
July 31, 1919	Constitution of the Weimar Republic approved by the Constituent Assembly.
March 11–17, 1920	Unsuccessful attempt by extreme right-wing paramilitary organizations to take over the Republic (Kapp Putsch).
January 11, 1923	French and Belgian troops occupy the Ruhr area of Germany in response to Germany's default on her reparation payments imposed by the Versailles Peace Treaty.
November 9, 1923	Unsuccessful attempt by Hitler to take over the Bavarian government (Beer Hall Putsch).
November 15, 1923	Peak of inflation: Reichsmark falls to 4.2 billion to one United States dollar.
April 10, 1925	Field Marshal Paul von Hindenburg, candidate of the center-right parties, elected President of Germany.
September 14, 1930	In elections for the Reichstag (parliament) the National Socialist Party wins 18 percent (6,400,000) of the votes and increases its representation from 12 to 107 seats, becoming the largest party in the Reichstag.
April 10, 1932	Hindenburg, this time the candidate of the center-left parties, re-elected President, defeating Hitler in runoff elections.

543

July 31, 1932	In elections for the Reichstag, National Socialist votes peak at 37 percent (13,750,000), and the National Socialist representation in the Reichstag increases to 230 seats.
November 6, 1932	In Germany's last free elections for the Reichstag, the National Socialist vote falls to 33 percent (11,737,000) and the National Socialist representation in the Reichstag to 196 seats.
January 30, 1933	Hitler becomes Chancellor of Germany.
March 23, 1933	Reichstag passes the "Enabling Act" giving Hitler's government dictatorial powers.
October 14, 1933	Germany withdraws from the League of Nations.
June 30, 1934	Hundreds of actual or supposed opponents of the Hitler regime, including many high-ranking officers of the National Socialist paramilitary "storm troopers" (S.A.), are executed without trial or warning, allegedly in response to a planned putsch by the S.A.
March 7, 1936	German troops reoccupy the Rhineland in violation of the Versailles and other treaties.
March 12, 1938	Germany invades Austria and incorporates it into Germany (Anschluss).
September 30, 1938	Munich Conference between France, Great Britain, and Germany accepts the dismemberment of Czechoslovakia by approving Germany's annexation of the Sudetenland.
November 9, 1938	Crystal Night—first major public program against the Jews.
March 15, 1939	German troops occupy Prague.
September 1, 1939	Germany invades Poland: World War II begins.
May 10, 1940	Germany invades France and the Low Countries.
June 22, 1940	France signs armistice.
July/October, 1940	Battle of Britain.
February 12, 1941	General Rommel lands in North Africa.
April 6, 1941	Germany invades Greece and Yugoslavia.
June 21, 1941	Germany invades Russia (Operation Barbarossa).
December 11, 1941	Germany declares war on the United States.
October 23, 1942	Battle of El Alamein begins.

November 8, 1942	British and United States forces invade North Africa.
January 31, 1943	German 6th Army surrenders at Stalingrad.
May 9, 1943	Axis forces in North Africa surrender.
July 5, 1943	Battle of Kursk begins.
July 9, 1943	Allies invade Sicily.
September 3, 1943	Allies invade Italy.
June 6, 1944	Allies land in northern France.
June 21, 1944	Russian offensive begins on the Central front.
July 20, 1944	Unsuccessful attempt by a group of army officers to assassinate Hitler and to overthrow his government.
December 16, 1944	Last German offensive (Battle of the Bulge) begins.
January 12, 1945	Russians launch their offensive across the Vistula.
March 7, 1945	United States troops cross the Rhine River.
April 16, 1945	Russians launch their final attack on Berlin.
April 30, 1945	Hitler commits suicide.
May 7, 1945	Germany surrenders unconditionally.

Index

ABOUT THE AUTHORS

General Johannes Steinhoff served in the German Air Force during the war and saw action in France, Norway, the Battle of Britain, Russia, Italy, North Africa, Rumania, and the skies over Germany. He was a commander of the first jet fighter wing to be formed in the German Air Force, and suffered severe burns, from which it took him years to recover, after a crash near Munich in 1945. Steinhoff, former Chief of Staff of the German Air Force and Chairman of the NATO Military Committee, authored *Messerschmitts over Sicily, The Final Hours,* and *Whither NATO.* He died in 1994.

Peter Pechel is the son of Rudolf Pechel, the former editor and publisher of *Deutsche Rundschau* who was imprisoned in a concentration camp by the Gestapo. Pechel fought in the German Army, reaching the rank of captain during the war, and saw duty in Poland, Greece, the Soviet Union, and France. He holds a doctorate from the University of Zurich and has been a foreign correspondent for German television in Britain, Africa, and the United States, and the host of many public affairs programs in Germany. He is the Vice-Chairman of CARE-Deutschland and a member of the Board of Directors of CARE-International.

Dennis Showalter has taught at Colorado College since 1969. He is joint editor of *War in History* and currently Vice-President of the Society for Military History. The recipient of numerous fellowships, he has served as Distinguished Visiting Professor at the U.S. Air Force Academy and held the Chair of Military Affairs at the Marine Corps University. His *Tannenberg: Clash of Empires* was awarded The American Historical Association's 1992 prize for military history.

Other DA CAPO titles of interest